I0655191

ED

The Nature of Social Work

ZOFIA T. BUTRYM

Senior Lecturer in Social Work
London School of Economics and Political Science

First published 1976 by
THE MACMILLAN PRESS LTD
London and Basingstoke
Associated companies in New York Dublin
Melbourne Johannesburg and Madras

ISBN 0 333 19124 2 (hard cover)
333 19703 8 (paper cover)

Produced by computer-controlled phototypesetting
using OCR input techniques and printed offset by
UNWIN BROTHERS LIMITED
The Gresham Press, Old Woking, Surrey

Contents

Foreword   vii

Introduction   ix

1 The Problem of Identity in Social Work   1

2 Models of Social-Work Practice   15

3 The Place of Values in Social Work   40

4 The Place of Knowledge in Social Work   63

5 The Social-Work Process   81

6 Social Work and Society   105

7 Some Current Issues in Social Work and their
    Implications for the Future   125

References   151

Index   163

Foreword

The views expressed in this book are the outcome of my thinking after twenty-five years in social work, first as a practitioner and later as a teacher. They inevitably reflect the totality of my experience, background and beliefs, and so, no doubt, my Polish origins, Christian upbringing and emotionally secure childhood will have contributed to my particular perspective.

I should like to pay tribute to all those who have influenced my professional development, whether at the L.S.E., the Institute of Medical Social Workers, the Tavistock Clinic, or in those social-work departments where I have been a student or have been employed. I owe special gratitude to Gwen Price and Enid Warren who have been of so much help to me both professionally and personally during my early years in this country. I am also indebted to colleagues and students, past and present, for all I have learnt from them, and to the many authors from whose writings I quote so extensively.

Last, I want to thank particularly those colleagues and friends who read chapters of the book at various stages of drafting, offered constructive criticism and gave me warm encouragement. Were I to mention their names the list would be long, and in a book expressing my personal views in a sometimes controversial context I thought anonymity might be preferred. I hope, therefore, that I shall be forgiven for not referring to them individually. One exception, however, that must be made are my thanks to Anne Deakins for her willingness and care in typing the manuscript and for her patience in deciphering my handwriting – renowned for its illegibility.

Z.T.B.

Introduction

The fact that it was considered necessary to devote a book to a discussion of the nature of social work is in itself worthy of attention. The nature of most of the other professions and occupations, such as those of the law, medicine, nursing, teaching and architecture, is far less ambiguous, and so the need for such clarification is less apparent.

The special position of social work in this respect can be put down to two interrelated factors. Social work is not only a relatively young profession but it is also one which derives more directly and more substantially from the particular society of which it is a part than is the case with other professions. Hence its functions and its modes of operation are substantially dependent on existing social structures and are to a great extent affected by the various processes of change within them. In addition, the preoccupation of social work with people and with their social circumstances creates its main occupational risk – that of a lack of specificity, of an inherent ambiguity – which makes it particularly prone to changes and fluctuations, not all of which are necessarily consistent or logical.

This ambiguity and ready exposure to external influences lays social work open to different interpretations regarding its nature and functions, and also encourages the expression of strongly held opinions on these matters not only on the part of social workers but also by others. Thus, on the one hand, there is a tendency for some people to view social work as little more than a matter of 'kindness of heart' and of 'common sense', thus potentially an opening for all men and women of goodwill. This conception of social work usually carries with it a marked reluctance to credit professional social work with any special or even additional expertise. In contrast, social work has been vested in recent years with increasing power and responsibility in the realm of containment, control and alleviation of some of the major problems facing contemporary society. The granting of such power and responsibility by society to social work implies a degree of confidence in its knowledge and capabilities which even many social workers would consider excessive.

This book will not attempt a historical review of social work because that is a task in its own right. However, where appropriate, references will be made to past trends and to their relevance to current issues. This will inevitably include criticisms of some of the writings about social work in the past when they present a simplistic or a distorted picture of the historical perspective. A good comprehensive history of British social work still waits to be written.

In *The Nature of Social Work* I shall try to focus on those characteristics of social work which make up its separate identity. I shall argue that this identity is largely derived from the nature of the relationship between certain value-based objectives and a unique amalgam of instrumental values, applied knowledge, practical skills and specific social context which constitutes the means by which these objectives are translated into action.

The book will therefore examine the nature of the objectives in social work, its value base, the sources of knowledge upon which social workers draw, the range of skills by means of which the values and the knowledge are made operational, and the effects of organisational settings upon social workers' functions. In addition, given the fact that social work is a social institution, and one which currently is vested with considerable importance in British society, the following additional structural issues will also be considered. What place does social work hold as an agent of both social caring and social control? What is the nature of the relationship between social work and the other social services? What are the implications for society and for social work of its expanding functions? Is there a need to draw more clear-cut boundaries within which social work is to operate and, if so, what should these be?

No great claims are made for originality in the approach to all these questions, and no ready solutions will be offered to the problems discussed. At the same time, no apologies are offered for the many expressions of personal viewpoint on the issues under consideration, and for a polemical rather than a 'purely' academic approach to some of them. This is because underlying the whole book is my interest in and commitment to social work as a humane and civilised form of expressing the responsibility of human beings for each other which would have invalidated any appearance of neutrality on my part. This is especially so in that, as will be argued throughout, social work is a 'value-ridden' activity, and therefore any serious discussion of it must incorporate moral issues.

A strong incentive for attempting this piece of writing was my growing realisation that whilst a large number of books about social work were coming from the North American continent, this was not being similarly matched by British writing, with the consequence that many inappropriate deductions were being drawn from the American scene about British social work, adding further to the widespread confusion about its nature. In the last couple of decades a number of useful books by British authors dealing with particular aspects of social work have appeared, but what remained lacking was a more comprehensive look. The only grounds on which I can hope that this work may fill an existing gap is that it attempts to present a holistic view of social work, a composite picture of all of its many interrelated and interacting parts which is difficult to convey when discussion focuses on any one or several of these parts.

The Nature of Social Work is not a textbook. It is not detailed enough for this purpose and pays relatively little attention to techniques as opposed to the more general considerations of a philosophical nature – a focus which is reflected in the title. For this reason, no attempt was made to provide a comprehensive bibliography, and the references quoted have been selected on the basis of their relevance to the discussion of the various themes in the book.

I realise that to attempt an approach to social work on these more comprehensive lines is to undertake a demanding task with a limited equipment. My justification for such an endeavour is not in assuming I have answers to the dilemmas posed but in my strong wish to encourage both social workers and others with an interest in social work to give time and attention to their serious consideration.

Chapter 1

The Problem of Identity in Social Work

Social work, in common with other 'helping professions', aims at promoting human welfare through the prevention and relief of suffering. Its particular concern has always been with human problems of living, but the manifestations of this concern have differed over the years for a number of reasons.

Intervention in problems of living calls for attention to both persons and the social circumstances in which those persons live. Given this general requirement, however, the balance between these two aspects of intervention can vary considerably under the influence of such factors as the prevailing social values and the nature of understanding concerning the causation of various human problems. The history of social work reflects a number of such fluctuations in the relative emphasis given to the 'inner' and the 'outer' aspects of human problems. Thus, for example, the early Charity Organisation Society social workers operated within an extensive framework of data collection in their attempts to form an assessment of their clients' material environment. Their social enquiries were the product of great care and thoroughness, and reflected a degree of objectivity having an almost 'scientific' flavour. In contrast, these workers' relative lack of sophistication in the realm of human psychology, combining at the same time with an awareness of the importance of that dimension to the understanding of individual and family problems, resulted in such moralistic judgements of their clients as are implied in descriptions of them as 'thrifty', 'lazy', 'self-respecting' or 'deserving'. Whilst the psychological crudity of these assessments is now generally acknowledged and extensively referred to in most accounts of the social work of those days, what is more frequently overlooked is the significance of the recognition inherent in these attempts at personality assessment, namely that human beings, as well as being shaped by their environment, are also the architects of it. As Octavia Hill put it:

> By knowledge of character more is meant than whether a man is a drunkard or a woman dishonest: it means the knowledge of the passions, hopes and history of people, where the temptation will touch them, what is the little scheme they have made of their lives, or would make, if they had the encouragement; what training long past phases of their lives may have afforded; how to move, touch, teach them. Our memories and our hopes are more truly factors in our lives than we often remember.[1]

However formidable the obstacles in the form of lack of an appropriate knowledge base in putting these sentiments into effect, the fact that these were not just empty words, not simply a poetic exercise, but guidelines for action, is demonstrated by Octavia Hill's own practice of taking to her most deprived clients bunches of primroses she herself had collected in the country. Surely, it would be hard to dispute that, in the light of our knowledge of this pioneer social worker, this was a tangible expression of her belief that man does not live 'by bread alone' and not a denial of the importance of bread (and of clean air or decent housing for that matter).

Much has been written about the 'psychiatric deluge' in social work following the availability of the insights derived from psychoanalysis, as a result of which the 'social' component in social work has been sacrificed at the altar of the 'psychological'. This aspect of the history of social work is the one to which most violence has been done in many writings (often by authors who are not social workers themselves and whose grasp of social work is limited, for example Wootton,[2] and Sinfield.)[3] I am not competent to judge the validity of the assertions concerning the damaging effects of the psychoanalytic influence upon American social work, but I am prepared to maintain with considerable conviction the fact that many of the analogies made in these writings, whether explicit or implied, between the developments in social work in the United States and in Britain, are not valid. In Britain, unlike the United States, social work has from its very early days been an integral part of various statutory bodies: general hospitals and magistrates' courts at first, followed by psychiatric hospitals and child-guidance clinics, and then, gradually, as the Welfare State came into being, becoming incorporated into many other public agencies such as local authority children's, welfare and health departments and education departments. This close association between British social work and statutory agencies has meant that social workers' functions have always been under the considerable influence of the values and the policies of the 'host' agency and those social institutions to which the agency was ultimately accountable, that is the law, central and local government and public opinion. Unlike their American colleagues in many of the voluntary family-welfare agencies, British social workers had a limited scope (too limited in many instances, as I have argued in *Social Work in Medical Care*[4] and *Medical Social Work in Action*[5]) for professional autonomy, and even had they so wished they could not disregard the various tangible factors in their clients' lives. They were expected to ensure, and were held accountable for so doing, that their clients had somewhere to live on discharge from hospital, that convalescence recommended by the doctor was arranged, that special diet allowances were secured from the National Assistance Board, that a probationer did persevere with the residence and the employment conditions of his probation order and that a child in care was visited regularly. The picture presented of social work during the two first decades of the post-war period by some writers, which is that of social workers devoted almost exclusively to personality change in their clients through the indiscriminate use of insight-promotion techniques, regardless of these clients' own needs and aspirations, feels as close to reality to the hospital, court and local-authority-based social workers of those days as holidays on the moon to the average holidaymaker!

To say this is not to deny the fact that individual social workers in such agencies as certain child-guidance clinics, where a primary emphasis on the personality aspects of social problems was both encouraged and was often quite appropriate, did not sometimes reverse the balance excessively in favour of the 'inner' factors with resulting neglect of the 'outer' aspects. One particular form of abuse of the new source of understanding was the attempt to apply the psychoanalytic treatment model indiscriminately to social-work practice.

To the vast majority of British social workers the availability of the insights derived from dynamic psychology into the motivations and behaviour of human beings, particularly in circumstances of stress, opened up a new vista for understanding their clients and their problems, and this provided new opportunities for informed and appropriate helping. Many of the formerly puzzling phenomena within the client/social worker relationship, such as clients turning down a much-coveted service when it was made available to them, or failing to return after what seemed to have been a particularly helpful interview, became comprehensible, and therefore more capable of being resolved.

What the foregoing discussion has illustrated, I hope, is both the historical continuity of social workers' concern with both the 'inner' and the 'outer' aspects of human existence, and the difficulties inherent in an approach which integrates the two.

The concept of social functioning refers to the interaction between a person or persons and their environment, both human and physical, a matter of great complexity. A comparison between Mary Richmond's relatively static view of the relationship between the client and his family and their social context, and Gordon Hamilton's clear recognition of the dynamic nature of this relationship as exemplified in the following statement – 'the human event consists of person and situation, or subjective and objective reality, which constantly interact'[6] – is a further illustration of the debt social work owes to dynamic psychology. Before its contribution was available, it lacked the means to make fully operational its concern with problems of human living.

Inherent in the concept of 'social functioning' is the recognition of the social nature of man and thus of the psycho-social nature of all human problems. It is a validation of such poetic insights as those of Donne – 'No man is an island' – or of the Polish poet Mickiewicz – 'My name is Million because I love and suffer for Millions' – and a constant reminder to social workers that to view a person simply in terms of his personality – its inherent strengths and weaknesses – and to ignore the world of people and of objects in which he lives, is to deny the reality of human existence, and therefore not a promising base for intervention in problems of human living. Equally, an approach to such problems which focuses exclusively on environmental amelioration, on social reform, on changing others, and which ignores the person or persons experiencing the problem – how it affects them, what attitudes they bring to it and its solution – what they have done to minimise its impact upon them (or to aggravate it) – constitutes a blatant denial of individual autonomy and therefore of human dignity. At its extreme it implies a view of man as a pawn totally at the mercy of forces outside himself, a creature incapable of making any choices or decisions concerning himself.

At this point, to avoid any risk of misunderstanding, it is necessary to emphasise that the foregoing discussion concerning the implications of this concept of 'social functioning' refers specifically to the practice of social work, for which the concept is being offered as central. It is not intended to imply any denigration of other forms of activity which focus primarily either on intra-psychic change, as in psychotherapy, or on environmental and social change associated with political action and social movements of various kinds aimed at particular social reforms. On the contrary, it is the realisation of the value and the importance of these activities, and of the different kinds of expertise and commitment for which they call, which prompts me to emphasise these differences. Without this distinction, social work may become discredited through failure to delineate realistically its own boundaries and thus clarify the areas in which it can claim specific expertise and be called upon to account for it by society. To acknowledge this is not to deny areas of overlap or to encourage demarcation disputes. On the contrary, a clearer sense of its own identity, and the resulting increase in confidence and security on the part of social work, should promote greater flexibility and readiness to collaborate with others in its practitioners.

As has already been emphasised, the appreciation of the importance of being concerned with both the 'internal' and the 'external' dimensions of human existence has been implicit in social work from the outset. The formulations of this appreciation have until recently, however, lacked clarity and sufficient sharpness. They have therefore not been effective in counteracting the vagaries of practice to which social work, as already suggested, is particularly vulnerable, owing to its weak identity and to the tentative nature of much of its knowledge base.

A useful analysis of the meaning and the application to social work of the social-functioning perspective is offered by Bartlett.[7]

Bartlett's aim in writing her book was to provide a unifying conceptual base at a time when recognition was fast growing within social work that both the separate fields of practice such as those of medical and psychiatric social work, child care and probation, and the different methods of intervention, for example casework, group work and community work, were parts of a whole rather than separate entities. This growing awareness of the 'generic' factor was accompanied by confusion regarding its nature which prevented any real progress being made in forming a conceptual frame for social work.

In Bartlett's view the main origin of these conceptual problems lay in the excessive emphasis put by social workers upon the methodology of their practice at the expense of the value and the knowledge bases for their activities. The focus on the 'how' of practice rather than on the 'why' of it has resulted, in her view, in the creation of rigid 'methods boxes' and a lack of a wider perspective.

Unlike many American writers in social work Bartlett makes a number of references to British social work which help to identify the particular features of both the earlier fragmentation and the 'generic movement' in this country, many of which differ considerably from those in the United States. One striking characteristic, for example, is the fact that 'casework', as a conceptual framework for social work with individuals and families, was a latecomer to this country, being an import from the United States in the 1950s. This obviously does not mean that casework was not practised by British social workers up till then; what it does mean is that it was practised alongside a good deal of community work (for example settlement work, work done by Councils of Social Service, and activities by individual practitioners in various agencies aimed at inter-agency liaison and collaboration) and a certain amount of group work (particularly with young people), neither of which activities was separately labelled. When formalised teaching in social casework was started in this country, this form of social work was 'dignified' and acquired a good deal of resulting prestige. Because there was no parallel 'dignification' at the time of either social group work or of community work, the latter activities atrophied rather than developed – throughout the 1950s and early 1960s – they were certainly not greatly discussed or written about.

It was the developments within social casework which led British social workers in the different fields of practice to realise that what they were all doing had a great deal in common, that they were in fact practitioners of a single art. It was this growing realisation which provided the basis for both the start of 'generic training' in educational establishments and the formation of a unified association of social workers.

Paradoxically, however, this coming together and closing of the ranks on the part of the 'caseworkers' made the incorporation into social work of both group work and community work in Britain more difficult once these were ready to make their voice heard and their claims for professional social-work status considered. This was because for nearly two decades professional social work (with the implicit criteria of education and competence) was seen as being synonymous with social casework.

However understandable this situation in the light of its history, it nevertheless underlines the conceptual confusion to which Bartlett has referred. To describe any activity in terms of its methods, rather than on the basis of its objectives, is to put the cart before the horse. This is as true of medicine, of architecture and of plumbing as it is of social work! The implications of such a confusion are particularly serious in a field of endeavour which addresses itself directly to human problems of living. Unless everything that social workers do is directly related to the central objective of promoting social functioning and the more specific objectives derived from it which are applicable in particular situations, they run a very real risk of turning their activities into ends in themselves. Although the end by no means justifies all means, and this is particularly true in social work where the means as well as the ends have to be ethically justifiable, nevertheless clarity about one's purpose and faithfulness to it are important elements of guidance and control over what one actually does.

Whilst emphasising the central importance in social work of 'social functioning' as the key concept, Bartlett acknowledges readily that the breadth of that concept makes it insufficient in itself to give social work its distinct nature. Her further elaboration of the concept as applicable to social work refers to several more specific characteristics. The stress upon the meaning of their situations to the people who experience them is the chief of these. Social work is concerned with people (be they individuals, families, groups or communities) exposed to actual life events, and not with either hypothetical human problems or with abstract issues.

The practical implications of this difference are in turn made clear by Bartlett's analysis of social functioning into the concepts of 'task' and of 'coping'. In her words, 'tasks refer to social phenomena, not techniques'.[8] They have to do with situations confronting people which have both social and psychological implications for them. The concept of 'coping' has to do with the other side of the coin: with the resources, both within the person, group or community and within the environment, which are available to draw upon in confronting the task or tasks.

Such a formulation brings the concept of 'social functioning' to a somewhat lower level of abstraction. The identification of social work with a focal concern upon the meaning of specific aspects of social functioning to actual persons, made operational through particular attention to the tasks inherent in these situations for those persons, and their coping abilities in confronting these tasks, provides a useful foundation on which to build a separate identity for social work.

The fact that this is no more than a foundation is clear when one considers the range of factors which influence the actual nature, extent and effectiveness of the encounters between social workers and people with problems in social functioning. Many of these will be considered in some detail in further chapters but some reference to them at this point seems appropriate. The nature of values in relation to the various problems and what constitutes a helpful approach to them is clearly a vital determinant. Of equal importance is the conceptual approach brought by social workers to these problems: what kinds of knowledge are they equipped with, and how adequate is it for a proper understanding of clients' tasks in living and of their coping abilities – after all 'the road to hell is paved with good intentions!' A framework of values and of knowledge, and the skills based on these, is not the only resource necessary for professional intervention in the lives of other people. An appropriate mandate to carry the job, legal, administrative and moral, and a range of such tangible tools as offices and equipment as well as supportive services from home helps, meals on wheels, day centres, remand homes, residential institutions, and others, are essential.

Inherent in the concept of 'social functioning' is that as problems reside in both the environment and the people, solutions to these problems need to come from both the environment and the people. To attempt to deal with a problem of homelessness exclusively by means of psychological support is as futile as trying to provide tempting titbits to a person suffering from *anorexia nervosa*.

Perhaps at this point it is worth pointing out how much easier it is to give lip-service to this notion of 'social functioning' than to be consistent in applying it in practice. There may be problems which do not entail such an interaction, and it is certainly possible to deal with most without focusing on it; however, where this is the case, whatever the nature of the intervention in the problem, it is not social work. To acknowledge this does not imply any automatic judgement as to what type of intervention is the more appropriate in a given situation, but the distinction is important to make for many good reasons, both conceptual and practical. A definition of social work as a form of professional activity concerned with intervening in problems of social functioning logically and therefore inescapably entails the need to attend to both the 'inner' and the 'outer' worlds of human persons, and to the relationship between them. Yet there is a good deal of evidence that not only people outside social work, but some social workers too, fail to recognise the implications of this. Currently, one cannot fail but witness the dual trend of more and more different functions being allocated to social work, and at the same time an increasing proportion of the time of many social workers being spent on activities which cannot meet the criteria of social work as above defined, however much one might try to stretch them. Where people are expected to carry excessive caseloads, where no differentiation is made regarding their competence in dealing with different kinds of problem and where no professional guidance is offered to those newly qualified or relatively inexperienced, there cannot be an adequate standard of assessment of the problems dealt with. Their meaning to the people concerned, the ratio of, and relationship between, personal and environmental factors, the ability to discriminate between the various forms of help that might be called for, are likely to be overlooked or lacking. In such circumstances, inevitably, social work turns into a routine administration of benefits, of advice, of channelling elsewhere; it becomes a form of residual social service, and thus ceases to be social work.

This dilemma currently facing social work has very serious implications for its future in that it is likely to add further to the problem of the identity of social work at a time when its expansion and the accompanying investment of public money and public trust in it call more urgently for a clarification of what social work is, what it stands for, and what it can achieve, than ever before in history.

It is possible to identify two current threats to the identity of social work.

One of these is the lack of an adequate job definition of social work, especially within the context of Social Services Departments (Social Work Departments in Scotland). They are by far the largest single employer of social workers with virtually a monopoly of their employment since the integration of hospital social work with local-authority-based social work as from 1 April 1974 (1 May 1975 in Scotland). This reflects, in turn, a more fundamental failure on the part of many people to differentiate social work from other social services as a specific service. This point was well emphasised by Butler.[9] In her view the various needs of clients of Social Services Departments can be divided into the following main areas.

(i) *Those 'beyond the agency's remit'*, for example 'housing, poverty, unemployment, and other major areas of social difficulty'. Social Services Departments 'were not set up to deal with such difficulties and have neither the sanction nor resources to try to do so'. The social worker's task in relation to these needs is to transmit them to appropriate institutions and to press for the necessary changes in policies and provisions on the basis of real information available to them.

(ii) *'Matters of right or entitlement'*. These, according to Butler, refer to 'the major service-giving elements of social services departments: meals on wheels, clubs, transport, bath rails, home helps, information and advice, the whole range of aids and aides, to enable people to live more comfortably and with less stress'. Whilst social workers need to know 'the range of services available, who to contact, and how, where to find the necessary information', the actual administration of these various services is not part of social workers' task.

(iii) *Needs for 'support and containment'*, which are derived from the problems experienced by certain groups of clients and their families who, for periods of differing duration, require someone to stand by them 'through thick and thin'. Many of these needs can be met by volunteers and others who are not trained social workers but the latter's involvement is often needed at the stage of assessment, initiating of help, and in providing over-all support and supervision to the 'supporters' and the 'containers'.

(iv) *'Provision for the quality of inner life'*. Butler includes a wide range of clients and of problem situations in this category: 'those who need some sort of alternative home care of special kind; adoption, fostering of the young or the old, therapeutic hostels, schools and homes ... marital reconciliation, or crisis-work; all such needs which have to do with people's relationships with each other and the quality of life and personal responsibility they may be able to move towards.' All of these call for social-work intervention and should therefore make up the bulk of social workers' caseloads.

A lack of proper differentiation between social work and other kinds of social service is not only grossly uneconomical but it is also conducive to a relative absence of job satisfaction on the part of social workers who resent having to spend a large proportion of their time in activities in which their professional education and training are of a peripheral relevance only. A further serious consequence of this is the continued lack of clarity on the part of many members of society, including large numbers of potential clients and referral agents, as to what social work is and in what types of problem it can assist. In terms of the public image of social work there is currently a very real risk that, by appearing to claim competence in so many different spheres and at the same time failing to show its effectiveness in much of what it does, social work will become discredited. This has already happened to some extent with regard to the care of the mentally ill in the community which many psychiatrists and general practitioners regard as having deteriorated since the disappearance of the 'specialist' mental welfare officer, and in relation to 'children at risk' following a series of deaths of a non-accidental nature by children in families known to social workers. More will be said about these issues of function and of specialisation in later chapters, but reference to them was necessary here in view of their direct relevance to the subject under consideration.

The other serious cause of confusion regarding the nature of social work is what, for the lack of a better term, can be called its 'politicisation'. This is by no means a unique British phenomenon – on the contrary, the articles by Specht[10] and Kendall[11] show how widespread it is. However, our concern here is with the particular manifestations of this current in Britain.

As has already been emphasised, inherent in the nature of social work is its vulnerability to distortion either in the direction of psychotherapy or of politics.

I have argued that, in the past, the threat of a 'psychotherapeutic takeover' of social work in Britain was more in the nature of a myth than of reality. Equally it would be mistaken to view the current 'psychotherapy in social work' movement as a denial of the distinct nature of social work. On the contrary, it is in my view a manifestation of the concern on the part of many social workers at the widespread neglect of the psychological component in the assessment of, and response to, human problems, especially by those who view social work as primarily a political tool.

The nature of the origins and the process of the new political commitment within social work are not easy to formulate. It commonly takes the form of an attack upon and a reaction against social casework, which is viewed on the basis of a misconstrued identity as solely an agent of social control and a reflection of the consensus view of society. Two major threads appear to run through these anti-casework arguments. One of these is that by being prepared to assist individuals faced by such social problems as those of inadequate housing, unemployment or inadequate income to manage better in their situation, social workers not only condone social injustice but assist it to continue. The other argument reflects even more clearly the underlying confusion regarding the nature of social work in general and social casework in particular because it equates intervention in individual problems of social deprivation with ascribing to those suffering from it the primary responsibility for their predicament. If one stretched this argument to its logical conclusion, presumably one should not intervene in helping a sufferer from an incurable disease have a somewhat easier time lest such intervention should be seen to imply his personal inadequacy.

There seems no doubt that there is a connection, and probably a close one, between this revolt against the individualisation of problems, and the discovery in recent years of the extent to which certain social problems of deprivation are widespread in our affluent society. Another important strand in the process is that of the re-emergence of community work and the close association of a large and vocal section of it with political action. The extent to which there is a widespread tendency among community workers to equate community work with such action, and to ignore the fact that it is but one element of it, is both recognised and questioned by Baldock[12] among others.

I very much share Butler's view[13] that there are no grounds for social work to claim a sense of special over-all responsibility for such massive national social problems as those of homelessness, poverty and unemployment. These are, by their very definition, problems for our society as a whole. This is not to say, of course, that in addition to the personal responsibility for these problems, which all individuals should acknowledge in virtue of their role as citizens, there are not groups of professionals and others with additional and more particular responsibilities. Social workers are one of these groups, but only one. Their responsibilities carry a differential aspect in virtue of social workers' particular knowledge and experience of, say, homelessness and its impact on individuals and families, but are not necessarily greater than the responsibilities of other groups, for example doctors and teachers, who, also, in the course of their professional work, come face to face with these problems and who know (or ought to know) what they do to people. I am thus arguing against social workers assuming their own omnipotence by seeing themselves as being more responsible for these problems than others.

On a more practical level, and this links with my earlier point regarding the proper functions of social workers, if an undue amount of their time and effort is spent on arguing about these general issues, then this must inevitably be at the expense of the requirements of their primary role – that of assisting people in their problems of social functioning. By making this point I am not arguing against social workers' involvement in social action; on the contrary, in my view, inherent in the responsibilities of any profession or other occupational group is to make available to society at large its cumulative experience of what it is which is lacking in that society and needs to be put right. More than this, that responsibility should not be confined to just producing the data and adopting a neutral attitude towards them; any responsible social group should argue and press for the utilisation of these data in ways which are conducive to the well-being of society. This social workers must do, just as doctors and teachers should be actively involved in the political aspects of health care and of education respectively.

To acknowledge this is not to suggest, however, that politics can be a substitute for social work – a stance which is taken by some people today. These appear to see no incongruity in wishing to have a primarily political role legitimised within social work whilst having little or no commitment to social-work practice. This point is dealt with well in the following statement in the British Association of Social Workers Report on Social Action and Social Work:

> Social Action, like any other part of social work, must be informed by social work values, perhaps the most relevant of which is the belief that people should be treated as ends in themselves and not as instruments. Thus the client is not to be regarded as an instrument of social change, but as a person who, in interaction with other people in similar situations, with social workers and with social work agencies, can bring about desired social changes ... [and] Social Action is of equal relevance to the caseworker, the group worker and the community worker as a supplement to, and not as a substitute for, other ways of working.[14]

In summary, the resolution of these twin issues of social workers' proper functions, and of the place of political action in social work, is an essential prerequisite to an establishment of a clear social-work identity. Such an identity need not be synonymous with rigidity or exclusiveness – two common by-products of professionalism feared by some social workers – and it is hard to deny the need for it on other grounds. Society has a right to know what it can expect and demand of social work, especially at a time when it invests increasingly heavy resources in it. I go all the way with Bartlett when she says that,

> For a profession like social work to be effective in to-day's society, it must identify an area of central concern that is (1) common to the profession as a whole, (2) meaningful in terms of the profession's values and goals, (3) practical in terms of available and attainable knowledge and techniques, and (4) sufficiently distinctive so that it does not duplicate what other professions are doing.[15]

Chapter 2

Models of Social-Work Practice

The concept of 'social functioning', as described in the previous chapter, provides social work with its basic terms of reference in relation to its broad objectives. It is, however, too abstract a concept for operational purposes and it calls for 'middle-range' generalisations for its application to social-work practice to be effective. It is not surprising, therefore, that an integral element in all conceptualisations of social-work practice has been an attempt to 'translate' the meaning of social functioning into some more tangible terms. An analysis of these different attempts provides valuable insights into the nature of the complexity of social work as a helping activity, and can thus serve as a useful supplement to some of the discussion in the preceding chapter.

The choice of 'models' for such an analysis has inevitably been an arbitrary one, partly for the reason that there is no general agreement within social work about which of the many formulations concerning the nature of social-work practice should be viewed as constituting distinct 'models'. There is not even absolute agreement as to what constitutes 'a model'. Thus in Roberts and Nee[1] no clear distinction appears to be drawn between 'theories' and 'models', and so the latter have been 'dignified' as 'theories'. In contrast, Reid and Epstein regard a model as 'basically definitional and descriptive', and as having 'a relatively low information yield'.[2] In their view, theory underlies and justifies models by providing an analytical framework for them, and thus enabling an examination of the 'whys' of practice.

In this discussion, the Oxford English Dictionary definition of model as 'representation of structure' is taken as a common basis for the inclusion of the various representations of social-work practice. In addition, Goldstein's criterion for the evaluation of models, namely that 'a model is useful only in its "goodness of fit" to the reality it is intended to represent',[3] is accepted.

Within the space available, the description and the analysis of the different models has inevitably to be limited. These are fully documented in their presentation by their own authors and so a detailed account of them would have entailed a good deal of repetition. The justification for their examination here rests, as already suggested, on their potential value in helping to clarify the over-all nature of social work.

The Problem-Solving Model

This model owes its existence to Perlman who has been elaborating it gradually over the years. Her formulations can be traced through her many writings, in particular *Social Casework: A Problem-Solving Process*,[4] 'The Problem-Solving Model in Social Casework',[5] and 'Social Casework in Social Work: its Place and Purpose'.[6]

The main emphasis in this model is on social casework as an extension of the processes of ordinary living. Life consists of problem-solving activities. For much of the time human beings are engaged in these activities without being consciously aware of their challenge to themselves. It is only when, for some reason, their usual equipment for meeting life situations fails them that they become aware of being faced with a problem. When this happens, new resources for dealing with the situation have to be mobilised. In some situations, for some people, this necessitates outside help. Potentially, no person is immune from being outfaced by certain demands made upon him by the exigencies of living. To whom this happens, and when, is dependent on a number of interrelated factors. According to Perlman these fall into the following three categories:

1. There are actual deficits of means by which to cope (e.g. material lacks, physical and intellectual deficits, emotional limitations).

2. There are discrepancies between what the role task or role relationship requires and the person's motivation and capacity; discrepancies between expectations held by the several persons involved in the role network; discrepancies between the actuality and the person's reading of it. Thus the persons involved are thwarted, blocked, or confused about how to cope.

3. There are disturbances or distortions of emotion, thought and/or behaviour symptomatic of personality difficulties that disturb or distort coping with person-to-person or self-to-task transactions.[7]

Social casework is a form of helping which is based on the acknowledgement that problems in living can only be resolved by those who experience them. There is thus no question of a complete 'takeover'. The social worker does not attempt to deal with the problem on behalf of his clients – what he does is to try to reinforce the existing resources within the client's own personality and his environment, both human and material, so that these can be more equally matched to the challenge of the problem.

The process of helping therefore incorporates the relationship between the client and the social worker as a major medium of helping. It is through this medium that the person with a problem is supported and nurtured, can experience respect, acceptance, empathy and caring, and can be offered hope in his current plight for an improved future. This is best summed up in Perlman's own words:

Within the problem-solving approach it is relationship that warms the intelligence, sustains the spirit, and carries the person forward in what would otherwise be a cool, rational process. Its rewards of nurture and steadfastness and recognition make it possible to bear the frustrations and compromises that problem-work involves, since there are few life situations that yield easily to problem-solving efforts and fewer still that may be completely 'solved'. Moreover, relationship developed offers the sense of oneness or identification of client with caseworker. In this there inheres the chance to 'borrow strength', to learn by both imitation and unconscious incorporation.[8]

Perlman is very explicit, however, about the fact that relationship is a means to the end of problem solving and not an end it itself. Thus, in her own words,

> No applicant comes to a social agency asking for a relationship. He does not say 'I want love' – or 'I want social affirmation', although his problem in interpersonal relationships may reveal such needs. He comes, as has been said, to get help with some tangibly identified problem in his social transactions. He hopes that the person who is charged with giving him such help will be competent, will be authorised, and will lend himself with concerned attentions to his needs.[9]

In her view, the process of helping consists of four interrelated elements: the person who has the problem; the nature of the problem; the place within which the helping takes place; and the process by which problem solving is carried out.

The main feature of her approach to 'the person' is her view of human nature as constantly in the making. This combines optimism about the potential feasibility of some resolution of even the most intractable problems with realism, which enables her to acknowledge the value of partial solutions and of amelioration as opposed to 'cure'. It also contains the dual recognition of the need to adopt a holistic approach to people and the validity of partialisation when dealing with particular aspects of their living.

Equally, her view of 'the problem' element is a pragmatic one. The emphasis is not on a search for every identifiable source of difficulty or deficiency but on the need to make the problem to be worked upon explicit, clearly defined and understood in relation to what can be done about it. No grand comprehensive diagnostic schemes are advocated.

The variable of 'the place' gives recognition to the importance of the organisational, structural and resource-providing framework inherent in the concept of agency function, although the elaboration of this dimension in Perlman's own writings is less than in the case of the other elements.

In keeping with her general stress upon the client being the ultimate resolver of his own problem, in her discussion of 'process' Perlman puts great emphasis upon the need to engage the person being helped in the problem-solving process, to help him effect transition from being 'an applicant' to becoming 'a client', to promote generally his right to self-determination and to make the exercise of that right more effective through increasing the range of his choices. The equal importance in problem solving of both cognitive and affective processes is stressed throughout.

The chief distinguishing features of the Perlman model, in terms of its particular interpretation and translation of the concept of 'social functioning', are in my view these:

(1) The view regarding the normality of problem-solving tasks, and therefore of the difficulties experienced in meeting these tasks, rather than upon the pathology of failure to manage;

(2) The degree of emphasis on the client as the main agent of change; and

(3) The attention given to social roles as the context within which problems in living both occur and need to be resolved.

All of these three 'value orientations' carry considerable implications for the knowledge base of social work and for its methodology. They certainly make social-work practice incompatible with an exclusive focus upon either the individual personality or the social environment, and consequently make it imperative for social workers to take serious notice of any theoretical contributions which can assist them to gain the necessary understanding of both. It seems to me, therefore, that the problem-solving model of social-work practice, besides making an important contribution to social-work thinking in its own right, has also laid the foundation for some of the more recent attempts at conceptualising social-work practice to which reference will be made later in this chapter.

The Psycho-Social Therapy Model

Hollis is the best known exponent of this model within which the central tenets of the 'diagnostic school' of social work in the United States have been incorporated. That school has a long tradition going back to Mary Richmond and counting among its exponents such well-known social thinkers as Gordon Hamilton, Lucille Austin, Annette Garrett and Charlotte Towle.

One of the chief characteristics of the psycho-social therapy model and its major contribution to social work has been the importance attached to the content and the process of 'psycho-social study' as an essential prerequisite to 'psycho-social treatment'. This has resulted in the considerable attention given by writers belonging to the diagnostic school to the various components of a social 'diagnosis' and how these can be elucidated. Although all of these writers have subscribed to the 'social-functioning' perspective and therefore saw 'the person-in-situation gestalt or configuration'[10] as the subject matter for the diagnostic approach, their model of social casework has increasingly become founded upon Freudian personality theory. Hollis explicitly acknowledges this in her account of the 'psycho-social approach', with the result that formulations concerning personality assessment and treatment of intra-and interpersonal conflicts have outstripped by a very considerable margin those relating to the social and the material environment of clients. This fact has come under increasing criticism in recent years both from within social work and from outside. What is equally important to recognise is that some of these criticisms do less than justice to the positive features of the model. They fail to appreciate that it is the very sophistication of the model in the psychological sphere that has made it such an easy victim of the unavailability and inadequacy of the parallel theories upon which to draw for an assessment of the societal dimension of social functioning.

Given this fact, the various implications of the use of the medical model implicit in the psycho-social therapy model of social casework are worthy of examination. As already suggested, such a model serves as an important source of encouragement to a thorough and a disciplined approach to the gathering of relevant information and to the drawing of relevant conclusions as a basis for planned and appropriate treatment of the condition or problem diagnosed. Such an encouragement has particular value in a sphere of activity as broad and as lacking in specific definition as social work, where the temptation to hide behind the basically unknowable nature of man and his problems, and so abstain from trying to comprehend what is understandable, is very real.

On the other hand, the model does emphasise the nature of the social worker as an expert to a potentially inappropriate degree. The extent to which the client himself is the ultimate judge of what troubles him, how much, and what he is prepared to do about the problem, could be overlooked. This could, in turn, reflect on the nature and the quality of the relationship established between the social worker and the client. Relationship plays a focal part in the psycho-social therapy process, and this includes the recognition of the element of mutuality in it. This mutuality is affected by the extent to which the client is seen as either an active participant in the process of understanding his problem and working on it, or as being a relatively passive respondent to the diagnostic enquiries of the social worker and a passive recipient of his treatment approaches. It is hard to deny that the psycho-social therapy model contains in it the occupational hazard of the social worker assuming too readily that he knows best what is good for his clients.

A criticism commonly levelled against the model is that it calls for such an extensive study of the problem and its various ramifications, in terms of both depth and historical perspective, that it is unsuitable for the large majority of problems which come to social workers. The validity of this criticism is not easy to assess. It would seem to be true that if the diagnostic requirements of the model were interpreted in certain rigid ways, this would require not only a good deal of time, but also a specific kind of motivation on the part of the clients to engage in a lengthy process of scrutiny of themselves and their life situation before being able to expect much tangible help and relief with their problem. However, there is no evidence that implicit in the model is the need to interpret it in such ways. On the contrary, not only the permission but the necessity for selectivity in what one is attempting to find out and understand is stressed by Hollis herself. Thus, whilst acknowledging the importance attached by many social workers of the diagnostic school to early childhood experiences, especially in problems of self-adjustment, she has this to say:

> Differential seeking of history, however, has always been recognised in diagnostic theory, and it received additional emphasis from the mid-thirties on. It is chiefly when the client's actions and responses in his current situation seem inappropriate that it becomes pertinent to inquire about aspects of his past life which our knowledge of human development leads us to believe may be influencing this inappropriateness and which therefore it might help the worker understand his reactions and know what help to offer.[11]

She also quotes with full approbation the well-known dictum by Gordon Hamilton: 'If a question is not pertinent, it is impertinent!'[12]

A major contribution by Hollis has been her various attempts to conceptualise the differential treatment approaches within the psycho-social therapy model. Her latest classification 'considers casework treatment as consisting of a series of verbal and non-verbal communications, and classifies these communications according to several dimensions'.[13] One of these dimensions differentiates between communications with the client ('direct treatment') and communications with others on behalf of the client ('indirect treatment'). The other major dimension is concerned with the dynamics of communication.

This classification of 'helping procedures' has been widely adopted in social work, reflecting both the degree of influence of 'diagnostic casework' within social work and the paucity of comparable classifications within other orientations. The imbalance within the model between conceptualisations regarding intra-psychic and interpersonal factors on the one hand, and those belonging to the social environment on the other, to which reference has already been made, is further reflected in the rather limited formulation of 'indirect treatment' as opposed to 'direct treatment'. The former is seen too exclusively as a modified version of the latter. Such an approach fails to take account of a number of important variables including the implications for the nature of the relationship between the social worker and those 'others' of their role differing from that of a client. It thus tends to contribute further to the current tendencies on the part of some social workers to reject the whole of the 'psycho-social therapy' model as being too exclusively concerned with the psychological dimension of psycho-social functioning.

One valuable contribution of the model which is in particular danger of being lost is its uncompromising assertion that, regardless of the nature and the origins of a problem, it is being experienced by a human person and therefore calls for attempts to understand the person and his reactions to the problem, as well as understanding the problem itself.

The Functional Model

This model represents the other major school of thought within American social work up to recent times. Smalley's formulation of it will be used here[14] but, like the diagnostic school, so also the functional school has had a number of other important adherents, including Jessie Taft, Virginia Robinson, Kenneth Pray and Alan K. Lucas.

Unlike the 'psycho-social therapy' model of social casework, the 'functional' model is by its very nature a much less cohesive one, and so in some ways quite elusive when it comes to attempts to describe it. It came into being as a reaction against an excessive influence upon social work of what was felt by some social workers to be a deterministic and mechanistic view of man as embodied in Freudian psychology. In its place the psychological foundations upon which the functional model was built were those of Otto Rank. The concepts in that psychology most relevant to the functional approach were those of the 'will' and the conflicting fears of separation and of death common to all human beings as a result of the birth trauma.

The concept of the 'will' is well conveyed in the following quotation from Smalley:

> The environment may influence, retard, divert, and complicate the development of the individual, but he remains in control of his own growth, central in his own development, and capable of continuing development throughout his life's course within the limits of his particular capacities and environmental opportunity at a given point in time.[15]

Both concepts, those of the 'will' and of the ambivalence over the respective fears of separation and of death, have led logically to the central importance with which the relationship between the social worker and the client has been invested by the functionalists. It is embodied in the concept of 'process', which has a unique meaning within the functional formulation, best conveyed in the words of Smalley herself:

> The functional school developed the concept of social casework as a helping process through which an agency's service was made available with the principles of social work method having to do with the initiating, sustaining, and terminating of a process in human relationship.[16]

As Smalley goes on to describe, such a formulation of the central objective for encounters between social workers and their clients has a number of important practical implications. One of these relates to diagnosis and treatment. Functionalists see themselves as operating to a 'psychology of growth' as opposed to the 'psychology of illness', which they claim underlies the activities of social workers who adhere to the diagnostic school. Therefore a diagnosis as a separate stage in the casework process has no place in the functional model. Instead, social workers of the functional school see their understanding of their clients' situations develop as an integral part of their giving a service and one which is subject to continuous modification. Equally, their view of the focus of change lying within the client and not the social worker, whose function is to facilitate the client's own potentialities for choice and growth, has made them reject the notion of 'treatment' in favour of that of 'helping'.

Given the somewhat esoteric nature of Rankian psychology and of the concept of 'process' as viewed by the functionalists, it is not easy to form a coherent picture of the 'functional' model. In spite of this fact there are a number of aspects of this model which have considerable value and relevance to the practice of social work.

One of these is the importance which the model attaches to agency function. Thus Smalley writes:

> The diagnostic group saw the purpose of social work as effecting a healthy personal and social condition in the clientele served, with the specific purpose of the agency not only secondary but also sometimes in a curious way parallel to, detached from, or even in opposition to the purpose of the worker. The functional group saw the purpose of the agency as representing a partial or concrete instance of social work's overall purpose and as giving focus, direction and content to the worker's practice.[17]

In this country, for reasons referred to in Chapter 1, there has always been a much more general recognition of the importance of the relationship between the agency (or setting) and social-work practice (see Timms[18] and Winnicott.)[19] In fact, Timms's emphasis on social casework as 'a means of fulfilling agency function' is almost open to being misinterpreted as denying social work any autonomy but as seeing it as a mere instrument for implementing agency policies.

Winnicott's approach to the relationship between social-work practice and agency function is more comprehensive and incorporates both sociological and psychological concepts. She clearly goes along with the late Professor Titmuss's view that 'the worker, the client and the setting are the basic components of action and must be viewed as a whole', by quoting him in the context of her discussion of this subject.[20] She expresses her own view regarding the nature of the relationship between social work and agency function thus:

Sometimes social workers talk as if the social services exist in order to provide a setting in which they can practice their casework skills. I can appreciate this keenness to establish professional skill – it must be present in every caseworker otherwise he or she will never achieve anything . . . But the question of emphasis arises. Is the caseworker aiming at practising a professional skill, or at serving the community? We know that in the interests of all, these aims must be complementary and integrated into the professional life of each social worker.[21]

In addition, Winnicott sees agency function as a means by which the relationship between society and its various members, subject to differing types of problem, is mediated in both tangible and symbolic terms. She thus argues that the primary social function of probation officers is to offer their clients a corrective experience of authority which is reasonable, consistent and based on concern for the other person, the type of authority which many of these clients have lacked in the past. Similarly, the functions of a child-care officer are to provide substitute parental care to deprived children and their depriving parents with all that this entails. Equally, medical and psychiatric social workers have their unique functions derived from the fact that they are an integral part of healing institutions, and thus represent the element of healing in their own work with their clients.

As will be realised, this formulation of social work in relation to agency function precedes the Seebohm Committee's Report[22] and the setting up of the generic Social Services Departments in local authorities. At first glance it is therefore no longer applicable, and of a historical interest only. However, without anticipating some of the discussion in later chapters, this should by no means be taken for granted. Being employed by the same authority need not be synonymous with working in one setting. In fact, the increasing number of social workers attached to general medical practice or schools, the continued presence of social workers in hospitals, and the dissatisfaction with lack of specialisation in such fields as those of mental health and child care, are but some of the indications that the relationship between the nature of social-work practice and the agency within which it occurs may soon become invested with renewed importance and interest.

The other element within the 'functional' model which deserves specific mention is that of the time factor. The model puts great stress on the potentialities inherent in the different phases of the contact between the social worker and the client, and provides considerable stimulus for a deliberate and an imaginative use of these potentialities. A failure to realise these was a common feature of much social work in the past, this taking a number of different forms. At the one extreme, the tendency to equate the length of contact with a client with the amount of help offered to him has tended to encourage a lack of critical evaluation of how the time was being used; at the other end of the continuum, brief contacts were often considered to offer only limited opportunities for meaningful exchanges, and this served as an excuse for not analysing their content and dynamics. For a number of reasons there has been a recent upsurge of interest in the time factor with regard to the practice of social work and there can be little doubt that some of these have a connection with the 'functional' view of the change process.

④ The 'Ministration in Love' Model

The formulation of such a model constitutes an attempt on my part to bring together and conceptualise a number of different orientations both within psychotherapy and social work which, however disparate and often non-specific, have nevertheless an important feature in common. This is the primacy given to the relationship as a source of helping, healing and growth in itself.

The foundations for this approach are largely derived from Christianity (or the 'Judeo-Christian tradition' as some writers put it) and existentialism as expressed in the writings of such thinkers as Kierkegaard and Buber. The concept of 'ministration in love' emerges most clearly from Halmos. *The Faith of the Counsellors*[23] is a book which, in spite of its largely polemical tone and its tendency to overstate the case, provides, nevertheless, some important insights into the ideology and motivations of 'counsellors', social workers included, and which in my view has been dismissed too readily by many people. The following few quotations convey Halmos's view of the values and the objectives underlying this form of helping:

> basic principles of work are, that human happiness and unhappiness are more or less autonomous conditions of the single individual, and

that their personal access to the single individual, seeking help, is the only method that could possibly make any marked and lasting difference to him ... The Faith of the Counsellors is a central feature of what is generic in all forms of counselling; all counsellors seem to be imbued with sentiments of worthwhileness in giving personal service to others ... The counsellor's identification with the role he constantly plays results in a rare and impressive accumulation of a sympathetic and caring attitude towards others ... the works of counselling are more Christian than most practices of our times ... [and] Counselling has brought back to the healing professions much of the humanity, which an advancing science has made precarious.[24]

The main tenets underlying these arguments are the primacy of love over science and technology, and hence the effectiveness of 'relationship therapy' over and above all other forms of intervention in human problems; tenets which are in turn derived from a view of human nature as constantly in the making and capable of growth and improvement, as opposed to a more deterministic orientation.

Halmos describes himself as an objective outside observer and critic of 'counselling' who is not a member of that 'culture' himself, and this fact is reflected in his approach to some of the operational issues in personal helping, for example that of 'the fiction of non-directiveness'.

Within the field of 'relationship therapy', the writings of Rogers are a good illustration of the application of the philosophy of the primacy of relationship. Rogers defines a 'helping relationship' as 'a relationship in which at least one of the parties has the intent of promoting the growth, development, maturity, improved functioning, improved coping with life of the other'.[25] Rogers sees as the main ingredients of a helping relationship warmth and an egalitarian attitude towards the other person; orientation towards the personality of the patient; promotion of a sense of trust on his part and a fostering of independence. His studies of the outcomes of various types of therapy have led him to conclude that a sense of mutual liking and respect between the patient and therapist was a much more potent factor in effectiveness than any particular method or technique adopted. His summary of all these attributes of a helping relationship under the four headings of 'empathy', 'positive regard', 'genuineness' and 'matched emotional response' are generally known and widely used in all discussions of personal therapy and counselling. What is worth adding is that the emphasis by Halmos on the extent of ideological commitment on the part of the 'counsellors' to what they are attempting to do seems to be borne out by much of what Rogers and his followers are expressing in their writings; for example Rogers writes:

> all of us who are working in the field of human relationships and trying to understand the basic orderliness of that field, are engaged in the most crucial enterprise in to-day's world . . . we are working on the problem which will determine the future of this planet. For it is not upon the physical sciences that the future will depend. It is upon us who are trying to understand and deal with the interactions between human beings – who are trying to create helping relationships.[26]

So far, in trying to look at the 'ministration in love' model, no specific reference has been made to its application to the field of social work. As will be realised, many of the formulations regarding the therapeutic use of the relationship between the helper and the person being helped are derived from the field of psychotherapy. This is reflected in the difficulties presented to social workers by the implementation in their work of some of the basic principles of 'relationship therapy' as conceived by Rogers, for example in relation to 'non-directiveness'. To Rogers this principle appears to possess an almost absolute value whilst it needs no great effort to show that many of the social workers' functions mandated by society, such as those related to the need to protect some people from others and from themselves, require a considerable degree of directiveness. There is, however, a more substantial and general reason why the acceptance of the importance of relationship as a major medium of helping in social work must assume its own characteristics, namely because its objectives differ from those of psychotherapy.

A fuller discussion of the specific place of relationship in social work will be left to a later chapter. In this context it is relevant to underline that a central place for relationships of all kinds, including those between the social worker and his clients, is implicit in the 'social-functioning' perspective of social work. This has always been recognised by social workers whatever form their formulations of this fact have taken. I also hope that the discussion of the 'problem-solving', the 'psycho-social therapy' and the 'functional' models has succeeded in conveying the central place of the social worker/client relationship in all three.

In addition to this common characteristic, what applies to all the models discussed so far is their general relevance to a wide range of situations, notwithstanding their particular strengths and limitations. In my view they are complementary rather than mutually exclusive as no one model does justice on its own to the complex nature of social work.

In contrast, the three models to which reference will be made next have certain inbuilt limitations which restrict their applicability to certain kinds of situations. The three models are the 'behaviour-modification model', the 'crisis-intervention' model and the 'task-centred casework model'.

The Behaviour-Modification Model

Underlying this model of social-work practice are the various learning theories which emphasise the importance of socialisation, show the extent to which human behaviour is learned behaviour, and trace the steps by which learning takes place. In terms of the model of practice itself this is founded on rather few selected aspects of learning theory, namely those which focus on actual behaviour to the exclusion of other factors. Thomas has formulated it thus: 'All behaviour is pertinent – "thoughts", "affect", as well as motor action – providing that it is discernible through the senses of the observer and can be reliably denoted.'[27] This means that such features of human life as the meaning of events to people and past influences on current functioning are of no relevance to the behavioural therapist. His focus is exclusively on current operant and respondent behaviour and on how this can be modified through either reinforcement or extinguishing. Hence in the behaviour-modification approach, more so than in any of the other approaches, considerable emphasis is put upon the technology of change and upon the particular behaviour-modification techniques. There is an accompanying lack of interest in, and attention to, the broader considerations regarding the nature of human life and functioning and the values surrounding it.

Because of these factors, the behaviour-modification approach has been severely questioned in terms of its basic compatibility with social-work philosophy and values. The main criticisms levelled at it are that it is based on a deterministic and a mechanistic view of man in which the biological components of human nature are given an excessively important place at the expense of the psychological and the spiritual components, and the degree of partialisation inherent in paying attention to symptoms only, and in not going beyond these, is incompatible with a holistic view and diminishes man in stature. In addition, some of the techniques of behaviour-modification, particularly those relating to extinguishing undesirable behaviour, for example token-economy and aversion-therapy techniques, are incompatible with the dignity inherent in human nature and are ethically questionable on that count and also because inherent in them is an acceptance of a philosophy that 'the end justifies the means'.

Some of these criticisms appear to be founded on a limited understanding of behavioural modification – both failing to recognise it as an inherent element in all human transactions and overlooking the range of choice it offers in social-work helping. Much of the literature on behavioural modification originates from psychological laboratories rather than clinical settings, and emphasises aspects of behaviour conditioning which are either inapplicable or unacceptable in social work. This cannot be said, however, of all behavioural technology, as is shown by Jehu[28] for example. Looked at from a more positive angle, a major strength of the behaviour-modification approach is that, because of its narrow and specifically defined objectives, the relationship between goals and results is more clear and more open to evaluation than is the case in much of social work. Another important point in its favour is the relative effectiveness of this approach in relieving in a relatively short time some acute and disabling symptoms which have been found not to respond easily to the more dynamically orientated treatment approaches. There is also the fact that, as people committed to a behaviour-modification approach argue (see Shaw),[29] some of the ethical issues raised by this approach, for example regarding manipulation, are relative rather than absolute. Control and influence are inherent in all forms of helping, even in the most non-directive, and some of the dangers involved in implicit and subtle manipulation in the context of a relationship of dependency can be greater than when the situation is more open and explicit.

The apparent irreconcilability of behavioural modification with other forms of helping in social work has been greatly affected in the past by the extent of the contrast in their respective approaches to the place of relationship. However, in recent years there has been increasing recognition on the part of the behavioural therapists that their relationship with their clients or patients plays a significant and an integral part in the therapy, and is not a mere incidental (or, as was perceived by some earlier, an obstacle).

This recognition has opened up new possibilities for the incorporation of behaviour modification into social work by both adding to its repertoire some of the specific techniques and making a more conscious and effective use of the more traditional elements in social work which involved behaviour modification, such as approval and disapproval, encouragement, example setting, and so on.

The question which remains unanswered in my mind is this. Given the practical value to social work of many of the discoveries made by behavioural psychologists and therapists about ways in which maladaptive behaviour can be modified, is this a sufficient reason for regarding behaviour modification as a separate model for social-work practice in parallel with models such as those discussed above, every one of which relates to an underlying body of values and has a fairly broad orientation to social functioning? Or, given the more exclusive technological orientation of behaviour modification, is it more appropriately viewed as one of the interventive methods of social work whatever conceptual model is being used?

The Crisis-Intervention Model

As implied in the title, this model refers to social work in crisis situations. Kaplan defines a crisis as 'an upset in a steady state'.[30] Rapoport refers to 'three interrelated factors' as producing a state of crisis: 1) One or a series of hazardous events which pose some threat; 2) a threat to current or past instinctual needs which are symbolically linked to earlier threats that result in vulnerability or conflict; and 3) an inability to respond with adequate coping mechanisms.'[31] She goes on to suggest that 'A hazardous event may be experienced by the individual as either a threat, a loss, or a challenge.'[32]

Crises are of two major kinds: crises of a traumatic nature entailing a 'threat' or a 'loss', and developmental crises such as adolescence or marriage which present a 'challenge'. Whilst opportunities for preventive work in relation to intervention in the latter type of crisis are generally recognised, and there are a number of references in the

literature to various preventive programmes of social work and other
services aimed at promoting this, most of the discussion around crisis
intervention and conceptualisations of 'crisis theory' have focused on
the traumatic type of crisis. The interest which crisis-intervention social
work has aroused in recent years can be traced to a number of different
factors. One of these, and a potent one, has been the growing
disappointment with much long-term work and the resultant questioning of its applicability and value in some situations. Coupled with this
was the growing need to 'dignify' short contacts in social work which
constituted in most agencies a large proportion of social workers'
caseloads. Developments in the realm of dynamic psychology, particularly the growing emphasis on *ego* psychology, and also contributions
from learning theories emphasising the importance of cognitive
processes in problem solution, and of such facets of change as
motivation, competence and modelling, were important influences in
rationalising and making instrumental these growing concerns by
practitioners.

An important specific feature of crisis intervention is the relatively
stronger focus upon the 'here and now' than upon the origins of the
problem which characterised much long-term work, although it is
important not to overlook the recognition by 'crisis interventionists' of
the potentiality inherent in current crisis situations for a more
satisfactory resolution of some residual past difficulties. As the
disturbance in the personal equilibrium created by a crisis is limited to a
period of a few weeks and after that period some adjustment to the
situation has to be 'found' by the individual, the time for intervention is
limited. In addition, because people in a state of crisis are in a very fluid
and exposed psychological state, this is the time when appropriate
intervention can be most effective. This optimum moment is passed
once a person has made an adjustment, and in cases where such an
adjustment was a pathological one (for example, in a state of
unresolved grief), the 'undoing' of it will require a great deal of time
and effort.

The central importance of an immediate, focused and time-limited
intervention has a number of practical implications for social work. One
of these is the need for the social worker to adopt a much more active
role than would be appropriate in other situations. He must be
prepared to accept a considerable amount of initial dependency on the
part of a person in a state of crisis by both offering the appropriate

psychological support and being prepared to intervene actively in that person's practical affairs. At the same time, the social worker must remember all the time that his intervention is both specific and temporary and that he must therefore foster the client's own problem-solving abilities and discourage regression which would put the worker into an increasingly parental role *vis-à-vis* the client. Thus the timing of the differential approaches based on sensitivity to fluctuations in the client's psychological state is in many ways a finer and a more delicate 'art' than when the situation is less acute and less exposed.

Carrying out crisis-intervention work has also important implications for the organisation and administration of the agency within which it is practised. Waiting lists, changes in personnel dealing with the client, rigid procedures regarding when, where, how frequently, and for how long clients are seen, are not compatible with the basic tenets of crisis intervention as outlined above.

It is this sharpness of focus which constitutes one of the most valuable aspects of this model. Its major weakness, on the other hand, is derived from the somewhat ambiguous theoretical base on which it is founded. As Rapoport puts it boldly, 'Crisis theory is not as yet a well formulated or holistic theory.'[33] It is an amalgam of insights derived from classical psychoanalytic theory, *ego* psychology, biology, social psychology, sociology and learning theory, which are far from adequately integrated. In practical terms this means that it is not always easy to define a crisis, and the concept lends itself to becoming stretched to the point where it will lose all its value through ceasing to be differentiated. This is a major hazard social workers need to guard against if they are to be successful in utilising the considerable potentialities of this approach to their practice.

The Task-Centred Casework Model

This model of casework practice was recently formulated by two American social-work theoreticians: Reid and Epstein.[34] It constitutes a very specific model of short-term social work. Interest in the latter, as has already been suggested, has been on the increase in recent years, and Reid has been instrumental in mounting, conducting and describing an experiment in short-term casework[35] which has aroused considerable interest by demonstrating the relatively greater effectiveness of short-term intervention over long-term work with clients experiencing interpersonal difficulties.

As the authors acknowledge, whilst the model of task-centred casework is derived from that particular experiment and is a form of short-term casework, it differs from the other kinds in a number of important ways. It not only limits the length of contacts between the social worker and the client to a maximum of twelve interviews over a relatively brief period of time, but it also requires that the problem to be worked upon be made quite explicit and adhered to.

The model does not incorporate a separate diagnostic phase but assessment is an integral part of the transactions between the social worker and the client in the course of clarification of the nature of the problem, translation of it into a specific task or tasks to be worked upon by the client with the assistance of the social worker, and in the on-going evaluation of how this task or tasks are being carried out.

The model has certain important features in common with both the 'problem-solving' approach and the 'psycho-social therapy' models. It shares with the former its use of the client's problem as the main focus, but goes further in its requirements of involving the client as the main change agent, with full understanding of the tasks to be undertaken in dealing with the problem and being motivated to enter into a 'treatment contract' and stick by it. The influence of Hollis's treatment methods is readily acknowledged by Reid and Epstein who comment that in their model greater use is made of the more directive procedures and of those which encourage a cognitive grasp of reality rather than those which are aimed at promoting the client's self-awareness.

In terms of its application the authors state that 'The targets to which the model is addressed are problems of: (1) interpersonal conflict (2) dissatisfaction in social relations, (3) relations with formal organisations, (4) role performance, (5) social transition, (6) reactive emotional distress, and (7) inadequate resources.'[36]

However, it is its claim to a very extensive application, for example 'The model is designed for use with the majority of clients currently served by social caseworkers',[37] which raises certain doubts about the model. It is not easy to reconcile its very explicit requirements regarding clients' involvement in, and commitment to, a specific 'treatment contract' with many of the clients whom social workers meet, a sizeable proportion of whom have neither come of their own volition nor have the necessary motivation or resources to operate in this way.

The authors' own discussion of the model's applicability to these types of client is not entirely convincing, nor does it take care adequately of certain kinds of problems which clients are unwilling or unable to perceive or accept, and yet which social workers cannot ignore.

Another query which this model raises is the extent to which it may encourage rigidity on the part of social workers in focusing on certain issues, and thus not making it possible for clients to move on to others which may have become of more importance and concern to them. Allied to this is the more fundamental issue of the extent to which such a degree of partialisation of human problems is compatible with a whole-person approach inherent in any form of helping which is based upon relationship. In this sense the task-centred approach paradoxically raises similar ethical issues to those which were discussed in relation to the behaviour-modification model. Its great strength, on the other hand, not unlike that of the behaviour-modification model, lies in the specificity of objectives and the consequent feasibility of evaluating the results of social-work intervention.

All the models of social-work practice so far discussed are predominantly models of social casework (although Smalley[38] makes claims to her model being of a more general application, and the problem-solving model is of direct relevance to both group work and community work). This is a significant indication of the primacy hitherto given to work with individuals and families within social-work practice and thought and of the range and the complexity of the issues involved in this type of work. The various models differ in scope, degree of abstraction, the nature and extent of theoretical backing, and their relative emphasis on particular aspects of social-work practice, such as assessment, differential helping approaches, place of relationship and importance of agency function. As has already been suggested, no one model is sufficient to cover all the exigencies of social-work practice with individuals and families faced with the multiplicity of problems inherent in living, and this is particularly true of the more specific models which are limited by their very terms of reference to certain types of problem or situation.

'Holistic' Models

Within the last few years attempts have been made to find broader models for social-work practice incorporating the different methods, or, to put it more correctly, cutting across specific methods. These have used, as their underlying theoretical basis, 'systems theory' as described by von Bertalanffy,[39] Buckley,[40] Thomas and Feldman,[41] and Janchill,[42] albeit to differing extents and with varying degrees of explicitness. Two of these deserve particular mention: The 'four-systems' model of Pincus and Minahan[43] and the unitary-approach model of Goldstein.[44]

The 'Four-Systems' Model

This discusses social-work practice in terms of four basic systems: (1) the change-agent system; (2) the client system; (3) the target system; and (4) the action system. The common objective of all social-work activity is seen as inducing change, and the more specific objectives determined by the nature of the problem relate to this central objective. There is a very comprehensive discussion in Pincus and Minahan's book of the various strategies for inducing change, including their applicability to the particular aspects of the four systems involved. Whilst this extensive technology constitutes one of the strengths of the book, the degree of emphasis placed upon it reflects also a major weakness. The feeling which is conveyed by both the largely 'technological' approach to social work, and the size of the canvas upon which its activities have been drawn, is that of a grand universal plan over which the social worker rules supreme by pulling the necessary strings to effect the results desired. Whilst I hasten to acknowledge this as an extreme way of voicing my misgivings, nevertheless the almost complete neglect of ethical issues, through a failure to discuss them explicitly, coupled with some implicit support for the maxim that 'the end justifies the means', for example where means of manipulating the target system are discussed,[45] raises important questions concerning the perception of the basic values underlying social-work intervention.

There is generally a discrepancy in this work, perhaps inevitable in view of its breadth, between an emphasis within the model on life tasks confronting people and upon the interaction between people and the various networks within the 'resource system', and the extent to which the different 'systems', as they are discussed, appear increasingly to assume an identity of their own and become depersonalised. This contributes in turn to the impression of a mechanistic approach to both problems in social functioning and to social-work intervention.

The assumption that all social-work helping has to do primarily with change is in itself open to misunderstanding although this clearly depends on how the concept of 'change' is viewed (and it is doubtless viewed from a very wide perspective by the authors). In some human situations in which social workers are actively involved, such as, for example, work with the terminally ill, other facts and needs might well be seen to predominate, and conceptualisation primarily in terms of change could distort priorities. This particular point reflects perhaps what seems to me an important feature of the book and which contrasts it quite sharply with the more restricted models previously discussed: namely, that in its desire to incorporate social-work activities with larger client units than individuals, it has gone to the other extreme and has sacrificed some of the depth of the considerations which are intrinsic to work with people, regardless of whether they are worked with singly or in groups, for the sake of breadth.

One should not, however, allow these criticisms of the model to detract from its usefulness in offering a comprehensive framework within which social-work practice can be viewed. The authors themselves maintain that their model is not in fact 'a single grand system of practice', and they acknowledge that it lacks some of the ingredients inherent in social-work practice, for example an adequate consideration of the ethical dimension and of the relationship. One cannot quarrel either with their statement that,

> when asked to choose between the medical model or the political model, treatment of the individual or changing of social institutions, social work should reject the premise on which such a choice is based. We propose that the formulation of the functions and objectives of social work practice focus on the interventions and linkages between people and social systems.[46]

This gives recognition to the essentially psycho-social perspective of social work, even if this recognition would have been enhanced by more emphasis being given to the moral dimension in helping people to negotiate the various systems, and by a somewhat less positivist approach to this and other issues.

The Unitary-Approach Model

The final approach to be considered in this chapter is that by Goldstein.

The author sets the tone for what is to follow in the following statement in his introduction:

> irrespective of the design and objective, whether practice is aimed at grand schemes for social change or the resolution of a common place problem, social work practice is ultimately concerned with persons as distinct individuals – their plans, hopes, ideals, needs, and the way they go about living them out. The final measure of worth of the professional act can only be found in the meaning it holds for certain persons, individually or in association.[47]

In keeping with this affirmation, the author devotes a great deal of attention to the place of relationship in social work. Thus, 'The medium for social work practice is generally some form of human association that differs from other social relationships in its purposive goal seeking properties.'[48] The sections dealing with the relationship, what is brought to it by both the social worker and the client, and what results from their interaction, are some of the most perceptive in the book and constitute a valuable addition to social-work thinking in this area through their successful blend of psychological and sociological elements. Both the social worker and the client are presented as operating within wider social systems, and Goldstein's application of system theory to his analysis of their interaction is discussed not only lucidly but reflects a dynamic approach, as appropriate in dealing with human systems. He makes this point quite explicitly: 'The ability of man to contribute to and alter his environment or even create new environments is as much a property of human behaviour as is his tendency to be affected by and to react to his environment.'[49] In consequence, in Goldstein's view, the systems concept facilitates the viewing of 'therapeutic' and 'social action' strategies not in political terms but as 'differential remedies',[50] and such a conclusion carries conviction in the context of his over-all approach.

The author views the objectives of all social work in terms of problem solving, and he relates this closely to the medium of social learning. His discussion of what is entailed in both, and why the two concepts are so interrelated, is in my view both original and valuable and fully compatible with the social-functioning perspective.

His 'Unitary Model of the Process of Social Work Practice' consists of three interacting dimensions or variables: (1) *Strategy*, which consists of 'the three major role activities of the social worker' – Goldstein calls these: 'study and evaluation; intention and intervention; and appraisal'; (2) *Target*, which he classifies into 'individual; family/group; and organisation/community'; and (3) *Phases* – these he divides into 'induction: core: and ending'.[51]

His discussion of all these variables succeeds in integrating a number of different contributions. Thus, for example, the analysis of the three time phases reflects the unmistakable influence of the 'functional' orientation, whilst discussion in other parts is influenced by other viewpoints and theories, for example those derived from both social and dynamic psychologies.

It seems to me that Goldstein's work constitutes a real advance in cutting across the separate methods of social-work practice, and thus contributes significantly to a clarification and establishment of a social-work identity. By the very nature of the task he has undertaken, much of his discussion, especially that regarding the three sub-models of his unitary practice model, that is 'a social systems model', 'a social learning or problem-solving model', and 'a process model',[52] is at a fairly high level of abstraction, and so presents a considerable challenge in terms of its practical application. However, the challenge is well worth accepting, because whatever may be the shortcomings of the book in succeeding fully to unify the various disparate elements of social-work practice, it has achieved, in my view, considerable success in a basic integration of what ultimately matters most; that is, of the values which motivate and justify the existence of social work with the framework of the knowledge, theoretical and practical, which guides its thinking and actions.

In some ways, the 'four-systems' and the 'unitary approach' models are complementary. The strength in the handling of the more 'technological' aspects of social work at the expense of value considerations in the former is matched by a strong value and humanistic base of the latter, which, however, pays much less specific attention to social structures. One cannot but wonder how far these contrasts are the result of the different starting points of the authors – community work in the case of Pincus and Minahan, and casework in the case of Goldstein.

If this is a correct assumption then one is also justified in deducing that a truly holistic formulation of social-work practice still remains to be achieved.

Chapter 3

The Place of Values in Social Work

Implicit in the discussion of the nature of social work in Chapter 1 was the fundamental importance of moral issues. This importance is derived from both the objectives of social work and the means by which it attempts to reach these objectives.

Concern with the quality of human living which, as I have argued in that chapter, is what social work is basically about, cannot operate in a moral vacuum, but on the contrary must be based on certain beliefs regarding what constitutes 'a good life' and also on ethical considerations in relation to the ways by which such a good life can be sought and promoted.

In emphasising the inherently moral nature of social work I do not intend to suggest that moral considerations do not play or should not play an important part in all human pursuits and preoccupations. Concern with moral issues is an inherent element of human nature derived from the fact of man's rationality and his ability to reflect upon himself in relation to his present, past and future. However, the greater the extent to which human actions are geared directly to persons rather than to inanimate objects, the more central the place of moral considerations. In social work both the ends and the means are more directly concerned with persons than is often the case in other types of activity. The promotion of a 'good life' by social work has to do not with some abstract or distant ideal, but with the tangible life situation of a human being or a human group. It is pursued primarily through the medium of the social worker's relationship with that individual or group and the client's own personality, as well as the goodwill of significant others, is an essential element in any actual change which is brought about. Human nature is thus the main and the most significant material with which the social worker is engaged – his own nature and that of others.

In one sense all this is very obvious, and therefore open to the danger of appearing condescending to the reader. My own belief that the obvious requires emphasis is derived from a good deal of evidence that there is currently a general reluctance in our society to acknowledge the prime importance of moral values and that this reluctance has also penetrated social work to a degree which calls for concern and reaction,

A number of reasons have accounted for this state of affairs.

One of these has been the decline in religious faith, and as religion and morality have been viewed by many people as synonymous, secularisation of society has resulted in a change in the importance given to morality. It would not be appropriate to discuss here how this equation of religion and morality has come about or to argue extensively about the errors of such an equation, except for stressing once again that morality is an inherent a part of human nature as is the physical body or the rational mind. A full discussion of this theme can be found in many writings on ethics, including those by Warnock,[1] and Downie and Telfer.[2]

Another factor which has played an important part in the recent lack of emphasis on the place of morality in human life has been the primacy given in Western Civilisation, since the end of the last century, to science and to what is considered to be 'scientific validity'. This has in turn resulted in a decline in the status of philosophy, and so the absence of adequate philosophical reflection upon the nature of scientific activity and its effects upon society have encouraged the myth that science is value-free, as well as consequently a dichotomy between scientific thought and moral considerations.

However, over the last few decades the untenability of such a rigid separation between science and morality has become increasingly obvious as the effects upon individuals and society of certain recent scientific achievements have raised complex moral questions and have necessitated the making of decisions and choices which could not be termed as anything but 'ethical'. I owe to Leonard[3] the following quotation from the French sociologist Goldmann which underlines the interdependence of science and philosophy:

> If philosophy is more than a simple conceptual expression of different world views, if apart from its ideological character, it also reveals certain fundamental truths concerning the relations of men with other men and of men with the universe, then these truths must be found also at the very basis of the human sciences and in their methods in particular ... If philosophy really tells us something about the nature of man, then every attempt to destroy it necessarily obstructs the understanding of human reality. In this case, the human sciences will have to be philosophical in order to be scientific.

I think that it is not inappropriate to paraphrase the last sentence of Goldmann's statement to read: 'In this case, social work has to be philosophical in order to be real.'

The appropriateness of such a paraphrasing is enhanced by the fact that the long-standing debate in social work regarding the art/science dichotomy, to which fuller reference will be made in the next chapter, reflects a tendency to think of knowledge and of values as separated into watertight compartments. The correspondence columns of social-work journals provide ample evidence that some social workers equate warmth and concern with a relative theoretical innocence, whilst considering conceptual sophistication as inevitably resulting in emotional coldness and distance.

Emmett[4] discusses the process by which the concept of 'doing good' to other people has gradually come into disrepute in social work, and suggests that reluctance to acknowledge that social work is concerned with doing good amounts to a denial of the core justification for its existence. She challenges social workers to drop their coyness in this respect and to have the courage of their convictions.

One is tempted to speculate why social workers have shown so much reluctance in recent years to acknowledge the basically moral nature of their activities. One reason for this may be related to the tendency among social workers, as well as other people, to fail to differentiate between 'acting morally' and 'moralising'. The early history of social work helps to explain the particular sensitivity on the part of contemporary social workers with regard to moralising. (It is interesting to note in this context that the definition of moralising in the Oxford English Dictionary does not impute any derogatory meaning to the word but reads as 'indulging in moral reflections, giving a moral quality, or affecting the moral quality of actions or feelings'.) However, one could also argue that, given the demands inherent in action guided by moral considerations, to claim a 'morally neutral' position (however mutually contradictory these terms) is to choose an easier option. This is implied in the definitions of morality as 'ethical wisdom; the doctrine or system concerned with conduct and duty' (O.E.D.).

According to Warnock the objectives of all morality are 'to contribute in some respects, by way of actions of rational beings, to the amelioration of the human predicament'.[5] This is, however, a general statement regarding the nature of moral behaviour by human beings, that is of behaviour concerned with the nature of conduct. Its particular application to social work calls for a reference to the philosophy underlying social work more specifically. This philosophy is derived from certain universal values inherent in the nature of man. Whilst these values can be formulated in a number of different ways, in my view they stem from three fundamental assumptions.

The first of these assumptions is that respect for persons is due to the inherent worth of man and is thus independent of his actual achievements or behaviour. This is the view contained in Kantian philosophy and can be summed up in the following quotation from Kant cited by Plant:

> A man deserves respect as a potential moral agent in terms of his transcendental characteristic, not because of a particular conjunction of empirical qualities which he might possess. Traits of character might command admiration and other such responses, but respect is owed to a man irrespective of what he does, because he is man.[6]

The practical significance of adhering to this value can be perceived particularly clearly if the view by Campbell,[7] supported by his references to other moral philosophers, is accepted, that the concept of respect is synonymous with that of 'agape', that it implies an acceptance of common humanity and requires appropriate rational and emotional investment.

The value of 'respect for persons' is considered by most philosophers to be the central moral value from which all other values derive. Plant states this quite explicitly when he writes that 'Respect for persons is a principle which is definitive of morality',[8] and argues that other principles such as those of acceptance and self-direction are implicit in it. Downie and Telfer put this even more strongly when they say that 'the attitude of respect for persons is morally basic . . . not only is it the paramount moral attitude but also . . . all other moral principles and attitudes are to be explained in terms of it'.[9] They also examine in relation to this value the frequently made assertion that the concept of 'a person' is an abstraction because personal identity is inseparable from social influence and people are moulded by the social roles in which they are placed and which they perform. They conclude that 'If the idea of a pure ego is an abstraction, so is that of a role which is enacted without leaving the imprint of the person who is in the role.'[10] They then refer to the analysis by Professor Williams of what constitutes respect for a person: 'each man is owed an effort of identification: that he should not be regarded as the surface to which a certain label can be applied, but one should try to see the world (including the label) from his point of view.'[11]

The limitations inherent in perceiving people exclusively in terms of their social roles are also recognised by Dahrendorf: 'The sociologist should make it clear that for him human nature is not accurately described by the principle of role conformity, that indeed the difference between this theoretically fruitful construct and his idea of human nature amounts almost to a contradiction.'[12]

In view of the foremost position given by philosophers to the value of 'respect for persons', my references to two further general values which social work assumes to be of a fundamental importance may be open to query. Whatever their correct place, however, in the conceptual ordering of values, it seemed to me that their implications for social-work practice were of a sufficient significance to justify their inclusion in a discussion which, after all, makes no claims to philosophical erudition but simply attempts to clarify both the nature of the assumptions and the beliefs underlying social work, and some of their implications for its practice.

The second basic value assumption on which social work rests is belief in the social nature of man as a unique creature depending on other men for fulfilment of his uniqueness.

The difficulties inherent in this fact of human life are clearly shown in the discussion by Plant[13] of the respective positions of the 'Individualist' (or 'Existential') and the 'Idealist' Schools of Philosophy. Adherents of the former (of whom Sartre is one of the best-known exponents) emphasise individual autonomy to the total exclusion of the validity of any form of outside controls or restraints. There is no place for social morality within this framework of philosophical thought, and it thus constitutes a denial of reality aptly summed up by Aristotle in his famous saying that 'He that could live apart from society might be a beast or a God but not a human being' (quoted by Plant).[14] Given this position of existentialism, one might well ask where does its attraction for many social workers lie. The answer to this question is probably to be found in the emphasis on human freedom and choice of which social workers' clients are so often bereft. For the existentialist, 'the sin' or 'immoral' behaviour is failure to exercise choice and the belief that one is wholly determined by outside forces.

The 'Idealists', on the other hand, who include such well-known current social scientists as Erving Goffman, by adopting an absolute view with regard to the dependence of individual behaviour upon social pressures, deny man an identity which is separate from the sum total of his various social roles. In doing so, they also deny him his intrinsic dignity and personal worth.

In his critique of these two philosophical outlooks, Plant writes that:

Neither kind of view can provide an adequate model of the relationship between man and society. The Existentialist must fail for the caseworker because the caseworker must see the difficulties in social functioning as problems and not as signs of maturity and freedom. The view of the Idealist cannot be adequate either, because it seems difficult to accommodate the casework values of respect for persons, and acceptance. It is necessary to preserve the concept of the individual who stands 'behind' his social role, but this does not entail that the individual is the basic category in terms of which we should look at modes of social life, as the Existentialist maintains. The Existentialist is incorrect insofar as he thinks that man can exist apart from his social roles, whereas the Idealist philosopher and the so called 'dramatic' sociologists such as Goffman are also incorrect in thinking that the individual is totally absorbed by his roles.[15]

Thus the problems inherent in the application of this basic value assumption in social-work practice are far-reaching and lie at the root of many of social work's difficulties and ambiguities regarding the respective function of 'individual growth promotion' and 'social control'. These will be discussed more fully later. However, to acknowledge the difficulties in this situation is not to deny the prime importance of the value or of the continued efforts on the part of social workers to come to terms with its requirements.

The third value assumption from which social-work practice derives stems from the belief in human capacity for change, growth and betterment.

Here too, in adhering to the values implicit in this assumption, social work is faced with considerable conceptual difficulties, particularly regarding the long-debated issue of free will versus determinism. In terms of the philosophical consideration bearing upon it, as Campbell[16] suggests, the outcome of arguments between the adherents of determinism and the champions of free will is inconclusive in that neither side can produce proof of the validity of its position and both sets of propositions start from certain assumptions which are taken for granted by their exponents. However, given that such notions as those of 'obligation' and 'responsibility' are integral to any discussion of human behaviour in a social context, in Campbell's view,[17] Kant's hypothesis regarding freedom in the moral sphere is a necessary and an acceptable one,

Downie and Telfer take issue with psychological determinism on the grounds that it fails to do 'justice to the epistemology of decision and action from the agent's point of view'.[18] They quote Stuart Hampshire's view that 'a man can have privileged knowledge of his own future actions which would not be possible on the basis of induction'.[19] Whilst recognising the conceptual difficulties inherent in substituting a 'purposive explanation' of human behaviour for a 'complete causal explanation',[20] they are 'forced to conclude that rational choice, and the concepts of action stemming from it, are not susceptible to complete causal explanation'.[21] They see a necessary connection between 'being a person, being purposive, and being morally responsible'.[22]

These various 'statements of belief' by philosophers regarding human capacity for rational decision and choice are of great importance to social work. Without such belief it would certainly be difficult, if not impossible, to find a good enough rationale for the objectives of social work which are primarily concerned with change and thus are intrinsically antagonistic to a deterministic philosophy of life.

Ewing's treatment of the application of determinism and indeterminism in human affairs has great relevance for social work and helps considerably, I believe, in responding to some of the dilemmas inherent in this aspect of philosophy and in its application to social-work practice:

> Practically it is perhaps a good dictum for most purposes that we should adopt the indeterminist attitude towards ourselves and the determinist attitude towards other men, in the sense that we should think of ourselves as capable of going against all the causes by which the psychologist would explain our conduct but be prepared always to look for the causes to explain the unsatisfactory conduct of other men. Even if he has some undetermined free will, we never know how much or how little the other man is to blame, and it is not our business (except where necessary in certain respects for practical purposes) to be his judge. Yet we must not of course carry out this maxim without qualification. It is the dictator or unscrupulous politician who takes a thoroughly determinist view of others to be moulded as means for his ends, and we may be unduly discouraged or else attempt the impracticable if we think too indeterministically of ourselves and take no account of the limitations imposed on us by our present character and past life. In any case, we must not think of the alternatives for a man as just being absolutely free apart from his physical limitations and as having no freedom at all: freedom is very much a matter of degree whether we think of it as consisting in independence of causes other than our own preference or in independence of causes altogether.[23]

The three value assumptions which have so far been discussed, respect for men, man's social nature and human capacity for change are, however, concerned with values of a very high order of abstraction, and in themselves not specific to social work, albeit, as I have already argued, indispensable to it. They provide a general justification for social workers' involvement in efforts at 'amelioration of the human predicament',[24] and suggest certain moral requirements that have to be met if these objectives are to be fulfilled.

In order to meet these requirements, guidelines of an instrumental nature are needed. Among the means which are available for the 'amelioration of the human predicament', Warnock considers that of 'good dispositions' as being the most important. His list of 'good dispositions' consists of 'non-maleficence; fairness; beneficence; non-deception'. In contrast, 'bad dispositions' are these: 'maleficence; non-beneficence; unfairness; deception'.[25]

Several writers on social work have also offered classifications of moral principles formulated with the view to the operational requirements of social work. Those of Hollis[26] and Biestek[27] are best-known. Both have been criticised on grounds of inconsistency with regard to the level of conceptualisation and instrumentality, and also, more seriously, on account of the weakness of their philosophical base. There have also been less well informed criticisms of these and other classifications on grounds which seem to imply that, because the critics were looking to them for specific rules of conduct, having failed to find these, they could see no value in guidelines of a more general kind.

My own position regarding middle-range conceptualisations of moral principles is that, whatever their limitations and shortcomings, they are nevertheless of considerable help in providing a framework for thinking about social-work practice in somewhat more concrete terms than mere 'first principles'. It is for this reason that I have chosen to analyse briefly some of these intermediate principles using as my basis Biestek's classification.[28]

The principle of 'acceptance' is a clear derivative of the basic value of respect for persons. It requires the social worker to extend unconditional love ('agape') to his clients regardless of the degree to which he finds them personally attractive or unattractive. Love in this moral sense is predominantly an act of will and not an emotional impulse; it is an expression of the obligation to treat others as one would like to be treated oneself, that is to recognise, respect and support their uniqueness and their worth.

It is obvious from the above description of acceptance that, in abstract, its imperatives are of an absolute nature and so it is an ideal unattainable in its fullness. Social workers are human and thus creatures of flesh and emotion, as well as rational beings, and so their capacity to give of themselves fully to others, to suspend their own needs and to control their egocentricity, is at its best of a limited degree. However, acceptance cannot be considered in a total vacuum: it implies accepting another 'I' and in that context it is, even in its absolute form, conditioned by the rights which the person who is 'accepting' has in relation to the one 'being accepted'. This fact has important implications for social work, not the least of these being the need to pay constant attention to the responses on the part of clients to social workers' offers of acceptance. One likely result of such feedback will be a greater awareness on the part of social workers that their ability as individuals to be accepting of different clients and various types of problem differs considerably. This might in turn encourage more attention being given to a matching of social workers and clients which would facilitate the exercise of acceptance between the two parties.

Whatever steps are taken to enhance social workers' capacity to be accepting of their clients, acceptance will never become easy to practice. However, this fact must not be allowed to lead to either despondency or complacency because respect for persons cannot be real without acceptance which is its most tangible single expression.

Non-judgemental attitude is a companion principle to that of acceptance, and some critics consider it is superfluous because it is encompassed in acceptance. However, given the complex nature of both acceptance and non-judgemental attitude, there is value in their being conceptualised separately. The latter is helpful in reminding social workers of their proper role, namely that it does not include sitting in judgement over their clients, who are the ultimate judges of their own behaviour and the motivations underlying it.

The confusion to which this principle lends itself is in being seen by some to incorporate an injunction against an assessment of people's actions. Such a confusion may well have contributed to the reluctance on the part of many social workers to form professional judgements regarding the nature of their clients' problems and the part played by the clients themselves in these, and to confuse a non-judgemental attitude with moral neutrality. For this reason it has been suggested by several social-work writers that 'non-condemnatory' might be a better substitute for 'non-judgemental'.

Whatever term is used it does not alter the inherent difficulty of this principle in terms of its requirement to combine a realistic view of human behaviour with abstinence from allocating praise or blame for it to the agent. Perhaps the most appropriate name for this principle would be that of 'humility' in that what it appears to intend to control above all else is the temptation to play God.

Like acceptance, individualisation implies a more absolute standard of practice than is attainable by any social worker. The principle is logically derived from the uniqueness of individuals. Hence failure to recognise that every human situation is also unique, that no two problems are alike, and to see that situation or problem through the eyes of the person experiencing it, constitutes a denial of that uniqueness and detracts from the respect due to the individual. And yet the very uniqueness of human beings entails constraints on one person being able to enter fully into the experiences of another.

As in the case of acceptance, it does not seem to me that our limited ability to individualise should detract from the value of the principle. On the contrary, by keeping it constantly in the forefront of their minds, social workers are more likely to improve the effectiveness of individualising clients and their situations than otherwise. Such an improvement can be enhanced by means of both fostering appropriate attitudes and the acquisition of knowledge. Paradoxically, just as individualisation constitutes an essential counterforce and safeguard to the dangers of classification of human problems and situations, so classification promotes individualisation by providing it with means to greater subtlety and sophistication.

The twin principles of 'purposeful expression of feelings', and 'controlled emotional involvement' constitute two sides of one coin, so to speak. They both relate to the mutuality inherent in the relationship between the helper and the person being helped, and are concerned with the rights in this situation of the latter and the obligations of the former.

Purposeful expression of feelings acknowledges the importance of the client being able to express and share his private thoughts and feelings, and stresses the difference which stems from such expression and sharing, reflecting the individual's own authentic needs rather than being a response to what the social worker is looking for, or wishing to hear.

Hence controlled emotional involvement requires of the social worker to suspend his egocentricity and relate instead to the needs of the other person. In a sense the term 'controlled' is a misnomer as it might be taken to imply that the only urge the social worker needs to control is that of an excessive emotional involvement, namely over-identification. In truth, however, under-involvement is an equally real hazard, as it reflects a lack of empathy and so prevents meaningful communication. It is therefore all inappropriate involvement, as manifest, for example, in trying to gain vicarious satisfaction from encouraging the client to expand on some aspect of his problem or past experience without due regard as to whether or not this is helpful from his own point of view, which should be guarded against.

One way in which 'confidentiality' could be described would be as having to do with people's rights over the 'property' of their secrets. The analogy with material belongings which such a definition implies can help to highlight the particular worth to persons of information concerning themselves and their lives, and the seriousness of the damage which can occur when their ownership rights in this area are infringed. 'Secrets' in this context do not necessarily concern some particularly dramatic events in an objective sense, but rather those feelings, events and aspects of a person's life to which he himself attaches particular importance and which he values as reflections of his identity. It thus follows that to extract these secrets from him under false pretences, or to pass them on to others when they have been entrusted in confidence, might constitute a more serious violation of personal rights than the stealing of a material object. The latter point indicates the inadequacy of the analogy between breach of confidentiality and theft, on account of the fact that invasion of privacy which results from failure in confidentiality frequently leads to a greater loss and one of a more fundamental nature than does theft.

The British Association of Social Workers' Discussion Paper on Confidentiality stresses the fact that confidentiality is 'in essence concerned with faith and trust, usually in a person',[29] and thus acknowledges the direct relationship between this principle and the basic value of respect for persons. However, as the Discussion Paper also acknowledges, confidentiality is not an absolute right in the sense that it can be in conflict with the equally valid rights of others, and it must relate to the reality of the 'social nature of man'. Hence the practice of this principle presents social workers with considerable dilemmas regarding the relative importance in particular situations of the rights of the different persons involved. Many of these dilemmas are similar to those regarding the practice of 'the principle of self-determination' which I shall discuss next, and so, to avoid repetition, I shall not elaborate on them here, except for referring to one major area of confusion which has been manifest in social workers' treatment of confidentiality. This has to do with an insufficient differentiation on the part of many social workers between principles concerned with basic human rights and those which are of a more instrumental nature. The former, whilst not being absolute require very good reasons indeed to be breached; whilst the latter justify a more pragmatic approach,

Confidentiality is a good illustration of a principle in the first category which had undergone a metamorphosis in the hands of many social workers. A recent small-scale study by Brandon[30] has revealed a most worrying degree of neglect on the part of social workers in Social Services Departments and Probation and After-Care Departments of their clients' rights to their 'secrets'. These workers readily provided information about their clients in response to telephone enquiries by unidentified 'social workers' and without even the slightest attempt to obtain the clients' permission for the sharing.

The paramount importance attached to the principle of 'self-determination' in social work for most of its history is only matched by the degree of confusion regarding its nature. As in the case of confidentiality, the focal point of this confusion has to do with whether self-determination is a basic value or an operationally useful principle. At the risk of over-simplifying the complex dialogue on this issue which has gone on among social-work writers over the years, it is my impression that there has been a gradual shift in the last few decades from a view of self-determination as an expression of negative freedom, that is as reflecting an individual's right to manage his own life and to make decisions concerning it, to its being regarded as a manifestation of positive freedom, that is of the human need for an extension of the range of choices available both within the personality and in the external environment. The latter view of self-determination has a much more utilitarian flavour than the former, and in the context of social work has inevitably shifted the focus from the client's right to non-interference, except when that right is in conflict with the rights of others, to his need for guidance by the social worker about how he can become more effectively self-determining. This is the view held by McDermott who says that 'those who identify the concept of self-determination with that of positive freedom tend to play down its status as a right, and to emphasise its role as an ideal or end to be pursued in the casework process'.[31]

His own preference for viewing self-determination as a basic human right is clearly expressed in the following statement:

> It is precisely because of the severity of the pressures to which clients are already subject, that the greatest care needs to be taken to ensure that they receive the respect they deserve as human beings. And this cannot be done without the most scrupulous regard for their right of self-determination.[32]

There is little doubt that the concepts of positive and negative freedom have a direct bearing on the place of self-determination in the scale of human values. Given the fact that the controversy regarding these two forms of freedom remains unresolved among philosophers, the task of formulating this principle in an unequivocal way for social-work purposes is virtually impossible.

The recognition of this difficulty does not need to detract from the importance of social workers taking self-determination extremely seriously in their dealings with people. Self-determination is not unique in presenting problems of application: on the contrary one can argue that this is a characteristic of all the great human values, including those of freedom and equality.

The recently published collection of papers on self-determination by McDermott discusses the concept of self-determination within a wider philosophical framework and is a most useful addition to the literature. It helps to dissipate some of the clouds of confusion which have increasingly surrounded self-determination in social work in recent years, including that of the relationship between self-determination and influence. This point, and the place of self-determination in social work more generally, is well summed up in the following passage by McDermott himself:

> If being self-determining, then, is not the same as being insulated from all normal exchange of ideas and influences between adult

human beings, it follows that the client's right of self-determination cannot be regarded as necessarily incompatible with the social worker's commitment to certain values, his intervention into the client's affairs, or his attempting to persuade the client of the desirability of adopting or avoiding a particular course of action. There may be other reasons for avoiding such things, but not that they violate the client's right to self-determination. The real threat to this right comes not from his exposure to the social worker's values, but from the opportunities for manipulation available to the social worker in the exercise of his authority – both his legitimate authority, and the pseudo-authority with which he is often accredited. And this threat will be resisted, if at all, not by abandoning the principle of client self-determination as unrealistic and unworkable, or transforming it into something compatible with manipulation and coercion, but by a sustained effort to grasp in all its ramifications the moral significance of the client's right of self-determination, and its bearing on the various methods and approaches open to social workers in their dealings with their clients.[33]

Biestek's classification of the middle-range principles of social-work practice was chosen, in spite of its shortcomings mentioned earlier, because it provides the most comprehensive and explicit formulation of these principles so far available, and thus constitutes a helpful basis and framework for thought and discussion. It seems also to me that it would be hard to dispute that what Biestek affirms and analyses are 'old verities' which have an inherent significance across the ages and cultural milieu and which social workers cannot afford to ignore under the pretext that the terms in which they are stated leave room for improvement.

The list of these principles refers specifically to social casework, and this fact necessitates, in turn, the question how far they are appropriate to other forms of social work such as work with groups, with communities and in residential settings. There is no doubt that the application of general value principles in different contexts does call for some differentiation but it is also clear that issues in the realm of values encountered in these other 'methods' or 'fields' of social work are no less real or less complex than is the case in social work with individuals and families. The recognition of this is clearly implicit in Goldstein's formulation of his 'unitary model' of social-work practice,[34] and it is well summed up in the following statement by him: 'Social work practice of any kind has to be conceptualised in inter-personal or transactional terms.'[35] Equally, Plant pinpoints in his recent essay[36] the importance of, and the need for, clarification of some basic value principles in community work which, more than other forms of social work, has tended to give precedence to the strategies and the techniques of practice over the ethical implications of these. In view of all these facts, I have no hesitation in asserting that all forms of social work can profit from the serious attention given traditionally to values by 'caseworkers'.

I began this chapter by arguing that social work is intimately concerned with moral issues, and I have then followed up this assertion with a discussion of some of the moral components of social-work activity. The recognition of the prominence and the all-embracing nature of these must result in the perception of social work as a fundamentally moral activity. To stress this, as opposed to simply recognising the widespread nature of moral issues within social work, is no mere difference in emphasis, but a substantial shift in the view of the nature of social work, carrying with it a number of important logical consequences. As these have to do with such a wide range of issues as the relationship to knowledge building and use, methodology of practice, the determining of priorities and professional education – to mention some – they will be discussed more fully in the context of appropriate chapters.

For the moment, I should like to elaborate on the concept of social work as a predominantly moral activity, with specific reference to Timms's Inaugural Lecture.[37] His view of the nature of social work is summed up in the following statement: 'I believe that we should consider social work as primarily neither an applied science nor simple good works but a kind of practical philosophising.'[38] He then goes on to argue that philosophy is integral to both social-work thought and practice. Timms has always been highly critical of the paucity of critical analysis by social workers of the concepts they were using, and he re-emphasises the need for such an analysis in the Lecture. However he goes on to suggest that 'The social worker cannot be content, in the manner of Hume, to leave philosophy in his study, because quite simply wherever he turns he is engaged in appraisals, his own and those of others.'[39] He therefore sees the intrinsic applicability of 'practical

philosophising' to the concern with values (both client's and the social
worker's own), to the meaning of different events and situations, and to
the whole host of the activities comprising social work. He refers to
Kant's concept of the 'middle-term' theory, and asserts the urgency of
the need in social work for such theory as a prerequisite to the 'practical
philosophising' of social workers being better informed and more
effective. This must include a clearer awareness of the separateness of
the client and the social worker and of their perceptions of a given
situation: 'In such a separation we can begin to explore social work not
as a straightforward mechanism through which money, goods or even
self-respect change hands, not as a kind of medicine, but as a search for
meaning, which has no end for either client or social worker.'[40] And
finally, Timms's philosophy on the nature of social work as 'practical
philosophising' is summed up in the following passage:

> The fact that we can never reach some grand general understanding
> either of a particular person or of people in general does not mean
> that the social worker and the client are engaged in nothing but
> perpetual and restless disappointment. Understanding is a process
> in which we engage and which produces results often sufficient for
> particular purposes.[41]

This statement in turn reflects Timms's distrust of 'the split between
feeling and the operation of intellect which seems to be a basic
assumption of many social work educators',[42] and thus has important
implications for the nature and the use of knowledge in social work, the
subject matter of the next chapter.

Meanwhile, the establishment of the fact that social work is
substantially a moral activity calls for an examination of the implications
of this in a number of practical respects. Given the fact that much of the
book is concerned in a more or less explicit manner with this task, I shall
confine myself here to those areas which will not be discussed
specifically in later chapters: the place of a code of ethics in social work;
the religious dimension; and the relationship between professional and
personal morality.

The slowness on the part of British social workers to formulate a
professional code of ethics is striking when viewed from the perspective
of social work as a predominantly moral activity. It is no doubt a
reflection of the more general reluctance to acknowledge that morality
and social work are indivisible – to which reference was made earlier.

An additional factor of considerable influence is the confusion and the lack of consensus with regard to the meaning of professionalism in social work. This subject will be discussed more fully later but it is relevant to refer in this context to the close affinity between many social workers' ambivalence towards the concept of professionalism and their lack of clarity or agreement about the nature of social work itself – this was discussed in Chapter 1. Recent debates within the British Association of Social Workers concerning various aspects of professionalism, including that of a code of ethics, do not convey an impressive picture of social workers' ability to think things through logically or consistently. Little attempt is made to define words so as to ensure a degree of common meaning; instead they are used in different senses to convey a particular stance or ideology. Certain representations of professions as, for example, those by some sociologists who view professionalism in an entirely negative light as institutionalising oppression by the powerful of the powerless, are equated with truth and are not often questioned. I believe that it is this ideological confusion which accounts largely for the very poor response to the draft *Code of Ethics for Social Work* which was drawn up by a B.A.S.W. Working Party and published as a Discussion Paper in 1972.[43] The response to it was very limited in terms of both quantity and quality of comment.

Given the fact that, by its very definition, a code of ethics provides only general guidelines to action and is not a book of rules which can be used as a substitute for personal decision-making, such a code needs the framework of a professional association to be meaningful and effective. There are two main reasons for this: an individual's adherence to the guidelines of a code of ethics is aided by the collective commitment to it of his elders and his peers; and the moral and psychological support derived from this fact.

It is important to recognise, however, that the formulation of any code of ethics, and of a social-work code of ethics in particular, presents very real difficulties in terms of a balance between stating general principles of a relatively high order of abstraction and laying down more specific rules of conduct. As I have already suggested, social work does not lend itself easily to many of the latter. The more abstract and general the formulation of the principles for practice, the more room for different interpretations of these and the greater the need, therefore, for some generally recognised and acceptable board of arbitration and discipline. It is difficult to conceive of such a board outside the context of a professional association or one where the professional viewpoint is strongly represented.

However difficult this is to achieve, a code of ethics in social work must aim at combining a meaningful and acceptable base for professional accountability with providing a framework within which an on-going discussion about moral issues can take place. The latter is an essential safeguard against an ossification and ritualisation of the code, resulting in its loss of meaning and credibility in a changing world. A professional code of conduct which allows adequate room for on-going debate is also one which makes much greater demands on the integrity and professional maturity of those who subscribe to it.

It is in the light of these considerations that such specific notes of guidance as those enshrined in the recent B.A.S.W. 'Code of Practice' for work with children at risk[44] have to be examined. In my view there is a lack of congruity between a general code of ethics like the one which was passed at the 1975 Annual General Meeting of the British Association of Social Workers[45] and a code of practice as specific as this. The latter appears to reflect much more societal pressures regarding social work with children than a professional concern with standards of practice. No other explanation comes readily to mind given the fact that no comparable code has been drawn up for social work with the aged, the mentally and physically sick and disabled, or any other group of clients about whom there is not the same extent of public interest and sympathy as there is about children. The most problematic aspect of this 'special' code is the implicit encouragement in it of a near absolute criterion of priority in relation to interventions where children are affected. This is difficult, if not impossible, to reconcile with the expectation of the exercise of professional judgement in determining priorities which should characterise a professional code of ethics.

The one recently adopted by the British Association of Social Workers defines its objectives in the following terms:

> Membership of a profession entails certain obligations beyond those of the ordinary citizen . . . Members of a profession have obligations to their clients, to their employers, to each other, to colleagues in other disciplines and to society. The degree to which these obligations are assumed is one determinant of the extent to which clients are accorded their rights.[46]

These objectives demonstrate how such a code, far from being an expression of attempts at enhancement of the status or the power of social workers themselves, is concerned with the safeguards of the rights of those with whom social workers transact in the course of their work. A code of this kind addresses itself directly to the value of respect for persons and its various derivatives: the central message of which reminds the social-work practitioners that all human beings are ends in themselves and must not, therefore, ever be used as means to other ends, however plausible. Social workers have always been more sensitive in the application of this value in their contacts with clients than in their dealings with other people on clients' behalf. The code is therefore a welcome as well as a necessary reminder that respect for persons does not allow for a classification of people into 'clients' and 'others', or of the 'others' into 'friends' and 'foes' who can be treated differentially. It is a worrying indication of the absence of a firm and consistent philosophical base shared by all social workers that there is a strong implication in the recent writings of some that such a differentiation is in fact a justified means for the achievement of a desirable objective.

At the beginning of this chapter, I asserted that morality was inherent to humanity and was therefore autonomous of religious faith. In making this assertion I was not being in the least original: it is a viewpoint which, as far as I know, is held by most contemporary Christian moral philosophers and theologians. For example, at an informal lecture given to a group of social workers, Bishop Butler, O.S.B., the well-known Catholic theologian and member of the Social Morality Council, stated that morality is not a specifically Christian thing but derives from being human. Equally, Fr J. Mahoney, S.J., lecturer in Christian Ethics at Heythrop College, University of London, maintains that 'Christianity speaks for human values', and that, in terms of morality, Christ did not teach anything original, but asserted human values previously acknowledged.[47] Christian Revelation, which is concerned with truths which are beyond the power of human reason to work out for itself, does not include 'moral mysteries' because, if such mysteries existed, morality could not be human.

What are the implications for social work of this reality? Does it mean that there is no significant relationship between the practice of social work and religious faith? I am only competent to discuss this question in the context of Christianity but I should be surprised if much of what is applicable in this context is not also true of other religions.

In a talk in 1963 on the subject 'Social Work: Professionalism and Catholic Reluctance', I suggested that 'it is . . . incorrect to talk or even to think of Catholic social work or Catholic social workers as distinct from Catholics who are social workers or social workers who are Catholics'.[48] ('Christian' could of course replace 'Catholic' in this quotation.) The distinction is of quite vital importance: 'Christian social work' suggests a particular brand of social work, with a possible implication of proselytising.

What then is the significance to a social worker of being a Christian? One of the important effects of Christian faith for the believer is that it confirms, deepens and enhances human moral values. The importance of this point is stressed by Macquarrie who states it as his aim 'to find a kind of basic common morality uniting Christians and non-Christians, and to look at the roots of this in our shared humanity'.[49] As it is not possible to separate entirely what one does from who one is, a social worker whose sense of commitment to human moral values has been strengthened by his Christian religion cannot fail to reflect this in his contacts with people, especially when his own person constitutes a major helping medium in work with his clients.

In my view, religious faith is a unique experience in virtue of its transcendental and absolute nature. The degree of confidence, security, and purpose it offers to those who believe has no equivalent within the secular world. At his best, a social worker who is a Christian should therefore be less prone to disillusionment and frustration in the face of difficulties or failure than his colleague who does not have a comparable faith to sustain him. He should also be able to combine more easily appropriate humility about his own limitations and shortcomings with conviction that it is worth trying his best within these.

His clarity regarding the social-work objectives, and his conviction regarding their value, should be logical derivatives of his belief in the Incarnation, Revelation and Redemption. The value of respect for persons assumes an additional dimension when perceived in terms of man's sonship of God. Human interdependence, too, with the implicit rights and needs of all people both to give and to receive, is given reinforced meaning. It would seem to me that there is no single social-work principle the importance and purposefulness of which is not enhanced by the spiritual dimension.

Like all ideals, the one of perfect Christian commitment to the service of mankind is seldom attainable by human beings, social workers included. It lends itself to abuse in many different ways, but it is hardly possible to think of anything of value which is not open to abuse as a result of human frailty, and in that sense religious faith shares the predicament of all human ideals and values.

Finally, before concluding this chapter, I must turn to the vexed question regarding the relationship between professional ethics and personal morality. In our complex society in which most individuals have to carry a multiplicity of social roles, some of which are mutually inconsistent, there is a tendency to view the behaviour required by these various roles as being distinct to them and entirely separate from behaviour in other contexts. I do not believe that such an extreme compartmentalisation of man is possible, although there is no doubt that we all adapt our behaviour to particular role requirements. It would seem to me that there is a fundamental difference between selective behaviour and behaviour which is basically alien to one's nature. This fact is well summed up (especially for social work) in a comment by Laurens Van der Post when he said in a B.B.C. broadcast in 1961: 'There is an important communication which we tend to overlook in life and that is the communication which comes not from what we say but from what we are.'

Social work, like any other occupation, entails the adoption of a special role which calls for behaviour appropriate to it which may be either inappropriate or not required in other contexts, for example within one's family. It is not, however, incompatible to recognise the instrumental aspects of the social-work role (as underlined, for example, in the already quoted foreword to the B.A.S.W. draft *Code of Ethics*: 'Membership of a profession entails certain obligations beyond those of the ordinary citizen') and accept simultaneously the validity of the following assertion by McDougall: 'We cannot make our professional life a nine to five persona. I know all about the need for other interests and for not taking the client problems home with us, and these warnings are important, but a profession is a way of life, it is not just a job of work.'[50]

I realise that the logical implications of this assertion for social work and social workers are serious and, perhaps for this reason, they are seldom faced up to. If they were, social workers might have to admit to themselves and to society that theirs is not only a profession but also a vocation – a truly embarrassing admission to make for many in this age of scepticism and materialism!

Chapter 4

The Place of Knowledge in Social Work

Social work is an 'applied discipline' in the sense that relevant knowledge acquired is for direct use in the pursuit of its objectives. The application of knowledge is, however, obviously far from being a mechanistic or simple process. As Stevenson reminds us,[1] knowledge is not synonymous with understanding or truth. The definition of wisdom by Socrates as 'knowledge of what it is one does not know' is echoed in modern times by Popper's assertion that our ignorance grows with our knowledge.

Implicit in all these statements is the warning to all who 'apply' knowledge of the considerable dangers which are inherent in an excessive or inappropriate investment in something which by its very nature is tentative and transitory. Another aspect of the elusiveness of knowledge, and one which seems of particular relevance to social work, has been stated by Magee in expressing Popper's view that 'Knowledge in the objective sense is knowledge without a knower: it is knowledge without a knowing subject.'[2] This emphasis on the selectivity of observation highlights the importance of the subjective factor in knowledge and its use.

Social workers, who are so constantly exposed to the subjective both in themselves and in their clients, cannot fail to have an intuitive awareness of the limitations of 'objective knowledge'. This explains partly the considerable ambivalence shown by many of them towards a conceptual approach to practice which Bartlett and Timms, along with other social-work writers, have consistently deplored. This ambivalence has certainly had a harmful effect on the development of social work in that it has prevented many practitioners from a wholehearted commitment to utilising the riches of their practice for the purpose of knowledge building and validation, in spite of being aware of the need, in social work, as in any other collective endeavour, to formulate current experience for transmission to future generations.

An influential factor in this reluctance has been the widespread confusion between the 'thinking' and the 'feeling' components within social work, This reflects the more widespread difficulty concerning the exact nature of the relationship between the cognitive and the affective aspects of human functioning. There is no doubt, however, that a dichotomy between these two, when taken to extremes and resulting in the belief that a warm heart and a cool head are not reconcilable, is totally antipathetic to the core nature of social work and its concern with the human predicament. The latter does not lend itself to a neat division between cognitive and affective elements.

What may be said in defence of social workers is that there is by no means universal agreement as to what constitutes either knowledge or a scientific attitude in its pursuit.

The question 'what constitutes knowledge?' has exercised philosophers from time immemorial, and very different answers have been produced for it at different periods and by different thinkers. Thus Descartes maintained that man is born with certain kinds of knowledge. His assertion was strongly disputed by the empiricists who asserted in turn that knowledge comes to man through the medium of his five senses only. The latter excluded from the realm of knowledge, therefore, such essential areas of human experience as cause–effect relations and proof of identity. According to empiricists, values are not subject to thought, and so they postulated a special sentiment to deal with the issues of right and wrong. The latter view was disputed by Kant who argued that values must not only evoke emotional approval but must convince men as rational beings. A look at the contemporary scene shows that the Linguistic School of Philosophy led by Ayer comes closer to the views of the empiricists than those of Kant in its insistence on a rigid separation of statements of fact – of 'what is' – from statements of value – 'what ought to be'. On the other hand, there is also evidence of a re-awakening of interest in moral philosophy, as exemplified by the writings of Emmett,[3] Warnock,[4] Downie and Telfer[5] and Campbell,[6] which by its very nature is concerned with the rationality of values.

Equally, definitions of what is 'scientific' vary considerably. There has been a growing tendency since the Renaissance and until recently to model all scientific activity upon the study of the natural sciences, and thus to invest with absolute values the methods of study characteristic of these sciences. The validity of this model is seriously challenged by Waddington[7] who, in discussing what constitutes a scientific attitude, emphasises the secondary importance of the methods of study in relation to both the nature of the material studied and to the scientist's attitude towards that material. In his view, the latter must be an attitude of respect and of readiness to be guided by the requirements of the material. It thus follows that the study of man must be appropriate to the nature of man and cannot be a mere replica of studies of other types of 'material'. To Waddington, science is but 'the organised attempt of mankind to discover how things work as causal systems'.[8]

What then are the main characteristics of the 'human material' to be considered in determining the appropriate methods for its study? Both the seventeenth-century philosopher, Spinoza, and this century's social psychologist, Mead, offer useful insights in this respect. Spinoza described three different levels of knowledge, each calling for different approaches for their comprehension. The first, and the lowest of these, is concerned with description – with 'what is': the second is about causal facts – 'the hows'; the third and the highest has to do with the typically human concern about purpose – 'the whys'. Mead reinforces Spinoza's reference to the existence of specifically human preoccupations which demand cognitive attention by emphasising the fact of the uniqueness of man among all living creatures in his ability to reflect upon himself and his experiences.

Inherent in such a viewpoint is the 'respectability' of trying to comprehend and conceptualise the less tangible manifestations of human life – such as feelings – which are by their very nature subjective and not open to verification by experimental methods. It is also implicit in such a recognition that the understanding of these can only be attained through such appropriate channels as interpersonal inter-changes within which 'feelings become facts'. It thus provides an important basis for social work to attempt a synthesis between the 'scientific' and the 'artistic' elements, rather than viewing them as essentially in conflict.

Support for such a position can be found in Popper who disclaims two separate cultures: one scientific and the other aesthetic, or one rational and the other irrational. In his view (as expressed by Magee):

> the scientist and the artist, far from being engaged in opposed or incompatible activities, are both trying to extend the range of understanding and of experience by the use of creative imagination subjected to critical control. They both use irrational as well as rational faculties in the pursuit of this objective; they are both exploring the unknown and trying to articulate the search and its findings; both are seekers after truth who make indispensable use of intuition.[9]

The particular point regarding intuition is of considerable importance to social work, which relies on it a great deal. Intuition is defined in the Oxford English Dictionary as a 'direct apprehension of reality' and, as Hollis pointed out, within this definition, intuition (or insight) is always accurate.

As well as acknowledging the importance to social work of its validation by such a concept of knowledge and study, it is equally necessary to recognise that the application in practice of such a 'philosophy of knowledge' is fraught with many difficulties. A common factor underlying these is the need to act decisively upon the understanding and knowledge available at any given point, Aristotle's statement (quoted by Emmett)[10] that 'the last step is not a proposition but an action' has profound meaning for every social worker who is constantly faced with the following dilemmas. Is this particular intuition of mine a true intuition or is it a false insight? What is likely to constitute a lesser risk to the client, my ignoring it, or my acting upon it? How do I weigh up the relative merits of facts observed and of the understanding derived through 'intuition' when these appear to be contradictory? Problems such as these highlight the interdependence of knowledge and morality. Given the relative nature of knowledge and its pitfalls, its use calls for a considerable degree of personal security. The latter is in turn dependent on trust: trust in the integrity of oneself and of others. Yet according to Dr Johnson (quoted by Stevenson), 'Integrity without knowledge is weak and useless and knowledge without integrity is dangerous and dreadful.'[11] – a statement hard to deny!

Provided integrity is present as a safeguard, social workers can no more afford to avoid making and using generalisations than any other group of people who seriously intend to improve the quality of their service by both learning from the experience and the mistakes of their predecessors and offering their own accumulated understanding for use by their successors. As already suggested in the preceding chapter, individualisation and classification are the two sides of one coin.

Social workers have a not wholly undeserved reputation for lacking sophistication in their use of theoretical constructs. They tend to confuse these with the reality which these artificial constructs are intended to represent. In this connection it seems not inappropriate to offer a definition of theory. Hall and Lindsey define theory thus:

> A theory is a set of conventions (terms, concepts, definitions), a creative, imaginative organisation by the theorist of his observations. It is an artistic arbitrary product. It is not and can never become true or false, although its implications may be either. A theory is either useful or not useful.[12]

That such a definition applies equally to all theories, not just those in the realm of the social sciences, is a point made forcibly by the mathematician Kline:

> We should regard any theory about physical space then, as a purely subjective construction and not impute to it objective reality, Man constructs a geometry, Euclidean or non-Euclidean, and decides to view space in those terms. The advantages of doing so, even though he cannot be sure space possesses any of the characteristics of the structure he has built up in his own mind, are that he can then think about space and nature and use his theory in scientific work. This view of space and nature generally does not deny that there is such a thing as an objective physical world, It merely recognises that man's judgments and conclusions about space are purely of his own making.[13]

Such utilitarian views of theory are of course incompatible with a rigid adherence to any particular conceptual formulation in the light of evidence that it has either outlived its usefulness or that it is insufficient

for the purposes of social work. Unfortunately, however, the history of
social work provides considerable evidence of both unjustified clinging
to outmoded theories and wholesale changes of allegiance as from one
theory or set of theories to others, as if these were governed purely by
the laws of fashion. One factor which has no doubt been influential in
this excessive adherence on the part of some social workers to particular
theories, and an equally excessive tendency on the part of others to a
wholesale substitution of new and fashionable ideas for the concepts
previously subscribed to, is the potential range of knowledge relevant to
and needed in social work. This knowledge is frequently subsumed in
professional literature under the umbrella terms of 'knowledge about
man' and 'knowledge about society', but such a shorthand is of limited
value in conveying either the complexity of the knowledge inherent in
the two labels of 'man' and 'society', or the dilemmas which stem from
the need to be selective in the choice of knowledge within these fields
and the need to integrate them appropriately. For example, there is an
inherent problem in the integration of knowledge of a sociological and
of a psychological nature due to the basically different terms of
reference of these two types of discipline, the former relating to
corporate social entities and the latter to individuals. However, the
problem is by no means confined to knowledge concerned with
macro/micro dimensions, In studying the individual, the concept of
'psychogenic illness' provides a good illustration of the difficulties
inherent in unifying knowledge from the physiological and the
psychological realms. Equally, in studying society the interactionist
perspective and that of Marxist determinism are not easy to combine in
promoting the understanding of social processes. In the face of realities
of this kind the temptation to equate certain kinds of knowledge with
dogma, and then to hide behind its authority, is understandable,
especially given the extent of the commitment to action inherent in
social work. It is this commitment which is probably the common
denominator in both kinds of 'intellectual extremism' to be met among
some social workers: the uncritical and inappropriate adoption of
certain psychological models, for example the psychoanalytic and in
recent years the behaviourist model, and a total allegiance to certain
sociological and political 'radical theories' to the exclusion of any
recognition of the relevance to social work of knowledge concerned
with intra-psychic processes.

A firmly rooted scepticism about the transitory and utilitarian nature of all knowledge would seem to be an essential prerequisite for social workers in avoiding the pitfall of confusing ideology with knowledge. This, however, will not resolve entirely the dilemmas inherent in having to acquire a degree of usable knowledge about 'man' and 'society'. How can these dilemmas be made more manageable?

Stevenson suggests that social workers abandon the notion of acquiring 'a body of knowledge' as this implies greater certainty and permanency with regard to the contribution of existing knowledge than is the case: 'to try and build a social-work house on the shifting sands of social science theory is asking for trouble. Social work should probably concentrate on erecting strong, portable, flexible tents rather than houses.'[14] Instead, she suggests that knowledge should be related to certain 'frames of reference' appropriate to social work, and that the various available theoretical contributions, both those that are complementary and those which appear to be in conflict, should be examined within their context.

This provides a way of partialising and rationalising the task of knowledge acquisition in social work, although it leaves unresolved the issue of what constitutes the appropriate frames of reference, and there is clearly scope for some controversy in relation to this. On the other hand, decisions as to what areas of knowledge have particular claims on social work can only be rationally made on the basis of the nature of social work and of its primary objectives. Given the degree of the lack of consensus regarding these, referred to in Chapter 1, it is hardly surprising that social-work education is currently in a state of turmoil and bewilderment. It is hard indeed to have a clearly formulated educational policy regarding priorities in learning when there is so much uncertainty about the tasks for which students of social work are being trained.

Notwithstanding these very real current problems in the realm of social-work education, it is possible to acknowledge the fundamental importance of certain general areas of knowledge. Bartlett has formulated these in the context of the following frames of reference:

1. Human development and behaviour characterized by emphasis on the wholeness of the individual and the reciprocal influences of man and his total environment – human, social, economic, and cultural.

2. The psychology of giving and taking help from another person or source outside the individual.

3, Ways in which people communicate with one another and give outer expression to inner feelings, such as words, gestures and activities.

4. Group process and the effects of groups upon individuals and the reciprocal influence of the individual upon the group.

5. The meaning and effect on the individual, groups and community of cultural heritage including its religious beliefs, spiritual values, law, and other social institutions.

6. Relationships, i.e. the interactional processes between individuals, between individual and groups, and between group and group.

7. The community, its internal processes, modes of development and change, its social services and resources.

8. The social services, their structure, organisation, and methods.

9. Himself (the social worker), which enables the individual practitioner to be aware of and to take responsibility for his own emotions and attitudes as they affect his professional functions.[15]

The list is truly formidable, and yet it would be difficult to deny the relevance to social work of any of these items, What needs to be faced, therefore, is the requirement of the acquisition of some basic knowledge in all these areas by social workers without their being overwhelmed with too much detail at the same time. This requirement raises in turn a number of subsidiary issues of considerable practical importance such as those of the nature of basic professional knowledge and its relationship to the more technical elements in training, criteria for the selection of priorities, the place of methods learning, and last, but not least, the relationship between general and specific knowledge. These will now be examined briefly in turn.

Whilst it is not possible to draw a rigid line of demarcation between 'professional' knowledge and 'technical' knowledge, in general terms the latter is subject to certain restrictions in that it relates to the demands of particular situations. In contrast, the former is primarily concerned with knowledge which can be transferred and with the ability to identify both similarities and differences in situations, and thus to know what is applicable to bring to a new situation from past experience, and what new knowledge it requires. According to Goldstein, 'What distinguishes professional competency from technical competency is the characteristics of autonomy and the ability to make critical decisions.'[16] The emphasis in professional knowledge is thus on acquiring a frame of reference within which to identify the characteristic features of disparate phenomena and on developing the ability to ask relevant questions rather than provide speedy answers.

The attainment of such objectives is obviously a demanding task and one which can only be achieved to a relative extent. As Gombrich has put it in another context, 'Do we measure it (knowledge) in relation to what is knowable or to what is worth knowing? After all, our knowledge is always superficial.'[17] However, given this intrinsic limitation, certain general requirements accompany attempts to acquire knowledge of a professional nature. An important one of these is the need to identify and transmit in education certain key concepts in each of the main areas of knowledge. Such a process entails not only grasping the knowledge content of these key concepts, but also an awareness of the appropriate ways of acquiring them. The above list quoted from Bartlett, for example, makes it clear that the various areas of knowledge referred to call for very different approaches. At the one extreme there is knowledge which can be best acquired through observation, reading or lectures. For example, item 8, 'the social services, their structure, organisation, and methods', is an instance of this kind of knowledge. At the other extreme lies knowledge which by its very nature calls for an intuitive approach and which it is not possible to acquire by other means. No amount of reading on self-awareness, for example, will enhance a social worker's insight into himself unless he is sufficiently free from personal insecurity and its by-products, such as rigidity and defensiveness, to be in touch with his feelings and behaviour and to learn from this source.

Even in the case of the two extremes I mentioned, the acquisition of knowledge is not confined to these media, however indispensable they are, but is dependent on other additional sources. Personal experience of a social service does help one to know more about it and, equally, reading about such matters as self-awareness or empathy does enhance one's understanding and appreciation of these attributes, thus making it easier to foster them in oneself and others, The range of methods by which most, if not all, knowledge is attained is increasingly recognised, and hence the growing interest on the part of social-work educators in the various aids to teaching, involving experience, such as projects, use of drama and other creative activities.

All these differing means reflect and refer to the three major aspects of human functioning: sensual perception, cognitive comprehension and affective experience, and so it becomes clear that the acquisition of knowledge is a process involving the whole person and cannot be confined to any one aspect. Whilst this is true of all learning, it is a truth of particular importance in social work given the range of knowledge involved and the varying nature of the different concepts encountered.

It is on account of this variety that the acquisition of professional knowledge in social work is dependent on some study in each one of the main areas, rather than on a concentrated study in a few. This is a necessary condition if transferability of knowledge is to be possible. Such transferability is much more viable in relation to concepts of a comparable level of abstraction and some general affinity than to those which do not meet these conditions. Thus, as already suggested, given the differences in the scale of approach between sociology and psychology, to expect a social-work student who confines himself in his professional studies to the acquisition of knowledge about society to be able to transfer this knowledge to an understanding of individuals, is to expect the impossible, and vice versa. The recognition of this important educational principle need not result in an obsessional preoccupation with a delicate balancing of the curriculum so as to ensure that every subject is given equal weight. Apart from the practical impossibility of this, such a policy would defeat its own ends because a 'balanced diet' does not consist of identical amounts of every possible nutritional ingredient, but is dependent on sufficient amounts of particular constituents.

It would be equally mistaken if the need for the acquisition of some knowledge in all the major areas of direct relevance to social work led to identical syllabuses on all social-work courses. Given the breadth of potentially relevant knowledge and the constantly shifting situation with regard to social-work practice, what is needed are various combinations of knowledge, taught with due regard to the nature of particular resources available to a course – both academic and fieldwork resources – and to the interests and needs of its students.

Provided the basic requirements of a 'core content' are met, there is everything to be said for a variety, some courses adopting a more 'clinical' focus, others emphasising community studies, and also for a differentiation being made on the basis of different client groups and methods of helping.

The latter point serves as a useful reminder that, so far, the discussion of the nature of knowledge, and the process of its acquisition in social work, has made little direct reference to the fact that this knowledge, like all professional knowledge, is for fairly specific use. An acknowledgement of this fact makes it necessary to give some consideration to the relationship between knowledge and methods of practice.

The usual definition of method as 'a systematic procedure' has been extended in social work (as Bartlett argues[18] and as is suggested in Chapter 1) to encompass much more. Methods have been viewed for a long time in social work as self-contained entities incorporating values, knowledge and skills. Chapter 1 discusses in more detail what the effects of this have been on the formation of a social-work identity transcending the separate methods so, to avoid repetition, all that needs restating here is that the primacy given to methods has been a considerable obstacle to the development of unity within social work in the realm of common values and a common knowledge base.

Bartlett suggests that in addition to the philosophical and conceptual objections to defining social work on the basis of its methods of practice, a division by methods is no longer viable on practical grounds, as it creates artificial boundaries between the various aspects of social-work activity. As has already been argued, no 'caseworker' can confine his activities to face-to-face contacts with individuals but is more or less extensively involved in various forms of group activity both with and on behalf of his clients as well as in aspects of 'community work'. Equally, a 'community worker' who wishes to justify his social-work identity can hardly refuse to become involved, to some extent at least, in the personal problems of members of his community groups.

But, even apart from the artificiality of the boundaries between work with individuals, groups and communities which a 'method orientation' entails, social work is a more complex and a more comprehensive activity than what results from the sum total of its separate 'methods' – as Bartlett argues. In her view, conceptualising social work in terms of methods has an increasingly restricting effect on the development of a fuller comprehension of the nature of social work and the range of its activities. Her alternative to 'methods' – 'interventive repertoire' – is no mere exercise in semantics but a substantial shift in emphasis from means to ends. This is well conveyed in the following quotation from the author: 'Interventive acts and techniques are means to an end and are only significant when the end is defined in terms of social work purposes and values and the situation is accurately understood through the use of social work knowledge.'[19]

If one acknowledges the validity of such a shift, then one has also to accept that however important the various aspects of technical expertise which comprise the effectiveness of the different 'interventive acts', their choice rests upon discrimination based on the application of value principles and cognitive understanding. These two, therefore, are an essential accompaniment to specific skills in an educational process aimed to equip social workers with ability to transfer knowledge and experience rather than to possess technical expertise only. To accept the primacy of values and knowledge over skills is not, however, to denigrate the latter. Among the definitions of skill given by the Oxford English Dictionary are the following two: 'Discrimination or discretion in relation to special circumstances', and 'A sense of what is right and fitting', underlines the important part played by knowledge in the use of these. The point being made here about the nature of the relationship between 'thinking' and 'doing' is that the latter must derive from the former and cannot therefore be an autonomous activity. It must have been this that Freud had in mind when he exhorted his keen disciples to 'set aside your therapeutic ambitions and try to understand what is happening. When you have done that, therapeutics will take care of itself.'[20]

The emphasis so far on the importance of a foundation of common general knowledge in social work as a prerequisite to its conceptual unity and coherence calls in turn for a clarification of the meaning of 'generic' and 'specific' in their application to social work,

Timms demonstrates aptly in his discussion of these concepts how many different meanings can be attached to them and the confusing effects of a lack of agreed definition of the terms used. Thus he writes:

> If, for example, we take 'generic' to mean 'general', then the complementary term would be 'specialised'. Adopting this definition has particular implications. It involves us, for instance, in thinking in terms of the general social worker, on the one hand, and the specialist, on the other. If, however, 'generic' is used in the sense of 'genus' we are led to think in terms of a common name covering a number of species. In this use of the 'generic–specific' idea a 'generic social worker' as a kind of person like 'the general social worker'

mentioned above would not be conceivable; the term 'generic' would refer to those characteristics which make it sensible and convenient to call social workers in different fields by a common name.[21]

The issue of 'genericism' in relation to social-work practice will be discussed more fully in a later chapter. With regard to the educational context, however, it is important to emphasise at this point the very fundamental difference between conceiving of generic as 'general' or as 'genus', that is shared, or common. The former interpretation might encourage the acceptance of an emphasis on 'the lowest common denominator' in order to ensure that everybody learns the same – a practice which is bound to have disastrous results on the intellectual standards of social work. The view that 'generic' means 'in common' must result, on the other hand, in a recognition that there is no inherent incompatibility between the 'generic' and the 'specific' but that, on the contrary, the two are complementary and interdependent. General concepts, such as those of loss or deprivation for example, can only become truly meaningful in a specific context such as loss of income or health, deprivation of freedom or affection. Acquisition of knowledge which leads to understanding requires both the grasp of the more abstract concepts and opportunities for their application in more specific contexts. Both the usefulness of the 'generic' thus conceived, and the dependence of that usefulness on the acceptance of the validity of the 'specific', is well formulated by Timms:

> the term 'generic' would refer to those characteristics which make it sensible and convenient to call social workers in different fields by a common name , .. [and] Any conclusions about the 'generic–specific' concept must recognise that social work practice at any one time concerns the specific: it is a question of understanding a particular situation confronting a certain client and worker in a particular organisation. This situation cannot be fully understood by discovering the appropriate general theory, if one exists, or effectively handled by recognising the correct covering principle.[22]

I believe that the relationship between the 'common core' knowledge and more specific content is of a crucial importance for the future of social-work education. The continued expansion of potentially relevant knowledge within the behavioural sciences, the widening range of functions being allocated to social work, and the resulting pressure of various vested interests for particular areas of study to be included in the curriculum, present a major educational dilemma. Unless a rational approach on the part of social-work educators can be adopted with regard to an appropriate balance between the 'generic' and the 'specific' content of teaching, and is accompanied by an informed selection of the concepts which warrant inclusion in the core content, the intellectual confusions within social work in the past will appear trivial in comparison with those to follow in the near future!

A discussion of the nature and place of knowledge in social work would be incomplete without some reference to the origins of such knowledge and the extent to which some of it can be regarded as social-work knowledge. What constitutes relevant areas of knowledge in social work is determined by the view of man as a complex entity with interacting needs in the biological, intellectual, social, emotional and spiritual spheres. It follows from this that any knowledge which contributes to a better understanding of man as an individual in the context of the society of which he is a member is potentially relevant and useful to social work. This certainly includes the whole range of the social sciences, including philosophy and economics and, in addition, those natural sciences, like anatomy and physiology, which foster the understanding of the biological aspects of human nature. Inherent in this required breadth of knowledge is the dilemma of how to ensure its acquisition without superficiality and dilettantism.

There can clearly be no easy answer to this, but the point made earlier about the need to identify central concepts in these different fields of knowledge, and become familiar with them without becoming submerged in the more detailed specific knowledge surrounding them, assumes particular importance in this context. In struggling with this very difficult issue, I am greatly encouraged by the approach to the same kind of dilemma in relation to social administration by Donnison. After having listed the various knowledge disciplines on which the study and practice of social administration have to draw, he asks the following question:

> But if the study of the social services demands so extensive an invasion of the territories of other disciplines, is anything distinctive left under the title of 'Social Administration'? Do we have a subject of our own, or are we merely a bunch of ex-economists, political

scientists and historians, would-be psychologists, philosophers and sociologists, who would be better employed in the purer atmosphere of these major disciplines?[23]

Donnison then goes on to answer his own question by suggesting that the absence of a distinct body of knowledge, theoretical structure, or methodology, is not incompatible with academic respectability. He sees the latter for social administration as resting with the distinct preoccupation with 'the development of collective action for the advancement of social welfare',[24] which calls for an appropriate application and integration of theoretical and methodological contributions from other fields.

In social work the answer to a similar type of question is in my view fundamentally the same, but of course different in specific terms. I am prepared to argue in fact that, given the service orientation of social work and its direct involvement with human beings, the task of appropriate borrowing and use of knowledge from other areas is particularly demanding and challenging in terms of both intellectual ability and professional integrity.

Viewed in such a context, the issue of whether or not there is a distinct body of social-work knowledge, which is frequently raised as implying that the credibility of social work rests upon this, becomes less real. However, this is not to deny the importance of social workers playing a more active part in the process of knowledge building than they have done hitherto. The importance of this is twofold.

First of all, if social-work practice is to develop and progress, the various experiences and insights of individual practitioners have to be made cumulative. There is a general recognition within social work that the accumulated 'practice wisdom' within it is not inconsiderable, but so far it has been insufficiently formulated into the concepts and generalisations which would allow it to be fully shared and passed on to future generations of social workers. This failure to conceptualise from the experience of practice has probably been a major contributory factor to the already mentioned dichotomy within social work between its 'scientific' and 'artistic' components. This is because inherent in professional practice is the need for both deductive and inductive types of knowledge. On the one hand, various theories and concepts need to be put to a practical test for purposes of their validation and modification; on the other hand, experience gained in practice should

lead to generalisations and should form the basis of new concepts and
theories. (Both the Law of Archimedes and Lindemann's Crisis Theory
are the results of such empirical findings.) Where the importance of
this process is insufficiently realised through either a mechanistic
application of theoretical knowledge, or a neglect of reflection upon the
more general meaning of the specific phenomena encountered, or a
mixture of both, theory and practice are bound to be felt to be at a great
distance from each other and only marginally related.

The other reason why neglect of knowledge building by social
workers constitutes an irresponsible attitude on their part is because it
denies the opportunity for other disciplines and occupations to benefit
from the experiences and insights of social work. I can see no better way
of conveying this point than to quote the concluding paragraph in
Emmett:

> I began by saying that social workers lived at the uncomfortable, but
> at the same time potentially creative point where social science and
> psychology meet and are brought to bear on practical problems. I
> have now claimed that moral philosophy in the sense at least of a
> considered view of moral judgment, also intersects this point. Social
> work can, I believe, supply a field laboratory for the combination of
> these different ways of thinking; and if social workers can show how
> at any rate some parts of these ways of thinking can be made relevant
> to practical problems, they may not only help themselves by their
> exertions, but also help moral philosophers and social scientists by
> their example.[25]

This is an inspiring challenge, and any attempts to meet it require a
consideration of the place of research in social work. It would be
difficult to deny the dependence of knowledge building in any field,
and so also in social work, on both inductive and deductive knowledge.
Although in recent years social workers have become more involved in
research activities, some of these have had a greater bearing on the
'field laboratory' functions advocated by Emmett than others. What
seems to be still badly lacking in social work, with notable exceptions
such as Goldberg[26] and Goldberg and Neill,[27] is both research
attempting to evaluate social-work practice itself and research aiming to
discover some common features of the problems dealt with by social
workers.

Bartlett[28] has emphasised social workers' failure to utilise their 'practice wisdom' in this way and, more recently, Davies[29] has both argued the potential value of social-work research of this kind and has shown some of the very real difficulties involved in it.

The fact that, in contrast to many other professions, social workers' record of research is poor, is not only due to these difficulties or even to their ambivalence towards the use of knowledge, to which reference was made earlier. The conditions under which most social workers practice are not conducive to serious and sustained intellectual effort. Failure to engage in research is but one manifestation of this. Inability to keep up to date with relevant reading, and absence of adequate reflection on what they are doing, are equally serious signs of the prevailing malaise which will be discussed more fully in a later chapter. What must be openly acknowledged is the very unsatisfactory and potentially dangerous situation in which social work finds itself as a result of the tenuous nature of the links between its broad theoretical foundations and actual practice.

This situation is not improved by the fact that social-work education, too, is in a difficult position and at a disadvantage in comparison with other academic disciplines with regard to its knowledge-building functions. Thus, given the lack of tradition of professional education in many British universities, social-work courses are still viewed with a degree of suspicion and with ambivalence. There is a widespread lack of recognition of the essential part played by fieldwork in social-work education, and this is reflected in expectations of social-work teachers which take no account of their extensive and intensive involvement in this aspect of their students' learning and the demands this makes on them in terms of time, administrative functions and public-relations work. (Unlike medical schools, social-work courses have no direct access to their 'field laboratory' but must create these opportunities for supervised practice and foster them themselves.) In consequence, no appropriate adjustments are made to staff/student ratios, the inability of social-work teachers to have the usual academic holidays is ignored, and criteria for promotion devised for staff on purely theoretical courses are rigidly applied.

This in turn results in a situation where social work within universities is predominantly under the leadership of professors of social administration or sociology – which perpetuates a distorted and a low image of social work within the academic community.

The most serious single outcome, however, of the vicious circle in which social-work education in universities and other institutions of higher learning finds itself, is the lack of opportunities for the large majority of teachers of social work to engage in research and creative writing and thus make the distinctive contribution which they only can make towards knowledge building in their own field.

Chapter 5

The Social-Work Process

Process is defined in the Oxford English Dictionary as 'continuous and regular action or succession of actions taking place or carried out in definite manner and leading to the accomplishment of some result'. The important features in this definition are the purposeful nature of a process and the complexity inherent in its being a construction consisting of a number of interdependent elements. These characteristics are certainly applicable to social work given the wide range of its activities, and this fact underlines in turn the importance of a unifying concept within which to analyse these separate elements.

There are a number of different and equally valid perspectives one could adopt in an attempt to analyse the social-work process. One of these is the interrelatedness of values, knowledge and skills to which reference has already been made in the earlier chapters. The perspective adopted for discussion here is that of the process of study/assessment/helping/evaluation in the context of a professional relationship in which it always takes place and in relation to the dynamics derived from the different phases in time through which the process operates.

Any discussion of social-work assessment (or social-work diagnosis) and of social-work helping (or social-work treatment) would be unreal without some reference to the medical model and its appropriateness. For various historical and structural reasons this model has been used widely in social work until fairly recently. Now, however, it is increasingly questioned. Some of these criticisms have more validity than others. It is certainly an over-simplification and a distortion of social work to suggest that the medical model has been used indiscriminately and without appropriate adaptation to the requirements of the situations with which social work is concerned. On the other hand, there is no doubt that excessive adherence to this model has been an obstacle to the development of a clear social-work identity. Given the various misconceptions and confusions in this area, it seems worth examining in some detail both the nature of the medical model and the extent to which it is applicable to the practice of social work. Perhaps this can best be attempted initially by looking at the nature of some common objections raised to the use by social workers of the medical model in their approach to problems.

One of these it that is places undue emphasis on abnormality or 'sickness', with the implicit assumption that the locus of the problem lies within the person experiencing it. From this follows the further assumption that there is a more readily available explanation for the 'disorder', and therefore a more clear-cut solution to it than is usually the case in social work. Further points of criticism have to do with the effects on the nature of the relationship between the social worker and his clients of the foregoing assumptions and the extent to which the social worker both sees himself in, and is vested with, a position of excessive authority *vis-à-vis* his clients. This was one of the major criticisms levelled by the 'functionalists' within American social work against the 'diagnosticians' during the period of controversy between the two Schools in the 1930s, 1940s and 1950s.

As already suggested, the adaptation of any model for purposes other than those for which it was originally intended is by no means an easy or a simple task, and social workers do not have a particularly impressive record of success in this area. However, before one can discuss in detail the application of the medical model to social work, it is important to be clear about its nature. In this respect a common mistake is to view the medical model as being much more homogenous than it is in reality. This was well argued in a recent article by Clarke.[1] He asserts that 'a medical model' does not exist and has never existed, but that there are instead a number of different models appropriate to the different kinds of illness dealt with in medicine. These call for such different approaches as relief of symptoms, keeping the patient alive until his illness has run its natural course, changing the patient's environment which is harmful to his health and educating him to lead a more healthy style of life, as well as the activities more commonly associated with medical treatment such as drug therapy or surgery. What the different models have in common is the recognition attached to the importance of observation and the use of other available methods of studying the problem as a prerequisite to appropriate action.

Viewed in this light it is hard to deny that social work can learn a great deal from the experience and thinking in medicine. Given the ambivalence on the part of many social workers towards an explicit and deliberate use of knowledge in their practice, which was discussed in the preceding chapter, the emphasis in medicine on the need to observe and reflect before one acts, coupled with a disciplined approach to the gathering of data and the acquisition of understanding, is of tremendous value to social work. (The well-known statement of Richmond's, 'When you study you keep your eyes open and you look, when you diagnose, you shut them and think',[2] illustrates the recognition of this fact within social work.) It seems to me that it is true to suggest that social work has gained a great deal from the contribution in this respect by medical and psychiatric social workers – the two groups which had the closest association with medicine.

As medicine adopts a more holistic approach to health, in which the importance of emotional and social factors becomes increasingly recognised, the range of aetiological and therapeutic factors with which it will have to concern itself will become hardly less than the variety which is so characteristic of social work. This highlights the importance of the two professions sharing a common framework of values and concepts, and thus being able to communicate and collaborate effectively and to learn from each other's experience. The importance of the latter point can be illustrated from the realm of the different nature of the client/social worker and the patient/doctor relationships. Given the valid differences in the nature of these two sets of relationships, certain 'occupational hazards' are contained in each which can be corrected by a reference to the other. Thus some social workers are prone to underplay in their dealings with clients the degree of the expertise and professional authority they bring to both the assessment of the problems and to their solution, whilst some doctors do not give enough recognition to their patients' own formulation of their problems and assume an excessively omnipotent role.

What I am arguing for here is the importance of distinguishing between the words we use and what they represent. The debate in social work regarding the concept of assessment of problems has centred far too exclusively upon the issue of whether or not the term 'diagnosis' should be used. The controversy in this respect has had an unmistakable political flavour, adherence to 'diagnosis' being associated with 'conservatism' and its rejection with 'radicalism'. This hardly seems an appropriate approach to what is conceptually a complex issue deserving serious and sustained intellectual attention.

There have been two major reasons why social workers have tended to avoid the intellectual challenge inherent in the subject of assessment within social work. One has had to do with the failure to distinguish sufficiently between an intellectual approach to the identification of problems in psycho-social functioning and a judgemental attitude towards the client. Some social workers have been prone to associate the expression of a professional opinion about a problem (which entails an assessment of the part the person involved has played in it) with an allocation of a degree of blame or praise to that person. This is a real difficulty in the realm of values, and it can only be resolved in the context of a differentiation between an unconditional acceptance of a person regardless of his behaviour and a realistic view of the behaviour which neither calls for, nor makes desirable, an attitude of moral neutrality towards the nature of that behaviour. Whilst it is important to recognise that 'to love the sinner and to hate his sin' is easier said than done, such a requirement is nevertheless quite inescapable in social work and cannot be shirked.

The second difficulty is derived from the degree of tentativeness which is inherent in any formulation of a social-work assessment due to the absence of clear-cut cause–effect relationships in the types of problem dealt with and to a resulting absence of any adequate system of classification of problems and of 'treatments' directed to these problems. There certainly are not the equivalents in social work of clear problem entities such as 'tuberculosis' or 'appendicitis' but, as already suggested, little of medicine now has the benefit of such definite categorisation.

There is no doubt that the major challenge inherent in making assessments of problems in social work stems from the lack of any specific framework for determining the particular configuration of relevant factors in a given situation. A doctor suspecting tuberculosis or diabetes knows that there are a number of quite specific tests which will reveal the presence or absence of these conditions. There are no analogous specific 'tests' in social work. This dilemma was well recognised by Richmond[3] when she made her famous comparison between a problem in social functioning and a pyramid, saying that if one thought of the presenting problem as the apex of the pyramid and of the exploration of the nature of that problem as a process of descent towards its base, then the closer the base and the greater therefore the width of the pyramid, the more intervening factors in the problem will have emerged, many of the roots of which remain hidden in the ground.

One other useful aspect of this analogy is the nature of the relationship it implies between past events and current influences. That both are important in any situation cannot be denied but their relative importance varies greatly. The dilemma is well presented in the two well-known dicta taken side by side: 'the child is the father of the man' (Wordsworth quoted by Freud); and 'only a dead man can be understood in the light of his past' (Jung). Some social workers have been guilty in the past of excessive preoccupation with past history at the expense of current reality. Within the contemporary social-work scene, the opposite extreme may equally be found. Social work is at present considerably influenced by general-systems theory, and this coupled with the extension of social-work functions and responsibilities encourages a truly panoramic diagnostic sweep of the client's life scene. At its best the acceptance of a more comprehensive approach to assessing the nature of problems should ensure a better understanding of them and lead to more appropriate intervention. This is conditional, however, on social workers having some clear framework within which to select for attention those aspects of the various relevant systems which apply in a given situation. There is otherwise a risk of adopting an inappropriate holistic approach which, by pointing to the relevance of everything, could result in total inaction.

As discussion of the various models of social-work practice in Chapter 2 has indicated, one widely accepted framework for the delineation of social-work functions has always been that of 'agency function'. It has been suggested with reference to the varying viewpoints regarding the differential significance of agency function that, whilst in Britain this significance has been either lost or is hard to identify, as a result of the unification of so many formerly separate social-work services under the aegis of one department, it may reassert itself in due course in some modified form because of its intrinsic importance. Some of the considerations implicit in this viewpoint can be taken a step further, by means of a brief analysis of the well-known framework used by Perlman,[4] namely the problem, the person, the place and the process. I have myself found them to be of help both as a concept and in practice in determining priorities in the assessment process.

The type of problem for which help is being sought, whether it is a housing problem, a shortage of income, a physical or mental disability calling for a major adjustment in the mode of life, or a problem of relationship, is a main factor in determining what needs to be ascertained before intelligent help can be offered. The age, sex, social class, intelligence, temperament, appearance and personality of the client will all influence the social worker's perception as to what is needed, what is realistic and what is likely to be acceptable. The nature of the agency and its resources, the range of its activities and its standing in the community, and the place of social work within it, are all significant factors. And last, but not least, the social worker himself, his orientation towards social work in general and to the type of problem in particular, the relative ease or difficulty with which he can establish a true rapport with the client or clients, the range and extent of his knowledge, expertise and practice skills, his ability to make available the various resources in the community which might be needed, and the dedication and persistence with which he pursues this objective, will determine the outcome.

Implicit in such an analysis of the effects of the four criteria of problem, person, place and process upon social-work assessment is their equal relevance to the nature and the extent of the help which the client is likely to receive. This fact underlines the interdependence of social assessment and social helping to a degree unparalleled in most other occupations. There are a number of reasons for this.

One of them derives from the relative nature of the understanding contained in any social-work assessment. Social-work diagnosis, unlike a medical diagnosis, has neither virtue in itself nor an identity separate from its function in providing justification and guidelines for action. In this context it is appropriate to quote Young: 'social diagnosis is a certain conclusion, or picture, always incomplete, made up of all the observed and understood facts at a given time, fitted together within a particular frame of reference, for a particular purpose'.[5] It is thus clear that it is not just the social diagnosis which influences social treatment. Social treatment facilities (interpreted broadly within the framework of 'the four Ps') will equally influence the content and form of social assessment.

The other important reason for the interdependence of social assessment and social-work helping stems from the central place occupied by the client in the process. In social work the client is both the main source of information about himself and his problem and he is also an important therapeutic agent. This derives from the focus in social work upon social functioning and hence the prime importance of the client's personality and his subjective view of his life experiences whatever their factual nature. More will be said about this in the discussion on the place of the relationship between the social worker and his clients later in the chapter, but for purposes of this discussion it is sufficient to note that the availability of information about a person's perception of his situation, and his reactions to it, is dependent on that person being prepared to share it with another. Such a willingness is in turn dependent on the client's confidence in the person to whom he is entrusting this information and on his belief that the information will be used for his benefit and not to his detriment. Therefore, an approach on the part of the social worker which conveys respect for the client coupled with an indication of both willingness and ability to help is an essential prerequisite and accompaniment of social-work assessment.

Some of the most important characteristics of the latter which have been discussed or referred to are aptly summed up in the following few quotations from Sainsbury:

> Social diagnosis is more than a simple collection or appraisal of facts about clients. Diagnosis demands at its outset some thought about the content and quality of agency function and the philosophical standpoint of each social worker ... It is not simply a balance sheet of information but a process [and] Diagnosis is a process of discovering patterns of significance in the information directly obtained or inferred ... [and] The caseworker's diagnosis must

include and respect the client's opinion about the source and content of his need.[6]

The indivisibility in social work of assessment and helping has sometimes been recognised to a degree which subjected the diagnostic element unduly to the therapeutic one. Bartlett[7] makes this point forcibly, and advocates a reversal of the balance, considering this to be a necessary condition for the development of a sounder knowledge base in social work. In her view, failure to differentiate sufficiently between the diagnostic and the treatment elements has in the past, not infrequently, reflected a reluctance on the part of social workers to engage in the demanding intellectual task of forming a coherent view of the nature of a problem and being prepared to put it to an open test by formulating it explicitly and acting upon it. I am sure she is right, and I do not think that the acceptance of the validity of her viewpoint and of its implications for practice needs to result in social-work assessment being carried out in a manner incompatible with a 'therapeutic intent'.

With regard to the social-work treatment or helping element in this process, many of the conceptual problems are derived from the same causes as those discussed in the section concerned with assessment. The absence of clear cause–effect relations in social work, which results in an inability to match particular helping interventions with specific problems, prevents an adequate classification of methods of helping. The difficulty is intensified by the current division of social-work practice into 'casework', 'group work', and 'community work' – a division which, as already stated, is proving increasingly unhelpful but for which no satisfactory alternative has yet been found. In the absence of a comprehensive and acceptable system of classification of the 'interventive repertoire',[8] all that can be done in this respect is to try to demonstrate the difficulty involved in any categorisation of this kind.

The following are some of the criteria which any system of classification would need to take into account, and the list of these is by no means comprehensive.

The time dimension is clearly one of these. Whether contact with a client, or a group of clients, is long term or short term, and what factors have influenced its length, is of considerable importance in determining the outcome of the helping process.

The targets for intervention are another obvious criterion. Is social work being carried out directly with the client or clients and their families, or is intervention focused on the client's immediate environment, human or material? The latter constitutes a very wide area, as the concept of environment (or social systems) includes the whole range of services and institutions (and all the people working in these) with whom social workers transact on behalf of their clients, for example general practitioners, hospitals, social-security departments, the police, employers, clergy, elected representatives or various voluntary bodies.

Intervention can also be aimed at effecting broader changes from which whole groups of clients or potential clients would benefit, such as, for example, matters regarding the policy of a housing department over rent arrears or of a hospital in relation to its waiting lists for different categories of patient.

Just who the client might be is a further factor of great significance. Is he an individual or is it a family in which, whilst one member constitutes the main focus of the work, the rest of the family are also involved in discussing the problem? Is it a marriage? – if yes the focus is on the marital relationship rather than on either of the two partners (but within this spectrum there are a wide range of different ways of working, for example both partners could be seen jointly, or separately, by one worker, or two). Is the client a family being assisted by social work through the medium of family therapy (here, too, as the literature on family therapy shows, the range of different permutations is considerable)? Is it a group of clients with some common handicap or problem (and, in that case, is it predominantly a 'talking' group or an 'activities' group)? Is the work being done with a community group or series of groups? (In the latter case, in addition to the various differences derived from the particular objectives of a community group, work with several groups within the same community is likely to involve arbitration between the conflicting objectives and different priorities of the separate groups, thus creating a conflict of loyalties for the community social worker.)

Social-work objectives cannot be ignored in this context. Social work as a profession has its over-all objectives with regard to assisting people in the task of living. These general objectives are then applied to specific situations and form the basis for more specific objectives. The latter could be classified in terms of attitudinal change on the part of either the client or some significant person (or people) in his environment, socialisation of a person or a group of people to further their social functioning in a given situation, behaviour modification of a more specific kind for the same purpose, environmental change of different types, such as improving housing, increasing income, securing a job or the services of a doctor, and support in a situation which cannot be altered but has to be borne and lived through whether permanently or temporarily, such as bereavement, a chronic illness, looking after a handicapped child or a senile relative.

The place where the social-work intervention takes place has considerable influence upon the process. Are clients seen in their own home, in the social worker's office, in his car, in a café, at a street corner, at a railway station, in a holiday camp, at a remand centre, in a prison, court, community home, hostel, hospital? – the list is endless. This is a differential feature the significance of which is not always sufficiently appreciated by social workers in terms both of their own deliberate choices and making the most of the circumstances under which they find themselves with their clients, and the opportunities inherent in the setting.

Given the availability of certain resources within both the worker and the client, the agency, and the wider environment, the differential use made of them constitutes a factor of great importance and a powerful means at the social worker's disposal to ensure the right kind of help to clients. The classification of casework treatment by Hollis[9] is well known and will not be repeated here, but some comment is perhaps appropriate in this context. Her categorisation of the work done directly with clients provides a fairly comprehensive coverage of 'relationship work'. One particularly valuable aspect is the degree of recognition given to the importance of cognitive insight. This was an important corrective, coming from an eminent exponent of the diagnostic school of thought, to the earlier impressions given by some of its writers that 'insight' is synonymous with psychological self-awareness. As Yelloly[10] has pointed out, it is important to differentiate between the different kinds of insight, and social workers in particular cannot afford to minimise the importance of cognition in human living. In my view one of the areas in social-work practice where new developments are badly needed is the adoption of a more 'educational' role with many of the clients, educational not in the sense of dogmatic teaching but in the sense of a deliberate widening of people's perceptions and understanding of the world in which they live with the view to an enhancement of their abilities to manage in it. This is surely a resource which many people need urgently and which social workers are especially well-equipped to provide, both directly and through the enlistment of other appropriate help, because of their dual concern with feeling and thinking and their interaction which are important factors in learning to be more effective in social living.

Hollis's categorisation of 'indirect treatment', of work done with others on behalf of the clients, and of environmental modification, is much less satisfactory, based, as it is, on the assumption that the treatment repertoire she had formulated in relation to work with clients is equally applicable to contacts with others. As I have already suggested, this is a difficult assumption to accept, given the important differential aspects of a number of various role positions. However, in spite of the number of criticisms of Hollis's formulation of social-work helping, no alternative classification of comparable comprehensiveness has been put forward. Instead, some forms of social-work intervention were 'dignified' by having new names attached to them, such as 'brokerage' and 'advocacy', although such activities have been an integral part of many social workers' repertoire since C.O.S. days. However, the central point which needs emphasising is that it is still of paramount importance for social work to identify the various 'helping' resources at its disposal and then to classify them.

The final category of factors which would need to be taken into account in any such attempt at classification is the very extensive one of client groups and their problems. No comprehensive listing of these is possible here and, given the infinite range of human problems, this would be a daunting prospect. A categorisation on this basis would need to be concerned with 'personal sorrows' as well as 'public issues', and the former, due to their subjective nature, do not lend themselves to this type of activity. Given this limitation, possible identifiable groups would include: children of different ages, people with different types of handicap, immigrants, people of different ethnic origins, culture and sub-cultures, the homeless, adolescents, the mentally ill, the physically sick, old people and delinquents. However, it should be remembered that both the client groups and the problems they experience result from, and are affected by, the broader social context of which they are a part and are therefore never static.

It was said at the beginning of this chapter that the social-work process of study/assessment/helping/evaluation took place within the context of a relationship. In my view this is the main unifying factor in the diversity of social-work functions and the actions which stem from these functions.

So much has been written about the place of the relationship in social work that it is difficult to approach this subject in a way which is not repetitious. However, the importance of the subject does not allow its neglect in a book on the nature of social work. In addition, there is a trend in social work at the moment to emphasise its political nature to the exclusion of the other aspects. 'Putting the relationship back into social work' may therefore not be inopportune. As has already been said, the primary reason and justification for the central place which has been given to relationship in social work in the past originated from the social nature of man and from his dependence on others for the supply of both material and psychological needs.

The nature of the latter is well described by Mead.[11] In his account of the process of development of individual personality he stresses the extent to which the sense of self is derived from a child's interaction with significant people in his environment. It is their actions of approval and disapproval which determine to a large extent his own conception of himself as worthy of respect and affection, or the reverse. This dependence on others for 'confirmation', and thus for the direction in which his personality development proceeds, continues throughout his life.

If a person's earlier relationships and experiences have been damaging (and this includes a wide range of unsatisfactory experiences such as punitive, inconsistent and neglectful handling, or an attitude of over-protectiveness as a compensation for inadequate loving), he will have been seriously hindered in the formation of a clear personal identity and will be prone to profound existential uncertainty and anxiety. At its extreme this could in turn take the form of either excessive withdrawal from contact with other people, or an immature identification with various representations of 'society', which in existentialist language is called 'transcendence'. Either extreme prevents the individual from feeling effectively a member of the human group and so encourages both an increasing sense of alienation and depersonalisation.

In this context the assumption that there is an inherent capacity within human nature for change and growth – discussed in Chapter 3 – assumes a central importance. Unless social workers believe that, however damaging earlier experiences have been and however crippled a person is as a result of these, there is a possibility of improvement in his situation given favourable circumstances, they have no *raison d'être* or justification to intervene in the lives of other people. This faith on the part of social workers has some affinity with the existentialist position which regards the human state as 'becoming' as well as 'being'. The position taken by Buber, for example, is of considerable relevance to social work. Unlike some of the later existentialists, including Sartre, the critique of whose views by Plant was quoted in Chapter 3, Buber's emphasis on the importance of the individual personality does not result in a denial of his dependence on others. Thus, in postulating the 'I–Thou' type of relationship as an ideal, Buber does not reject the value of the 'I–It' relationships because they fall short of this ideal. On the contrary he sees the two kinds of relationship as complementary in reflecting the dual nature of human needs: the need for uniqueness and the need to belong. The following quotation from Righton conveys very clearly Buber's stance in this respect:

Buber sees life in this world as a state of affairs in which all men are to some extent alienated, and therefore, not free to engage at will in unconditional personal commitment. It makes no sense, therefore, to work or plan for 'I–Thou' relationships: they are but rarely experienced and when they happen they are 'unattended moments', spontaneous and unpremeditated. At such a time (or rather in reflection afterwards), we realise that *this* is what we mean by 'being', by freedom from self-assertiveness or self-transcendence; but we cannot command it. For most of the time our relationships with each other are in fact less than fully human; they are calculating, automatic, circumscribed by regulation, convention or fear: in short, role performances. This is an inevitable consequence of the human condition, and Buber makes no bones about his belief that we should all strive to make our role performances (including therapeutic ones) as effective and as technically competent as possible – it is not a question of scrapping 'I–It' relationships but of searching for all feasible means of improving the quality of 'I–It' relationships. But – and this is Buber's main teaching – it is only through our experience of living at an 'I–Thou' level, however fugitive, that we can gain insight into the ultimate purpose of our strivings in the world of 'I–It'. Without vision of this kind, our work, our social planning, our research, our theories, our therapeutic experiments – are all so much groping in the dark. It is not much use thinking out sophisticated treatment methods for sick people if we have no notion of health more positive than a mere absence of painful symptoms: still less if those methods sometimes make the sickness worse.[12]

Formulations such as this help us to appreciate the potential for healing inherent in helping and helpful relationships. Implicit in this recognition is also the acceptance of two facts of great practical significance: the first of these is that any relationship has this potential within it and, in consequence, no group of people, be they psychotherapists, counsellors of various kinds or social workers, has, or should have, a monopoly of helping by this medium. Thus the concept of 'community care', properly understood as care by the community rather than merely as care in the community, implies a recognition of this capacity within the network of relationships in a community (conceived as *Gemeineschaft* and not as a *Gesellschaft*).

However, the recognition of the above fact should not exclude an appreciation that some kinds of 'relationship work' demand considerable knowledge and skill if the potential inherent in a purposeful and appropriate use of helping relationships is to be fully realised. The book by Ferard and Hunnybun[13] provides a good illustration of this point.

Social work is an activity which is both uniquely well-suited to carrying out some of this particularly demanding work, and its nature and effectiveness depend on its ability to fulfil this task. There are several reasons for this.

The most obvious of these is, of course, the fact that given the various functions allocated to social workers by society, they are engaged more frequently and on a more regular basis than many others in the community in work with large numbers of people who suffer from the effects of earlier deprivations in terms of their limited ability to function in society. This presents social workers with many opportunities to correct some of the damage resulting from earlier experience and to reverse the cycle, so common to human beings in this type of predicament, of difficulty in relating to others due to earlier rejections resulting in further rebuffs, leading to greater withdrawal or more inappropriate aggression. In emphasising the importance of this role, I am not trying to suggest that it is an easy one. On the contrary, my arguments in favour of professionalism in social work in the next chapter are founded on the recognition that the demands inherent in this type of helping are such that social workers cannot afford, for the sake of their clients and the community as a whole, to neglect proper preparation for it. They must take advantage of opportunities for on-going learning and mutual support, thus safeguarding themselves to some extent against major failures due to inadequate knowledge.

Furthermore, the preoccupation with the meaning of experience inherent in social work which emphasises the importance of the 'how' as well as of the 'what' makes it imperative to pay serious attention to the effects that 'being helped' have on the individual. It is not only whether or not a social worker has succeeded in securing a badly needed 'commodity' for his client which counts. Equally important is whether the acquisition of what was needed and desired has been a positive personal experience, enhancing his sense of self-respect and worth and giving added confidence for future living, or whether it has had the opposite effect of undermining him further, making him feel barely tolerated or pitied, a social liability carried grudgingly but inevitably by a 'responsible society' through its social-work agent.

Space does not allow exploration of the various reasons why being at the receiving end of any service presents psychological difficulties for most people. Clearly the nature of the need and the threat it constitutes to a person's well-being is a major factor which influences the degree of this vulnerability. Social values with regard to different kinds of problem are also of major importance. Thus, in our society, on the whole, being in need of medical care is socially acceptable and evokes a response of sympathy; in contrast, having to accompany one's child to a juvenile court on account of his delinquent or unruly behaviour is usually looked upon with disfavour. Previous experience of dependency is also very influential in how a person views and approaches his present need for help.

Some of these factors serve to illustrate the extent to which, in our society, people are judged and are expected to be judged in terms of what they do, or have failed to do, rather than what they are. Such an instrumental view of persons encourages a false sense of security, on the basis of some specific success which may be short-lived, as well as a sense of failure arising from difficulty in meeting the requirements of a particular social role or task. This major distortion of a basic human value both stems from, and is constantly fed by, an excess of 'I–It' type of relationships and the inadequacy of the 'I–Thou' elements within them. So many people transact with each other exclusively in terms of their role performance and not as persons to persons.

One of my reasons for stressing this fact is that it helps to highlight the importance and the value to the clients of social workers of a relationship which, whilst fully acknowledging and accepting its instrumental features, namely that it is purposeful and there is a job of work to be done within a limited span of time, carries with it an equally full acknowledgement that a relationship is an interaction between persons entailing mutual involvement at a deeper and more meaningful level than a mere interchange of words. It is only in the context of such a relationship that the various values which were discussed in Chapter 3 can assume any real meaning. That meaning is in turn enhanced by the professional nature of the relationship. By this I mean its purposeful nature, its limited scope in terms of its duration and objectives, and the authority vested in the social worker due to his role within society and his particular agency, his knowledge and experience in dealing with human problems, and that personal authority which a given client may invest in him.

As space does not permit me to consider the range of the various more specific objectives in the service of which such a relationship is used, the only other aspect which I should like to emphasise, because I believe it to have been underplayed in some of the writings, has to do with some of the implications of the mutuality which is inherent in all 'real' relationships. This fact of mutuality is not invalidated by the fact that the role of the client carries with it a degree of dependency which is in contrast to the responsibility for the provision of a service which is vested in the role of 'social worker'. Neither ceases to be human in virtue of his particular role, and the interchange which takes place in the context of the relationship is an interchange between two human beings as well as between a client and a social worker. This is so obvious that it might well be asked why the point is made. However, it needs making in order to emphasise the crucial fact that unless the social worker is prepared to receive from the client as well as to give to him, he cannot be of real help to him. This is because denial of one's dependency in a relationship introduces falsehood into that relationship and, more particularly, constitutes a denial of the common humanity of the participants. Social workers' clients have often had a superfluity of false (as opposed to 'authentic') experiences in their lives.

A prime function of the relationship that the social worker establishes with them is to provide both a corrective experience to the past and a prophylactic for the future. Adding more inauthenticity, and that in the context of a relationship vested with social significance, would be more than irresponsible.

One general and significant way in which social workers depend on their clients is in being allowed to assume a helping role with regard to them – a truly substantial 'gift' for those who fully recognise the privileged nature of such a role.

Inherent in any consideration of relationship is consideration of the communication which takes place within it. The two concepts are basically inseparable: a relationship is a necessary condition for effective communication and the quality of a relationship can be largely judged by the effectiveness of the communication between those concerned. The main reason for this lies in the neutrality of words as media of communication and their dependence on the social and emotional context within which messages are being conveyed and received. This limitation on words as a channel of communication is well-conveyed in Cherry's comment that 'words are slippery customers', and in his quotation from Oscar Wilde that 'England and America are two countries separated by a common language'.[14] The implications of this limitation for social-work practice are immense, and highlight both the relevance of the insights of communication theories and the importance of establishing some means of communication which supplement, correct and clarify the message carried by words.

The effectiveness of communication is greatly dependent on both the clarity on the part of the person transmitting a message as to what it is he wishes to communicate, and an open approach on the part of the person receiving the communication to the message carried. A degree of ambivalence on the part of either results in confusion and distortion. Given this fact and that clarity, lack of ambivalence and openness are all relative rather than absolute qualities, feedback is an essential element in all communication. Ruesch defines feedback as 'the process of correction through the incorporation of the effects achieved'.[15] A good illustration of the results of failure to incorporate feedback into a system of communication is provided by Mayer and Timms[16] in their discussion of the reasons why some of the clients studied had not been helped in spite of the good intentions on the part of their social workers. These acted on certain assumptions without checking these against their clients' perceptions of their needs and their reactions to the help being offered.

The importance of feedback in the communication process highlights in turn the importance of evaluation as an integral part of the social-work process – a fact which is not always given enough recognition by social workers. In this context, evaluation does not mean formal research in the sense of attempts to validate certain procedures or ways of working with a view to the drawing of generalisations; it concerns every individual practitioner reviewing his activities with every client or group of clients in relation to the objectives which were defined on the basis of his assessment of the problem. Although evaluation constitutes logically the final stage of the social-work process of study/assessment/helping/evaluation, and every piece of social work should end with it, it is by no means confined to the final stage. As in the case of assessment and helping, evaluation is (or ought to be) a continuous element in the process. Stock-taking is needed at regular intervals, following every significant activity, be it an interview with the client himself or contact with someone else on his behalf. It is essential to see whether the original objective is being carried through and whether it still holds good or needs modifying in the light of new understanding gained about the problem, or a change in the client's situation, or in the availability of resources, or in all these areas. It is only through an incorporation of such a reflective activity as an integral part of all his work that the social worker can ensure that what he does is purposeful and responsible and not a hit-and-miss endeavour guided by fluctuations of mood or fashion, by what is easier or more convenient.

The importance of the time factor in the social-work process was mentioned earlier. This is a subject which, like so many in social work, is surrounded by a good deal of confused thinking particularly with regard to a failure to differentiate between principle and expediency.

The significance of this factor was recognised from the outset by the adherents of the functional school of social work, as described in Chapter 2. In contrast, the diagnostic school has been guilty of a relative degree of neglect of the subject.

Decisions regarding the desirable length of time for working with an individual client or a group of clients are an integral part of the social worker's professional judgement reached in the course of his study of the problem and formulated at the stage of social assessment. They are thus subject to the same kinds of considerations which apply to all the decisions regarding appropriate help. Of these, the primary one relates to the needs of the client himself, derived from the nature of his problem and his personal characteristics. The point needs stressing because just as in the past some social workers operated on the basis of the assumption that the longer the period over which they saw their clients, the more beneficial this would be, currently short-term work of different kinds is seen by some as *ipso facto* superior to long-term work regardless of the objectives of the work as implied by the client's needs. Neither of these 'ideologies' is compatible with a caring and professional approach.

In considering the characteristics of the different phases of the contact between the social worker and his clients it is clear that the beginning phase is the one which has been documented more fully. This is the stage of getting to know each other, of establishing mutual trust, and of reaching a more or less explicit agreement on the objectives of the work together. This last aspect of agreement, of a contract between the client and the social worker, is the one which has often been neglected in the past and to which considerable attention is currently given, largely under the influence of Reid and Epstein[17] whose contribution was discussed in more detail in Chapter 2. This is an important and welcome development which should contribute towards a more active involvement of clients in decisions regarding the process of helping, whatever particular form it takes. Like all new developments, there is some risk of its being invested with greater versatility and more universal application than the specific 'task-centred' model warrants, but giving clients a more prominent position in the process of solution of their problems is not dependent on either this particular model or on any other specific contractual arrangement. It is primarily a matter of intention supported by an understanding of what constitutes appropriate ways of putting this intention into effect in particular circumstances.

The middle stage is the time when the major effort at working on the problem or problems takes place. The task originally set out often proves more difficult than envisaged by the client, and sometimes also by the social worker. Ambivalence is a common feature of this phase: ambivalence towards both the problem and one's partner in the working relationship. For the client much of the ambivalence evolves around change, which is implicit in the situation in which he is engaged. Change always carries with it an element of threat and raises the question, 'is the known evil not better than what might result from change?' This is a very understandable question given the fact that not all change is necessarily for the best. This point is brought out very clearly by Szasz[18] who warns against too ready an assumption on the part of therapists that in dealing with psychosomatic symptoms the translation of these into a more 'real' language will automatically result in an improvement. On the contrary, such a premature translation unaccompanied by effective measures of help could lead to suicide or acute psychosis.

However, if the difficulties and threats inherent in change can be faced successfully by the client, this will not only be of immediate benefit but will be a greatly strengthening experience for the future. The confidence gained in the course of the present experience – confidence in both himself and in the goodwill and helpfulness of the social worker – will stand him in good stead in facing future problems and in utilising other helping resources within society.

The end phase, or that of termination, has also been rather neglected in social-work literature, and even writers of the functional school give it less attention than to the other two phases. One cannot but wonder to what extent this apparent reluctance to formulate the characteristics and the requirements of this phase reflects an avoidance of the pain which is inherent in all parting. As Lamartine said, '*partir c'est mourir un peu*', and how true an insight this is. However, it is because partings are painful and yet constitute such a common and frequent feature of human life that social workers can particularly ill afford not to use the opportunity of the ending of their contacts with clients to help the latter deal with loss and not be overwhelmed by it. In this connection, it is particularly important to realise that, paradoxically, it is easier to part from people with whom one has had a satisfactory relationship free from excessive ambivalence and guilt. Unresolved grief reactions which lock people within themselves are usually due to the latter. Thus a satisfactory relationship with a social worker can provide a helpful base enabling the client to face the reality of living: namely that nothing lasts permanently, that people one loves move away and ultimately die, that moving forward entails leaving something behind and that there is no advance without loss.

A particular feature of the opportunity provided by the client/social worker relationship to help the former accept change more easily is the degree of dependency on the social worker experienced by most clients at some stage and how this is resolved. In spite of the desire of most people for dependency on others, dependency also carries an element of threat. As Winnicott has put it, 'the hallmark of maturity is an individual's capacity to identify with the community without loss of identity and sense of self'.[19] Few people, if any, manage to achieve such a hallmark of maturity, and with the majority it is a case of trying to achieve a reasonable balance between being capable of depending appropriately on others without feeling too threatened by this, and managing to be independent and self-sufficient when this is called for.

That it is often easier to give than to receive is well-recognised. This is because the former act puts a person in a position of power and supremacy whilst the latter implies inferior status and dependency. The clients of social workers are therefore in an intrinsically difficult position; they need to depend, and the extent of that need makes dependency on the social worker initially, at any rate, threatening. This situation can easily result in a degree of resentment during the early and middle stages of the contact. Where this is accompanied by guilt, as commonly happens, the need to make reparation will be one of the characteristics of the end phase of the relationship.

It is thus clear that how social workers approach and handle their clients' dependency is of vital importance. A genuine recognition on their part of the reciprocity inherent in the relationship is crucial. This should lead to a readiness to acknowledge their own dependency on the client and to accept his various 'gifts' in accordance with the varying stages and degrees of his ability to give in their relationship. The main results of such responsiveness will be enhanced self-respect by the client, his ability to terminate the relationship without guilt and excessive distress, and lessened fear of future separations. These are clearly no mean achievements, and if the phase of the termination of the contact between the client and the social worker is viewed against their perspective, it cannot fail to be recognised as being of crucial importance to the whole of the helping process. It has within it the potential for both enhancing the recent experience and invalidating much of what had gone on before.

It would be wrong to assume that the importance of the relationship in social work applies exclusively to social casework, and yet the anti-casework stance of a number of people could lead them to such an assumption. It is therefore necessary to dispel some of the myths about social casework which play a part in creating confusion and prejudice, such as that social casework is synonymous with an almost exclusive concentration on intra-and interpersonal dynamics viewed from a psychoanalytic point of view and entails a concentration on insight promotion and work of a long-term nature.

The earlier part of this chapter, in which both the nature of social assessment and the range of methods of helping were fully discussed, has shown the lack of justification for such a premise. Implicit in this discussion was the view (not in the least original!) that what differentiates social casework from other forms of social work is that its focus is upon work with and on behalf of individuals and families. If the common and the unifying bond of all forms of social work is concern with problems in social functioning, as has been argued in Chapter 1, then the only valid difference between casework, group work and community work is the unit of attention. The unit of attention in both group work and community work are certain groupings of people. These still consist of individuals, and the ultimate objective of all social work is to promote human well-being which, in the final resort, has to do with people. To acknowledge that groups develop an identity of their own is not to deny that their members will retain their individuality. It is surely just as much the ultimate responsibility of a group worker or a community worker, as of a caseworker, to foster individual welfare, although the objective is reached by different means. I have heard many a community worker consider as a major achievement the fact that he has succeeded in helping a depressed member of a community group lacking in confidence to discover hidden talents of leadership and organisation.

By emphasising this point, I am not attempting to deny the difference in skills required in working with clients of different numbers and in different constellations. What I am trying to stress is that if the major and the common feature of all social work is concern for human beings in the context of their life situations, then an understanding of people and a degree of ability to work with them through the medium of relationship must also be shared. This needs stressing if for no other reason because, in my view, the denial by some non-caseworkers of the relevance of relationship work in their engagements with clients has been an obstacle to the conceptualisation of the differential uses of relationships in contexts other than that of casework.

A more fundamental question exists regarding the place of the three separate 'methods' of 'casework', 'group work' and 'community work' within the social-work process. How useful is this division still? On the credit side, it helps to identify the client 'unit' upon which a social worker's attention is focused – but does this outweigh the various disadvantages?

The chief of these is the compartmentalisation of social work into 'methods boxes' with the lack of flexibility this implies in terms of both obstacles to mobility as between these methods and the absence of a framework which would allow for the addition of new developments within the 'interventive repertoire' such as, for example, the various forms of day care.

How can the basic unity of social work be reconciled and the needs of social workers' clients best met if social workers belonging to the different 'methods' see themselves as operating in fundamentally different ways?

There does seem to be an increasingly strong case for breaking down the divisions separating the various 'methods' and thus removing the emphasis on their different aspects and their self-sufficiency. On the one hand, no one 'caseworker', 'group worker', 'community worker' (or 'residential worker' if residential work is seen as a method rather than a setting) is competent to practice with equal effectiveness the full range of the skills which comprise each one of the 'methods'. On the other hand, as already stressed, there are very few, if any, skills exclusive to any one 'method'. These facts should be conducive to an abandonment of structures which have outlived their usefulness in favour of a more realistic classification of the range of differential helping encompassed by social work. For this to be possible, there has to be, however, a degree of consensus about the nature of social work and the core characteristics of its helping process. Flexibility and differentiation at the boundaries are dependent upon clarity, firmness and consistency of purpose at the centre. It is my sad but strong conviction that the quality of social-work practice is currently being adversely affected by the lack of a clearly formulated and generally agreed distinctive core, and that this will continue for as long as it is missing. At present, too frequently, rigidity of a doctrinaire character serves as a substitute for a commitment founded on adherence to basic values; and equally chaos derived from confusion masquerades as flexibility in spite of the obvious fact that the latter can only exist against a background of a relative clarity about objectives and of decisiveness in their pursuit.

Chapter 6

Social Work and Society

Reference was made in the 'Introduction' to the extent to which social work in particular is a product of the society within which it functions and is affected by both the nature of the problems occurring within that society and the attitudes governing the response to these problems. A brief look at some of the recent legislative and other social provisions and their effects on social-work services will therefore be taken to underline this point.

The Mental Health Act of 1959,[1] which shifted the emphasis from the custodial care of mentally ill and subnormal persons towards treatment and prevention, has also introduced the concept of 'community care' for this group of patients and, by implication, for other types of client as well. 'Community care' entails both care in the community and care by the community, both of which aspects have considerable and direct implications for the numbers of social workers required to implement them as well as the nature of their activities.

The Children and Young Persons Act of 1963,[2] by laying upon local authorities the responsibility for promoting the well-being of children by attempting to prevent family breakdown, has extended the concept of child welfare embodied in the original 1948 Children's Act to that of family welfare. The resulting reinterpretation of social workers' functions, not the least, of these being the provision of financial resources as a means of preventing family breakdown, has greatly added to and changed the nature of the powers invested in social workers.

The Children and Young Persons Act of 1969[3] has further added to these powers by transferring some held previously by the courts to local-authority social workers. Thus, the abolition of Approved School Orders and their replacement by Care Orders has meant that it is no longer the courts who decide on the form of appropriate treatment, but social workers instead. The new provision of 'intermediate treatment' in that Act has immensely widened the scope of the activities required to be undertaken by social workers if this new form of 'treatment' is to be effective and fulfil the spirit underlying its introduction.

The Social Services Act of 1970,[4] which implemented most of the recommendations of the Seebohm Report,[5] has undoubtedly been the most influential single piece of recent legislation in terms of its effects on the place of social work in society. Not only did this Act provide for the unification of local-authority social-work services, thus creating administrative structures of a size and complexity previously unknown to social work, but by its emphasis on total community needs and the contribution which it saw social work as making towards the meeting of these needs, it invested social work with unprecedented responsibilities. Because neither the Seebohm Report nor the Social Services Act of 1970 gave adequate recognition to the need for considerable additional resources as a necessary condition for the fulfilment of these new expectations of social work, most of the criticisms of these two 'documents' by social workers and others have centred on this particular failing. What has not attracted sufficient questioning and debate, in my opinion, is the appropriateness and feasibility of some of the more global objectives stated. For example, on reading the Seebohm Report it is possible to identify sources of some of the confusion among local-authority social workers as to the exact nature of their responsibilities in response to such national problems as shortage of adequate housing for low-income families, the inadequacy of social insurance and supplementary benefits, as well as others of comparable scale. I am convinced that considerable unproductive guilt, with resulting wastage of creative energy among a sizeable proportion of these workers, follows from such uncertainties.

Another very important effect of both the Seebohm Report and the 1970 Act has been the relative shift in emphasis within local-authority-based social work towards the administration of social provisions, planning of services and their management. This, initially, in many areas, was at the expense of sufficient attention being given to the quality of the social-work service being offered to the client at the grass-roots level. With so many of the most experienced practitioners having been recruited into senior- and middle-management posts, direct work with clients was inevitably left to inexperienced new recruits and trainees. 'All generals and no troops' became a common and not a wholly undeserved comment on the situation.

The 1970 Chronically Sick and Disabled Persons Act[6] provides not only an illustration of a specific and extensive area in which the involvement of social workers is expected, but it can also serve to demonstrate in a specific context the regularly recurring phenomenon of new legislation extending the responsibilities and powers of social workers without these being accompanied by any commensurate provision of necessary resources for the effective implementation of these new responsibilities and powers.

This is equally true of the Criminal Justice Act of 1972.[7] A number of provisions within the Act carry important and direct implications for the Probation and After-care Service. For example, both Community Service Orders and Day Training Centres as alternatives to imprisonment constitute a considerable increase in both the volume and the range of probation officers' tasks. These, coupled with the more established but constantly expanding functions of providing social-enquiry reports for the courts, supervising clients on probation, acting as parole officers, doing after-care work, offering marriage guidance and other forms of 'voluntary' help, are bound to contribute to a further increase in the discrepancy between the manpower needs of the Probation and After-care Service and the actual resources at its disposal.

In addition to the legislation mentioned above, various proposals for future changes and current debates implying future developments are likely to have considerable impact upon social-work practice.

The controversial new Children Act 1975[8] concerning adoption services and other provisions for children deprived of normal family life, given the amount of disagreement a number of its provisions have generated, is bound to place social workers at the centre of the conflict between the needs of deprived children and the rights of their parents, conflict which has been highlighted already in recent cases of non-accidental injury to children.

The Department of Health and Social Security (D.H.S.S.) Working Party on Fostering Practice,[9] which is expected to report shortly, will undoubtedly recommend that an improved standard of service should be offered by social workers in this area; this will have considerable implications in terms not only of manpower resources but also of the knowledge and skill which will need to be acquired in order to meet these additional expectations.

Equally, the long-term implications for social work of both the Younger Committee's recommendations[10] and of the White Paper on Better Services for the Mentally Ill[11] are considerable.

The Central Council for Education and Training in Social Work has produced a number of Documents including some on social work in different areas of practice and with various client groups. Of these, the Report on Training for Residential Work[12] and that on Training for Social Work with Handicapped People[13] are of particular importance. They rightly emphasise the present discrepancy between the needs of clients both in residential settings and those suffering from the different disabilities, and the availability of trained social workers to meet these needs. Given the low percentage of social workers currently involved in work in both these contexts, the sheer numbers of new recruits needed is staggering, without the further essential consideration of the quality of the services offered.

As a further illustration, in what is by no means a comprehensive list of examples of the increasing demand in our society for social workers with ever more widely ranging functions, the Report of the D.H.S.S. Working Party on Social Work Support for the National Health Service[14] must be mentioned. The Working Party was concerned with both the general implications for social work of the unification of the National Health Service, and the specific issues resulting from the transfer on 1 April 1974 of hospital social workers from the N.H.S. payroll to that of the Social Services Departments of local authorities.

The Working Party's recommendations reflect their conviction, shared by an increasing number of people within both the health and the social-work professions, that the effectiveness of a comprehensive and holistic health service to the community is dependent on its ability to draw on the resources of a sufficient number of social workers attached to the various parts of the health service.

At the moment the position in this respect is a long way from meeting such a requirement. Not only did the situation on 1 April 1974 reflect an acute shortage of social workers in the health field which would take a great deal of effort and new resources to alleviate, but there are grounds for fears that in view of the pressures on Social Services Departments from so many different quarters, the priority given to the health sector may not be high. This could in fact result in a widening rather than a narrowing of the gap between need and provision of services to meet it.

What has been said about the place of social work in health care could be equally true with regard to education. In view of the growing evidence of the close interdependence between influences at home and at school in shaping children's behaviour and future happiness, it is hard to deny the potential contribution of social work in this sphere however negligible it is in most places at present.

The above instances have been discussed with a view to demonstrating in more detail the very wide range of functions now vested by society in its social workers. In demographic terms it entails a coverage of clients of all classes and of differing cultures from 'the cradle to the grave'. The areas of difficulty in which social work intervenes directly range from family relationship problems of all kinds to problems created by various forms of material deprivation. Psycho-social problems inherent in physical and mental illness, in physical and mental handicap, and in old age, form another large area of concern. Social workers' involvement in relation to the different kinds of anti-social behaviour, which is highlighted in most of the functions of the Probation and After-care and Prison Welfare workers, is by no means confined to them. Social workers in all settings meet and attempt to help people who for a variety of reasons have 'opted out' of their social roles and whose alienation from society creates problems for themselves and for others.

Many social-work functions, in addition to 'direct work' with clients, call for an involvement of other 'helpers' within the community – volunteers and others – including members of other professions, and this constitutes in turn an important and distinctive social-work function, not always sufficiently recognised.

What must be increasingly apparent is that, within the last twenty years or so, social work has emerged from a relatively insignificant small-scale activity to becoming a social institution of considerable size and importance which continues to grow and to expand.

However, the recognition of the powerful nature of social work, and of its origins in the social mandate which determines the scope of its activities and the extent of its intervention in the lives of others, must lead inevitably to the acknowledgement of the many problematic aspects of this situation.

The most obvious one of these derives from the abstract nature and the ambiguity of the concept of 'society' itself. When we use the term 'society', what do we mean? Do we think of the government of the day, or of particular influential groups in society? Do we use the concept of 'society' consistently, or do we differentiate it in particular contexts depending on what we consider to be the appropriate 'reference group' for us or for others in a given situation?

This leads to the the next problem, which is partly derived from the first, namely the false implication of consensus which the term 'society' carries when, in fact, there are often strong differences of view among the different social groups over the same issue. Thus, for example, an official policy of community care for the mentally handicapped or certain kinds of offender frequently meets with considerable difficulties of implementation because of protests from local citizen groups against plans to locate a hostel in their area. People who resent or who fear having a group of 'social deviants' housed in the vicinity of their homes are not infrequently the same people who, in another context, such as that of political party or church membership, have expressed 'progressive' and 'humanitarian' views favouring such developments in general.

Thus a further factor of great importance in observing the clarity of society's mandate to social work is that of ambivalence. Society as it expresses itself in the attitudes of various individuals and groups is both benevolent and punitive. Our feelings towards people who are under-privileged or specifically handicapped in some way are mixed. On the one hand, most of us are able to draw upon the humanity we share with these 'others' to a sufficient extent to feel genuine compassion. On the other hand, few of us are entirely immune from a reaction of pity which signifies an attitude of superiority and reflects a 'we–they' distinction. Paradoxically, like compassion, pity too stems from a degree of identification with the other person but, unlike compassion, pity is an attitude of defence against the acknowledgement of the possibility that a similar event could have happened to oneself and that one is not immune against similar or comparable dangers. It is pity and not compassion which frequently motivates measures for the care of the 'problem' groups in the form of their segregation from the 'normal' population. The avoidance of a personal close involvement with those who threaten one's own precarious sense of wholeness can be compensated for by generous gifts of money or the conduct of public campaigns for improved conditions.

Pity is by no means the only form of defence by members of a society against a full recognition of their shared humanity with its deprived members. Punitiveness is also more often than not derived primarily from fear rather than malice. If society can justify another's predicament in terms of its resulting from that person's own shortcomings or misdeeds, then it can feel safer. As previously mentioned, the categorisation of problem groups into either 'delinquent' or 'sick' reflects society's ambivalence towards those who deviate from the 'norm', but, as has already been suggested, such a categorisation is always precarious and incomplete – hence the constant changes in emphasis and boundary between what is seen to constitute 'badness' and 'sickness' respectively. The differences in perception with regard to the nature of the mental illness in medieval times and the present day is a good illustration of such a shift, and both alcoholism and drug dependency constitute a contemporary example of this uncertainty.

Given this situation it is not surprising that social workers get a double message from society, whether or not this is expressed in legislation.

Inherent in society's ambivalence towards particular groups of its members is the expectation that social work will act as both its conscience and its protector. What I want to emphasise (because even social workers do not always appear to realise it) is that both these expectations are equally genuine. Society both wants and seeks ways of expressing its concern and its responsibility for those less fortunate than the rest; it also desires and seeks some means of protecting itself against what it perceives as constituting a threat to its values and its stability. To acknowledge this is not conditional on the acceptance of a 'consensus model' of society but a recognition of the reality of social living.

As Fowler has pointed out,[15] social workers are expected by society (and this includes most if not all social groups ranging from those who legislate in Parliament and the Judiciary, to the various groups of citizens representing particular interests) to be both caring and controlling. The real issue at stake, over which there are divergencies of views, is the relative weighting of the two in particular circumstances.

Before looking specifically at the position of social work itself with regard to its caring and control functions, it seems necessary to comment on something which may seem obvious to many but which could be overlooked, namely the 'phenomenon of contagion'. It would be surprising if, given the extent of the ambivalence towards many of the people with whom social workers are concerned, some of this ambivalence did not rub off on to the social workers themselves. There is no lack of evidence in fact that this is the case.

Society's ambivalence towards its social workers takes various forms. A 'double-edged idealisation' is one of these. This is an attitude of high praise for doing the 'dirty work' of society accompanied by some kind of hurtful denigration. My study of medical social work in a teaching hospital[16] provided me with a good demonstration of this. In talking to some of the doctors I came across a fairly consistent level of high praise of medical social workers for their personal qualities of dedication, patience, tact, kindness, and so on, coupled with an almost complete denial of the applicability of intellectual knowledge and learning in their sphere of work.

Conflicting expectations about what social work can achieve is another frequent reflection of such ambivalence. These sometimes combine a view of social work as omnipotent with resentment at any claims by professionally trained social workers to possess a degree of expertise beyond that found among lay people.

The fact that both the clients of social workers and social work itself are subject to such conflicting and inconsistent attitudes on the part of society points, albeit in a somewhat negative way, to the importance of social work having a stance of its own. It cannot be a mere agent of society any more than it can ignore its social mandate. Heraud points out the need for social work to have its own identity very succinctly: he sees social work as a distinct social sub-system which both 'performs functions on behalf of the wider social system and stands for values and goals which may represent a critique of the dominant system'.[17] One aspect of the distinctive nature of social work which Heraud stresses is its role as an 'institution of the truce'. Heraud derives this concept from his critique of the orthodox Marxist view of social conflict as inevitably resulting ultimately in revolution. In his view, social change and reform can be achieved by means of compromise, and social work has an important part to play in its achievement and maintenance: 'social work "faces both ways" in its advocacy of therapy or individual measures to ameliorate social problems and reforms, or structural changes which would seek to eradicate these problems at their source.'[18] He then goes on to emphasise that ambivalence towards an institution of truce is an inherent feature of its role.

Morrell adopts a similar stance:

> If it is part of the social worker's function to help people adjust to the expectations of the society in which they live, it is equally part of their function to criticise these expectations, describing some as unrealistic or irrational, and others as unethical. Society has no business to expect social workers to further a one-sided process of adaptation, all the change being demanded of the clients and none at all in social expectations. On the contrary, society must expect the social work profession to derive from its experience of working with the clients understandings about society's responsibility for the attitudes and behaviour which it finds damaging or inconvenient. And it must expect to be told by social workers that their role is to mediate an active reciprocity of relationships involving social as well as individual change; it is not that of engineering a passive conformity to unchanging social norms.[19]

He went on to coin the phrase 'constructive critics of an imperfectly loving society' as a way of describing this function.

I find these concepts of social work as an 'institution of truce' and 'constructive critic' interesting and meaningful. Inherent in them are the notions of 'social institution' and 'professional autonomy', both of which are central to social work. They also help to explain why there is a conspicuous absence of social work in totalitarian countries, be these of the right or the left, in which conflict is dealt with rather by suppression than by compromise.

However, as Heraud himself is the first to acknowledge, the function of 'truce-maker and maintainer' is by no means an easy or a comfortable one, nor is that of a 'constructive critic'; both call for

...y, wisdom and maturity. How well equipped is social work for ... emanding role? What are the necessary prerequisites to enable its ... ment?

The first and the most obvious one is the need for social workers to recognise and accept that they are involved in both caring and controlling, and that far from being incompatible the two are complementary. Love is meaningless if not accompanied by concern aimed at preventing the loved person from harming himself – this involves various methods of control. Equally, control, unless intended and experienced as an expression of concern and love, is unlikely to prove effective and lead to the desired effects. Nowhere can one see the complementarity of love and control/protection more clearly than in relationships between parents and children. Whilst it would be incorrect to draw a close analogy between parent/child and social worker/client relationships, a degree of comparison is not inappropriate. Thus one of the functions which parents and social workers have in common is that of assisting socialisation in terms of coping skills.

The recognition of the control element in social-work practice should not result, however, in complacency regarding either its ethical implications or the intellectual demands inherent in knowing what constitutes appropriate and acceptable control in a given situation. In work with any individual client or group, the fundamental question which has to be posed is, 'for whose benefit is the control being exercised' – followed closely by the further question, 'by what means is that control being carried out and is this justified in itself, as well as being justified by the ends desired? The extent and the nature of the client involvement in the social-work process, which were both discussed in the previous chapter, are as applicable in relation to the control aspects of the social worker's role as in all other respects. The client has the right to be aware of the nature of the social worker's control functions and of the means by which the social worker plans to exercise these: whether they entail decisions in relation to the allocation of scarce material resources of one kind or another, or have to do with access to specialised forms of help such as a psychiatric or a marriage-guidance service. The issue at stake may be the conflicting needs or rights of someone else; for example, the client's child being neglected by her; or the social worker's control may lie in the authority of professional knowledge and skills and the intention to use these for the achievement of some change in the patterns of clients' response to others. The list of possibilities is endless but the examples given should be sufficient to underline the fact that the element of control in social work cannot be confined to control derived from legislative powers or carried out by some specific means, such as taking a client to court for breach of probation or applying for a 'place of safety' order for a child. It must also be clear that to exercise control by means of manipulating clients is not compatible with social-work values. This in turn means that a client or a group of clients must be free to reject control, although it is also important to realise that for some such a rejection may not constitute a real choice.

The difficulties and dilemmas for social workers which arise from these dual functions of social caring and social control are considerable and should not be underestimated. It must be recognised that they are inseparable from social-work practice and that they are a characteristic of its nature. The danger of denying or minimising this reality is that no adequate attempt will be made to grapple with the dilemma. The relevance of both values and knowledge to this task is obvious. What may be less obvious and more controversial is the view that, given 'the truce function' of social work and the resulting importance of its having a clear and a separate identity of its own, a strong commitment to professionalism is essential.

In recent years the terms 'profession', 'professional', and 'professionalism' have become, in certain quarters, particularly among 'radical' sociologists, virtually terms of abuse. It would not be appropriate or particularly profitable to go into the reasons for this development, but what needs pinpointing is its idiosyncratic nature. The Oxford English Dictionary defines these three terms as follows:

Profession –
> a public declaration; a business or profession that one publicly avows; any calling or occupation by which a person habitually earns his living; the body of persons engaged in a calling.

Professional –
> applied to one who follows, by way of profession or business, an occupation generally engaged in as a pastime.

Professionalism –
> a professional quality, character, method, or conduct.

It is clear from these definitions that the terms concerned are neutral in themselves, and that consequently any derogatory meanings attached to them (for example Pearson's view of professionalism as 'learning the catechisms of a closed order'[20]) must stem from certain specific assumptions. The assumptions which have given rise to the negative view of professions and professionalism currently encountered include the following three:

(1) that the model being used by all professions is that of the three 'ancient professions' of the law, the church and medicine, and that this is an outdated and inappropriate model;

(2) that professions are primarily concerned with the pursuit of the vested interests of their members at the expense of others in society – the more powerful a profession and the greater its monopoly over the provision of a service, the more socially harmful it is;

(3) that professionalism encourages distance between the provider of the service and the receiver and is thus antipathetic to equality.

The following discussion of professionalism in social work will be largely concerned with the attempt to refute the validity of these assumptions and with putting forward an alternative conception of its nature and its primary characteristics.

The assumption that the appropriate model for all professionalism is that derived from the three established professions is widespread. One of its manifestations is the emphasis in much of the sociological literature on the professions on the various 'professional traits' and the measuring of occupations in terms of the stage of their development on the road to becoming professions against these traits. Etzioni's concept of 'semi-professional'[21] is but one illustration of this approach. Depending on the traits listed and the relative importance attached to them, social work has been considered by different writers as either a profession (for example by Greenwood),[22] a semi-profession (for example by Etzioni),[23] or an activity which can make no claims to a professional status as yet although it may attain it one day (for example Flexner).[24]

The limitation of the 'traits approach' in my view lies in the abstract nature of the underlying preoccupation and in its failure to make sufficient allowance for the dynamic nature of professions. Thus one of the traits still generally associated with the medical and legal professions is that of private practice whilst in this country there are currently relatively few doctors who are solely engaged in such practice, and very large numbers of doctors are full-time employees of the National Health Service. With regard to legal practice too, the employment of solicitors in increasing numbers in Legal Advice Centres and other salarised posts brings into question the appropriateness of this criterion.

I therefore think that Heraud is right when he says that the process of professionalisation is more important than whether or not social work has achieved full professional status.[25] Without taking up a position on the issue whether or not social work is a fully fledged profession, I shall concentrate on discussing the central components of the process of professionalisation which I consider to be an essential condition if social work is to be true to its nature and its demands.

To provide a framework for such a discussion I have chosen two separate statements about the nature of professions. The first of these is by Merton, according to whom 'the concept of a profession' is made up of 'the threefold composite of social values'. These values are: 'first, the value placed upon systematic knowledge and the intellect: knowing. Second, the value placed upon technical skill and trained capacity: doing. And third, the value placed upon putting this conjoint knowledge and skill to work in the service of others: helping.'[26] The second statement is by Carr-Saunders: 'A profession is an occupation based upon intellectual study and training, the purpose of which is to supply skilled service or advice to others for a definite fee or salary.'[27]

Between them these two views of professions and professionalism pinpoint four major components of the process of professionalisation, or to put it differently, of the process of socialisation into professionalism.

Commitment to professionalism entails a service orientation, a primary concern to give of one's best in trying to meet the needs of the recipients of the service. This does not preclude self-interest in terms of promotion, remuneration, conditions of service and so forth, but it does not allow these to be pursued at the expense of the interests of the recipient. Flexner calls it 'professional spirit' and maintains that it is this that matters most in professionalism.

It is worth noting in this context, however, that recent instances of industrial action by nurses and doctors have provided a dramatic illustration of the difficulties involved in establishing and maintaining a right balance between 'professional spirit' and self-interest. A further significant point was the absence of any fundamental difference in the behaviour, in the face of this dilemma, by members of an 'established profession' and those belonging to a 'semi-profession'. This fact would appear to validate criticisms made of 'trait-based' distinctions between professions as, for example, that by Heraud which was referred to earlier.

Closely linked to the 'service orientation' of professionalism is its socially functional nature. The provision of a skilled service is in response to society's needs and it therefore entails both social rights and obligations. The former include the payment of regular fees or a salary; the latter a serious and responsible commitment to providing a regular service in response to expectations.

Concerning the functional nature of a profession, reference must be made to the currently fashionable attacks on the professions for fostering inequality and promoting elitism. Such criticisms can be found with reference to social work in a number of recent writings (for example Richan and Mendelsohn)[28] and they are usually accompanied by pleas for the removal of all differentials between social workers and their clients.

Several comments can be made in response to the more extreme approach adopted by the exponents of this 'egalitarian' philosophy, which has already been challenged effectively by Specht,[29] among others.

One of the basic problems inherent in such a 'philosophy' (and which is by no means confined in its application to social work) is the confusion between equality and uniformity. By implication, its exponents appear to view all differences as constituting inequality, a viewpoint difficult to reconcile with either the notion of human worth as derived from uniqueness or the social requirements for diversity inherent in different roles.

Another strand visible in this form of rejection of professionalism is a manifestation of a more radical rejection of social work as a social sub-system. This is the view implicit in Seed,[30] whose plea for social work to retain its original character as a social movement seems to ignore to a large extent the realities inherent in the institutional nature of social work and all that this entails in terms of both authority and social accountability.

At its most extreme the view that professionalism is intrinsically socially divisive overlooks the needs and the expectations of the consumers of professional services. These usually evolve around efficiency, reliability and expertise, and the majority of clients of social workers faced with a crisis in their lives are no more anxious to view these workers as their 'equals' in the context of their problem solving than are most patients to decide on the relative merits of medical or surgical treatments (see Mayer and Timms).[31] The point is made to emphasise the danger of personal ideology masquerading as the championship of the rights of others. The reality of such a danger is highlighted by the fact that in many of the arguments in favour of a greater identification on the part of social workers with the needs and aspirations of their clients a very partial view of social work and its functions is conveyed, apparently without this being recognised by the authors.

Furthermore, a rather naive conception is often reflected in many of these writings concerning what constitutes both 'distance' and 'closeness' in the context of human relationships. As this was discussed at some length in Chapter 5, it will not be elaborated upon except to reiterate that the functional aspects of the social-work professional role cannot of themselves determine the quality of the transactions between social workers and their clients.

The functional nature of professional activity requires that the social purposes for which it is undertaken are carried out well and effectively; society has a right to the assurance that its expectations incorporated in the mandate given to a profession are in fact fulfilled. This fact underlines the important part played by knowledge and its acquisition as an essential prerequisite to the specific expertise which is characteristic of professionalism.

A feature of professionalism which is largely derived from the three preceding characteristics is the guardianship of social trust. This is an inescapable and a logical outcome of a profession having distinct social functions and being equipped with specific expertise and authority to carry these out. Furthermore, beyond a certain point others are not able to judge the quality of professional behaviour and actions, and a proper assessment of these remains the domain of the individual practitioner and of his professional peers. Lest this should be seen as reflecting professional defensiveness and as a method of ensuring that failure by professionals is concealed from public gaze, the point needs emphasising that where professional conduct is officially prescribed, and is thus subject to formal and external controls, only conduct of a very specific and limited kind is involved. But professionalism does not stop at the permissible and the expected but strives after quality and perfection, matters for which only individual conscience aided by professional knowledge and values can legislate. This is what Lord Kilbrandon had in mind, I think, when he said: 'But what the doctor and the lawyer each have in common, namely the acceptance of a moral standard more exacting than the obligations which legal rights enjoin, is owed to membership of a profession.'[32]

The limits to the 'public accountability' of professionals are a matter of great seriousness and importance. It cannot be denied that they are potentially subject to abuse, and the reports that are published of disciplinary proceedings against some doctors and lawyers, for example, amply demonstrate that they are in fact occasionally abused. However, if one were to dismiss as unacceptable everything which is subject to abuse, one might be left with little that is worthwhile. Avoiding problems in this way is unrealistic if not immoral, analogous to restricting education for the many lest it give dangerous ideas to some.

I believe that it is only by acknowledging this reality that the necessary safeguards can be devised for the protection of society against the iniquities and the vagaries of its professionals; to the extent to which an ostrich-like attitude to the problem is adopted, it will remain largely untackled. In considering possible solutions one faces again the primacy of both informed judgement and moral integrity in the individual practitioner in ensuring professionally sound and ethically desirable behaviour, qualities which are neither easy to acquire nor are capable of simple validation. The recognition of their essential importance is, however, a necessary condition for ensuring that appropriate means are devised to promote them; among these clarity regarding the social expectations held of a profession, appropriate investment in a sound professional education geared to those social expectations, and proper controls over professional practice, including controls by peers, are of the utmost importance. The place and the functions of a professional association as a medium for the enhancement of the quality of the service provided to the public is particularly relevant to the latter point.

Carr-Saunders saw such associations as an integral part of professionalism:

Professionalism has its problems of organisation. It has its weaknesses and its dangers. But taking all in all, the growth of professionalism is one of the hopeful features of the time. The approach to problems of social conduct and social policy under the guidance of a professional tradition, raises the ethical standard and widens the social outlook. There is thus reason to welcome a development of which the result will be to increase the influence of professional associations upon character, outlook and conduct.[33]

In his view professional associations have four major functions:

(1) to ensure competence by excluding the unqualified;
(2) defining and enforcing rules of professional conduct;
(3) improving the status of the profession; and
(4) taking appropriate public action.

Whilst he recognised that some of these functions were open to abuse in that they could be made to serve the vested interests of the professionals at the expense of the interests of the general public, he did not regard such abuse as by any means inevitable but, on the contrary, 'the advancement of the status of the profession and the extension of the craft in the public interest on the whole do go together'.[34]

If social work as a corporate body is to be serious in its acceptance of the social mandate as discussed above, it must accept responsibility for ensuring the means by which a proper carrying out of the mandate is made possible. It is difficult to see how this could be attempted without ensuring a recognised minimum of common educational background and adherence to basic values against which professional practice can be evaluated and on the strength of which the profession can accept a degree of corporate responsibility for the professional conduct of its individual members.

It is in the light of these facts that the logical weakness of the position of those who argue against the membership of a professional association of social workers being based on appropriate qualifications is apparent. There has to be a congruence between the membership of a body and its objectives. Had the primary function of a professional association been the interests of its own members, as is the case with a trade union for example, membership based on employment rather than on qualification would have been appropriate. Given the objectives of a professional association as outlined by Carr-Saunders and others, effective fulfilment of these is dependent on membership being restricted to those who have a common qualification and who can be held accountable on that basis.

A recent Discussion Paper by the Membership Committee of the British Association of Social Workers,[35] raising the possibility of extension of the membership of the Association to all those who are employed as social workers, justifies this partly by asserting that the absence of a shared professional training by members need not prevent them all from subscribing to a professional code of ethics. This seems to me to be a difficult argument to substantiate as it appears to be based on a sharper and a more complete differentiation between knowledge and values than is possible in reality where values are informed by knowledge and knowledge is made convincing and instrumental by values.

The credibility of an association claiming to be professional without seeking to maintain and enforce professional standards of practice would be particularly hard to maintain in the area of public or social action. This is generally seen as one of the major objectives of any professional association and has particular significance for a professional association of social workers because of their dual concern with the relief of current problems and with social reform.

In a society in which pressure groups assume an increasing importance in affecting policy decisions, it would constitute failure on the part of social workers not to draw on their cumulative experience of human problems and the part played by various social institutions in their causation, exacerbation and perpetuation in order to press for appropriate changes. However, for such social action to be effective, it must not only represent strength in numbers but it must carry the professional authority of those who exercise the pressure. It is therefore important for social workers to distinguish between social action undertaken in virtue of their professional know-how and experience, for the advocacy of which they have the appropriate authority vested in their social function, and the type of social action which any socially conscious citizen might feel under an obligation to promote.

Some of these points were made by Richards in her Chairman's address at the British Association of Social Workers' recent conference on decision-making in social work. For example, after having emphasised the importance of credibility as a condition for being listened to, she stated that:

Credibility as conferred on us externally is influenced more by the quality and authority of the statements we make than by the numerical strength ... It is essential therefore that the Association continues to meet its responsibilities to bring together and use knowledge gained by social workers in their practice which is relevant to major social policy making ... only if we apply the knowledge, skills and values that social workers gain in their training and their practice can we as an Association, contribute effectively and with credibility to ongoing developments in social work practice.[36]

Given the fact that Merton's and Carr-Saunders's view of professionalism, and the latter's perception of the functions of professional associations, could be seen as reflecting concepts no longer appropriate to the present age, or as inapplicable to social work, especially by the adherents of anti-professionalism within it, it is not irrelevant to refer back to the time of the creation of the British Association of Social Workers and to those objectives with which by common agreement it was invested at the time. These were spelled out quite specifically by McDougall:

We have a constitution and it is prefaced by a statement of aims and objects. These are important; we spent a long time agreeing them and getting them into the right priority. They are not a list of double-talk planned to satisfy the Board of Trade and then to be disregarded. I would like to remind you of them. BASW has been started as a *professional* association. This is a deliberate choice. Standing Conference of Social Work, I would remind you, arose from a committee called out of concern for standards of training. As a professional association, aim number one must be the promotion and maintenance of standards of service. Of course a profession is also concerned to protect the interests of its members but this cannot be its first aim ... It follows from the nature of the first responsibility of a professional association that training, the active participation in training and a vital say in approving training, must be a major activity of the new association. We need a major say in training because the profession and the public needs protecting as much from the whims and fancies of academics, as from the expedient decisions of ministries. Standards, training, service to the community, these must be our major objectives.[37]

The extent of attention given to professionalism is derived from my conviction that in a complex and a pluralistic society there must be a logical connection between particular social functions and appropriate social institutions in the context of which these functions can effectively take place. Social work is a major social institution or sub-system related to a number of other systems including those of education, health care and central and local government. Its maintenance and evolution as a social institution depend on both the influence of various forces which are outside it and on its own inner functioning as a social system. The latter includes both the ideological commitment and the means by which this commitment is made operational. I see the concept of 'professionalism' as central to this process. The following quotation from Lord Kilbrandon is chosen as a summary of my argument:

> I find it strange that there should be misunderstanding of a fact so obvious as this: that the duties laid upon a man in consequence of his acceptance of professional standards are owed by him to the world at large. They are not evidence of a private or corporate privilege. Bernard Shaw in one of his rare foolish passages describes all professions as a conspiracy against the laity. This is like calling compulsory pilotage in narrow waters a conspiracy against the ship's passengers . . . It is not as a monopoly that a profession demands the right to lay down rules for the conduct of its members in the interests of those they serve, together with the conjunct right to exclude from membership those who do not conform to the standards their brethren lay down.[38]

Chapter 7

Some Current Issues in Social Work and their Implications for the Future

This final chapter will be concerned with a more practical and a more detailed consideration of the issues which were alluded to at the beginning. The line of argument adopted in the discussion of these issues will reflect the approach taken throughout the book about the nature of social work and its place in society, following on and elaborating the view expressed in the preceding chapter.

As already suggested, contemporary social work finds itself in a paradoxical situation in which an ever-increasing demand for its services is coupled with unprecedented criticism because of its failure to fulfil society's expectations. This is a position which obviously calls for some analysis of the reasons which have given rise to it as well as suggestions for action which could result in changes. To attempt such an analysis is a complex and a difficult task as so many different factors have varying degrees of relevance to the problem under examination.

It seems important to recognise at the outset that many of the issues influencing both the effectiveness of social work and its public image are reflections of a general malaise within our civilisation. This is so universally recognised and acknowledged that it would not be profitable to engage in a lengthy discussion of the phenomenon itself. It is, however, relevant to mention several of its characteristics which have particular bearing on the position of social work. These include a widespread sense of disillusionment with most social institutions, including political institutions (see Halmos),[1] a disinterest in the past, coupled with a lack of confidence in the future, all of which result in an orientation predominantly to the present and a strong distrust of any form of institutionalised authority.

The emphasis in this book has been on the extent to which social work must adopt a stance similar to Janus if it is to fulfil its dual function of concern with individual well-being and with social conditions which would promote and enhance it. Such a dual concern implies the need for a careful and appropriate balance between the elements of 'creative, or individualised justice' and 'proportional or equitable justice'[2] which is extremely difficult to achieve. It is not altogether surprising that social workers have frequently been unsuccessful. In the past (although not in the days of the early social-work pioneers!) when casework was seen as the almost exclusive method of helping, the swing tended to be in favour of 'creative justice' with relatively little interest being shown in wider measures aimed at social change. In recent years, the pendulum has swung in the opposite direction. A number of factors have contributed to this: the greatly enhanced powers of social work; its widened functions and the accompanying discovery of the extent to which large numbers of the population are disadvantaged as a result of failure in the realms of 'proportional justice' concerned with income, housing, education, health, and so on; and the greater political consciousness of many of the new recruits to social work, particularly to community work.

As a result of this shift in emphasis, some social workers have developed a perception of social work which puts in question the very core of its identity, namely its concern with actual persons rather than with abstract ideals. This distorted perception takes a number of tangible forms which have one characteristic in common: they lack a consistent and a tenable base. Thus the emphasis on the primary concern of social work being with social reform and the accompanying hostility towards most of the contemporary social institutions – their policies and their organisation – is not recognised as inconsistent with entering employment in these institutions. A historical perspective of social work as an evolving activity in response to social needs and social change is often lacking. Even such commonly fashionable expressions as 'radical social work' or 'new social work' reflect a preference for slogans over concerns with issues of substance. Thus it could be argued in response to those who regard the encouragement of clients' awareness of their disadvantaged positions as constituting 'radical casework', that it is neither more nor less 'radical' than was the embracing by the social workers of their day of psychoanalytic insights with the resulting attempts to enhance their clients' self-awareness. Equally, 'new social work' implies a denial of past changes within social work and makes claims about the qualitatively different nature of current changes which are not self-evident.

One serious result of this type of confusion is the omnipotent nature of the claims which social workers appear to be making when they imply that the salvation of society rests with them. Like all such claims this one is transparently unreal, and is thus conducive to distrust and suspicion. Specht has summed this up well:

> it is the passionate but uninformed quest for 'relevance' and activism that has helped convince others of social workers' naivete ... ideology without the means to achieve ends – without competence and institutionalised means to translate that competence into action – is futile for a profession.[3]

Whilst Specht's remarks refer to the situation which prevailed in the United States in the 1960s, Fowler gives a similar warning to British social work:

> social work is in danger of becoming ... all things to all people, and taking upon itself a responsibility not only for individuals, but also for the quality of the society in which we live ... To foster the notion that almost any activity of a socially ameliorative character can be embraced by social work is a myth, and a dangerous one at that.[4]

One indication of the nature and the form of the differential contribution social workers can make to social reform comes from Morrell:

> It is an illusion to think that society can be renewed on any basis other than attitudinal change. Institutional change is of value only if it places new tools of social organisation in the hands of people who have already accepted that they need such tools in order to pursue new values. Without such acceptance, widely shared by those whose

lives will be affected, institutional change is simply a formula for altering the rules for containing conflict: it is not a formula for resolving conflict towards greater reciprocity. The proper stance of social workers towards social reform is, therefore, to see themselves not as revolutionaries, nor even as people who, by virtue of their professionalism, have any special competence in the design of formal institutional structures. It is rather to remind society, constantly and insistently, that such structures are mere tools; and that they stand in constant need of renewal to reflect and support a process of evolution towards ever greater reciprocity in relationships between people, and between people and their total environment.[5]

The importance and the urgency of social workers defining their functions, including functions concerned with the promotion of social change, in realistic terms which would allow constructive action and public accountability seems hard to dispute. I have deliberately emphasised social workers' own responsibility for such a clarification because, even though all social roles are subject to social transaction and negotiation, the acceptance of a role entails a degree of moral commitment which is inconceivable if the role is inconsistent with one's own values and objectives. Similarly, in response to the degree of uncertainty and confusion within society regarding the nature of social work and of the contribution it can make to the well-being of society, it is incumbent upon social work to present an image of itself which is clear enough to dispel the current confusion and which fosters realistic expectations.

I believe that a major obstacle at the present time to such a clarification of what social work is, and what it can do, is the lack of differentiation between social-work and social-services provision. There are many examples of this. In Scotland it is institutionalised in the name of the local-authority departments under the 1968 Social Work (Scotland) Act as 'Departments of Social Work' in spite of the fact that social work is but one function among many carried out by these departments. In England and Wales, although the equivalent departments are described more correctly as 'Social Services Departments', and although social-work staff constitute only about 10 per cent of their total work-force, their ethos is generally social-work orientated and there is often no clear delineation of the functions which social workers are specifically expected to carry out. Given the acute shortage of social workers, this results ironically in a situation where only a proportion of the posts designed as 'social-work posts' are in fact filled with people who are qualified for these (the latest figure, according to D.H.S.S. returns is 42 per cent of basic grade staff and 60 per cent of senior staff). More often than not, the same type of work is expected from all the incumbents of these posts, regardless of whether they have had professional training or not. Surely, a situation is anomalous in which claims by a group of people regarding competence and the need for high degree of skill as prerequisites to the provision of an adequate service exist side by side with such a complete lack of differentiation of functions and tasks. It is a situation which would not be tolerated by any guild of craftsmen or a trade union representing skilled workers.

These problems of differentiation are linked to the ambiguity and conflict to be found in the relationship between 'individualised' and 'proportional' justice referred to earlier. As Stevenson has emphasised in the context of her discussion on the relationship between social work and provision of supplementary benefits,[6] although social work has been traditionally associated with 'individualised' justice, increasingly aspects of 'proportional' justice have had to be accommodated within it. Much of the recent social legislation referred to in Chapter 6, under which social workers have been given discretionary powers to grant financial aid and a range of material help under a variety of circumstances, is a clear illustration of this. Administration of scarce resources and social work have thus become increasingly linked. This development necessitates a very careful look on the part of social workers at the nature of this connection and its justification in different contexts. Extremes at either end of the continuum must be avoided as they are not tenable in terms of either principle or practicality. Jordan raises many pertinent issues in this respect. His assertion that 'The transformation of local authority departments from casework agencies into public welfare relief authorities is already under way, and has already transformed the functions of the local authority social worker'[7] cannot be dismissed, even if his subsequent quotation from Brill – 'His historical ancestor is not the psychiatric social worker who returned to England from the States in 1940 after training, but the old relieving officer'[8] – needs to be taken with a pinch of salt!

Jordan's discussion of the extent to which social-services departments have been gradually taking over from the Supplementary Benefits

Commission the responsibility for income provision in emergencies and financial assistance in situations of chronic poverty is in keeping with the problems experienced by many social workers employed by local authorities and causing them confusion and frustration. Whilst some people, including some senior administrators in social-services departments, ascribe these feelings of discontent to social workers' preference for personal satisfaction from their job over the provision of services required by clients, Jordan questions very powerfully the appropriateness for social work of income provision and maintenance functions and he marshalls considerable argument in support of this view. This has largely to do with the danger in confusing problems of personal adjustment with those of poverty and other forms of material deprivation. Jordan regards social work as primarily concerned with the former, to which it can bring the individualised and humane approach called for and which is its intrinsic contribution to human well-being. In his view, the equation of poverty or poor housing with personal failure, which an involvement of social workers implies, encourages a negative stigmatisation of deprived groups in the community. Thus it contributes to the vicious circle in which certain behaviour is expected of people in these groups which their various responses to their social plight then confirm. The role which is expected of social workers in this situation is particularly ironic and even tragic if Pinker's assertion that 'the most personal forms of social service are likely to be the most humiliating for the beneficiary' (quoted by Jordan)[9] is in fact correct. Jordan himself is quite unequivocal in considering that, 'It is the mixture of public assistance and social work that is so fatal to the social workers' professional task, and to the interests of their clients in need of either kind of service.'[10]

The increasing involvement of social workers in the administration of means-tested benefits of various kinds has profound implications for the nature of social work, its public image, the kinds of functions it carries out, the ways in which it is organised and administered and for the education and training of social workers. These will now be examined briefly.

An important consideration with regard to the provision of any professional service is that of its quality. Whatever the nature and the degree of the expertise vested in a profession, one of its characteristics is the importance attached to public accountability in response to the public trust vested in it, coupled with the fact, mentioned previously, that an essential part of that accountability is derived from 'internal' controls residing in the individual practitioner and his professional group. It is therefore imperative for any individual subscribing to the professional ethos of a service orientation, and a sense of personal responsibility for how it is enacted, to ensure that the expectations others hold of him are not incompatible with his ability to subscribe to these imperatives. It cannot be denied that, in this respect, many social-work practitioners at present find themselves in an untenable situation. Appeals are made to their 'spirit of service', they are encouraged to feel themselves excessively responsible for the various ills of contemporary society, which can only be tackled on a national or even an international level, and they are put to exercise their 'humanising influence' in conditions which are often so inhuman in themselves that automatically they become party to them.

One aspect of this discrepancy between the requirements of professional practice and its reality is the size and the nature of the case loads. As has been argued throughout, social work stands or falls by its ability to identify and respond to the meaning of experiences to persons, whatever these experiences may have been. This requires in turn the kind of approach which was discussed in Chapter 5, on the social-work process; an approach based on attempts to identify the specific and often unique features of a situation and which calls for a degree of personal involvement on the part of the social worker in both cognitive and affective terms. What happens to social work when it is asked to process clients at a rate and in circumstances which make such an approach to them impossible? It reduces it to a routine activity, focused on the obvious and the most urgent, which may or may not be the most important aspect of a human situation. The paradox and the tragedy of this lies in the fact that a quick, efficient and routinised provision of many types of service is what is often required. Lady Wootton had a valid point[11] when she argued against casework being offered as either a substitute for, or an unnecessary addition to, the provision of a specific service asked for. Equally, Jordan[12] provides evidence from his involvement with claimants' unions of the extent of the resentment on the part of clients at social workers' enquiries into their personal lives in the course of dispensing specific material provision. The degree of this resentment was greater than in the case of contacts with officers of the Supplementary Benefits Commission. The reason for this lies, as Jordan has stated, in the abuse of both social work and material assistance resulting from failure to differentiate between them and to acknowledge the validity of their separate existence. Lest I be misunderstood as arguing against social workers 'soiling their hands' by attending to their clients' material as well as psychological needs, I must make it clear, or rather reiterate what I said earlier on, that this is far from being the case. The criterion in social work for providing material aid should be the same as it is in any other form of need. It should be aid offered in the context of a personalised, creative type of service, and not as a form of administration of proportional justice. This distinction is not based on a judgement of the respective importance of these two types of service or their different status, but simply upon the fact that they call for differing approaches and are not easily combined. This difference is valid from both clients' and workers' points of view. Clients have a right to straightforward receipt of services when this is appropriate, and they have a right to be heard unhurriedly, and their personal needs carefully considered, when they experience a state of disorganisation, confusion or distress. Equally, the fact that social workers are trained to look for the distinctive and specific which lie behind generalisations and labels does not make them the most effective people to administer services on the basis of categorised entitlements.

As Stevenson has already shown,[13] an acceptance in principle of the differences inherent in administering 'creative' and 'equitable' justice will never mean that social workers will have no responsibility for making discretionary judgements regarding allocation of scarce resources. Similarly, however bureaucratised the administration of 'entitlements', those responsible for it will not be spared the need to consider the 'exceptional case'. The recognition of this cannot, however, serve as a justification for failure to recognise the basic difference which is inherent between a service based on the provision of specified needs and rights, and one which exists largely for the purpose of discovering what these needs and rights are in particular instances.

The confusion of social work with the relief of poverty and with material assistance of other kinds is not the only cause of the excessively large or inappropriate case loads carried by some social workers. The assumption of unrealistic and excessive responsibilities on the part of social workers themselves has already been referred to. It reflects both confusion on the part of many social workers about the nature of their contribution and an abdication of responsibility on the part of the various other institutions and groups within society for the problems in its midst. One particularly worrying manifestation of this trend is the assumption that social workers should somehow be cognisant of every potential human tragedy in their area and should be able to avert it. Thus, when an old person who has been living alone is found dead after several weeks or months, the common public response is to criticise the local social-services department for its failure to prevent the tragedy. No questions are usually raised as to the nature of the local community and the quality of neighbourly relations within it which makes such occurrences possible. Similar social expectations and attitudes prevail in relation to other vulnerable groups in society, particularly children, as the nature of recent publicity in relation to 'battered children' clearly illustrates.

It is significant that these unrealistic expectations of social workers are mainly confined either to these groups or to those who are experienced as a threat to society, delinquents for example. In contrast there seems to be limited recognition of the large numbers of people in society with other needs: marital problems, unresolved grief, isolation, chronic depression and alienation of various kinds, towards whose improved well-being and happiness social workers have an equally great contribution to make. One cannot but see this difference in the extent of social concern as reflecting society's own need to protect itself from its guilt in producing social casualties. Those which attract public notice and serve as a reproof are the visible ones; the hidden types of unhappiness can be confined more easily to the category of 'private sorrows' and thus ignored.

My reasons for emphasising this point are twofold: first, to stress the danger of social workers colluding both with the power vested in them with regard to certain kinds of problems and groups of clients and with the determination of priorities being made for them by others; and, second, to underline the importance of refusing to play the 'numbers game' at the expense of the quality of the service provided. Professional accountability cannot operate if professional standards of practice are lacking, and unless social workers accept such accountability and therefore assert the needs for standards they can be no more than bureaucrats. The latter term is used in its descriptive sense and not in a derogatory way in order to make the point that, whatever the strengths of bureaucratic services in certain contexts, effective social work cannot be offered through this medium. Intrinsic to its nature is the need for imaginative individualised responses to ever-changing circumstances for which no rules can be prescribed and for which the ultimate responsibility must rest with the individual practitioner, whatever sources he may choose to consult to guide him in the making of the particularly difficult decisions.

If society wishes to give top priority to the eradication of certain social ills, such as those of poverty, homelessness, and lack of adequate work and leisure facilities for young people, it must find appropriate means to do so. This may include the reallocation elsewhere of some of the resources which are now invested in social work. What makes no sense, however, is social work being asked to carry out functions for which it is singularly ill-equipped, and having in consequence to neglect those which it can carry out effectively.

In broad terms, any functions carried by social work must meet the criterion of being focused on persons rather than on particular events or provisions. It was this criterion which motivated medical social workers during the period between the introduction of the National Health Service and the beginnings of the post-Seebohm era to relinquish such tasks as providing surgical appliances, arranging hospital transport and payment of fares on behalf of the then National Assistance Board, and to abandon such procedures as the routine interviewing of all patients on admission. It is probably true to assert that before the setting up of Social Services Departments social workers in most of the social services had, to varying degrees, succeeded in distinguishing between work which required their own intervention and that which could be carried out by non-social-work staff or volunteers. It is not surprising that the service in which this differentiation was least clear was local-authority welfare departments in which the number of professionally trained social workers was low before the establishment of two-year social-work courses in Colleges of Further Education and similar institutions following the recommenda-tions of the Younghusband Report.[14]   Some of the reasons for the confusion about functions in some social-services departments are connected with the problems of social workers' increasing involvement in the administration of material provisions, which was discussed above. In addition, the broad and ever-widening terms of reference of these departments create particular difficulties in identifying the range of functions carried out by the departments, and in then deciding where the different functions belong within them. The urgency of the matter is, however, increasingly recognised, as witnessed by the research into the functions of social workers employed by local-authority social-services departments, sponsored by the Department of Health and Social Security and carried out by Olive Stevenson. Additionally, the B.A.S.W. has set up a working party with the following terms of reference:

> to identify, describe and define the social work task, and to make recommendations concerning the implications of their findings for practice, with particular reference to the appropriate functions of trained and untrained social workers and of other staff providing field work social services, and to the development of specialisations.

A Preliminary Report of the Working Party published in March 1975[15] reflects the difficulties of the task. Good in parts, like the 'curate's egg', it incorporates both helpful thinking and a good deal of confusion. Its major limitation is that it confines itself to a discussion of social work within the context of social-services departments, thus reinforcing the assumption, only too common, that social work and the work of social-services departments are synonymous. One example of this assumption is the increasing frequency with which the public media talk and write of 'social workers' *and* 'probation officers'.

The statement in the Report that 'there is a marked tendency for social work and social services work to be regarded as synonymous. This is both erroneous and dangerous', is followed by an attempt to delineate the particular contribution of social work in the following terms: 'the use of social workers is but one of many, to be utilized when there is some perceived problem of social functioning requiring a more personalised intervention in the interactional situation between the client and his environment'.[16] Once the discussion moves beyond generalities of this nature, it becomes much less clear or consistent. Although a distinction is drawn between 'trained' and 'untrained' social workers, there appears to be a good deal of ambivalence about the respective tasks of these two kinds of worker, understandably in a situation where the reality is that both are expected to undertake comparable activities. The division in the Report of the 'social-work task' into specific roles is particularly unhelpful in this respect as it conveys an oversimplified view of social work and focuses too heavily on what social workers do at the expense of consideration of what clients need.

It is not surprising, therefore, that in a strong attack on the Preliminary Report a group of social workers has rejected the validity of the definition of social work by its roles because 'many of the roles mentioned . . . could well be undertaken by people with a degree of information, intelligence and compassion. Nowhere does the report mention the uniqueness of the individual social worker in using himself/herself as a resource to help the clients.'[17]

The reference in the Preliminary Report of the Working Party to 'trained' and 'untrained' social workers raises one of the more complex and yet crucial issues in social work. What does the term 'social worker' stand for if this kind of differentiation is made? Are we talking about expediency, about a temporary situation in which, as a result of the expanding demand for social workers, their supply cannot keep up with the demand for the time being? Or are we implying that, however desirable and conducive to an enhanced quality of service offered, training for social work is an extra or a luxury because this type of work can be carried out adequately without a specific educational preparation for it?

These are fundamental questions and yet, surprisingly, they have not been faced fully or consistently by any of the bodies responsible for the provision of social-work services. New legislation calling for additional numbers of social workers is seldom accompanied by a corresponding increase in resources for the employment and training of social-work staff. Increasing demand on the part of employers for trained social workers does not go hand in hand with any steps being taken to ensure their most rational deployment. Exhortations by the Central Council for Education and Training in Social Work for both a broadened base of common-core teaching on qualifying courses and increasing amounts of teaching on the specific needs of different client groups and the range of services to meet these, do not take sufficient count of the time constraints imposed by one-or two-year courses – the duration of most social-work courses at present. Another factor, largely ignored at present, is the difference in both the recruits and the products of different training courses. Whilst at the end of their courses all those who complete them satisfactorily qualify as social workers, there are differences amongst them in terms of academic background, achievements and competence as practitioners in differing contexts. In spite of these, for reasons of either practical convenience, functional confusion or from confused notions of equality, no distinction is usually made by employers regarding the nature of the responsibilities allocated.

The drawing of distinctions between trained social workers presents formidable obstacles. The recommendation of the Younghusband Report[18] that there should be two distinct categories of social worker: university-trained and non-university-trained, each carrying different types of work determined by the degree of complexity of the problems dealt with and of the skills required, proved impossible to implement and was abandoned in practice from the outset. This was only partly due to the great shortage of social workers, which was not conducive to differentiations of this kind; another, and more important reason, was the fact that the Younghusband Committee underestimated the difficulties involved in distinguishing between social work of differing degrees of complexity, particularly at the point of intake.

Whilst no easy solutions to this problem of extreme heterogeneity among professionally qualified social workers can be suggested, it is nevertheless important to recognise that it exists. What also remains is the problem of the relationship between quantitative and qualitative considerations in the professional education and training of social workers with which the Younghusband Committee had to grapple. Given the ever-increasing complexity of social-work tasks, a strong argument can be made in favour of a lengthening of the training of many social workers even at the risk of such precedence given to quality resulting for a time in a decrease in the total numbers qualifying. The validity of 'fewer but better' cannot be totally dismissed when some of the realities of current social-work practice are examined.

As far as the relationship between trained and untrained 'social workers' is concerned, the issues are very different. Here it would seem that the essential preliminary step for all to take is to acknowledge boldly the expediency of the present situation in which such a large proportion of people in designated social-work posts in many departments are untrained. In the absence of proper job analysis, and given the confusion already fully discussed between social-work tasks and the administration of social benefits, it is difficult to know the extent of the real as opposed to the manifest shortage of social workers. This is far from clear with regard to field-workers but the difficulties inherent in reaching any realistic estimate are compounded when the areas of residential care and day care are considered. In the latter the relevance of a social-work contribution has only recently been recognised and there are bound to exist considerable differences in the interpretation of its exact place and nature.

Whatever the numbers, there is no doubt that in all these and other areas in which social workers are employed, there are a very large number of tasks which do not require a trained social worker to carry them out. What is surprising is that it has taken such a long time for this fact to be recognised within some social services departments, especially in view of the evidence available elsewhere, especially in hospital social work (see Moon[19] and Butrym)[20] regarding the large proportion of work within social-work departments calling for the services of a welfare assistant or administrative worker rather than a social worker.

The recently announced scheme by the Central Council for Education and Training in Social Work[21] for a distinct form of training for non-social-work staff within social services, culminating in a 'Certificate in Social Service', reflects a recognition of this fact and is thus an important step forward in the establishment of a clearer distinction between social-work and social-services provision. Success in achieving this objective will depend, however, on a realistic recognition of the differences of knowledge and skills between professionally trained people and those whose skills are of a more specific or technical nature, thus resulting in an appropriate division of work between them. There is a potential danger in the C.S.S. scheme in that it may too frequently be viewed only as a stepping stone to professional training and thus fail to provide adequate job satisfaction and career investment incentives for many of those entering it. The other possibility which needs to be guarded against is the scheme resulting in those workers with a different type of service to offer, including 'indigenous workers' and 'volunteers', finding their contribution undervalued. The nature of the training envisaged for C.S.S. workers is ambitious and will require the injection of considerable resources, particularly in terms of manpower. It remains to be seen whether these will be available to the extent needed for such a scheme to be viable.

For all these reasons, a crucial condition for the success of the objectives underlying the introduction of the C.S.S. scheme is a clear working out of the relationship between these workers and social workers. One important consideration in this are the circumstances in which the new type of worker will be operating, whether within the context of social work or outside it. This in turn is dependent on more general considerations regarding the structure of social-work services and their relationship to the other social services of which they are a part.

The literature on the relationship between professional services and bureaucratic organisational structures is extensive and no attempt will be made to review it here. What needs to be discussed, however, is the current position of social work within local authorities, and the extent to which its present organisation and administration are conducive or otherwise to the fulfilment of its objective – an effective provision of services to the community. The following quotation from Jordan conveys a depressing but probably not an entirely untrue picture of the situation prevailing in most social-services departments: 'a large organisation staffed by young, disaffected and relatively inexperienced workers, under the close administrative control of a large hierarchy of well-organised bureaucrats and confused, alienated, senior professionals, bemoaning their lack of contact with clients.'[22]

Jordan goes on to suggest that one manifestation of the overwhelming frustration felt by basic-grade social workers placed in such situations is their attempt to resist administrative controls by means of a 'trade-union' style of resistance – motivated by considerations of financial gain (for example confrontations over stand-by duties), rather than by a 'normative' type of resistance – resistance related to service values and objectives and the means being adopted to operationalise these.

He also quotes some of Spencer's reflections concerning the application of organisational theory to the bureaucratisation of social-work services within social-services departments: 'both theory and research findings point to the importance of delegating decisions to the professional on the job ... attempts to programme the field worker's decisions for him are only likely to weaken his commitment to the job.'[23] Spencer then relates the extent of bureaucratic control over social workers' decisions in social-services departments to their involvement in administering scarce material resources, as the latter are usually subject to this type of control, and concludes that 'Bureaucratic controls are largely irrelevant to the orientation of social workers to the job, although they may safeguard some minimal standards of service.'[24]

There can be no denying, in the light of both theoretical considerations and current reality, that social work finds itself in a very problematic situation. The discrepancy between its manifest role in society and the expectations accompanying it, and its actual ability to function in a way which is true to its spirit and effective in fulfilling its functions, is far too wide to be tolerable for much longer. At the risk of sounding dramatic, it appears to me that there is a real possibility of a total disillusionment with social work on the part of society if some radical remedial action is not soon taken.

For changes in the right direction to be possible, concerted action is required by all concerned: it is unlikely that unilateral action from whatever source could achieve the desired results. Social workers themselves have, however, an essential part to play in stating unequivocally what it is they stand for, what they can offer and what is the limit of compromise beyond which they will not be prepared to go. The relevance to this of a professional attitude and outlook as described in the preceding chapter is in my opinion indisputable. A recent recognition of the need for change which, if supported by the majority of social workers, could become a turning point in the history of social work in this country, is the B.A.S.W. Career Grade Working Party Report.[25] This begins with a firm commitment to 'improving standards of social work practice' and a reiteration that 'Helping people with problems individually, in groups or in communities, requires knowledge which is not just accidental and skills which are not just routine, but which are developed through training and experience.'[26] The Report then goes on to highlight the current anomaly in social-services departments where 'social work assistants spend more time than social workers with clients, social workers in their turn spend more time with clients than senior social workers, and so on'.[27] In criticising an organisational structure which creates such a state of affairs, the Report states:

> A model which ensures that as a worker gains experience and improves in competence his opportunities to practice diminish, is a strange one indeed ... many social workers who enter the profession with a strong motivation to practice social work ... find that direct work with clients is devalued and that status depends upon moving into social work administration or teaching ... Management has been seen as the ultimate goal, leading inevitably to a devaluation of the actual practice of social work and perhaps to a

devaluation of the client too ... The quality of service to clients inevitably suffers, as does public confidence in social work and morale within the profession ... For a profession which works primarily through relationships and which requires such a high level of maturity and continuity for its successful practice there appears to have been an abandonment of basic principles ... the social worker has only limited accountability for his work – a principle which is sharply at variance with the normal precepts of a profession, of the practitioner accepting individual responsibility for his practice ... the main factor ... is confusion about the professional identity of the social worker – is he primarily a social worker, or primarily a local government officer?[28]

These selected quotations convey the degree of concern expressed in the Report and the responsible and perceptive nature of the analysis of the problems. It concludes with the following sobering comments:

Somehow the situation has got turned on its head – the administration which is theoretically designed to service the carrying out of practice has become the master and the controller of practice ... as the local authority stranglehold over the development of social work becomes more of a monopoly this situation could become even more general than it now is.[29]

The Report does not stop at having diagnosed the disease but it proceeds to suggest an alternative pattern of organisation for social work. After having stated that

We cannot accept ... that this system is the only way of administering a social work service ... No other profession is structured in this way. All other professions draw a clear distinction between administration and professional practice, and reward and value their distinguished and experienced practitioners, [the Report goes on to suggest that] a radical restructuring of social service departments, with a clear distinction made between professional practice and administration ... A parallel might be drawn with the medical profession in hospitals ... The hospital is administered by a separate profession – that of hospital administrator.[30]

Given the current unpopularity of the medical model in social work, the use of this particular analogy in the Report would appear to reflect both the strength and the courage of the convictions of its authors. They bluntly acknowledge that

> This model is a hierarchical model, but the hierarchy is a professional rather than an administrative one. The managerial responsibility of the consultant is focused upon enabling junior colleagues to improve their professional practice, not at removing accountability from them ... An hierarchical structure is not necessarily anti-professional. Indeed it can help to facilitate professional development.[31]

Their conception of the application of such a model to social work is conveyed in the following quotations:

> The 'consultant' in social work terms would be a practitioner with a few years ... post qualification supervised experience ... He would work in close co-operation with other personnel from the social services department ... and the whole would be administered by local government officers, whose role would be to facilitate the work of the professionals ... If all social service administration were taken over by administrators, releasing social workers to resume professional practice, would there really still be a dire shortage of social workers in the field, or insufficient talent available to institute something like the hospital consultant scheme?

> For at least two years following qualification the social worker should be seen as completing his apprenticeship or basic training. He should not be expected to undertake the full range of responsibilities or to be fully accountable for his work. He should work under close supervision with a limited caseload, and this should be designed primarily as a continuing learning experience.[32]

The Career Grade Working Party Report has been quoted so extensively because it provides one of the most explicit and articulate acknowledgements to date of the seriousness of the predicament in which social work finds itself, as well as offering some concrete suggestions as to how the situation might be tackled which are consistent with the nature of social work as a personalised rather than a bureaucratic service. It will be interesting to see what response the Report will evoke from social workers in Britain. To some extent this is bound to be mixed because of the tenuous nature of professionalism within social work and the vested interests of some individuals – those in management posts whose social-work identity may have been diluted by their involvement in bureaucratic practices, and those whose 'radicalism' prevents them from recognising the value to clients, as well as to social workers, of professionalism rightly conceived. One must, however, hope that what the Report says will make sense to many social-work practitioners who will see in its recommendations some hope for the end to their worst frustrations.

It would be foolish to expect that the radical changes advocated in the Report could take place on the strength of social workers' action alone. Their validity has to be accepted also by others: the policy-makers in central and local government, senior administrators, educationalists, fellow professionals in other fields, and the various sections of the public. The difficulties involved in bringing these changes about are considerable as they entail some 'unscrambling' of the complex organisational and administrative apparatus which was created in the course of the implementation of the Seebohm Report.

Although the setting up of social-services departments was greeted with a considerable degree of enthusiasm by many people, social workers included, in retrospect some of this enthusiasm is more difficult to account for. Jordan has referred,[33] for example, to the irony inherent in the setting up of a family-focused service coinciding with its becoming responsible for the administration of a plethora of means-tested benefits and thus becoming an agent of the stigmatisation of these families. The current clientele of social-services departments consisting largely of the most socially deprived individuals, families and groups in the community is certainly a far cry from the ideal of a social service 'directed to the well-being of the whole community and not only of social casualties' (Seebohm Report).[34] There is in fact considerable evidence that the image of most social-services departments as catering for 'social casualties' acts as a strong disincentive to those who do not wish to be viewed in this light, and that some citizens are thereby deprived of opportunities to receive social-work help when they need it. The prophecy made by the late Professor Titmuss a few years before he died, namely that social-services departments were running a very real risk of taking the place of supplementary benefits departments as a residual social service, appears to be uncomfortably close to fulfilment.

When viewed in this light the 'one door' as the route to help of

various kinds, considered as such a great gain for potential clients by
the Seebohm Committee, begins to assume a different picture. It does
not call for much imagination to appreciate the plight of an individual
(or a family) who, for whatever reason, feels himself to have
antagonised an influential member of the staff of a social-services
department. If he no longer has confidence that his need will be judged
objectively and sympathetically, where can he turn as an alternative? In
such circumstances many people needing help are bound to fail to take
up the opportunities available to them. This is an inevitable by-product
of the position of near monopoly which social-services departments
have developed, even without additional disincentives such as the
quality of the reception offered in some of them (see Hall).[35]

In retrospect it seems strange that a structure of the size and
complexity of local-authority social-services departments should have
been considered to be the most opportune base for social work. In this
connection a brief reference to the relationship between social work
and health care is not inappropriate. It is commonly assumed that the
decisive factor in the transfer of hospital social workers to social-services
departments was the criterion formulated in the Green Paper on the
organisation of the National Health Service,[36] that the right basis for
the location of different professionals with a contribution to make to
health care should be determined by the nature of their contribution
rather than by the type of client served. However, what is not always
sufficiently recognised is that the decision regarding hospital social
workers had been pre-empted by the nature of the reorganisation of
local-authority social services and the National Health Service respectively. Once the responsibility for the community care of the mentally
and the physically sick and disabled and the elderly was vested in the
new social-services departments, a separate hospital social-work service
became both professionally non-viable and organisationally unsound.
No serious consideration appears to have been given, however, in the
course of these two mammoth reorganisations to the possibility of the
unified National Health Service embodying the World Health
Organisation health-care ideal by incorporating as an integral part of its
structure a social-work service. Such a service, combining responsibilities for the mentally and physically sick and disabled and the aged, in
both hospitals and other kinds of institutional settings, and within the
community, could not only make a significant contribution to health
being viewed as 'a state of complete physical, mental and social

well-being and not merely the absence of disease or infirmity',[37] but could serve as a valuable alternative to social work provided within social-services departments. The latter, by being able to concentrate on the needs of local communities, and those living singly or within families in these, could in turn make a real impact in promoting the ideal of 'a living and a caring community' envisaged in the Seebohm Report, and which, by general agreement, is sadly lacking in many places to the detriment of the quality of life of the residents.

Given the existence of social-services departments with all their complexities of structures and uncertainties regarding functions, what can now be done to free social work within them from the grip of bureaucracy and enable it to fulfil more adequately its role in society? It would seem to me that changes are needed on several levels and in a number of respects. The first of these, as advocated by Jordan[38] and the B.A.S.W. Report,[39] should be a separation of social work from social-services administration. Something on the lines of a social-work department or division within the total social-services department structure should be created and run by social workers on professional lines. Certainly a great deal would need to be worked out in terms of that department's accountability to the over-all administration, and also of determining which functions would belong to it and which not. In relation to the latter, there would be difficult issues to resolve, especially in the realms of residential and day care, but this should not be beyond the possibility of a collective effort on the part of all concerned, provided there was enough conviction about the importance and value of the task.

The creation of a separate professional administrative service within social-services departments, which such a change would entail, should prove to the mutual benefit of social workers and social administrators. Currently, relations between the two are often strained, and this detracts from effective collaboration. Students of social administration at both undergraduate and postgraduate level lack clear career openings, which sometimes results in the somewhat absurd situation that many social-administration courses serve largely as a source of pre-professional training for social workers, although they are reluctant to acknowledge this. In turn, social-work courses admit a proportion of students whose primary interest is in social administration rather than in social-work practice. Specific career opportunities for those with a specific training in social administration would serve the needs not only of clients but also of the discipline itself.

Assuming the existence of a separate social-work section within social-services departments, the next important issue concerns the deployment of its staff. In this connection, it is important to note that there seems to be a growing disillusionment with the area-offices structure within social-services departments. This is on several grounds. Thus, the B.A.S.W. Report suggests that

> The area office represents a departmental presence in the area – not necessarily the provision of professional social work services at those points where they are most needed: schools, surgeries and clinics, hospitals, community centres, factories, etc. A community based service can become as isolated from the community as an institutional-based one if it represents an organisation's presence rather than springs out of the needs of the community it serves.[40]

Other criticisms emphasise the discrepancy between the objectives of area offices – 'to bring the services to the people' – and the size of the areas covered, which in many cases are far too large for any meaningful community focus to be possible. It would therefore seem that if one of the functions of local-authority-employed social workers is to promote community spirit, to mobilise, on the one hand, deprived groups within a local community for social action and, on the other, the more privileged members for helping their fellow citizens, and to be easily accessible to those families and individuals who cannot be expected to seek help outside their home territory, some analogous structure to general practice needs to be considered. The 'patch' must be small enough for the local community and its ills to become known to a team of social workers, and for the latter to become familiar and trusted figures in the community. Such a team would need to have a truly generalist orientation: it should not start from any preconceived assumptions regarding either the nature of the problems or methods of helping but be prepared and able to become involved on a community, specific group, family or individual basis as appropriate. Whether or not one should conceive of generalist workers, who like G.P.s can intervene up to a point on each one of these levels and in relation to most problems – as opposed to a team of 'specialists' – is an important issue for consideration. My own preference would be for 'generalists' at this level, by which I mean social workers with a sufficiently broad conceptual base to enable them to make proper assessments of need and of the type of intervention called for. It would be difficult to conceive of a team of social workers servicing a small 'patch' being able to include in its midst all the relevant specialities and, even more important, if the initial assessments were made by workers with a specific orientation either regarding problems or methods of helping, this could slant the nature of the assessments made. Although a broad 'generalist' orientation is not incompatible with some differentiation of knowledge and skills among the team members, inherent in a 'patch system' of the kind outlined here is that work requiring a specialist approach would be carried out elsewhere.

A prerequisite to the effectiveness of community-orientated teams of this nature will be the availability of strong supportive specialist social-work services. The exact nature of all these specialisations is difficult to predict, and they are bound to change with the changing nature of the problems, the growth of knowledge and differences in functions. Some of these are, however, obvious, and there is a good deal of current public demand for them. The various aspects of work with disadvantaged children and their families – both natural and substitute; social work with the mentally disordered; work with the physically sick and disabled; marital work, work with adolescents; these are some of the obvious examples of specialisation in relation to the nature of problems or conditions in which clients find themselves. But there are also other bases for specialisation in social work, for example, with reference to particular practice skills and to settings in which practice takes place. There is a growing recognition within both social work and elsewhere that the concept of 'generic practice' has been badly misconceived and that the effectiveness of social workers' interventions is greatly dependent on the possession of some expertise in a defined area.

Another consideration of great importance in ensuring a social-work service which is both accessible and acceptable to people in need of it, is that it should somehow overcome the dangers and risks inherent in the present near-monopoly provision by local-authority social-services departments. One way of loosening the identification with 'the Town Hall' would be the setting up of small specialist units away from it. Another, about which more will be said shortly, is to encourage the attachment of social workers to other agencies.

Where a voluntary agency exists in the area, it should be to the advantage of the clients in most instances for that service to be used by social workers in the local authority either as a substitute for a local-authority-based service or, more likely, as an alternative and a supplement to it.

As already suggested, some of the disadvantages inherent in the local authority holding a virtual monopoly over the employment of social workers (with the exception of Probation and After-care Officers in England and Wales) could be minimised if as many social workers as possible were attached full time at various strategic points, or 'crossroads' as Meyer[41] calls them. These certainly include hospitals, general medical practices, health centres and schools, but, resources allowing, one could think of many others, including social-security benefit offices and work places. The emphasis on full-time secondment is quite deliberate given the extent to which social workers' distinct contribution in these various 'places of attachment' is bound to be concerned with the exercising of an individualising influence in a given institution and with regard to the service it offers. This requires a degree of commitment on the part of the social worker to his host agency and of knowledge of its particular culture which is not possible to achieve on a part-time basis. Such a whole-hearted commitment is also necessary for effective teamwork with other professionals.

A framework for the delivery of social-work services on the lines suggested here has much in common with what Meyer suggests[42] within the American context. Where I part company with her is over the extent of the comprehensiveness of the coverage by social work. If I understand Meyer correctly, her realisation of the nature of the predicament facing residents of urban societies, coupled with her view of the social-work contribution having to do with the 'democratisation' and 'individualisation' of services provided by the various social institutions, has led her to invest social work with an almost exclusive responsibility in this area. She thus advocates a complex network of social-work services, staffed by different grades of worker under the supervision of trained and experienced social workers, at all the 'crossroads' she could think of. Such a conception of the role of social work in society contains the serious danger, in my opinion, of vesting social work with a monopoly of caring and of capacity to individualise, which is difficult to reconcile with the objective of promoting the caring content within all the manifestations of social living. Such an objective would surely be defeated if social work, however unintentionally, encouraged the development of an excessive and inappropriate dependency upon itself analogous to the 'medicalisation' of society which Zola[43] and Illich[44] have deplored. Although the case has doubtlessly been overstated (by Illich in particular), the validity of the basic argument is not easy to refute, and social work will do well to heed the implicit warning in relation to itself.

Meyer's conception of the place of social work within society stems partly from her great faith in prevention and the high priority she allocates to this function within social work. Whilst she partly acknowledges that primary prevention in the public-health sense is not applicable to social work, she is nevertheless anxious to create structures which would make early prevention possible. The plausibility of such an objective cannot be denied, and it is salutary to remember the strength of emphasis in the Seebohm Report on prevention. However, social work must guard against excessive ambitions which it is not capable of fulfilling. There is also the issue of priorities, given that resources will always be limited, and that, within the sphere of social services, supply appears to stimulate demand.

Although it is natural to prefer to prevent an evil from occurring to having to deal with it when it comes about, nevertheless realism makes it imperative to acknowledge that however 'good' a society and however much better it may become, short of Utopia it is not possible to conceive of a situation where there will be an absence of human problems. It is my view that, whatever else social work does, its primary function is to respond to the predicaments which currently exist and which cause personal suffering. Social work cannot afford to abandon this function of relief of suffering for the sake of any other task, however worthwhile it may be in itself. To do this would be to betray the ideals it professes, and this would in turn result in a loss of identity and *raison d'être*.

To adopt such a stance is not to deny, however, both the value of preventive work and the opportunities within social work for it by means of early intervention in problem situations before they have had time to escalate. There is considerable evidence in support of this from social-work practice in crisis situations (see Parad)[45] and in such settings as that of general medical practice (see Forman and Fairbairn[46] and Goldberg and Neil).[47]

Besides their being placed in strategic positions, prevention can perhaps be most effectively pursued by social workers by their drawing on the evidence from their practice of the various societal deficiencies and feeding it, via their professional association and by other collective means at their disposal, to those who have the power to change structures and reallocate resources. This is the policy which Dame Eileen Younghusband, among others, has advocated.[48] The close relationship between informed social action and prevention, and their interdependence, does not always appear to be fully realised by the advocates of both.

The underlying theme of this last chapter has been the need for a greater congruity and consistency between the nature of the contribution which social work has to make to the well-being of society and the institutionalised means by which that contribution is made. It has been emphasised in this context that social work cannot usefully serve as a substitute for the shortage of other services or make up for their deficiencies. The distinctive characteristic of social work lies in the personalised nature of all its activities. Whether it deals with individuals, or client or community groups of differing sizes and composition, it can only be effective and meaningful if it relates to actual persons. Social work cannot therefore make an impact on crowds or operate primarily through the medium of ideological movements or political programmes. 'Small is beautiful' is very much the case with social work, including its community-work component.

To recognise this is not to deny the considerable potential within social work for effecting important and lasting social change. Social work is always concerned to a considerable extent with attitudinal change: with change in how clients feel about themselves and about others and with change in the attitudes of others towards clients. Whilst these changes are not of great dimension, they are cumulative, as Halmos, among others, argues. Whilst many would see his optimism as reflected in *The Personal Service Society*[49] as excessive, the ideal he puts forward is surely an important one, well worth striving for. I, for one, believe that social work has its part to play in bringing our society closer to that ideal provided it remains true to its nature.

References

Chapter One

1. C. E. Maurice (ed.), *Life of Octavia Hill* (London: Macmillan, 1913) p. 258.

2. B. Wootton, *Social Science and Social Pathology* (London: Allen & Unwin, 1959).

3. A. Sinfield, *Which Way for Social Work?*, Fabian Tract, 393 (1969).

4. Z. T. Butrym, *Social Work in Medical Care* (London: Routledge & Kegan Paul, 1967).

5. Z. T. Butrym, *Medical Social Work in Action* (London: Bell & Sons, 1968).

6. G. Hamilton, *Theory and Practice of Social Casework* (Columbia University Press, 1951) p. 3.

7. H. M. Bartlett, *The Common Base of Social Work Practice* (New York: National Association of Social Workers, 1970).

8. Ibid. p. 95.

9. B. Butler, unpublished paper given at a short course on 'Specialism and Genericism', by the Central Council in Education and Training in Social Work (1972).

10. H. Specht, 'The Deprofessionalisation of Social Work', *Social Work* (March 1972).

11. K. A. Kendall, 'Dream or Nightmare – Future Social Work Education', *Social Work Today*, no. 16 (1972).

12. P. Baldock, *Community Work and Social Work* (London: Routledge & Kegan Paul, 1974).

13. Butler, paper on 'Specialism and Genericism'.

14. *Report of the Working Party on Social Action and Social British Association of Social Workers (1974).*

15. *The Common Base of Social Work Practice,* p. 86.

Chapter Two

1. R. W. Roberts and R. H. Nee (eds), *Theories of Social Casework* (University of Chicago Press, 1970).

2. J. W. Reid and L. Epstein, *Task Centred Casework* (Columbia University Press, 1972) pp. 7, 10.

3. H. Goldstein, *Social Work Practice: A Unitary Approach* (Columbia University Press, 1973) p. 187.

4. H. H. Perlman, *Social Casework: A Problem-Solving Process* (University of Chicago Press, 1957).

5. H. H. Perlman, 'The Problem-Solving Model in Social Casework', in *Theories of Social Casework*, ed. Roberts and Nee.

6. H. H. Perlman, 'Social Casework in Social Work: its Place and Purpose', in *Casework within Social Work*, ed. J. Parker (Department of Social Studies, University of Newcastle, 1973).

7. Perlman, 'Social Casework in Social Work', pp. 13–14.

8. Perlman, 'The Problem-Solving Model in Social Casework', pp. 151–2.

9. Ibid. p. 152.

10. F. Hollis, 'The Psycho-Social Approach to the Practice of Casework', in *Theories of Social Casework*, ed. Roberts and Nee, p. 35.

11. Ibid. p. 48.

12. Ibid. p. 46.

13. Ibid. p. 65.

14. R. E. Smalley, *Theory for Social Work Practice* (Columbia University Press, 1967) and 'The Functional Approach to Casework Practice', in *Theories of Social Casework*, ed. Roberts and Nee.

15. Smalley, 'The Functional Approach to Casework Practice', p. 93.

16. Ibid. p. 80.

17. Ibid. p. 80.

18. N. Timms, *Social Casework: Principles and Practice* (London: Routledge & Kegan Paul, 1964) ch. 1.

19. C. Winnicott, 'Casework and Agency Function', in *Child Care and Social Work* (Welwyn: Codicote Press, 1964).

20. Ibid. p. 62.

21. Ibid. pp. 61–2.

22. *Report of the Committee on Local Authority and Allied Personal Social Services*, Cmnd. 3703 (London: H.M.S.O., 1968).

23. P. Halmos, *The Faith of the Counsellors* (London: Constable, 1965).

24. Ibid. pp. 26, 27, 28, 182, 190.

25. C. Rogers, 'The Characteristics of a Helping Relationship', *Personnel and Guidance Journal*, no. 37 (1953) p. 6.

26. Ibid. p. 16.

27. E. J. Thomas, 'Behavioural Modification and Casework', in *Theories of Social Casework*, ed. Roberts and Nee, p. 187.

28. D. Jehu *et al.*, *Behaviour Modification in Social Work* (New York: Wiley, 1972).

29. M. Shaw, 'Ethical Implications of a Behavioural Approach', in ibid.

30. D. Kaplan, 'A Concept of Acute Situational Disorder', *Social Work* (April 1962).

31. L. Rapoport, 'Crisis Intervention as a Mode of Brief Treatment', in *Theories of Social Casework*, ed. Roberts and Nee, p. 277.

32. Ibid. p. 277.

33. Ibid. p. 267.

34. Reid and Epstein, *Task Centred Casework*.

35. J. W. Reid and A. W. Shyne, *Brief and Extended Casework* (Columbia University Press, 1969).

36. Reid and Epstein, *Task Centred Casework*, p. 20.

37. Ibid. p. 20.

38. Smalley, *Theory for Social Work Practice*.

39. L. von Bertalanffy, *General Systems Theory* (New York: George Braziller, 1968).

40. W. Buckley, *Sociology and Modern Systems Theory* (Englewood Cliffs, N.J.: Prentice-Hall, 1967).

41. E. J. Thomas and R. A. Feldman, 'Concepts of Role Theory', in *Behavioural Science for Social Workers*, ed. E. J. Thomas (London: Macmillan, 1967).

42. Sister Mary Paul Janchill, R.G.S., 'Systems Concepts in Casework Theory and Practice', *Social Casework* (February 1969).

43. A. Pincus and A. Minahan, *Social Work Practice: Model and Method* (Illinois: Peacock, 1973).

44. Goldstein, *Social Work Practice: A Unitary Approach*.

45. Pincus and Minahan, *Social Work Practice*, pp. 247–71.

46. A. Pincus and A. Minahan, 'An Integrated Framework for Social Work: Some Implications for Education and Practice', in *A Unitary Approach to Social Work Practice*, ed. F. Ainsworth and J. Hunter, Conference Report (University of Dundee, 1975) p. 48.

47. Goldstein, *Social Work Practice*, p. XIII.

48. Ibid. p. 54.

49. Ibid. p. 55.

50. Ibid. p. 118.

51. Ibid. p. 188.

52. Ibid. p. XIII.

Chapter Three

1. G. J. Warnock, *The Object of Morality* (London: Methuen, 1971).

2. R. S. Downie and E. Telfer, *Respect for Persons* (London: Allen & Unwin, 1969).

3. P. Leonard, 'Social Work: Science or Mystique', unpublished lecture given at a study conference held under the auspices of the National Institute for Social Work (1969).

4. D. Emmett, 'Ethics and the Social Worker', in *Social Work and Social Values*, ed. E. Younghusband (London: Allen & Unwin, 1967).

5. Warnock, *The Object of Morality*, p. 16.

6. R. Plant, *Social and Moral Theory in Casework* (London: Routledge & Kegan Paul, 1970) p. 12.

7. A. V. Campbell, *Moral Dilemmas in Medicine* (London: Churchill Livingstone, 1972).

8. Plant, *Social and Moral Theory*, p. 20.

9. Downie and Telfer, *Respect for Persons*, p. 33.

10. Ibid. p. 31.

11. Ibid. p. 32.

12. R. Dahrendorf, *Homo Sociologicus* (London: Routledge & Kegan Paul, 1973) p. 83.

13. Plant, *Social and Moral Theory*.

14. Ibid. p. 40.

15. Ibid. p. 43.

16. Campbell, *Moral Dilemmas*.

17. Ibid.

18. Downie and Telfer, *Respect for Persons*, p. 101.

19. Ibid. p. 101.

20. Ibid. p. 112.

21. Ibid. p. 114.

22. Ibid. p. 113.

23. A. C. Ewing, *Ethics* (English Universities Press, 1953) pp. 164–5.

24. Warnock, *The Object of Morality*, p. 16.

25. Ibid. pp. 71–93.

26. F. Hollis, 'Principles and Assumptions underlying Casework Practice', in *Social Work and Social Values*, ed. E. Younghusband (London: Allen & Unwin, 1967).

27. F. Biestek, *The Casework Relationship* (London: Allen & Unwin, 1961).

28. Ibid.

29. *Confidentiality in Social Work*, Discussion Paper No. 1, British Association of Social Workers (1971) p. 3.

30. D. Brandon, 'Clients have a right to hope for better Privacy than this', *Community Care* (23 April 1975).

31. F. E. McDermott (ed.), *Self-Determination in Social Work* (London: Routledge & Kegan Paul, 1975) p. 7.

32. Ibid. p. 14.

33. Ibid. pp. 135–6.

34. Goldstein, *Social Work Practice*.

35. H. Goldstein, 'A Unitary Approach: Its Rationale and Structure', in *A Unitary Approach to Social Work Practice*, ed. F. Ainsworth and J. Hunter, p. 21.

36. R. Plant, *Community and Ideology* (London: Routledge & Kegan Paul, 1974).

37. N. Timms, '. . . and Renoir and Matisse and . . .', Inaugural Lecture (University of Bradford, 1971).

38. Ibid. p. 3.

39. Ibid. p. 4.

40. Ibid. p. 6.

41. Ibid. p. 6.

42. Ibid. p. 4.

43. *A Code of Ethics for Social Work*, Discussion Paper No. 2, British Association of Social Workers (1972).

44. 'Children at Risk – B.A.S.W.'s Code of Practice', *Social Work Today* (4 September 1975).

45. 'Code of Ethics for Social Work', *Social Work Today* (18 September 1975).

46. Ibid.

47. Both references, to Bishop Butler and Father Mahoney, are in respect of unpublished talks at study conferences for social workers.

48. Z. T. Butrym, 'Social Work: Professionalism and Catholic Reluctance', *Blackfriars* (October 1963) p. 419.

49. J. Macquarrie, *Three Issues in Ethics* (Student Christian Movement, 1970) p. 45.

50. M. McDougall, 'The Obligations of a Profession', *Social Work Today* (September 1970) p. 20.

Chapter Four

1. O. Stevenson, 'Knowledge for Social Work', *British Journal of Social Work*, vol. 1, no. 2 (Summer 1971).

2. B. Magee, *Popper* (London: Fontana, 1973) p. 72.

3. D. Emmett, *Rules, Roles and Relations* (London: Macmillan, 1966).

4. Warnock, *The Object of Morality*.

5. Downie and Telfer, *Respect for Persons*.

6. Campbell, *Moral Dilemmas in Medicine*.

7. C. H. Waddington, *The Scientific Attitude* (Harmondsworth: Penguin, 1941).

8. Ibid. p. 9.

9. Magee, *Popper*, p. 68.

10. Emmett, 'Ethics and the Social Worker', p. 11.

11. Stevenson, 'Knowledge for Social Work', p. 225.

12. Quoted by Bone in S. Arieti (ed.), *American Handbook of Psychiatry* (New York: Basic Books, 1959) p. 94.

13. Quoted in C. R. Rogers, 'Toward a Science of the Person', in *Behaviourism and Phenomenology*, ed. T. W. Wann (University of Chicago Press, 1964) p. 128.

14. Stevenson, 'Knowledge for Social Work', p. 226.

15. Bartlett, *The Common Base of Social Work Practice*, p. 223.

16. Goldstein, 'A Unitary Approach: Its Rationale and Structure', p. 36.

17. E. H. Gombrich, *The Tradition of General Knowledge* (London School of Economics, 1962) p. 16.

18. Bartlett, *The Common Base of Social Work Practice*.

19. Ibid. p. 78.

20. Quoted in N. Timms, *Casework in the Child Care Service* (London: Butterworths, 1962) p. 20.

21. N. Timms, *The Language of Social Casework* (London: Routledge & Kegan Paul, 1968) pp. 27–8.

22. Ibid. pp. 28, 29–30.

23. D. V. Donnison, *The Development of Social Administration: An Inaugural Lecture* (London: Bell & Sons, 1962) pp. 20–1.

24. Ibid. p. 21.

25. Emmett, *Ethics and the Social Worker*, p. 21.

26. E. M. Goldberg, *Helping the Aged* (London: Allen & Unwin, 1970).

27. E. M. Goldberg and J. E. Neil, *Social Work in General Practice* (London: Allen & Unwin, 1972).

28. Bartlett, *The Common Base of Social Work Practice*.

29. M. Davies, 'The Current Status of Social Work Research', *British Journal of Social Work*, vol. 4, no. 3 (Autumn 1974).

Chapter Five

1. P. R. F. Clarke, 'The "Medical Model" Defended', *New Society* (9 January 1975).

2. M. Richmond, *Social Diagnosis* (New York: Russell Sage Foundation, 1917) p. 347.

3. Ibid.

4. Perlman, *Social Casework: A Problem-Solving Process*.

5. L. Young, 'Diagnosis as a Creative Process', *Social Casework* (June 1956) p. 275.

6. E. Sainsbury, *Social Diagnosis in Casework* (London: Routledge & Kegan Paul, 1970) pp. 6, 17 and 7, respectively.

7. Bartlett, *The Common Base of Social Work Practice*.

8. Ibid.

9. F. Hollis, *Casework: A Psycho-social Therapy* (New York: Random House, 1964).

10. M. Yelloly, 'Insight', in *Behaviour Modification in Social Work*, ed. Jehu *et al.*

11. G. H. Mead, *Mind, Self and Society* (University of Chicago Press, 1970).

12. P. Righton, 'Social Work: Science or Mystique', unpublished

lecture given at a Conference under the auspices of the National
Institute for Social Work (1969).

13. M. L. Ferard and N. K. Hunnybun, *The Caseworker's Use of
Relationships* (London: Tavistock, 1962).

14. C. Cherry, *On Human Communication* (M.I.T. Press, 1957) p. 10.

15. J. Ruesch, 'General Theory of Communication in Psychiatry', in
American Handbook of Psychiatry, ed. Arieti, p. 898.

16. J. Mayer and N. Timms, *The Client Speaks* (London: Routledge &
Kegan Paul, 1970).

17. Reid and Epstein, *Task Centred Casework.*

18. T. S. Szasz, 'Language and Pain', in *American Handbook of
Psychiatry,* pp. 982–99.

19. Winnicott, 'Casework and Agency Function', p. 62.

Chapter Six

1. *Mental Health Act, 1959* (London: H.M.S.O.).

2. *Children and Young Persons Act, 1963* (London: H.M.S.O.).

3. *Children and Young Persons Act, 1969* (London: H.M.S.O.).

4. *Social Services Act, 1970* (London: H.M.S.O.).

5. *Report of the Committee on Local Authority and Allied Personal Social
Services,* Cmnd. 3703 (London: H.M.S.O., 1968).

6. *Chronically Sick and Disabled Persons Act, 1970* (London: H.M.S.O.).

7. *Criminal Justice Act, 1972* (London: H.M.S.O.).

8. *The Children Act, 1975* (London: H.M.S.O.).

9. *Report of the Working Party on Fostering Practice, 1975* (London:
H.M.S.O.).

10. *Report of the Advisory Council on the Penal System, Young Adult
Offenders, 1974* (London: H.M.S.O.).

11. *Better Services for the Mentally Ill, 1975,* Cmnd. 6233 (London:
H.M.S.O.).

12. Central Council for Education and Training in Social Work,
Residential Work is a Part of Social Work, Paper 3 (1973).

13. Central Council for Education and Training in Social Work,
People with Handicaps Need Better Trained Workers, Paper 5 (1974).

14. *Report of the Working Party, Social Work Support for the Health
Service, 1974* (London: H.M.S.O.).

15. D. Fowler, 'Ends and Means', in *Towards a New Social Work,* ed.
H. Jones (London: Routledge & Kegan Paul, 1975).

16. Butrym, *Medical Social Work in Action*.

17. B. Heraud, *Sociology and Social Work* (Oxford: Pergamon Press, 1970) pp. 196–9.

18. Ibid. p. 199.

19. D. Morrell, 'Does Social Work Hinder Social Reform?', an unpublished paper (1969).

20. G. Pearson, 'The Politics of Uncertainty: A Study in the Socialisation of the Social Worker', in *Towards a New Social Work*, ed. H. Jones (London: Routledge & Kegan Paul, 1975).

21. A. Etzioni, *The Semi-Professions and their Organisation: Teachers, Nurses, Social Workers* (New York: Free Press, 1969).

22. E. Greenwood, 'The Elements of Professionalisation', *Social Work*, vol. 2, no. 3 (1957).

23. Etzioni, *The Semi-Professions and their Organisation*.

24. A. Flexner, 'Is Social Work a Profession?', *Proceedings of the National Conference of Charities and Corrections* (1915).

25. Heraud, *Sociology and Social Work*, pp. 219–48.

26. R. K. Merton, 'Some Thoughts on the Professions in American Society', *Brown University Papers* (1960) p. 9.

27. A. M. Carr-Saunders, *Professions – Their Organisation and Place in Society* (Oxford: Clarendon Press, 1928).

28. W. C. Richan and A. R. Mendelsohn, *Social Work: The Unloved Profession* (New York: Watts, 1973).

29. Specht, 'The Deprofessionalisation of Social Work'.

30. P. Seed, *The Expansion of Social Work in Great Britain* (London: Routledge & Kegan Paul, 1972).

31. Mayer and Timms, *The Client Speaks*.

32. Lord Kilbrandon, 'Ethics and the Professions', *Journal of Medical Ethics*, vol. 1, no. 1 (April 1975).

33. Carr-Saunders, *Professions*, p. 31.

34. Ibid. p. 17.

35. British Association of Social Workers, 'Eligibility for Membership', Discussion Paper, *Social Work Today* (24 July 1975).

36. K. Richards, 'Social Work Decisions – A Continuing Responsibility', *Social Work Today* (30 October 1975) p. 456.

37. K. McDougall, 'The Obligations of a Profession', *Social Work Today* (September 1970) p. 18.

38. Kilbrandon, 'Ethics and the Professions'.

Chapter Seven

1. Halmos, *The Faith of the Counsellors.*

2. Tillich quoted in O. Stevenson, *Claimant or Client?* (London: Allen & Unwin, 1973).

3. Specht, 'The Deprofessionalisation of Social Work', pp. 4–5.

4. Fowler, 'Ends and Means', in *Towards a New Social Work*, ed. Jones, p. 93.

5. Morrell, 'Does Social Work hinder Social Reform?'.

6. Stevenson, *Claimant or Client?* chs I, II.

7. B. Jordan, *Poor Parents* (London: Routledge & Kegan Paul, 1974) p. 11.

8. Ibid. p. 11.

9. Ibid. p. 99.

10. Ibid. p. 181.

11. Wootton, *Social Science and Social Pathology.*

12. Jordan, *Poor Parents.*

13. Stevenson, *Claimant or Client?*

14. *Report of the Working Party on Social Workers in the Local Authority Health and Welfare Services* (London: H.M.S.O., 1959).

15. 'The Social Work Task', Preliminary Report of the Professional Development and Practice Committee of the British Association of Social Workers, *Social Work Today* (6 March 1975).

16. Ibid. p. 748.

17. Staff and students at the Central Hospital, Warwick, 'The Social Work Task', *Social Work Today* (12 June 1975) p. 190.

18. *Report of the Working Party on Social Workers.*

19. M. Moon, *The First Two Years* (London: Institute of Medical Social Workers, 1964).

20. Butrym, *Medical Social Work in Action.*

21. Central Council for Education and Training in Social Work, *A New Form of Training: The Certificate in Social Service*, Paper 9:1 (1975).

22. Jordan, *Poor Parents*, p. 110.

23. Ibid. p. 109.

24. Ibid. p. 113.

25. 'Report of the Working Party of the British Association of Social Workers on Career Grade', *Social Work Today* (24 July 1975).

26. Ibid. p. 283.

27. Ibid. p. 283.

28. Ibid. p. 284.

29. Ibid. p. 284.

30. Ibid. p. 284.

31. Ibid. p. 284.

32. Ibid. pp. 284–5.

33. Jordan, *Poor Parents.*

34. *Report of the Committee on Local Authority and Allied Personal Social Services,* para. 474.

35. A. Hall, *Point of Entry* (London: Allen & Unwin, 1975).

36. Department of Health and Social Security, *The Future Structure of the National Health Service* (London: H.M.S.O., 1970).

37. World Health Organisation, *Official Records,* no. 2 (1948) p. 100.

38. Jordan, *Poor Parents.*

39. 'Report of the Working Party on Career Grade.'

40. Ibid. p. 284.

41. C. H. Meyer, *Social Work Practice: A Response to the Urban Crisis* (New York: The Free Press, 1970).

42. Ibid.

43. I. K. Zola, 'Medicine as an Institution of Social Control', *Sociological Review* (November 1972) pp. 487–504.

44. I. Illich, *Medical Nemesis – The Expropriation of Health* (London: Calder & Boyars, 1975).

45. H. J. Parad (ed.), *Crisis Intervention* (Family Service Association of America, 1965).

46. J. Forman and E. Fairbairn, *Social Casework in General Practice* (Oxford University Press, 1968).

47. Goldberg and Neil, *Social Work in General Practice.*

48. E. Younghusband, 'Social Work and Social Values', *Social Work Today* (September 1970).

49. P. Halmos, *The Personal Service Society* (London: Constable, 1970).

Index

acceptance, principle of 48–9
administration
   local-authority social services 138–41, 143–6, 148
   social 76–7, 145–6
   social-work 139, 141–3, 145–8
adoption 107–8
after-care 52, 107
agencies 3, 24–5, 85–7, 148
alienation 92, 109, 139
ambivalence 99–100, 110–13
anxiety 92
Approved School Orders 106
area offices 146
art/science dichotomy 42, 65–6, 77
assessment, social-work 84–8

Bartlett, H. M. 6–8
behaviour, moral attitude to 84
behaviour-modification model 29–31, 68
Biestek, F. 48, 54
British Association of Social Workers 14, 51, 57–8, 122–3, 135, 140–3, 145–6
bureaucracy 133, 139, 143, 145

Care Orders 106
Career Grade Working Party Report 140–3, 145–6
case loads 9, 131–2
casework 6, 12, 16, 21–3, 54, 101–3
   model, task-centred 33–5, 99
caseworkers 55, 73
categories of social worker 136–7
Central Council for Education and Training in Social Work 108, 136, 138
Certificate in Social Service (C.S.S.) 138
change 100–1, 126–8, 150
   capacity for 46–7, 92–3

change-agent system 36–7
Charity Organisation Society 1
child-care officers 25
children 58, 133
Children Act 1975 107–8
Children and Young Persons Acts 105–6
Christianity 26–7, 59–61
Chronically Sick and Disabled Persons Act 1970 107
classification 48–9, 67, 88–91, 103
Code of Ethics for Social Work 57–8, 61
coercion 54
cognitive/affective dichotomy 64–6
communication 97–8
community-orientated teams 147
Community Service Orders 107
community work 6–7, 12–13, 39, 55, 73, 89, 94, 102–3, 105, 150
compassion 110–11
competence, differences in 9
conduct, code of 57–9
confidentiality 51–2
control
   element in social work 114–15
   social 46
'coping', concept of 8
counsellors 26–8
Criminal Justice Act 1972 107
crises, social work in 149
crisis theory 33
crisis-intervention model 31–3

data collection 1, 21
day care 138, 145
Day Training Centres 107
democratisation 148
Department of Health and Social Security Reports 108, 135
Departments of Social Work 128, 144–5
dependency 95–6, 101

depersonalisation 92
deprivation 12–13, 94, 130, 143
determinism 46–7
diagnosis, social 87
diagnostic approach 19–22, 24, 82, 84, 98: *see also* assessment
dispositions, good and bad 48
dogma 68

education
of clients 90–1
of social workers 69–72, 74–7, 79–80, 108, 121, 136–7: *see also* training
social-work contribution to 109
egalitarianism 118–19
elitism 118
emotional involvement, controlled 50–1
environment 23, 89, 131
amelioration of 3, 5, 13, 91
ethical issues 30, 35, 36, 40–2
ethics, professional code of 56–8, 61, 122
evaluation 98
existentialism 26, 45, 93–4
experience, personal 92, 95, 96–7, 101, 131
extremism, intellectual 68

family therapy 89
family-welfare agencies, voluntary 3
feedback, communication 97–8
feelings 50, 65
fieldwork 79, 137, 139
financial
assistance 130, 131–2
resources 106–7
Fostering Practice, D.H.S.S. Working Party on 108
'four-systems' model 36–7, 39
free will 46–7
freedom, positive 52–3
Freud, S. 23
functional model 22–6
functionalists 82
functioning, social 4–9, 15, 19–20, 28
functions of social workers 12, 14, 17, 24–5, 28, 49, 85, 106, 109, 113–14, 137–8, 140, 146: *see also* scope of social work
Working Party on 135–6

generic practice 6, 25, 147
generic–specific concept 74–6
generalisation 67, 77–8
generalist workers 146–7
Goldstein, H. 37–8
'good life', promotion of 40–1
group work 6–7, 73, 89, 102–3
groups, categories of 91
guidance, professional 9
guilt feelings 100, 106, 133

Halmos, P. 26–7, 150
Hamilton, Gordon 4
Handicapped People, Report on Training for Social Work with 108
health field, social workers in 108–9, 134, 138, 144
helping
process of 17–18, 21–4, 30, 86–91, 94–5, 99–101, 103
relationship 27–8, 35
hierarchy, professional 141–2
Hill, Octavia 2
history, client's 85
holistic approach 18, 35–9
Hollis, F. 19–22, 48, 91
homelessness 13
hospital
administration 141
social work 108, 134, 138, 144
human rights, basic 52–3
human sciences 42, 65
humility 50, 60

idealism 45–6
identity
in social work, problem of 1–14
of social work 8–11, 14, 82, 112
ideology and knowledge 69
income provision 130–2
indigenous workers 138
individual growth promotion 46
individualisation 50, 67, 148, 150
insight 90, 97, 102
institutions
changing 127–8
disillusionment with 126
interventive repertoire 73–4, 88–91
intuition 66

judgements 2, 49–50
justice 126, 129, 132

Kant, I.   43, 46, 56, 64
knowledge   63–9, 122
   in social work   8, 56, 63, 67–80

legal profession   117, 120
legislation   105–8, 128, 129
Linguistic School of Philosophy   64–5
local authority
   administration   139–45
   services   106–8, 128–30: *see also*
      Social Services Departments
   welfare departments   134
love in moral sense   48

mandate for social work   8, 10, 105–8
manipulation   30, 54, 115
material aid   130, 131–2, 134
maturity   101
means-tested benefits   129–30, 131–2,
   143
mechanistic approach   30, 36, 78
medical model   82–5
medical practice, social work in   149
medical profession   117, 120
mental health   11, 25
Mental Health Act 1959   105
Mentally Ill, White Paper on Better
   Services for the   108
methods of practice   6–7, 73, 103
Meyer, C. H.   148–9
'ministration in love' model   26–9
models   15–16
   social-work practice   16–39
moral activity, social work as   55–6, 84
moral issues   xi, 40–4, 48–9, 55
moral philosophy   65–6, 78
moralising   42–3
moralistic judgements   2
morality, religion and   59–60

National Health Service
   Social Work Support for the, Report
      of the D.H.S.S. Working Party
      on   108
   Green Paper on Organisation of
      144
natural sciences   65–6, 76
needs of clients   10
neutrality, moral   43, 49
non-judgemental attitude   49–50

objectives, social-work   89–90, 96, 99,
   104, 106, 148–9
old people   133

Perlman, H. H.   16–19
personality
   assessment   2, 3–5, 20, 22, 87
   development   92
persons, respect for   43–4, 49, 51, 53,
   59, 60, 87
phases of social worker/client contact
   99–100
philosophising, practical   55–6
philosophy   43–6, 64–6, 78
philosophy/science interdependence
   41–2
Pincus, A. and Minahan, A.   36
pity   110–11
place of social-work intervention   90
politicisation of social work   11–14, 92,
   126–7
poverty   13, 130, 132
practice, social-work
   code of   58
   methods of   6–7, 73, 103
   models of   15–39
pressure groups   122
preventive work   31–2, 149–50
Probation Service   25, 52, 107
problem-solving model   16–19, 39
process   81
   model   39
   social-work   81–104
professional associations   120–4
professionalisation   117, 121
professionalism   57–8, 61, 95, 115–20,
   124, 130, 133, 140–2
   abuses of   120–1
psychiatric social workers   83
psychoanalysis   2–4, 68, 102
psychological
   assessment   2–3
   determinism   46
   support   9
psychology   23–4, 78
   dynamic   4, 32
psycho-social
   perspective   37
   therapy model   19–22
psychosomatic symptoms   100
psychotherapy   5, 12, 28
public accountability   119–20, 130–1

punitiveness 111

radical social work 127, 143
Rank, Otto 23–4
Reid, J. W. and Epstein, L. 15–16, 33
reform, social 5, 113, 126–8
relationship
  agency/social-work practice 24–5
  doctor/patient 84
  in social work 17, 20–2, 23–6, 28–9,
    31–4, 38, 49–51, 83–4, 92–5,
    96–101, 102–3, 114–15, 119
  role 17, 93, 96–7
  therapy 27–8
religious faith 59–61
research 78–80
residential care 138, 145
Residential Work, Report on Training
  for 108
residential worker 103
resistance to administrative control
  139
Richmond, Mary 4
Roberts, R. W. and Nee, R. H. 15
Rogers, C. 27–8
role
  activities 39
  definition of social work 135–6
  relationship 17, 93, 96–7
  requirements 61

science 65–6: *see also* social sciences
science/philosophy interdependence
  41–2
scope of social work 3, 5, 9–11, 126–
  34, 144, 148–9
Scotland 128
secondment 148
secularisation of society 41
Seebohm Report 25, 106–7, 143–4,
  145, 149
self-determination principle 52–4
Shaw, G. B. 124
Sinfield, A. 2
skills 74
Smalley, R. E. 22–5, 35
social
  administration 76–7, 145–6
  conflict 113, 115
  control 46
  functioning concept 4–9, 15, 19–20,
    28

  nature of man 44–6, 51
  reform 5, 113, 126–8
  sciences 69, 76, 78, 135
Social Services Act 1970 106–7
Social Services Departments 10, 25,
  52, 109, 128–30, 134–5, 138–48
'social systems model' 39
socialisation 29, 114
society
  differences within 110–12
  expectations of 125, 128, 133–4, 140
  secularisation of 41
  social work and 105–24, 148–9
  social workers as critics of 113
specialisation 11, 25, 74, 147
statutory agencies 3
supplementary benefits 129–30, 131,
  143
supportive services 8, 147
systems theory 36, 38

task-centred casework model 33–5, 99
'task' concept 8
teaching, social-work 6, 140
technical expertise 74
theory 67–9
  models and 15–16
time factor in client/social worker
  contact 26, 32, 88, 98–9
Timms, N. 24
training 7, 69–70, 108, 121–3, 129,
  134, 136–8, 142, 145; *see also*
  education
transcendence 92
treatment
  indirect 91
  intermediate 106
  medical 83
  social-work 87–8
truce in social conflict, social work as
  institution of 113, 115

unemployment 13
unification of social-work services 92,
  106
unified association of social workers 7
unitary-approach model 37–9, 55
United States of America 2–3, 148
  models of social-work practice in
    19–26
universities, social-work courses at
  79–80, 136–7

values 64–5, 122
in social work 8, 19, 40–62
vocation 62
voluntary agencies 3, 148
volunteers 138

Waddington, C. H. 65
welfare: *see also* material aid
agencies, voluntary 3

assistants 138
departments 134
Winnicott, C. 24–5
Wootton, B. 2
World Health Organisation 144

Younger Committee 108
Younghusband, Dame Eileen 150
Younghusband Report 134, 137

Social Administration: Social Work

THE EVERLASTING STORY
OF NORY

The Everlasting Story

of Nory

a novel

Nicholson Baker

Chatto & Windus

LONDON

Published in 1998

2 4 6 8 10 9 7 5 3 1

First published in the United States in 1998
by Random House Inc., New York

This edition published in Great Britain in 1998 by
Chatto & Windus
Random House, 20 Vauxhall Bridge Road, London SW1V 2SA

Random House Australia (Pty) Limited
20 Alfred Street, Milsons Point, Sydney
New South Wales 2061, Australia

Random House New Zealand Limited
18 Poland Road, Glenfield
Auckland 10, New Zealand

Random House South Africa (Pty) Limited
Endulini, 5A Jubilee Road, Parktown 2193, South Africa

Random House UK Limited Reg. No. 954009

A CIP catalogue record for this book is available from the British Library

ISBN 0-7011-6690-8

Papers used by Random House UK Limited are natural,
recyclable products made from wood grown in sustainable forests.
The manufacturing processes conform to the environmental
regulations of the country of origin

Printed and bound in Great Britain
by Mackays of Chatham PLC

For my dear daughter Alice, the informant

The Everlasting Story
of Nory

1. What She Liked to Do

Eleanor Winslow was a nine-year-old girl from America with straight brown bangs and brown eyes. She was interested in dentistry or being a paper engineer when she grew up. A paper engineer is an artist who designs pop-up books and pop-up greeting cards, which are extremely important to have easily available in stores because they make people happier in their lives. Lately Nory was in a stage of liking to draw pictures of Chinese girls wearing patchwork Chinese robes with their hair up in a little hat, or held on the side with a pin. She told a constant number of stories to herself in the car while they drove to Stately Homes. She also told them to herself in the bathtub or in the mirror. Sometimes she and her friends made up stories together, but that of course depended heavily on the friend. Another thing Nory liked doing was making up new designs of dolls that she wished you could have the opportunity to buy but you can't and probably never will.

For example, she drew a doll named 'Riena.' Riena had straight hair parted on the side and puffy sleeves. She was not stretched out with a teenagery figure or short with a massive rounded head. Her hands and wrists could bend so she could hold a miniature carton of eggs, and every egg would have a realistic crack in the middle. You would help Riena put the egg down on the saucing pan, and shuffle it around, and after a while the egg would break by itself, because it would be filled with a special substance that expanded when you jostled it. A little folded-up rubbery thing that was an egg would goosh out, probably sunny side up, in the pan. Or you could have the second option of scrambled style, or an omelette. Riena had an apron with a pattern of spoons and forks. Sadly she didn't exist except as a drawing.

Nory was tall for her age, especially in the city of Threll, in England, where she and her mother, her father, and her brother, who was two, were living for a certain amount of time. There were quite a number of girls at her school, the Threll Junior School. She was hoping she would meet a good friend.

2. An Important Building

Threll Cathedral was the biggest thing in the city, by any means. It was an old cathedral that had a tower on it that had the unique ability to look close to you, and yet be very far away. Airplanes can do that, too. They seem close but aren't, unless it isn't your lucky day. Inside the cathedral was almost as beautiful as outside except that there were modern things like wires and plugs that looked as if somebody had made a careless mistake, and modern-day loudspeakers up on the columns looking pretty indistinct. There were also some big tombs carved out of a certain kind of black and red stone that was not precisely frightening but was certainly alarming, because it was so vividly black, and of course there were corpses buried here and there in the walls or in the floor, some of which might be quite mummified. Saint Rufina, a famous woman who had been a very lovely young princess with long black hair who decided to give up her jewelry and become a nun and wear only the roughest clothes, and who died in a terrible way, by being eaten to death by wild dogs that ran through the church in the dead of wintertime, was in a special chapel all to herself, where one arm of her was set aside, that someone had scooped up and saved from the dogs, because everyone had loved her for her kindness and her healing ability. Nearby her chapel was a very tall thin window with pictures of tanks and warships and bombers on it. War pictures didn't seem like a perfect idea for a subject in stained glass in a famously holy cathedral, but on the other hand if you're going to have a stained-glass tank or battleship, this was probably the most beautiful tank you would ever find. The caterpillar treads were made of tiny scribs and scrabs of green and blue glass. The window was in honor of some of the people from the city of Threll who had died at war.

Way, way up in a tower above the stone floor of the Cathedral was the Jasperium. It was a kind of a stained-glass window in the form of a dome, right over where the two pieces of the cross met. A cathedral is usually arranged in the shape of a crucifiction, because Jesus died up on the cross. 'But why,' Nory wondered sometimes, 'do they have to concentrate on the awful way he died? Why not have a cathedral in the shape of a G, for God, a squared-off G with an inner courtyard with a wishing well and herbs growing to make tea for the sick, for instance?' A thousand upon a thousand pieces of green glass were up there in the Jasperium in a little circle—a pretty big circle, actually, but it was little from the distance away you were standing when you looked up at it. When the sun was bright outside, it sent the green light down in a soft green stalk onto the

floor of the Cathedral. They had a group of black chairs
specially positioned so you could sit in a chair and wait for
the green light to come over you like a spotlight on a slug,
and supposedly at that moment you could almost think
God's thoughts. You were not really thinking God's
thoughts, of course, but the thoughts God wanted you to
think. If you didn't believe in God, you were thinking what
others thought of God, or what they thought God wanted
them to think. At least you were thinking the Cathedral's
thoughts in some fashion, which was a pretty worthwhile
thing to be able to do on its own.

3. A Story About Beetles

The owners of the Threll Cathedral, who were the
Anglican Bishops and Deans, had just spent millions of
dollars, or pounds, to clean all the glass in the Jasperium
and make sure it wasn't going to fall down. But while they
were doing that, they had discovered that Death Watch
Beetles had chewed through the lead that covered the ends
of the beams of wood that attached the Jasperium to the
tops of the stone columns. So they had to replace some of
the wood, but not all. Death Watch Beetles were called
that because in former times, when a person was very sick,
if his family heard any of these beetles banging their small
heads against the wood of a house—chk, chk, chk—it
meant the sick person would die soon. Nory, because she
wanted to be a dentist, had a specific thought about this,
which was: 'Their teeth must be extraordinarily strong to
have chewed through lead. They must be hidden away
normally and then fold out when they open their mouths.'

Crocodiles grow twenty-four sets of teeth in their lives and they can perform for two years without food. But Nory severely doubted that the Death Watch Beetle had more than one set of teeth. 'It must be a difficult way of life up there,' Nory thought, 'generation after generation of Beetle, trying to find enough to eat in the old, horrible, chewed-over wood. They must be down to the bare gristle.' Near the Cathedral was a very good tea shop that had an extremely good chocolate fudge cake. The cake was served with a little cup of whipped cream, by the way.

Nory didn't like a certain picture in one of the brochures that her parents bought about Threll Cathedral that showed a man wearing a mask putting a metal tube into one of the old pieces of wood under the Jasperium in order to squirt powerful bug-killing foam inside. She had to make up a story about a family of Death Watch Beetles who learned of the approach of a squirt of the poison and packed up their household and made little parachutes out of some candy wrappers one of the bug-killing men had left in the scaffolding and parachuted down, down, down, smuggling through the cool empty air of the inside of the cathedral, swaying, their feelers curled up tight in fear, until they landed in a huge stone land of green light on the cold floor near a little girl with bright eyes and black hair named Mariana.

Mariana was sitting with her eyes closed, waiting to see if she could think the thoughts God wanted her to think. She opened her eyes to see how close the light was to her feet, because she thought that as soon as the light touched her feet she would start to feel the sacred holiness, and she was just creeping her feet a little closer to the light, so that the holiness would get there more quickly, when she thought she noticed something. Yes, she did notice something: four tiny creatures, carefully folding up a chewing-gum wrapper. 'Oh, who are you?' she said, bending toward them and letting them hop onto her palm.

'We're Death Watch Beetles,' said one of them. 'A bad man is squirting our country full of terrible poison.'

'Oh,' said Mariana, 'he isn't a bad man, I'm sure, he just wants to be sure that the Jasperium doesn't fall down. You see, when you eat the wood, the wood becomes weaker and weaker, and finally the whole thing would turn to crumbs and fall. You wouldn't want that to happen to the Cathedral, would you?'

'Well,' grudged the Death Watch Beetle, 'if they'd just explained what the problem was, and given us another piece of wood to live in, we would have left on our own. As it is, look at little Gary, he has gotten sick from chewing on the lead.' And indeed Mariana saw that little Gary was lying on his back and he did not look at all well. He looked as pale as a bug can look, and near death. Mariana gently put all four beetles in her pencil case and walked out to the forest. She knew where a special fallen tree lay. There was a pool of rainwater in a groove of this tree, and she picked a certain kind of flower as she went, singing a mild song, and crushed the petals in the water. It was a special kind of flower that could cure any kind of lead poisoning, and it was called the Montezuma flower, because it could grow in really hot or very cold places, so that it was a great survivor. Then she opened the pencil case. The three healthy Death Watch Beetles carried Gary, the sick one, out. 'Wash him in the water,' said Mariana gently. She was a tall girl with dark brown hair. 'The potion will help him.'

At first the beetles weren't sure, and they sniffed the water and tested it with their feelers and that sort of usual behavior. Then gradually they lost their fears and dipped

Gary freely in, not head-first but gently, tail-first, and they all went in, one by one, and splashed in the water contentedly. They had spent so many centuries cooped up inside the old Norman beams of the Jasperium that they had forgotten that rainwater could be so clean and pure, and they were overjoyed. Gary sat up in the water and said he felt much better. Then all four of them found a place in a spot of sun to dry their bodies and when they were toasty and warm again, they waved goodbye, and began chewing their mazes in the huge tree trunk. 'Lovely layers of wood!' they said. 'Rings and rings and rings! It'll be a long time before we chew up this enormous country! Don't tell anyone you brought us here.'

'I won't,' laughed Mariana. 'Good luck!'

'Thank you, Mariana,' they called, giving a last happy wave. 'Bye! Bye! Bye!'

That was a story she had made about them. In real life Nory had never even seen a Death Watch Beetle. But there were definitely some unusual creatures in Threll. The worst one was a huge spider that her mother spotted in the shower curtain while Nory and Littleguy were in the bathtub setting up a store to sell pretend cappuccinos, with bubble foam. Her mother suddenly jumped up with her magazine and hurried them out and called Nory's father.

'What is it?' said Nory, who hadn't gotten a look because she was shoveled out of the bathroom so quick.

'Don't look,' said Nory's father. 'It's a loathsome Anglo-Saxon bug. It's huge.'

'I won't be disgusted,' said Nory. 'I promise, I won't be.' She peered in, then instantly wailed out in a misery of disgust and hugged her mother. 'Oh, awful!' It was an enormous thing, like a black crab, with the dastardliest hairy legs Nory had ever seen on a spider, and not like a daddy longlegs's legs, which are quite graceful, but hairy in an ugly thick fearful way. Normally Nory liked all insects, even earwigs, and especially ladybugs, and she did not appreciate any killing, because of the important rule of Do Unto Others, and how would you like it if a huge scrumple of toilet paper came down on you and stole your life away? But this spider in particular was just too hideously hairy-legged to get any empathy from her.

Nory's father came out.

'Is it dead?' they all asked.

Nory's father said that yes, it was dead.

'Good,' said Nory, although immediately she felt a little sad, not to mention embarrassed about shrieking to pieces when she saw it. 'What did you do with it?'

'Flushed it into the depths,' Nory's father said. 'The worst part is I always feel I have to open up the toilet paper to look.'

'Not to dwell,' her mother said.

That was their first adventure in Threll. Nory had some trouble sleeping for two nights, but then she got quickly over it. The only problem was that now she didn't like going to the bathroom in the middle of the night because she sometimes worried that a second-cousin-once-removed of that big black spider was lurching under the seat. But gradually she got over that worry, too. It was a wooden toilet seat—the landlady said that she had bought it for five pounds at an auction from a Stately Home, and that the Duke of Tunaparts, or someone quite obscure like that, had sat on it every day of his life, which was not really a point to its favor.

4. Littleguy Had a Sensible Fear of Owls

Nory was a day student at Threll Junior School, where she used a medium-nib fountain pen with a kind of blue ink that you could make disappear completely from the page with a two-ended instrument called an ink-eradicator. Even when the ink had had a chance to dry for three weeks, the ink-eradicator still had the power to make it disappear. Threll School was started by a kind-looking person with a fur collar whose picture hung on the stairs going up to the dining hall. Pamela Shavers, who was a girl in Nory's class, said he was called Prior Rowland because he lived prior to Henry the Eighth. The dining hall used to be the barn for the monk's cows, another older kid said, but Nory couldn't understand why the monks would have wanted to drag cows up and down stairs twice a day. Then her mother explained that they had built in a second floor when they shipped out the cows. There was still sometimes a slight barny smell about the place, though. The wood had twisting beams, like driftwood, but no Death Watch Beetles that Nory could see; of course she couldn't possibly have heard them banging their heads since kids at lunch make tons and tons of noise.

Prior Rowland began the school to honor the memory of Saint Rufina, something like two thousand years ago, or 'early this morning,' as Nory's brother used to say. Littleguy he was called, although his name was really Frank Wood Winslow. To Littleguy 'long ago' and 'early this morning' meant pretty much the same thing, because his head was still basically a construction site, filled with diggers and dumpers driving around in mushy dirt, and it was hard for him to tell what were the real outlines of his ideas. He knew how to say 'construction site,' and 'traction engine,' and 'coupling,' and 'level crossing,' and 'hundred-ton dump truck,' and 'articulated dump truck' and 'auger driller,' because he loved those sorts of things. But he sometimes held up a very simple object, like a fork or a candle, and said, 'I forgot the word for this.' And he still called a pillow a pibble. But that was a normal thing to expect, Nory thought, because you have to spend your whole life learning more and more about how to draw a difference between one idea and another idea and how to keep them separated out rather than totally dredged together in a sludgy mass. For example, if you say that you're doing something to the honor of someone's memory, say to the honor of Saint Rufina's memory, you don't mean that you're honoring the wonderful memory they might have, as in they can dash off the names of every kid in the class by heart, because they don't have any memories at all, since they're dead. And you don't mean that they have wonderful happy memories of picnics and chicken sandwiches and feeding the ducks that you're honoring, because they don't have those, either. You can't mummify a nice memory in someone's head—no magic herbs will do it. And you don't mean you're honoring any particular other person's memories of the person that is being honored, because the people who are honoring him may not even have known him or met him. Or her, in the case of Saint Rufina. You're just simply honoring the basic idea that this person once lived her life and you're trying to convince the world not to forget her. But any person who remembers her is going to die also, obviously, so you have to keep convincing people from scratch—'Remember this person, remember this person, remember this person.' It isn't easy, but it may be satisfying work.

Littleguy liked having Nory read books to him. However, she had to be careful about certain books. He was not frightened of spiders so much. But owls were a different bowl of fish! To him the nighttime was full of owls rustling and blinking their huge staring eyes. In Nory's house, they couldn't even say 'owl,' they had to spell it out. When Nory read Littleguy a book like *The Country Noisy Book* and they came to the page with an o-w-l sitting in a tree at nighttime, she would bustle to the next page. If she tried to casually cover the owl up with her hand, it never worked, because he knew it was under there. Sometimes Littleguy would try to be brave. 'I like owls very much,' he would say. 'But I don't like just *that* owl.'

Once Nory's mother found Littleguy in the Art Room late at night trying to color over the yellow eyes of a scary owl with a red marker, because he didn't like coming across it in his *Winnie the Pooh* magazine, which he had been flipping through before he fell asleep. Another time he told Nory that two very bad owls were wanting to look in his window, behind the curtain. When Nory heard that, with the frightened seriousness on his face, she also felt a little twizzle of fear down the back of her neck and places like that, because she especially did not like the idea of things waiting outside for her and staring in through blank, black windowpanes at night. The first and one of the few early, early things she remembered about her life was of running down a long hall and stopping at the edge of a window. Then bang: she thought she saw the ugliness of the Tweety Monster with its frown-eyed face, on the other side of the window, and she screamed 'Mommeeeee!' The Tweety Monster was just simply a monster version of Tweety-bird in a *Sylvester and Tweety* tape—Tweety turned into it when he drank a special potion. No reason to be scared of a casual little cartoon. But it *was* scary, and when Nory screamed and dashed away from the window Nory's mother said gently, 'I know, I know, but it's just drawings. There's no Tweety Monster out there, no bad thing, only the gentle night and the squirrels all fluffed up to keep from getting too cold, and the raccoons having a pleasant chew of garbage. Everything's all right.' Her mother's eyes were the most soothing, nicest, softest, deepest eyes that any mother could ever have. They were, to be specific, blue. Sometimes instead of two owls Littleguy had a bad dream about two old, old trucks from the scrapyard with huge tires driving around the living room with their bright lights on. And yet in real life, Littleguy loved trucks more than anything, except trains. One time Littleguy even said he had a nightmare about sitting on the toilet and not having a book to read.

That was one thing that Nory really thought was not quite fair about bad dreams, when they went ahead and took something you loved, like trucks, or mirrors, or your mother, or were proud of, like sitting in the bathroom all by yourself, and made them scary. If Nory had a library, she would not allow any Goosebumps books in the children's department, because just the covers were frightening, never mind the dreadful insides, and kids weren't even aware how frightened they were sometimes until later that evening. There was one book with a picture of an evil doll that she really thought was a bad idea. Why ruin the idea of something nice, like a doll, by making it so horribly scary that you couldn't think about it and couldn't trust it? Your dolls aren't going to do anything bad to you. Your dolls should be trusted to be in your room with you in the middle of the night. Goosebumps books got kids much more scared than they ever wanted to be, or ever expected they would be, and they didn't need that help anyway, since their own dreams would do a superb job of scaring their dits off just on their own. But still, Nory's cousin Anthony and her friend Debbie loved reading Goosebumps books and couldn't think of a funner thing to do. So not everyone had the same reaction.

Nory especially disliked when she had teeth-dreams. Say, for example, a beautiful graceful fluffer-necked duck that was just sitting away the time in the reeds by a river, its feathers being fluttered by the wind, and when you came up to it in the dream to hold out your hand to it to say hello and give it a piece of bread it would suddenly curl back its beaks and show huge fangy teeth. Or a horse with pointy teeth and bug-eyes with white rims would chase her. Or cows with pointed teeth. But those dreams were mostly ones she'd had long ago and gotten adjusted to. Another fairly old dream Nory had was of being chased through various shades of colors by a queen who was determined to cut off her arm for a punishment. Nory dashed away from her, but the Queen came chugging closer, with some of her men, and Nory realized she couldn't escape. So she made them a compromise. She said to the Queen, 'Okay, okay, don't chop off my arm, you can chop off my head.' That way, she wouldn't experience the pain. The Queen said, 'All right!' And *wham*, the ax came circling. 'Ah, how nice,' Nory felt. She didn't have to bow or anything. She didn't even have to put a paper bag over her head.

The moral of the dream was: Better to be dead than armless in agony. It wasn't a perfect moral, though, Nory thought afterward, even for a dream—which isn't too surprising since it's too much to expect of your dreams that they would end up giving off good morals—but really, you can learn to do almost everything you would need to do without arms: play cards with your toes, and that kind of thing. You might hesitate for a moment if your dentist wanted to work on your mouth holding the tools in his toes, true. That might not be the world's most raging success.

5. A Slight Problem After Lunch

At least if Nory had a bad dream she could go into her parents' room and poke at them gently until they woke up enough to comfort her back down. Not every kid had that kind of luck. Some of the kids at Threll School were there all day and all night, twenty-four hours a week. Roger Sharpless was a very short boy with an intelligent face like a detective who cried on the first day in the Cathedral during service during the first week. 'Why are you crying?' Nory asked, in a whisper. 'Sometimes I cry during the day,' he whispered back. Afterward, when they were walking to the Junior School building, he said that he missed his parents horribly. He said that the sight of the little white pillow on his bed in his room reminded him of his old room and that made him cry, because think about it, going away from everything you know, your rugs, your windows, your parents, your driveway, your exact look of street, can be quite a shock to a nine-year-old. He also told her a fact that he said he would never forget in his whole life, because he had gotten it wrong on a test one time: the Greeks wrote by making marks on wax. Nory felt that it was kind of him to tell her, because now she would never forget it either.

The day after that she had a much less good experience. She dropped her tray in the dining hall when it was full of fresh food. Kira, one of her new sort-of friends, said, 'Oh, don't worry, somebody else will get it.' But Nory didn't feel right about leaving the mess in a lavish plop on the floor and walking on. The jacket potato did not look its best. An older girl scooped down to help her, and finally a woman came by with a mop. But by then all the other kids from her class had gone off and were eating merrily along, chew chew chew, getting far ahead of her. Not only that, but the line had gotten very long, because a whole conjugation of older boys had come in. She didn't want to cut in, so she went to the back and waited all over again. The line was so long it even went down a few steps of the stairs, which gave her a chance to look at Prior Rowland's fur collar.

Finally she got a new tray of food, and she sat anonymously down. People in her class were leaving to go back to the Junior School building. One after another they were going. Nory had her eye on them the whole time, except when she was looking down at her plate. She thought, 'Ah, but she's still there, so it's okay.' And then when that girl left, she said to herself, 'Ah, well, *she's* still there, so when worse goes to worse, I can go back with her.' The problem was that the Junior School was far away from the dining hall, across two streets, and Nory had an awful if not atrocious sense of direction and knew she would never find it by herself. So she ate and ate and finished up and whammed out the door of the dining hall, hurrying to be with a girl who was in her class. Dorette was her name. Dorette said, 'Sorry I can't talk, I'm meeting a friend.'

Nory said, 'Oh, okay.' The other girl came up. It was a girl Nory didn't like very much because she had said that Nory had a 'squeegee' accent on one of the first days of school. Nory stood a little way behind and started following them as they went around the buildings toward the old gate.

Dorette turned and said, 'Go away. Why are you following us?'

'Because I don't know the way home,' said Nory.

'Home? Home?' the girls said.

'I mean, the way back to the class,' said Nory.

'Oh, go on, you know the way,' the two girls said. 'You lead us, and we'll follow.'

So Nory started tenderly walking in front of them down the street, not vastly sure she was pointing in the right direction. There was a road curving up a hill that didn't look familiar. There were no crosswalks. She turned around and noticed that the girls weren't behind her. She started to feel scattered and scared. Then the two girls jumped out from behind a bush with red berries and laughed. She started following them again, and they told her to go away. Fortunately just at that point a teacher came out from a door in the building and the two girls said, all nicey-nicey, 'Hello Mr. So-and-so.' They began chatting with him. Nory was worried that they would tell the teacher that she had been following them and she would get in trouble, but they didn't. So she could sneak along, pace by pace, some distance behind, from bush to bush. That was how she was able to get back. Later that day, on the playground, another girl said, 'Hah-hah, you were sent back, you were sent back.' Nory had no idea what the girl was talking about, so she said, 'What are you talking about?'

'For dropping your tray,' the girl said. Nory said, 'I was not. I went to the end of the line because you shouldn't cut in. And I'm from America. We don't say *sent back* in

America to mean what you mean. We don't say *bin* in America, we say trashcan. We don't say *crayons* when we're talking about colored pencils, we skip to the case and say *colored pencils*. Got it?'

The girl made a rabbit-nibbling face and shuffled off to Buffalo.

In history class that day, the teacher was talking about the Crusades, and he suddenly said, in the weirdest cowboy accent you ever heard, 'And they went in, shootin' and hollerin' and plunderin' up tarnation, by golly.' Then he said to Nory, 'I'm sorry. I should have asked your permission first. Do you mind if I make fun of the way Americans talk?'

Nory said, 'If you think that's the way Americans talk, go right ahead.'

The teacher said, 'Thank you. And I give you permission to call us limeys whenever you like.'

'Thank you,' said Nory. 'But why would I want to say that?'

'In the States, that's what you call us, is it not?' said the teacher.

'I don't know, but I don't think so,' said Nory. 'What are limeys?'

'Ah, they're an ancient seafaring people who eat limes on shipboard to keep their teeth from falling out,' said Mr. Blithrenner.

6. Be Careful About Fluoride

Besides History, there was I.T., which were the initials of Information Technology, where they were learning the middle row of letters on the keys of the Acorn computers. And there was French, and Geography, and Music, and Netball, and Hockey, and other classes, too. There were a surprising amount of teachers at Threll School all together. Even the headmaster of the Junior School was the teacher of a class called Classics. He started off one class by reading in a deep, roly-poling voice about the trickles of blood of the Trojans mixing with the muddy water that collected in pools at the base of the walls of the ruined city. It turned out to be the story of Hercules. Or, not Hercules precisely, but someone with a name quite a bit like Hercules, although it wasn't Hector either. Anyway, whoever he was, he was dipped in magical waters when he was a baby except for where he was held by his ankle.

A few days after that, the headmaster spoke to the whole Junior School in Hendall Hall, which was the place the whole school got together, except when they went to Cathedral once a week. He told them about a painter who had not believed in himself and had been so hungry that he had squeezed tubes of oil paint into his mouth. The paint had lead in it, and it affected his brain in a negative way, and soon enough he gruesomely shot himself in the chest. Now his paintings were worth millions of dollars, which would probably be billions of yen.

Kids want to eat lead because it tastes sweet, Nory knew, which is also why they want to eat toothpaste. You're only supposed to put a pea-sized amount of toothpaste on your toothbrush but many kids put more. Nory thought that what they should make is a tube of toothpaste that squirts out green until you've squirted out just the right amount, and if you try to squeeze more out after that, the color turns red, meaning stop: Green light, red light. If you eat too much toothpaste, the fluoride in it will turn your teeth gray, but there was a kid at the Junior School who had a bad cavity or some sort of medical thing gone wrong in one of his pointy side teeth, one of the bicuspids maybe, that made it completely gray 'from smokebox to buffer,' as Littleguy would say. You only saw it when his mouth made a malicious laugh, as in 'Hah-hah-hah, hah-hah-hah, I'm going to revenge myself on you for that!' If that boy, who was really a fairly nice boy, had had a sweet tooth and eaten tube after tube of toothpaste, that same tooth would be just as gray as it was now, but he wouldn't have the cavity to worry about, and the rest of his teeth would match the color exactly so it would blend in and wouldn't be so noticeable. Nory's own teeth were sometimes a little yellow, she thought, but then she went on a rampage brushing them individually one by one and got them to look pretty white. They looked white in photographs, anyway, which made her happy.

The moral of the story about the child who was dipped in magical water was: nobody is one hundred percent immortal. Except God, for those who believed in God. The moral of the story about the painter was: you never know who will be famous and talented, so try not to get discouraged, and don't allow handguns. The moral of the story about gray teeth was: sometimes by trying to do a good thing, you do a bad thing instead.

7. Fables in the Car

Aesop's fables were where the idea of having a moral came from, but some of them made no sense whatever. Before bed, Nory's parents read to her in alternation with each other, so one night her mother would read something, the next night her father. That first week of September, while Nory was listening to her mother read *A Hundred and One Dalmations,* she was listening to her father read Aesop's *Fables.* He very often fell asleep a few minutes into reading. You could tell he was beginning a doze because he would start pronouncing the words in a hurrying murmur and then stop. Murmur, then stop, murmur, stop. And phrases would get into the story that had nothing to do with anything. If Nory gave him a nudge in the arm, he would bob awake and squinch his eyes shut very tight and flare them open them very wide and forge off into another page. Then very gradually his voice would fall away into a mutter again. 'Seward's folly hima hima hima cartouche hima hima Barcelona hima hima hima.' Sometimes he read for pages that way, it was really quite remarkable, mixing giblet after giblet of totally unrelated nonsense into the story. 'And the canisters could use some priming,' is something that he said one time, in the middle of the story of the crow and the stones. Nory wrote it down and told them all at breakfast. If the story was good, Nory's father didn't fall asleep nearly as fast as if the story was going through a boring stretch. Then the nudging didn't work and she finally had to say, 'Daddy, you're tired, aren't you?'

'How did you guess that?' Nory's father would ask, from deep in his doze.

'Well, for one thing, the book seemed to be flopping.'

'Was it flopping?'

'Yes, it was.'

And then Nory's father would say, 'Well, I guess that just about wraps it up,' and shut the book and say goodnight. The next time that it was his turn to read, he wouldn't remember any of what he had already read, and he would go through several pages, saying 'Did we read that? Did we read that?' Nory usually could remember because she had a not-too-shabby memory for things that were read to her. It was very rare for Nory's mother to fall asleep reading to Nory. Sometimes Nory almost fell asleep when she was reading to her dolls but almost never when she was being read to.

One night Nory's father managed to read three Aesop's fables in a row that just weren't up to sniff. Aesop had had a very bad fable-writing day. Maybe the wax wasn't smooth enough for him to concentrate. Nory's father fell asleep after about ten minutes of reading and slept until Nory's mother woke him up by coming in to give Nory a K and H and a G of W. That anagram stood for a 'Kiss and a Hug and a Glass of Water.' The next day, they drove to Wisbech to see Peckover House, a Stately Home, and on the way Nory had the idea of getting each one of them to think up a fable, as something to do in the car.

Her mother's fable was about an ivy plant that overdoes himself and stays green year round, even through the freezing snows of winter. First he was evergreen for the pure joy of it, and then he was a little less happy and a little more bitter because the other plants failed to follow his lead of staying green and even made little jokes about the ivy plant and his odd winter habits. Finally the ivy got so upset with the rest of the garden for sleeping through the lonely cold months that his anger made his leaves turn brown at the edges and his tendrils stop uncurling. The gardener, who was used to his being green and healthy all year, pulled him up by the roots and threw him in the compost dump. And the moral was: Stay out of politics.

Nory's father's fable was about a cat who loved tuna catfood in cans and refused to eat the whitefish or the beef or the liver in cans, even though he was starvingly hungry, in order to try to force the girl who cared for him to give him tuna every day. The girl got so worried about the cat's not eating that she took him to the vet. The vet said he was healthy, but he said that she must feed him only dry catfood from now on. And the moral was: He who wants only tuna, may end up with only dry.

Nory's fable was about two Korean girls. Once there were two little Korean girls. Their parents had died in a car accident, because the ambulance had not had the Jaws of Life to use to save them. The Jaws of Life are, as you know, huge scissors that can cut through metal and pull an injured person from a car. So the poor, tired little girls were sent to an orphanage. There they put up signs that said 'Help!' because they were treated very badly. Seeing their signs, a kind woman, who wanted so much to have a little girl, adopted them. They were very grateful. But one day the mother, whose name was Nanelan, had to go to a different country to the Queen's birthday party. She asked the only couple she could get in touch with to watch her children. But she did not know that these were evil people. The first day she was gone they spilled a puddle of water to make the children slip and hurt themselves and go to the hospital, so that they would not have to pay for the children's food. The next night the couple, dancing with evil joy, fell into the puddle. Hearing this, the insurance company refused to pay the hospital, and the couple lost all the money. And the moral is: Do not be selfish or your curse will come back.

They asked Littleguy for a fable, too. He came up with two. His first fable was called 'Bulldozer.' Once upon time was a train. A train on a track. It saw a diesel train coming

on the track, too, and they crashed. The two went *kssssh!*
All the pieces came off they. The puff-puff broke, and the
wheels broke, and the track broke. Everything broke. But
they went to the shop and got fixed and they got painted,
and went to the station and people came on them and they
set off. The end.

Littleguy's second fable was called 'Browned.' Once
upon time was a bulldozer, pulling a trailer filled with all
kinds of choo-choos, digger-trucks, and auger drillers, and
dump trucks. And the other ones that have round things,
cement mixers. The bulldozer saw a car pulling a trailer by
it. And they didn't crash, they just went right by they. The
bulldozer drove and drove and drove and drove and drove
and drove and drove. The bulldozer's name was Browned.
The end.

Since there were no morals in Littleguy's two fables,
Nory added them on. The moral of the first fable was:
sometimes when there's a crash, it turns out all right in the
end. And the moral of the second one was: sometimes
things don't even crash at all.

At Peckover House, Nory got a National Trust eraser
from the gift shop after they had tea.

8. *About Debbie*

Nory was proudly born in Boston, Massachusetts, in
America. A lot of houses looked like Peckover House in
Boston. Boston was old in a beautiful way and it was
especially important to Nory because it was frankly the
only city she had ever lived in, except Venice for three

weeks when she was three years old, where she was baptized with a surprising splash of water in a huge cold church, holding her own candle, that later got broken and had to be thrown out even though it was wrapped in tissue paper. In Venice she also ate pitch-black spaghetti. The black was squid ink and it was quite good. Long ago, they used to use squid ink to make real ink, for using in Medium Nib fountain pens, but probably it would make a kind of ink that no ink eradicator would eradicate. Ink eradicators were made from pigskin and pig-waste, according to a girl at Threll Junior School, who said her sister once visited an eradicator factory.

Threll was just a town, not a city, and Palo Alto, California, was just a town, too, although it had quite a seedy neighborhood in the way that real cities do. You might imagine a French person going around Palo Alto, California, with an American person. The American would say, 'As you will notice, there are some seedy areas.' The French person would say, in his very strong French accent, 'Oh, is this—city area?' Pronouncing it of course the way the French teacher at the Junior School pronounced it. And the American would misunderstand and say sadly, 'Yes, I'm afraid it is seedy. There's just no getting around it.' Maybe that's how the idea that cities were seedy came about, if it happened quite a number of times. Also when people don't cut their grass, it grows so long that it shoots out a tassel of seeds, which was a sign that the people in that house didn't care about their yard. Maybe they were caring for a sick person who was cooped up in the house, or maybe they were busy giving themselves shots of drugs and alcohol and didn't have the energy to walk out their front door and cut the grass. That's another way the idea that cities were seedy could have come about.

Nory's favorite street in Palo Alto had a number of stores on it, including the toy store. Nory spent half an hour there one Saturday in the summer while Littleguy played with the breakdown train at the Thomas the Tank Engine table. She looked through every one of the Barbie outfits, because her new best friend, Debbie, said she liked Barbies with black hair and blue dresses. Debbie had given Nory a friendship locket to celebrate that they were new best friends, and Nory was extremely happy about that and wanted to give Debbie a Barbie from money she earned selling hand-lettered signs to her parents. She looked and looked, and finally tucked away behind a whole lot of other outfits she found a dark blue Barbie dress with lighter blue sparkles on the front, and she hung it back on the hook as the very first one and went to get her mother. When she came back, though, another girl was there with *her* mother, and the girl was holding the blue dress outfit in her hand. Nory stood there and tried her best to hint by the sad hopeless way she was flopping her arms and looking at the blue dress in the girl's hand that she had just spent a whole half an hour going through every outfit to find it, but the girl and her mother ignored her, or didn't know what she was flopping about, and she didn't want to say anything, because of course the girl had found it all by herself, it's just that the girl wouldn't have had hardly a chance of finding it if Nory hadn't found it and put it on top where it got the special feeling of being the first outfit on display.

They went to another toy store a week later, but there were no blue dresses that were right. Blue was not in fashion at that moment. So Nory got Debbie a tiny glass panda bear posed on a branch, all made of droops of light blue glass, because Debbie was devoted to pandas and had about thirty of them in her room. Nory wrote Debbie a letter soon after they came to England that said:

Dear Debbie,
How ary you? How is your school? I went to the Fitz Willyham museum, where there was a fan room, and there is a fan launguage for things you're not allowed to say in public if you place the fan behind your head it means 'Don't forget me'! There was a fan that I preticularly liked, It is made from coal and mother of peal. I went to Pecover House, but I think it should be famous for its garden more than the house. It has a wunderful statue of a girl and a dog made from stone, and a green house with a fern that will crumple-up when you touch it. I miss you and your dog Sharpy, how is that shoe consuming feind? I hope to be seing you again soon. Love Eleanor PS Please write back.

She drew a picture of a girl holding a fan behind her head at the bottom of the letter.

The best dream Nory had ever had was about Debbie. Nory had died, although she didn't come to that conclusion until a different part of the dream. She whispered in Debbie's ear, 'Debbie, Debbie, it's me.' Debbie recognized Nory's voice and looked up. Debbie had a very wide face, and she could get a look that was kind of still, kind of unnerved. Her mouth looked bigger because her lips were over the wiring of her braces. She made that unnerved look at Nory. She said, 'Nory! Nory! Is that you?' She recognized Nory's voice, even though she couldn't see her.

'Don't worry, Debbie,' said Nory, in a calm gentle voice. 'Don't be scared. I would be too if I were you.' Debbie seemed calmer. Nory showed her the newspaper, which said on the front page ELEANOR DIES IN A FIRE. Not her family, not anyone else. Later on in the dream Nory said Boo to Garrick, a kid in her class, sort of fakily: 'Garrick? Boooooo!'

Garrick said, 'No way, she can't be a ghost, she's dead already.'

'Oh, yes I can!' said Nory and fumed out in her full ghostiness. Garrick started running out of fear and tripped. That was funny because Garrick was a ten-year-old and usually extremely confident and pleased with himself and made fun of Nory's spelling, which wasn't very good. In fact it was a 'bosaster,' as Littleguy would say. But the wonderful part of the dream was when Debbie looked up, hearing the voice, and knew it was Nory nearby her.

9. A Strange Vegetable

'It's sometimes kind of impressive,' Nory thought, 'to try to envision how many bricks there are in a city.' You could tell a city was old by the colors and crookedness of its bricks. In Boston Nory noticed that usually the bricks were red, but in Threll they were usually, not to be disrespectful, kind of a dirty yellow, and they were even less straight than in Boston. You wouldn't expect dirty yellow crooked bricks to look pretty, but they did, especially where you could see places in the walls where there had been old windows or old doorways that had been stuffed with other bricks and stones and pieces of old buildings.

That was what a certain memory that you had forgotten felt like—you knew that a window had been there but it wasn't now, just an old brick wall, so you couldn't see through it. There was a very tall brick wall around the garden of the Bishop's Palace at Threll, with pointy stones on top, so that the poor people couldn't sneak in at night and steal the cauliflowers, which might have looked tempting in the moonlight to a very hungry mouthwatering person of long ago. At Waitrose, the supermarket, they sold darling little dwarf cauliflowers in the 'Dwarf Food' section. It wouldn't be called dwarf food in America because that would hurt the feelings of a real dwarf, who would feel not too pleased about being compared to a vegetable.

Waitrose also sold a mysteriously pointy green plant, halfway between a cauliflower and a pine tree, called a Romanesco. Nory's mother said that 'Gothico' would be a better name for it. It was intended to be eaten for dinner, but it looked like a screensaver on Nory's mother's computer called 'Permafrost II.' 'Worms' was the neatest of all the screensavers, though.

Nory gave the Romanesco to the Cathedral to be a part of the arrangement that was done by Threll School in the South Door, for the Harvest Festival. Kids had carried in carrots in bunches, and zucchini, which were called courgettes in Threll, and broccoli, apples, and sugar beets. But luckily nobody else in the school had given a Romanesco, which made hers easy to see. Nory's father took three pictures of Nory in her school jacket and tie standing to one side of an open bag of potatoes. The potatoes were shaped just like the stones they put on either side of a lot of the sidewalks in Cambridge to remind your feet in a polite way that you were getting close to the grass. Cambridge was, as you may know, where you go to get a Ph.D. After they went to the Fitzwilliam Museum, in Cambridge, Nory told herself a story in the car, holding one of her dolls.

10. The Story of the Fan

One day, there was a little tiny baby. She was born too early, so she was really, really tiny. She should have gone into an incubator, but her parents weren't rich enough, so she couldn't. They just had to raise her as being a really, really small little person. She had a big soft-spot because she was so early. And her umbilical was too long. And so on. She was, on the whole, too small. Just a tiny little person.

When she was about three weeks old, she could already do her grasping. She couldn't really turn yet, but she could turn her head, ever so slightly. She turned her head ever so slightly. She could almost grasp. She couldn't have handled it yet, because that would be just impossible, so amazing that it would be a fairy tale, which this is, of course, but she seemed to be trying to grab for her mother's fan. And ever since, she seemed to be totally interested in fans. Just completely interested in them. Her parents named her Colander.

When Colander was full grown, she was a midget, because she was just a tiny person. When she was twelve, the tallest she ever was, she was as tall as Frank is. She was really short. So one day—it was really hard for her to go to school and museums and because people might tease her because she was so short—but one day they went to a museum. It had a lot of different things in it, china and armor and sculpture. They wandered here and there. She said: 'I see that dark room. What's in that dark room?'

They went into the dark room she had looked at. And there were the most beautiful fans that she had ever seen. So many different kinds, shapes, sizes. In the corner of each glass case was a little yellow box of some kind of mold killer to keep all the fans from being eaten by a strong fan-eating fungus.

But the fan that really caught her eye was one that was carved from mother-of-pearl, when you opened it up. When you closed it, it had beautiful ivory carvings of children, and then the ivory was put on top of jade. And there was beautiful gold-plating, where the hair of anything would be. For instance, if there was the hair of a mother it was gold-plated, all the hair was true gold plate. And there were also some diamonds put here and there on the fan. There were many other fine fans in the room, but that one was her total favorite.

She wanted most of all in the world to have it. She wanted to start a collection, and she wanted that fan in the centerpiece of it. That was all she wanted. She thought about fans, she drew pictures of the fan, in school she doodled 'fan' on her hand when she'd gotten totally bored with the conversation the teacher was giving to them. It was a long conversation in Latin and she hadn't been studying Latin all that carefully because she was thinking about the fan. The fan was what entertained her.

They went back to the museum on her birthday. Her parents asked, 'Is it possible, you know, to get a model of that fan?'

The museum people said, 'Oh, well, I'm sure we can have a model made.' The owner of the museum was really really nice.

Her parents said, 'Yes, but we don't have much money.'

And the museum man said, 'Oh well, it's only fifteen dollars.'

Colander heard that and said, 'Wait, I have fifteen dollars, I've been saving my allowance to get the real one, but now that you say it's only fifteen dollars, I happen to have fifteen dollars!'

'No, no, that was your allowance,' her parents said.

'No, I want to,' Colander said, 'I'll get the money.'

So she paid the museum the fifteen dollars.

But her parents said, 'No, no, no, little child, you shouldn't be spending your own money, it's your birthday present, we should get it for you as a birthday present.'

'You can get me other things,' said Colander, 'but I'll pay for this.' Because she knew that her parents really didn't have very very much money. She had tried to save up fifteen dollars for ages. She was only given about a nickel each time she completed her work, a nickel or two.

Anyway, Colander forked him the fifteen dollars the next day, and he—the museum owner—said, 'Oh thank you very much, but you should have this. I can see that this is well-earned money. You should have it. I'll give the fan to you free as grass, for your good work.'

Colander said, 'Oh no, you shouldn't. Keep it, keep it.'

Finally, after a lot of persuading, the museum man got Colander to keep the fifteen dollars. So he was actually giving her this wonderful thing free. 'I'll give it as my own birthday present for you,' he said. And so he had a duplicate fan made, in a factory in Bombay, and it was to some people even more beautiful than the first. It was so gorgeous you wouldn't believe it.

The museum owner was exceptionally rich. He was very, very rich. So this was nothing to him. 'Pshaw. Oh, just a thousand dollars, pshaw.' So he spent a ton of money making this one tiny little fan. He put it in a box, wrapped it up, very very nicely, and wrote 'For Colander, from Mr. Harvonsay.' And on her birthday Mr. Harvonsay looked in the phone book and found their address, and said, 'Is this little Miss Colander's house?'

Colander said, 'Yes it is.'

So he gave her the little box.

'Oh, great,' she said. 'Oh, thank you.'

She opened all her parents' presents, and they were excited to see what was in the little box wrapped so neatly, so her mother said, 'Now open the little box.'

Everything she'd gotten up till then was a fan to put in her collection. In the box from Mr. Harvonsay was the fan. Everyone gasped out loud, it was so superb. Then her parents said, 'Oh, and one more present for you.' In her room there was a glass case and little stands to put fans in. She had a whole little mini fan collection of her own.

She was very happy, but the glass case had to be very low, or she'd have to tell her parents where to put everything in it, because she was short. Her parents were relatively short, but they weren't as short as she was. And so, the end.

11. Feeding the Swans

As for the Bishop's Palace garden, across the street from the Cathedral, it was definitely not owned by a Bishop in the Catholic Religion. Nory was a Catholic because her mother was a Catholic, and Nory's mother was a Catholic because her father was a Catholic, and her father was a Catholic because his mother was a Catholic, or had been.

They only went to church on rare times, but they said grace every single night. If it had been a Bishop in the Catholic Religion—which was one of the most popular religions of the world, though Christianity was probably slightly more popular—there wouldn't be a huge garden hidden out of sight, because Catholic bishops would devote all their money to the church and pray the day away, and care for the poor, and wash the poor's wounds with hot rags. No huge grand house, and no greedy high brick wall for a Catholic Bishop.

The way you make bricks is by baking them like brownies in an oven, or pouring the mixture into thousands of small molds and drying the shapes in the sun if you don't expect it to rain terribly much where you live. If it does rain and you haven't baked your bricks, you may end up with drooping walls. The bricks that are used to build a brick oven must get so totally baked into brickness that they almost can't bear it another minute, since they heat up, on one side, that is, every time they bake the bricks inside, hundreds of times over, like a drip of black cheese in the microwave.

Brick is a good word for bricks because it has the sound of the sharp, crunchy edge in it, pulling across. They were looking into Force and Friction in Nory's science class at the Junior School, and finding out that a brick creates a ton of friction. Ricki Ticki Tavi, the mongoose who saved the little boy, got his name from the rick-ticking sounds he made. Near the end, when Ricki Ticki disappears down the hole with Nagaina, the Queen Cobra, with 'his little white teeth clenched into her tail'—animals often had surprisingly white teeth—you're supposed to think that he might be dead. Usually with a story there is a moment at which you're supposed to think some person or animal has died or some other really sad failure has happened—and if you don't know that that's how stories are supposed to work you can become quite upset and have to run out of the room to escape the squeezing feeling in your chest, like at the end of *Lady and the Tramp,* when the movie tries its hardest to make you think the old dog who couldn't smell very well anymore had gotten run over by a carriage-wheel and died.

But the time of worrying that Rikki Tikki is dead didn't last quite long enough, in Nory's opinion. It could have lasted a little longer, and since they're supposed to be having a terrible battle down in the hole you need some sign that something's going on down there, like little faint struggling sounds, or every so often a whiffle of dirt flying out of the hole.

The other small problem with the story—not that there are any real problems with the story, it's a good story by a man who lived in Africa for many years, not an African American man but just a man who lived there, or somewhere like Africa—but it's sad to think of such a likable mongoose eating holes in the baby cobra eggs. The baby cobras hadn't killed anything or frightened anyone. They would when they hatched out, because that's what cobra snakes are designed to do naturally. But a story should not have a small, tiny, curled-up barely alive animal be killed unless it has done a terrible thing, which it can't have done because it hasn't even uncurled itself from the egg. And the story isn't about what cobras do naturally, anyway, since it has the cobras speaking. In real life they don't speak, at least in English. A cobra couldn't call itself 'Nag' or 'Nagaina' because the cobra's tongue is so thin it couldn't make an N sound. A cobra would probably just call itself 'Lah,' if anything.

The swans on the river made a pretty frightening sound when Nory fed them. They came up out of the water and started walking toward her, shrugging up their wings, and no matter how many pieces of bread she threw their way, they kept coming towards her, because they wanted the bigger piece of bread in her hand. When Nory said, 'Hold your horses, back up, back up!' they opened their beaks and made a nasty sound, like a hissing cat. Their necks were like cobra necks, somewhat. Nory's father was alarmed and didn't want to feed them anymore and was shooing them away with his briefcase, but it wasn't fair, Nory thought, that just because a bird was somewhat alarming he should not be fed, whereas the ducks, which weren't alarming, should be fed. There was a group of ducks that were so cute, a mother and about fifteen babies, each with a dear fluff of brown on its head. They crossed the street, just like in *Make Way for Ducklings*, which was the first book Nory ever read. Nory gave them some crackers. A girl at the Junior School, Kira, who was turning out to be a nice friend, said that her parents didn't let her feed the birds any bread, because it wasn't what they would normally eat if they were wild. Nory told her that she fed the birds sesame crackers, at least sometimes, and sesames are seeds and birds eat seeds. But both the ducks and the swans ate grass. There was a lot of grass-eating, which wasn't very natural either, because there didn't used to be so much grass in the world.

There was a lot of attention paid to grass in England. Cows used to keep it short, long ago, but now they used lawn mowers, of course. Sometimes they mowed it very short in a crisscross, so that it looked like a plaid cloth. One large field below the cathedral near Nory's school was totally bare earth, because they were putting in new grass.

One day when she was walking home with her mother they saw five men walking in a row on this field. Each man had a big white plastic thing attached around his waist, like a drum in a marching band in a parade, and they reached into their drums and got handfuls of grass seed and threw it out over the brown field. Nory's mother thought it was a beautiful sight, and it was. There were some interesting holes in one of the fields they used for sports at Junior School, but nobody seemed to know what was inside them. Not cobras and mongooses, but you never know. You don't want to reach your hand down in there. Even if you poke a stick in, sharp teeth could suddenly grab the stick, which would be startling. In some fields, people might have been buried there long ago. For instance near the South Door of the Cathedral it was now all grass, but in the map of the way the Cathedral was during Prior Rowland's lifetime it said 'Monks Graves.' Did they move the monks, or just forget about them?

12. *Ladybugs, Butterflies, and a Hurt Thumb*

Nory used to not like the idea of burying people terribly much. Now she had come to gripes with it as a fact of life. When she was four she dictated a letter that her father typed out for her:

> To Whom it May Concern:
>   Eleanor Winslow does not want to be buried under the ground.
>
> > Sincerely,
> > Eleanor Winslow.

She scribbled a fake signature, since at the time she had not known how to write, and she put a stamp on the piece of paper and scribbled on the stamp and it looked official. When her hermit crab lost all its claws one by one, very forlornly, and died only a few weeks after they got her, Nory buried her with a grave marker that said:

TO HERMIONE
Soon Gone

She wanted a dog or a rabbit or a kitten, anything warm-blooded, except possibly a cow, but her parents said that they couldn't have one for various reasons.

The field at the school that Nory used for hockey had no holes at all, whatsoever, because it was made of Astroturf. There was lots of sand sprinkled in the Astroturf. Nobody knew why. If you were an animal, digging a hole, and you dug and dug and then dug up to the surface intending to make a South Door for your hole, and you came up under the Astroturf, you would be pretty unhappy about having done all that work for nothing. Maybe there were dead monks under there. Once Nory found a ladybug in the Astroturf and carried it to the edge, and set it on a leaf. That was on a fairly embarrassing day, the second time they played hockey, when Nory's skirt fell off twice. Luckily hockey was all girls. And another girl had the same problem, too. While Nory was carrying the ladybug off the field, she was worried that it would fly off. If it flew off, it might just land in more Astroturf, where it couldn't live.

Nory said to it, very confidentially, 'Don't fly yet, Ladybug. Ladybug, if you try to fly, I'm going to have to confiscate your ability of flying. I can't confiscate you, but I can cup my hand over you and confiscate your ability of flying.' Confiscate was a word she'd learned from a boy who walked back with her from lunch one day. He said that it was a good thing she wasn't in Five-K, because in Five-K the teacher was awful. If you write in pencil and you were supposed to write in pen, or do something of that level of badness, the teacher would confiscate your pencil and tell you she was going to give it back the next day, and then she never gave it back. The boy said he stole his pencil back. He said, 'And rightly stole it!' He opened up the teacher's drawer and had to fumble through it to find his pencil because it was bursting at the gills with confiscated things.

Ladybugs are very useful bugs because they eat aphids. Nory used to think, 'Poor little aphids.' But aphids eat the ladybugs' eggs, so ladybugs have a right to hate them. It was something a little like Rikki Tikki Tavi and the snake. Nory's mother said that when a gardener bought a whole jug of ladybugs they had to let them out at night so they don't know where they are and settle down with those particular aphids as their enemy. Otherwise they might try to escape to the other aphids, which they know better and hate more, because those were the ones who actually ate their eggs. Human beings have an unusual amount of power over the lives of bugs. Kids kill thousands of bugs every day without dropping a hat. Once Nory was looking at a ladybug that was either dead or alive, she couldn't tell, maybe playing dead or just relaxing or sunbathing or burnt in the sun. But then someone came walking along, not thinking about what she was doing, but just walking along, and she smashed the ladybug, without even seeing it. A green spread out. Insects have green blood. Now, if that had been a child who had been squushed, everyone would be tearing their hair out. Even if a small thing happens to a child, she remembers it and talks about it for a long time.

Maybe insects' blood is white or some other color, and only turns green when it is exposed to air. We think human blood is red but it's blue just before it comes out of a cut. The very second it reaches the edge of the cut, it changes, in the twinkling of an eye, because of the air.

They were watching a pianist one night, Nory's mother, Nory's father, and Nory, because when Nory called her friend Kira, Kira said 'You've got to watch this great piano contest.' Littleguy was playing with James the Red Engine. One of the people in the contest played the piano so hard he got a red spot on the back of his thumb. He was from Yugoslaw. Nory saw it and said, 'He's hurt himself.'

'Oh, I think it's just a shadow,' said Nory's father.

But it wasn't. There were little spots of blood on the piano keys. Then the next person had to play. Think of him sitting down and seeing ladybugs of blood all over the piano. He can't wipe them off because the wiping would make an ugly sound and the judges might remember the ugly sound very well, since it was the very first thing he played, and give him a bad result. His eye would be distracted by the blood and he would make more mistakes, maybe. Or he might think, 'Hah hah! I won't bleed, no sir!' It was sad to think of the people in the contest who practiced so hard their whole lives long and still eventfully lost.

That little thing, a bleeding thumb, was a big thing for a person. For an insect or some other small creature it would be minor. One time Nory scrumpled up a leaf to put it on the compost pile in Palo Alto. She didn't know that there was a snail on the other side of the leaf. So she accidentally crunched the snail, and she got snail slime all over her hand. It was awful. She hadn't meant to scrumple the snail. From then on, whenever she picked up a leaf, she turned it over to see if anything was on the other side. Very

often there was. Another time she caught a butterfly and
was trying to put it in a jar with some grass blades. Its body
was in the jar, but its head was accidentally outside, and
she didn't know that, while she was turning the lid of the
jar. She looked over and there was its head outside the jar.
She snatched the lid away and the head was still partly
attached. The butterfly flew away. But she felt the guilt of
the idea of having done that pull at her horribly.

Nory's father said that feeling guilty was useful because
when you felt it you had a piece of useful knowledge: you
knew that you didn't want to do that thing, whatever it was,
that made you feel guilty, so the guiltiness was a way of
teaching yourself what you ought to do in the future. In
some cases that was true but Nory felt horribly guilty about
having scrumpled the snail and screwed the lid on the
butterfly's head even though she hadn't meant to.

But the guiltiness did stay in her mind and make her act
differently. For instance, three kids found a butterfly on a
tree near the dining hall at Threll School one time, near
the beginning of term. They were trying to make it fly, but
it wasn't cooperating. One of the girls wanted to put it in
her backpack. Immediately, Nory thought, 'If it goes in
there, with all the heavy books and notebooks, it will end
up like one of the cookies that I put in my backpack that is
now just a dust of crumbs. It will be the death of that
butterfly.' So she said to the girl, 'Here, take my pencil case
and put the butterfly in there.' The girl carelessly took it
and put the butterfly in. That meant that Nory was totally
without a pencil case. The pencil case had pencils,
including a Barbie pencil, her medium nib pen, her ink
eradicator, her National Trust eraser, ruler, protractors,
everything. She had to borrow pens from kids, and at first
they were nice about it, but after a few days they were

really mean about it and said, 'Are you going to beg for a pen again? I'll tell you right now you can't have one.'

Of course one of the reasons she'd given the girl her pencil case was not just to protect the butterfly, but probably more because she wanted the girl to be impressed by her generous act of handing over the pencil case. Finally her mother said, 'You *must* get that pencil case back from that girl or you will have to buy another pencil case out of your own allowance.' So Nory asked the girl for the pencil case back and got it at the end of the day, feeling huge relief.

Another story about a pencil case was a more horrible one. Daniella Harding said, and Nory wasn't sure if she was telling the truth, but she said that she got the pointy end of a protractor stuck through her cheek. Kira asked, 'Did you scream?' Daniella said that she'd had to go to the san. She got a little scar on her face. But Nory had had a friend at the International Chinese Montessori School in Palo Alto who was always making things up, and ever since then she was not so quick to believe everything every kid told her, especially if they told the story a certain way. She could have gotten the scar from poking herself with a pencil. Or it just could have been a simple fall-down-and-scrape-your-face.

13. *Close Calls with Crying*

A lot of Nory's stories used to be about her most beloved stuffed animal, a puppet raccoon called Sarah Laura Maria, who was often being stolen away by a bad witch and helped by a good witch, stuff like that, but lately Nory had

begun a whole set of stories about a girl named Mariana
who has a very sad but in some ways good life. Coochie,
which was Nory's other name for Raccoon, still was in
some stories of her own, too. Cooch had recently begun
attending a boarding school as a day student in the dresser
in the guest room of the house in Threll they were renting.
Samantha and Linnea and Vera, other dolls, were going
there as well, each in its own drawer. They were full
boarders. There were quite a number of flying squirrels at
the school, who would climb on the play-structure and fly
off in great arches. Coochie tried to do it but she had eaten
too many jacket potatoes for lunch and she fell down and
got badly scraped and bruised. It wasn't the sort of scrape
you get when you scrape your knee on the Astroturf, which
makes it completely red, it was more of a real cut. A girl in
Nory's class named Jessica—the one who said Nory had a
'squeegee accent' on one of the first days—fell on the
Astroturf and got two red knees when they were playing
hockey.

'Oh, are you okay?' Nory asked her.

'If I were "okay," would I be sitting down with tears
pouring down my face?' Jessica said.

'No,' said Nory. Almost all children were rude
sometimes. Nory herself was quite rude from time to time.
Once she had told a boy who had said her teeth were too
big that his shoes were dusty. He had turned bright red and
looked so hurt that she felt bad afterward.

It wasn't a good idea to stop any possibility of liking a
person because of one single thing they did. Sometimes
people forget themselves. Sometimes, though, what a child
did was so bad, so severe, that you lost all your ability to
keep up any friendly feelings toward them. Such a thing

happened last year at International Chinese Montessori School, when Bernice wrote Nory a folded note that said 'I'm sorry' on the front, after they had an argument, and then inside it said, 'Dear Eleanor, I'm sorry, but I am not going to live with you in a house when we grow up, I'm going to live with my *first* best friend.' That was just the limit, that 'first'—Nory couldn't now detect one tiny scrabjib of friendship for Bernice in her heart when she thought of her. Her best friend now was Debbie, probably, who was shyer and nicer.

Littleguy occasionally said rude things that could hurt your feelings, but he was two and usually it was a question of him just not understanding what he was saying. Once on Saturday afternoon for instance Nory tried to teach Littleguy how to play field hockey, after having spent some of her morning on Astroturf learning the basics. He hurt her feelings when he rejected a hockey stick she especially made for him out of a wooden pole, a toilet-paper tube taped on at an angle, and some green ribbon from her Samantha doll as decoration spiraled around. She had been rather pleased with this homemade stick.

'Littleguy—so do you like it or do you hate it?' she asked him, wanting to jostle him into saying a little thank-you.

'I hate it,' said Littleguy, but in a pleasant, good-natured way. 'I want *that* stick,' meaning Nory's real stick.

'That's not the right way to talk to Nory,' called out Nory's father from inside. 'She made that hockey stick especially for you and used a whole green Samantha ribbon and a toilet-paper tube to decorate it.'

'I'm sorry, Nory, I'm sorry, Nory,' kind little Littleguy said, very nicely, looking up at her with his serious little mouth and hopeful eyes.

Nory said, 'Thank you, Littleguy.' She loved the open feeling you got when someone said I'm sorry to you after you were mad or hurt-feelinged at them—the feeling of the scrumpled paper of the unhappiness going away from your chest. It made you almost burst with generousness toward them. 'But it's really my fault,' she said. 'I'm sorry to *you* for asking the question confusingly in such a way that you couldn't tell which way was the right way to answer for politeness.'

'Me, too,' said Littleguy. 'Do you want to see my gooseneck trailer? It's had a bad mergency. It's stuck in the mud.'

Littleguy of course cried a hundred times a day—he had about eight different kinds of crying, several of them rather ear-gnashing—but Nory almost never cried because she had learned a few years earlier that it more or less ruins your reputation to cry, even if someone says something that makes you want to. It's very embarrassing to cry. Boys especially will like you more if you don't cry, and want to be your friend. Jessica cried when she fell on the Astroturf but it was a pretty bad fall, two knees at the same time. And she said the rude thing to Nory partly just because she was purely a rude girl some of the time, but partly because she was embarrassed, and she was very serious about boys, in almost a teenagery way, or not quite in a teenagery way but in a double-digit kind of way, and she probably worried that her enemy-friend, Daniella Harding, would tell Colin Deat that she had cried on the hockey field. Not as many people cried at this school as at Nory's old school.

There were two times this year so far Nory almost, almost cried. One was when Shelly Quettner found out that Nory kind of liked a boy by the name of Jacob Lewes.

Nory told it to Daniella Harding, who turned out to be Shelly Quettner's sidekick in the whole process. Shelly started saying to Daniella, 'What did she say? What? What? What?' And she squeezed it out of her. Or maybe Daniella wanted to tell her all along, it wasn't so clear. Instantly Shelly Quettner was saying to the class, 'Nory fancies Jacob Lewes!'

Everybody said, 'Is it true? Is it true?' Jacob Lewes immediately turned dead red and stared at his pencil case. Nory was red, too, but only in the places that she got red, which were on the sides of her cheeks, so that her blush turned into long sideburn-things. People said, 'Well? Do you fancy him?' Nory thought seriously about denying it, because honesty may be the best policy at times but it certainly does seem painful at other times. But it's painful the other way, too, because if you say, 'No, I certainly do not fancy Jacob Lewes, whatever for?' then Jacob Lewes's feelings might be a tiny bit hurt, even though he would also act very relieved to hear it, and also you then right away think, 'Oh, I shouldn't have tolden a lie,' and you have to say, 'Well, actually, yes, I mispoke, I do fancy him.' So you have twice as much pain as if you had just gone ahead and admitted it, because you have the pain of feeling the guilt of lying and the pain of admitting that you do fancy him.

So Nory said, 'Well, I do think he's nice.'

Julia Sollen said, 'You're blushing!'

'Yes, I know that,' said Nory. 'Any further questions?' It was all quite terrible and there was a sliver of a moment when Nory thought, 'This is so bad that I have a slight feeling in my lips of wanting to cry, should I cry?'

Luckily one girl came up and said, 'You know you should tell everybody that Shelly Quettner fancies Colin Deat,' because that was what Shelly had told someone, and Nory thought about it and almost did it but then she thought, Do Unto Others. Nory's conclusion was that Daniella Harding was definitely not going to get told any of her secrets anymore.

It turned out that Nory didn't really fancy Jacob Lewes so much as all that. First, he said tiresome things about how he hated Barbie dolls, which is what American boys do, and then especially after he started to make fun of Pamela Shavers. By the way, 'fancy' was the word they used for it in England, and it was an idiotic, dumb, stupid word, *fancy*, but not as horrible as if Shelly had said, 'Nory loves Jacob Lewes.' The good thing about experiencing that horribleness, though, was that because she'd already gone through the 'Nory fancies Somebody' business, she could talk to a boy like Roger Sharpless and nobody would think a thing of it. One time Nory was fighting around with Roger in a playing way and Roger got a little vicious and swopped her in the side of the face with a rolled-up geography booklet. He didn't know it would hurt as much as it did, because when you roll up something like a magazine or a thin floppy book you think it will be kind of soft and springy, like a rolled-up piece of paper, but actually it can feel as hard as a metal pipe, just about. Nory said, laughing, 'Roger, you're going to give me a black eye, now.' And she thought, 'Oh dear, oh dear, they're going to see my eye, it's full of water.' And then she remembered that one time at her old school she'd thought her eyes would look terribly full of water and she went into the bathroom to check and she found out that you couldn't even tell unless you were really looking. So she thought, 'No, I don't think they'll notice.' And Roger didn't seem worried at all. But he did nicely say he was sorry to have swopped her with his geography booklet.

Those were the two times she almost cried so far, but didn't.

14. Fire Safety Tips

Nory left Boston and moved to the Trumpet Hill house in Palo Alto when she was still one year old. So the only reason that she had any memories about Boston and its bricks was that they had been back to visit. That was before she had Cooch, her only daughter from her marriage to Sylvester the Cat, who later sailed away to Africa. It was before she knew almost anything, for instance that long ago sailors threw pigs overboard to see what direction they would swim, because whatever direction they swam in was land. Or that if a cat is bred without a tail he won't be able to feel where he's going to the bathroom, since the tail is their sense of where they're going to the bathroom. Without a tail a cat will just go all over the place, not knowing, like dogs who leave their dog leisures here, there, and everywhere.

Nory didn't even know the word for elbow back then, when she was one. They had a video of her first learning 'elbow' in the yard, much later on. Really almost the only thing she kept with her from Boston was a tiny scar on her nose that she got in the bathtub when she picked up the plastic razor that her mother used to shave her legs and looked at it, and somehow, before she knew it, presto, she had cutten herself with it. Even that tiny scar was gone, almost. And now Littleguy knew the word 'elbow.' He said 'Elbows help you jump!' and he would then jump to demonstrate. He was right, elbows do help you jump, especially if you jumped the way he did, with a lot of arm motion to make it seem like a very high jump.

Littleguy did not seem to know the word 'ankle,' however. Babies learn the words for their feet and toes and fingers quite early because they can hold them close to their faces, and they learn about their eyes and nose and mouth because they are *on* their faces, but for some reason they are never terribly interested in their ankles. The word is weaker in their mind. That might have something to do with the strange myth of dipping Achilles.

It wasn't Hercules who was dipped. Nory learned his proper name in another Classics class—Achilles. Achilles's mother was unhappy that Achilles wasn't completely immortal, so she dipped him head-first into the Watersticks. The Watersticks led from the Alive to the Unalive, in other words to the Dead. She held him by pinching hard on the back part of the foot, above his heel. 'But wouldn't that hurt the baby tremendously?' Nory wondered to herself. 'Wouldn't there be a big chance of it falling right out of your hand?'

She imagined a tiny naked baby hanging by one leg, terribly frightened, bright red in the face from screaming, kicking the other leg wildly. The cold water would make the poor thing gasp desperately and it would pour right up its nostrils, because they would be upside down. Water in your sinuses can be really painful. If the goddess really loved her baby, she would have gotten in the water herself and then gently lifted the baby by its waist from the shore, right side up, one hand on either side, and lowered him in, and where her hands were covering his skin, once he was almost floating, she could just let one hand go for a second, then close, then let the other hand go, then close. You have to be careful to hold up the head, too. The ankle was just not a practical or safe choice of place to hold a newborn child.

But they were much less careful about things like safety in ancient times. Nowadays safety is a major concern but back then the sky was the limit with danger, really. Nory's first school was called Small People, and one of the first things they learned at Small People was the safety tip 'Stop, Drop, and Roll.' That was what you were supposed to do when your clothes caught on fire. If you ran, the flames would flare up, and you would probably get a third-degree burn. A third-degree burn is when the skin is black and charred.

'Should you hide from the fireman?' the teacher asked.

'No,' said the kids.

'If he has a big mask on, should you be frightened into thinking he's a space alien?' asked the teacher.

'No,' said the kids.

'And what do you do if your clothes catch on fire?' asked the teacher.

'Stop, drop, and roll!' the kids shouted.

At first Nory was very happy to know that rhyme, but then she was taught it again at her next school, the Blackwood Early Focus School, where three firemen came by for a visit. That teacher was not in a good state of mind and shouted all the time, because the class was so wild. One kid spent every minute of his day rolling around on the floor, so there wasn't much need to ask him to drop or roll. Stopping might be nice, though.

Nory's parents took her out of that school, which was a public school, when they noticed that Nory had learned to write one more letter in three months, G. One letter in three months was just not acceptable, they said. So they put her in the International Chinese Montessori School, and presto, the alphabet was in her brain in a jiffy and she was learning songs in Chinese about Sung O Kung, the ancient monkey.

And then one day a fireman came in with some blankets and had two kids hold a blanket low to the floor. The blanket stood for the thick, thick smoke that you were supposed to crawl under. Crawling was fun but it also gave you a panicky feeling because you could imagine being in a room and unable to know where the window was because the smoke was so thick, except for a tiny layer just above the floor. How would you possibly know where the windows were? You'd need to tape a card with an arrow on it pointing up at the window, so you'd know that there's where you'd need to take a breath and plunge up into the hot smoke and smash out the window with a pillow. 'And what do you do if your clothes catch on fire?' asked the fireman.

'Stop, drop, and roll!' shouted the kids.

That and don't smoke, don't take drugs, don't talk to strangers, and the rainforest is burning to the ground, were the things that it seemed like every kid was taught over and over and over, to an endless limit. You got told them *so* many times, on TV ads as well—wasn't there anything else in the world that kids should know? For instance other safety things, like: Be careful when you play with your little brother because his head is quite hard and it could break your nose. Or, don't run in fancy black shoes because their soles are nine times out of ten extremely slippery. Or, don't try to pull down a wooden Chinese-checker set from a shelf above your head because it can fall straight on your toe and make the toenail turn dark purple and almost completely fall right off. Or, don't chew too wildly or you might bite your tongue, which really hurts.

Or what about things that were not about safety at all, such as for instance salting meat, or about the three layers of the tooth, the inner layer, the middle layer, and the outer layer, called the crown, or the three layers of the coffin in Egyptian times, the layer of gold, the layer of silver, and the layer of something else, like bronze? Everybody's gotten the idea that when somebody died, the Egyptians mummified them. Well, does that mean everybody got to be mummified, or does that mean ten out of a hundred? Why not spend some period of time answering that kind of question, rather than endlessly 'Stop, drop, and roll'?

Long ago they used to preserve meat by stuffing it into a barrel with tons and tons of salt. The salt was so salty that the germs that are dedicated to making meat go bad couldn't do what they were planning to do, because of the gagging taste, and the meat just sat there, month after month, getting saltier by the minute. The history teacher at Threll Junior School told that very interesting thing to the class, and when a boy began talking loudly and interrupting, the teacher said, 'Be quiet, or I'll stuff *you* in a barrel of salt.' The boy turned bright red. Another time the teacher, Mr. Blithrenner, said to Roger Sharpless, 'Roger, if you put your finger any deeper into your nose it'll come out your ear.'

Nory hated added salt, but she loved Parmesan cheese, and when she was littler she used to pour out a big pile of Parmesan cheese on her plate and dab it up with her finger, if nobody was looking. Her cheeks got bright red when they had spaghetti because of a reaction to the cheese crumbs on them, not because she was embarrassed to eat cheese. She had no embarrassment whatever about eating cheese. Pamela Shavers said Parmesan cheese had lots of salt naturally in it. Crisps were naturally quite salty, as well. Once two bothersome boys found an empty package of crisps in a bin, or trash can, and they went up to Pamela Shavers and said, 'Oh, Pamela, would you care for a bag of crisps?' Pamela took the bag and squeezed it and when it went flat they laughed.

But there was something different than Parmesan cheese about pure salt sprinkled around on food—the wicked little crystals—as opposed to mixed *into* food, that Nory really wasn't such a fan of. Also sugar sprinkled in with vegetables—if she didn't know that there was added sugar in a pan of carrots, then it was fine, but if she knew, then she couldn't bear to think about it. Nowadays Littleguy was a tremendous fan of any kind of sprinkleable cheese. He and Nory had their own individual miniature cheese dispensers, labeled 'E' for 'Eleanor' and 'F' for Frank. Littleguy ate the cheese by pouring out a little hill of it on his plate when their parents were talking about something like the history of table manners and not paying any attention, and then he licked his spoon so that it was sticky and rolled it in the cheese so that the little scribbages of the cheese stuck to the spoon.

Well, so far, nothing about 'Stop, Drop, and Roll' at Threll Junior School, not a hint of it, which was a relief. Because really how much use would it be to know that rhyme in a fire? It depended on the kinds of clothes you were wearing whether that would be a good safety tip or not. For instance, say you were trying to dash across some burning piece of wood to escape through the front door, and the hem of your nightgown caught fire. It wouldn't be a good idea to throw yourself on the floor and start rolling around, because the floor might be burning, and if you had on a stretchy soft nightgown, you could pull it off and scamper out of it through the hole in the neck, when if you rolled around with it on, your legs would surely get burned.

They had had two fire drills already at the Junior School—one on purpose, and one by mistake. In a fire, the whole class was supposed to line up in a double row and the person at the front of the line called out the name of each child and checked it off on a piece of paper to make sure they were in line. The problem was that some kids would make a run for it, and the person calling out the names would wonder if those kids were hurt back in the back of the class and couldn't call out, when actually they were already outside, flopped out on the Astroturf gasping in that farm-fresh air. What if there was terrible smoke, would they all line up lying down, and have their names called that way?

Drama class was turning out to be very good at the Junior School. In drama class they were paired off, a boy and a girl together, and they were learning to die in various ways. One person poured boiling oil on the other and the other had to act out what it was like to have boiling oil poured on him. Then they switched off. The drama teacher was very, very good. The first week they learned how to die by being shot, and they practiced fake falls. The teacher said, in a very sweet voice, 'Oh dear, a sad, sad, thing happened to me today. So sad. I forgot my popgun. So I'll just have to shoot you without it, like this.' And she pointed her finger at each kid and said 'Bam! Bam! Bam! Bam!

Bam!' Everybody pretended to get shot and died. To do a fake fall, you begin standing up—of course—and you slide one of your knees down, down, almost touching the ground, then turn your head, and fall on the side, slide your whole arm down, then go still and dead. It's easy to do it slowly, but to do it quickly, as if you're really dropping dead, is not such an easy project. That was why it was so important to learn how in drama class.

In drama they also did a little skit where two people go to a pub, which is a bar, and one asks the other if he or she would like a drink, and then tells him to look somewhere off—'Oh, look at that interesting menu over there, how fascinatingly interesting'—and then, plip, poisons the person's drink by dropping a little tiny red pill into it. Nory poisoned Stefan's drink first, and he writhed around on the floor until she thought he was going to sprain something. (A sprain is worse than a strain—they are two totally different things. A lot of kids didn't realize that.) Then, when it was Nory's turn to be poisoned, she acted the part of a princess who drinks the drink, realizes that it's poison, because so many evildoers are wanting to steal the kingdom from her family, feels the stabbing of pain in her stomach, knows she is going to die within a manner of minutes, puts her hands together in a quiet adjustment on her lap, stretches out on the floor, and dies with the barest flutter of her eyelids.

In drama they never did act out one of Nory's secret ideas of a terrible disaster, though, which was, What would it feel like to be caught in a burning rain? That was just as well, because Nory had already put that idea in one of her Mariana stories. She had become totally emerged in telling it to herself on the way home from Oxburgh Hall, which was more of a Stately Castle than a Stately Home.

15. The Story of the Deadly Rain

When Mariana was only about eight or nine years old, she experienced something that one out of twenty people in India would have experienced. It was The Deadly Rain.

She had gone on trips to the Sahara deserts before, for she went on many different trips, and this was one of them. She had built a shack there for her summer house, or her father and mother had.

But what she had not heard, or that was not known among the people, was that the rain was going to be so hot, so very hot, that with the first touch of it, your finger would be burned black or blackish purple. If she had known this she would have picked a different time to come for sure. But she did not.

She got off a little horrible airplane and stepped with her first step into the orangish yellow sand of the Sahara deserts. The first thing she noticed was the tremendous amount of snakes, lizards, and different animals. She dropped and rolled over in the soft, comfortable sand. And she looked around. It was five minutes after that that the rain started. It rained solidly all night. It was horrible. Burning rain.

The next day, when it was still raining, she wandered, wandered, walking for home, home, all she could think about was getting to her home, out of the Sahara. Now what you may not notice about this, is that she could not just go into her house, or stand under the shade of a tree. She was alone in the desert, with only the wild snakes to accompany her. She stepped into the sand, each step making a mark that would soon vanish because of the heavy marks of the rain. It was not really raining from the sky very hot, but what happened was that the heat wave was so much hotter than the coldness of the rain that when the rain got down to a certain point, it started to boil, sizzling, poppling—sizzling, poppling. Animals scurrying here and there underground. Oh, how she wished she could go underground with them, be sheltered with them. She was too big.

Her slow walk now turned into a fast run. Tears streamed down her cheeks, and her hot face began to sting even worse than it had before. She was noticing that the rain was turning into balls of hot ice.

'But wait,' she thought, she stopped for a moment to look up at the sky. The heat wave was stopping, and huge pieces of hail were coming down from the sky. This made her happy. So she lay down and fell asleep, predicting that the next morning would be just as bad as the first, and took this chance to sleep.

'It might be my only chance,' she thought, lying down on the soft sand once again, this time happily. But just as she was about to shut her eyes, she noticed something— something that she'd never seen before.

It was a little girl, about the age of four. Of course she'd seen many little girls before, but this one was tired and hungry and dirty and blinded by the hot rain and hail. She was stumbling, bumping into sharp cactuses, there was nothing she could do. Mariana thought, 'How could I let her stay here? I've been that sick, I've been that lonely, but I've never been blinded in a hot rain and now hail like this. And, boy, would I have liked somebody to come and help me. I must go and save her,' she thought. 'I must carry her back to my house. I must.'

She got up and picked up the child. The child's heart stopped beating so fast. She calmed down. Her eyes for the first time opened. She looked up at Mariana with such happy eyes, sparkling eyes of pure glee, as if to say, 'You have saved me, Mariana, you have done well.'

Mariana looked back at her, as if to say, 'I've only done what people should have done for me.' She started walking. Each footstep she took now felt heavier and more uncomfortable. But the child was not the burden to her. The only thing that made her upset was the child's tears. The child was crying, not out of pain, but out of happiness. But Mariana had no idea that a child so young could be happy in the midst of something so horrible.

The next day, as she predicted, it was hot rain again. But this time not just boiling like the first, but so hot half of it was turning to steam. Steam only meant hot drips covered her face—both of their faces, rather. Their steps were heavier. The girl was crying, crying with pain, not from herself, but from looking into a face that had so much pain.

But now Mariana had come to a part of the desert where she was not alone. Many other people like herself were suffering, adults. She tried dragging one of them along, but it would not help. She was not strong enough to carry a three-year-old and a sixty-year-old. She found a shawl on a cactus. She took it off and wrapped it around the little girl. The little girl smiled. Then she took another shawl and wrapped it around herself this time. She thought she could walk faster if she had something to protect her from this awful rain, but it seeped through. She thought that this should be her punishment, to suffer this horrible rain, and to carry this heavy little girl, her punishment for being so selfish and taking the best spot she could pick in the year and taking the plane instead of walking.

She knew that she could, of course, because she had done it before. She had walked through places so full of trees and sticks carrying heavy buckets of hard metal for the princess Malina, in India. Finally she tried sticking a hollow stick into one of the cactuses, by cutting with her pocket knife a hole in it. She sucked and it burnt her mouth terribly. For an animal had died, a black-skinned animal, on the cactus, where she had struck in her stick. It was then that she decided that there was no way of getting water, she was stuck, she had to go home.

The little girl spoke for the first time. 'Do not carry me,' she said. 'You have to take care of me and find a place for me when you get home.' And as if she had read Mariana's mind, she said, 'A cactus would be a better burden for you. It would punish you even more, because of the spikes. And you could easily saw one off and carry it home, and then you wouldn't have an extra punishment of taking care of me when you get home.'

But the girl had begun to love her, Mariana, that is, and Mariana was not apt to let the girl go away and die. For she knew she would. She walked on, quicker, quicker now, the hot rain got hotter and hotter. Her face started bubbling it was so hot. Her sweat turned red with blood. The girl cried blood in looking at a face that seemed to have so much pain again. Mariana spoke softly to the girl. 'Do not cry, dear, do not cry, it takes blood from your precious body.' The girl wiped her tears. Mariana, seeing the girl wiping her tears, remembered her own face, and how much it hurt. She touched it. It felt more pain, and what the little girl saw is what you should see in your mind. She saw pain: the face was very swollen and she touched it. The air-filled skin broke, very thin now, because it was full of air, and blood gushed out. It was painful-looking and definitely was painful for Mariana.

She was almost at home now. Of course she couldn't see it, but she had gone two quarters of the way. Only ten miles to go, but her feet were so sore. Her hair was dyed almost red. Walking farther and farther and farther and farther, tired to beat the band. The girl looked up again, like she had done the first time Mariana had picked her up. Now with swollen cheeks but a happier face. She looked wise. 'We are almost home now,' she whispered, 'I can tell by that cactus.' She pointed to the tallest cactus Mariana had ever seen. Mariana stepped back. She forgot about her pain, the heavy child she was holding, and all the hot rain. It reminded her of when she was a baby. She was born under a tall, tall sequoia tree. The tree had been cut down to build a nice beautiful house, but in her mind it was not cut down, but was still standing there, in Australia. The sand was getting more shallow now. It would have hurt more now for me or you but to her it meant home. It meant getting the little child safe, finding her new parents, or finding the old parents, if they had not died, and getting home to her own mother and father out there. In the bottom of her heart she thought they might have died, but I can tell you now that they hadn't. But in her heart she also thought something else. She thought, 'I can adopt her. She can be my own child, I can take care of her.'

The child read her mind once again. 'You are my mother now,' she said. 'My parents have died.' Wisely she said this, not as a three-year-old, not as an old person, but as Mariana's own mother would have said it. Mariana remembered the Australian look of her mother now. Long beautiful black hair, and now she also noticed something else about the child. She, too, was an Australian. Mariana hugged the child tight now, with the child upright in her arms, as she had seen women in Australian doing.

Finally she came to the wooden house. The sight of it was miracly happy-making for her. She lay the child down on the couch on the front porch. Her mother and her father hugged her. Then she fell, her knees bending. They gently took her to her bed. She slept a gentle sleep. It felt like it lasted twenty days and twenty nights. In later years, she raised the child, with her parents' help, and the two of them became best friends.

And that was only one of the stories of the amazing, everlasting Life of Mariana.

16. Something Needs to Fail

The idea of everlasting life came partly from the kinds of things you say in Cathedral, and partly from a movie called *The Neverending Story,* which was an extremely good movie in many ways, one of which was that it was unusually rare to have a two-part movie and have the second part be just as interesting as the first, basically. 'Neverending' and 'everlasting' were good words for the job because they last and last when you say them, like 'forevermore.'

Nory had saved up a few stories from the Everlasting Life of Mariana, and she was wondering how in the world she would remember them, since they were too long to write down. Some were definitely a touch on the gruesome side, but that was what you might expect since if it's a gruesomeness that comes from your own private brain when you're awake it's not the least bit the same as the kind of gruesomeness that somebody else might offer you in a book or a movie. On the other hand, the scary things your brain decides to show you at night are totally different, they can be *very* bothersome, definitely, but the things that you think up on purpose are usually not as bad, because they were just teetering at the exact limit of frighteningness that you wanted them at, and you didn't have to worry that they were going to slip over the limit.

You really need something to fail in a story, because then when it fails it has to get better. The way Nory thought of the burning rain story was that she once noticed that sometimes rain, when it was falling very lightly, would give you pins and needles on your face. Very very light rain, *ting, ting, ting,* could hurt surprisingly. Just tiny, tiny drops of sharp rain, coming down very quickly because they're so small they slide right past the bigger softer raindrops.

Another time, on the way back from Blickling Hall, Nory told a story to her very small Felicity doll. It ended up being about a little brother because her own brother, Littleguy, was right next to her in his car seat, transfixed in his sleep. The story was gruesome, but not *as* gruesome as the story about the burning rain, which was probably the most gruesome one she'd ever told.

17. A Story About a Girl Named Era and Her Brother

There was a little girl named Era. She lived in a beautiful cottage near Blickling Hall with her brother. It was so lovely, everything was perfect. Her mother and father were perfect, they never were angry, and always were nice to them. Era was walking in one day, after playing outside in her favorite place to play. But, ooh, she fell into horrible mud.

'Oh no,' she said, 'I have just spoiled my lovely dress. Oh no.' And she began to cry. She got up out of the ditch and walked over to her mother.

'Oh dear,' said her mother, 'your favorite dress, too. Well, I'll just have to make you a new one, and patch up that one.'

'Thank you, Mother,' Era said, and bowed politely, or curtsied, as you might say. She walked along, putting her school things away in the proper places. 'Mother,' she said, 'is Father out of the hospital yet?'

'Yes, he is, he's in the breakfast room, if you go in there, you'll see him.'

Era walked in, and there was her father. He smiled brightly at her. She played games all morning. But her dress getting mud on it was not the only tragedy of that day. She was walking on the street with her brother, who was eight, coming back from the market with all the goods. She put her brother down, and she, being a thirteen-year-old, went off to do some homework, or prep.

Her mother was making dinner, and went off in another room to get her laundry, and her father stayed in the breakfast room, unable to walk still, because of his injury about a month ago. She walked happily through the living room as she went to her room. There was her brother, taking out the matches slowly one by one.

'Oh no,' she said, 'Help, no!' And she grabbed the matches away from him. But just as she grabbed it away, the match in his hand flung against the matchbox, and a fire started. She dropped the matchbox and called out. But her mother could not hear her. She was covered in laundry from head to toe, bringing it into the kitchen.

'Fire!' screamed Era, pulling her brother out with her. But they tripped over her matchbox and he burned his legs badly. She carried him out, quickly, but she tripped again, falling on him, then picked him up and ran out with him screaming in pain, from fire. She had stepped on a knife that had cut through the back of her shoe. Oh, she was scared, running. It was horrible. They had tripped on the thing where you scrape your shoes, when the snow and dung had been there. 'Oh no,' she thought, 'my poor brother, my mother, my father.'

Her father, unable to walk, and her mother, unable to hear, sadly died in the fire. It was awful, she wiped tears from her face and sobbed. Her brother was bleeding terribly now. She picked him up and got out. He was screaming with pain again. Oh, she could almost feel the pain herself. 'Oh,' she said, 'brother, don't cry, don't cry.' And she wiped his tears. She could see the pain in his face, but he was very obedient, he did whatever his sister would ever wish him to do. He quietly was carried by her. She could see the pain in his face, easily. She could see that he was struggling.

'Oh, brother, you may cry.' She saw a small tear drip across his face, which was wiped back by his shaking hand. He could not resist that tear, she knew, there was no way of helping it.

'Oh, sister, I can walk,' he said.

'You will fall,' she said, because he could only barely walk with his injuries, and tumble over himself. She brought him carefully to the hospital, with blood stained all over her white and now brown dress.

'Oh, no,' she cried, going in the revolving door. She walked slowly over to the desk, carrying her lovable brother. 'Oh, no.' She wiped her tears away and tried to fix her hair, which was horrible now. The curl was coming out, the one that was in the back. It hung almost straight down now. She was scared. Her hair always hung straight down when she was scared. Maybe it was the sweat that pulled it down by getting it wet, dripping. Her brother was horrified. The doctors took him.

And for a while after that you never got to see her clean white prim dress or her nice hairdo, but you saw blood and mud and things like that on her dress. She became very poor, without the tiniest bit of money. She walked to a stone. In the stone, she carved her mother's name, sadly. She couldn't do it, but the stone was covered with mud, so she tried scratching a message in the mud. She walked along, four days she spent without her brother. Finally she went over to the hospital and picked him up. Fortunately he was better. Soon he was well enough to be picking berries and peeling oranges again, and they had lovely suppers together.

She carried him wherever he went. And, the end.

18. A Little About Raccoon

The thing that had failed in Nory's own life was that right now she didn't have a best friend in England. And she honestly missed her best friend from America, Debbie, who hadn't written back. Some kids are not so good about writing letters, though. Another sad and unfair thing was that Nory had only gotten a tinily short time to have Debbie as her best friend, since she'd only met her very recently, in about the past two years.

The great thing that was important to know about
Debbie was that she love, love, *loved* telling stories with her
dolls. She had four stuffed kitten dolls that made a purring
sound when you turned them at an angle, not quite
identical in their faces but almost identical, and she had an
extraordinary imagination that just went on and on and on
to an endless limit. Nory and Debbie played the Samantha
game together, which was an everlasting game, in which
disaster after disaster happened to Samantha and
everybody else who took place in it. One time Samantha
was hanged by her foot on the lampshade because a dog
named Fur was going to burn her. Fur was actually a very
good dog, he was a puppet dog that Debbie loved most of
all her animals and slept with. (Debbie loved her pandas,
too, but her pandas were more of a collection.) But they
had to have a bad creature in the story or it wouldn't have
the feeling of something failing, so they had the idea that
he had been given a pill by this wandering bad person that
made him bad for a short time. So the result was that he
was being quite dreadful, temporarily, and wanted to kill
the kitties and Samantha. That allowed him to be bad for
the sake of the story but not overall bad for the sake of
Debbie's dear animal that she slept with. The four
adventurous kitties figured out a way to save themselves by
pretending there were only two kitties and getting the dog
Fur to take a second pill that would make him go to sleep.
When he woke he was his old warmhearted self again.
Telling those stories with Debbie was so miracly much fun.

Before she knew Debbie, Nory told her stories by
herself. It was hard to remember how she began, but it
appeared to her now that she might have begun with little
snibbets of stories she told in different voices in the bath,

or looking in the mirror, because those were some of the most important storytelling situations. She had a rubber raccoon that had hundreds of adventures in the bath. Obviously she couldn't take Cooch herself because Cooch was (speaking of things you shouldn't speak of) *sewn:* she was a cloth puppet and couldn't get wet.

Sarah Laura Maria Raccoon was one when Nory found her, abandoned by her parents lying cold and numb by the road. She and Sylvester had adopted her, and then it turned out that Cooch was their own lost child. A witch had taken away their own child long before. The witch came pouring up from the steam of a grilled cheese sandwich one day, an ugly thing, and stole their dear Coochie away, and their hearts were broken, or 'juken down' as Littleguy would say, since that's how he pronounced broken down. Heartjuken for many long years they lived in their small cottage, until one day they found an older Raccoon cold and abandoned by the road. 'We must adopt her, she looks so much like our own long lost Sarah Laura Maria,' they said. When she revived a little she told them what had happened, that she had been living a perfect life with her two parents when a wicked witch came along and took her, but fortunately she escaped by throwing salt in the witch's eye and dashing out of the witch's boat and jumping overboard, where the mermaids took her to their castle and cared for her and tried to teach her as best they could to be a mermaid raccoon. She had grown very thin when she was with the witch but she grew plumper now, feeding on sea salads. And sometimes—if by chance someone in a boat threw it overboard—a good old potato. She did her best and she wore long flowing dresses made of the finest kinds of seaweed found near Africa, but she was a land-raccoon in her heart and finally she thanked the mermaids with many hugs and waves and swam ashore. There the husband and wife, out on a walk on the beach, found her.

'Darling, do you notice how much this Raccoon looks like our own dear child?' the mother asked.

'Yes, yes I do,' said the husband. 'I wonder if she'll want to play with some of the toys that our dear little child used to play with.' Sadly he went upstairs and got down the box of things. There was a Fisher Price Main Street, with a set of five letters that you could put into a mailbox, and a set of foam numbers that fit together, and many other things.

'I had just that toy,' said Cooch. 'And just that toy.'

'You did?' said the parents, in amazement. 'Could she be . . . ?' they wondered. 'What is your name?'

'Sarah Laura Maria,' she said.

'But that is the name of our own daughter, who was stolen away by a witch many years ago!' said the mother and father.

'I was stolen away by a witch, too,' Coochie told them shyly.

'You're our daughter! Oh, come here, oh my!' And they hugged her and kissed her and were overjoyed forevermore.

19. A Chinese Monk

So Nory did tell stories like that before she met Debbie, to herself, but Debbie was a wonderful friend because she was willing to let the story go where it preferred to go, and she could think up disasters for Samantha that Nory couldn't conveniently think up by herself. Debbie had a very wide, wide face, and long black hair that was shiny and perfect, because her parents were Chinese and Filipino, although she spoke only American, plus the Mandarin Chinese they learned in the International Chinese Montessori School, which was also called ICMS. Neither of them could speak Cantonese, which was a totally different bowl of fish from Mandarin. When the two of them were drawing something together, though, they would sing a song in Mandarin that their Chinese teacher taught them, called 'Namoowami tofo.' The song went something like

> Xie er po, mao er po,
> Shen shang de jia sha po.

What it meant was basically, 'His shoes are broken, his hat is broken.' Or rather, that was the translation that the teacher gave them. The problem was that their teacher hardly knew a giblet of English. Nory's translation to herself was, 'Shoes are torn, hat is torn, his whole outfit is torn.' The song was about a crazy monk. The best part was just a sound, 'Namoowami tofo,' which was the prayer to the Buddha that the monk used to do his magic. He was born from the Buddha. His name was Ji Gong. He was very free, even though he was a monk.

Nory still sang the song quite often, because some Chinese songs are so great that how can you not sing them? But she was at the point of forgetting a lot of the Chinese characters she used to know, such as

木

which means 'wood,' or

which means 'spill.' She never wrote Chinese now. Nobody in her class now at Threll Junior School was Chinese, even though there were some Chinese kids in the Senior School, and so there was nobody who even understood what a Chinese character was, and what pin yin was, and how you had to memorize the order of the strokes.

Her parents originally thought they might get a Chinese tutor for her in Threll, but Nory had school on Saturday mornings here, and plenty of homework, and that left her only one day off. If a Chinese tutor came on Sunday, Nory wouldn't be exhausted so much as thinking, 'Oh, my poor scrabjib of a weekend!' When would they have time to drive to a castle or a palace, which is what they did every weekend? At Oxburgh Hall, high up in the tower where the princess stayed and sewed, they saw a little brick place where the Catholic priest would have to stuff himself when the government inspectors came sniffing.

So that was just the fact of it: Chinese was going to grow faint in her mind. She hadn't known all the characters in the world, anyway. Four years was how long it took her to learn Chinese, as much of it as she knew, which wasn't all that much compared to what an adult or an older child would know, so she thought that in French it might take her about two years to learn it, because it wasn't as difficult as Chinese. But still, French was nice and hard—nice and hard. *Dix* was a very meaningful word. 'It already means ten, in a sensible way,' Nory thought. When she first heard 'dix,' she thought, 'Oh, puff, that's not like ten.' But very soon it meant ten in quite a sensible way. And *Je* was actually quite a better word for 'I' than 'I.' No language was easy. It was a bad mistake to think so. English was about the most blusteringly hard language you could get. Verbally Chinese was much easier than English.

Certain languages from Africa weren't as complicated in some ways, though, Nory thought. They didn't do 1, 2, 3, 4, 5, 6, 7, 8, 9, 10, drrrrrr, their numbers didn't go for infinity. They went one, two, three—and then 'many.' For instance: 'There were many people at the store.' Well? Does that mean four, or does that mean twenty-five? Their next-door-neighbor in Palo Alto, who spent a whole year in Africa, in Bombay, told Nory that about the numbers. Nory told it to Debbie, who said it couldn't be true, because how could they have phone numbers or know how much things cost? Say you went to see *The Little Mermaid* with your family in Bombay, and the person said, through the little hole in the glass, 'Two adults and two children? That will be many dollars, please.' Or hickles, or gumbobs, or whatever Bombayan dollars are called. Many dollars? How many dollars?

Nory had to agree that her friend Debbie had a worthwhile point. Debbie was very smart and talented at a lot of things, including the piano. She was an all-around wonderful friend, the kind of friend you think finally just *has* to be your best friend, because there is no other choice but to have her be your best friend. Especially when Bernice said she was going to live in a house with her 'real' best friend, which was rude and mean. Bernice had a two-color retainer with a picture of a silver mermaid on it. Debbie had silver writing in her retainer that said 'Debbie.' When Debbie got her retainer, it left Nory as the last girl in the class not to have a retainer. That was one reason she thought, long ago, when people started getting their retainers one after another after another, 'I know! I'll be an orthodontist, and design people's retainers for them.' She would design one with the image of a big teethy smile on it. If Littleguy needed one, she'd do one with a steam train. You could think of the teeth as a train chuffing around the jaw.

In England it would be almost impossible to be a professional orthodontist, because almost nobody in school had retainers to speak of, or rather 'false palates,' as they were known by the select few. Probably the reason nobody had them was exactly because of that awful, queasy-making name, false palates. You might as well call them 'bladder-stones' and get it over with.

20. A Report About the Teeth

The idea of designing people's retainers was part of what first got Nory interested in teeth. Then she found out that the whole subject was more fascinating than you could ever predict. In Ms. Beryl's class at the International Chinese Montessori School she did a report, 'Teeth.' One of the things she wrote about in the report was a two- or three-inch model of a tooth that was carved centuries ago to show the horrible pain of a toothache. There were different pictures on this large ivory tooth, sort of like the different pictures that are in stained glass. Stained glass was invented to tell stories in pictures because so few people could read back then. Now we have to read twenty-five books just to figure out what the stained glass is saying, so it's the opposite of before, when you didn't read but just looked around and thought, Ah, King Solomon, I see. Ivory was a good choice for the model tooth because ivory is the tooth of the elephant. The model showed people throwing skulls in a fire, probably to illustrate the horrible burning pain of a toothache, and a picture of something bad happening to a woman, some drastic tooth operation. It had a hinge. It was a box, which you opened up. 'Maybe if you stored candy in it,' Nory thought, 'you would eat less candy because you would see this horrible carved picture of the skulls going into the fire and think, No, I won't have that lemondrop, not just yet.'

Also in the report—which was probably the best thing she did in Ms. Beryl's class by far—Nory drew a diagram of the layers of the tooth. For years she had thought, 'There must be layers to the tooth, there *must* be, it can't possibly be all the same substance.' It worried her for a very long while, and then, presto, when she drew the diagram, copying from the encyclopedia, she was happy to discover that there were. She liked when things had layers—the earth has layers, the trunk of a tree has layers, the atmosphere has layers. A conker has layers, too. It has a green spiky outer layer and a very shiny wonderful layer which is the conker itself, which is like the finest, smoothest wood in a very precious table or the knob of a chair or something like that, in a great palace like Ickworth House, where the floorboards are curved. (They were somehow bent into curves with the help of steam engines, which pleased Littleguy.) And then inside that there's the growing part of the conker, which is like the nerve of the tooth. Sometimes you can find a double-conker. 'Conker' is the English way of saying horse chestnut, and it's a very good way because they can suddenly conk you on the head. After the sermon in the Cathedral at Harvest Festival they were all crossing the street and Nory spotted tons and tons and tons of freshly fallen conkers. She rushed over and started gathering them. They're very rare in general because as soon as they come off the tree, people come over and get them. Everyone was really happy to find more conkers had fallen, just during the short time they were in the Cathedral. They sang a song in service that went: 'Think of the world without any flowers, think of the world without any trees.' Then it went, 'The farmers spread the good things on the land, but it is God's almighty hand, that waters them, but,' then there was something Nory couldn't remember, 'but more to us as children, he gives our daily bread.' The English way of singing was quite different from the Chinese way of singing. In the English way, you had to hold one note for a very long time, and you didn't woggle the note so much. The English had extremely high singing voices and their songs were meant to be sung in an English accent, so when one child out of dozens was singing them in an American accent it didn't always have a pleasant outcome.

Sometimes when they had sung the flower-gathering song in Chinese class Bernice would sing it with her retainer halfway out of her mouth, which was rude and disgusting, and it made the Chinese teacher furious. Bernice had to go on time-out once for doing that. (Time-out didn't exist in England—they had detention, or DT, instead.) Bernice also talked baby talk with her retainer halfway out. Once she bit it so hard it broke and half of it went up into the part of her nose that connected to the back of her mouth and the doctor had to go in and pull it out, or it would have stayed there forever causing trouble. Debbie would never think of chewing her retainer in half— she was a very sweet girl in many ways. Her braces made her mouth wide and gave her that thinking look that was the most noticeable thing about her besides her hair. Of course her whole face was quite wide. Nory's face was a smashed, squashed, shriveled little thing, she felt. It seemed shriveled partly because she spent her time with Debbie and other Asian kids, who are, you just have to say, the most beautiful type of kids in most ways. Nory would draw a self-portrait and be not perfectly content with it, thinking, 'Well, it's a bit of a squished head on the sides, but all right.' And then she would look at her face in the mirror and think, 'Well, no wonder I drew a squished head.' Her parents said she was a beautiful child and sometimes she did think she looked pretty, but it was not polite to brag that out loud. It was quite all right for parents to tell a child she was beautiful, just as long as they didn't tell her she was beautiful in front of other children. If they announced it in front of other children it would put the other children in an awkward position, because they would be just sitting there, odd man out.

One day at her new school, the Threll Junior School, Mrs. Thirm asked the class to write the first paragraph of a story with each child as the main character. Nory started off with: 'Marielle was a young girl with brown hair and brown eyes who was forty-three inches tall.' But she wasn't entirely happy with this. What she had been tempted to write after the 'who was' was not that she was forty-three inches tall, but something similar to the scene in *The Little Princess*, where the girl is being shown around the school, and she acts as a 'bright-eyed, smart, quiet little girl most of the time.' It wasn't exactly, persistently those words, but at least that was the feeling of the scene. And the girl who played the Little Princess in the movie looked a tiny bit like Nory. Nory really wanted to write that Marielle, who stood for her, was a 'quiet little girl, most of the time, very quiet, and mysterious—or not really mysterious, but if you took a little bit away from the meaning of mysterious, or add a little more to the scene in *The Little Princess*, an almost mysterious girl.' But she wrote none of that because even though Marielle was not her own name, it would be clear that she was writing about herself and it would be kind of bragging to say those things.

21. What You Might Have to Do, Though

The time when Nory most thought about how she looked was, of course, when she looked in the mirror, which was just before bed when she was brushing her teeth. They made a mistake, Nory thought, in advertisements when they showed a long, long stretch of toothpaste starting at the very tip of the toothbrush and going to the other end of the bristles, because that's really not the amount you should have. It's way too much. If you put that much on, it burns your whole mouth, since there are a lot of nerves in the gums, so what happens is that you are desperate to want to spit it out immediately, without brushing your teeth at all. Then you could claim, 'Oh, yes, I brushed my teeth' without really brushing them. Or you do it very quickly and you do a really, really bad job. That was what was so important about the idea of a pea-sized gob.

And always while she brushed she made a toothful smile, because you almost have to, which put her in the mind of pretending to be another person. That was one way she would start telling stories: she would talk to the twin toothbrusher in the mirror, and then she would play a game that there were twins, asking each other questions, and then triplets. She would act out each one's personality, and something sad would have happened to one of them. One time she played a mirror game in which there were five duplicates of her. That was back in America. Each person had strange bracesy things in their mouths that were made shaped like candy, and flavored like candy. So each twin would come on and describe how great her braces were. 'Hi! These are raspberry-flavored braces! They're astonishingly good braces!' 'Mine are apple-cinammon! They're superb!' And so on. They would take turns advertising their braces. And then they would get into a conversation, and that would lead to a story about some trouble one of the twins was having. Then Nory's mother and father would call upstairs, 'Nory? Are you in your night-costume?' Nory would shout back, 'Oops! Sorry! I was dawdling, I'm afraid!'

Nory wanted to work for an advertising campaign, like her grandfather, while she was trying to get her certificate of dentistry, because she loved advertising campaigns. She wanted a Ph.D., though, most of all. Nory's mother told her about Ph.D.s, and she was determined on getting one. She positively *had* to have that Ph.D., because for one thing it makes you feel smart to have one and it's something that basically all people get. She was not going to be kept away from getting one just because she would have to get some strange badge of dentistry. So she would probably need to be something more, like a dental surgeon or a dental botanist, who does research into why teeth grow or get cavities, in order to need to get that Ph.D. But she would still have to go to a dentistry school. That surely would still be a necessity.

Nory wouldn't mind working with a corpse if it meant dentistry. Doctors have to operate on corpses, she had heard, and if you're going to be a dental surgeon, you definitely might have to use a corpse, because dead people have teeth, too, don't they? If you're going to pull the teeth from anyone, it might as well be from a corpse. The school could make a huge plastic figure, like a voodoo doll, and have the students pull teeth from that, but it would be very expensive and you'd have to create all those parts of the body from scratch out of clay or better yet FIMO. The teeth would have to snap in and out somehow. Why not use a dead person, since they're available? Nory wouldn't mind doing it, because she wanted to be a dentist so much. On the other hand, she did get quite disgusted by doing math. Math, math, math. One pencil lead used up, then another, then another. Then you're out of pencil leads and you have to use a regular pencil. Sharpen, sharpen, sharpen. Whole huge erasers used up madly erasing things you did wrong. Her National Trust eraser had no corners left now. It was a pathetic egg of an eraser. The idea of all that math she would have to do in order to be a dentist gave her an extremely carsick feeling.

But: 'Don't count your bad lucks before they happen.' That was a saying that she had made up. It was kind of like 'Don't count your chickens before they hatch,' except the opposite.

22. For Some Reason, People Were Bad to Pamela

In real life there were identical twins at her school. They didn't have braces. At first Nory thought they might become her good friends. But it was hard to be friends with them, because you don't want to talk to both of them at the same time, as if they're one person, because they might not like that, so you talk to one, and then you have to instantly talk to the other, so that you don't seem as if you're ignoring her, which wouldn't be polite. So you ask her a question, and then the other twin asks a question, and you answer that question, and you ask that twin a question about what activities she's going to sign up for, table tennis or French knitting. So then that twin begins talking about activities. Then you have to ask the other twin about her activities. They do mostly the same thing, but not exactly the same thing. And sometimes you can't keep track of which twin you asked what. Even if you didn't want it to be, it was sort of like, 'If I ask you one question, you ask me two questions.' They seemed to have mostly the same friends, and really it didn't matter which one you talked to because they were both equally as nice and equally as interesting, and they both looked pretty much the same, pretty much blond, that is, and sweet-smiling. So you felt just as comfortable talking to one as to the other.

But it didn't turn out that Nory became friends with them. The twins had other friends from last year they relied on heavily. Sometimes, as a matter of fact, they were a bit irritable with Nory and fair-weather-friendish. Once they were even part of a whole gang-up of girls who were bad to Pamela Shavers. Pamela Shavers, for no reason at all, was selected to be that certain someone that everyone should laugh at and say quite sharp, mocking things to. She had skipped ahead one year, so she was in Year Six when really her age was Year Five, which is to say, fourth grade. So? What was bad about that? Pamela lost her prep book in the changing room and was rushing trying to find it and four other girls from one of the older classes started saying they'd used it as loo paper. Not very likely. The twins weren't really a part of that group, though, they were just watching and laughing. Their older sister, though, was one who was saying things like 'Are you sure you didn't bake it in a pie in Kitchen Arts?' Pamela was just on the edge of crying, saying 'I'm going to miss my train!' Nory couldn't stand it and said: 'Stop. You're being horrible to her. Stop it, stop it, stop it.'

'Oh, oh, you're friends with her?' said one of the girls to Nory. 'You don't know better, you're from America, you have no idea how squeegee your accent is.'

'Yes, I am American, I have an American accent,' said Nory. 'Your accent, let me inform you, is dreadful. You bark like a sea lion.'

People giggled a little at that and that made Nory well known and made the girl furious, but the important thing was that Pamela had a chance to look some more for her prep book, which she found.

Another time Pamela lost her jacket, or maybe someone hid it. She was frantically looking, and nobody was willing to help. They just told her rude things. 'Well, we don't know where it is, we gave it to an old drooling man who came to the door who gave it away to Oxfam.'

Pamela kept saying, 'I have to catch my train!' There was the same sound in her voice that seemed to Nory as if she certainly was going to cry, but she didn't. It was just the quality that came into her voice when she was angry—although maybe there was some crying in it. (Nory's own record was still perfect: she had not cried. Had not and would not.) Pamela couldn't leave without her jacket on because Mrs. Derpath stood by the door, totally on the watch-out. She would nip you by the neck, throw you around, toss you back into the classroom, if you did not have your blue blazer on. So Pamela had to find that blazer.

Nory helped her, she rummaged and scrummaged, she found it under a pile of backpacks, and she said, 'Here, Pamela, here's your jacket.' But it was completely trampled over and disgusting. Kids had been practically been doing the Majarajah on it, stamping back and forth without noticing. Nory helped her dust it off. 'Thanks,' said Pamela and she hurried away for her train. She ran in a crouching run, her backpack bouncing like a kangaroo, but her eyes looking down and a little forward on the sidewalk. It was not exactly the way a happy girl would run.

Even Nory's friend Kira, who was turning out to be a good friend in England, didn't want Nory to be nice to Pamela. Pamela had been quite nice to Nory in one of the early days of school, when Nory had forgotten how to get back to the Junior School building from the dining hall, once *again*. Nory had an atrocious sense of direction—about as atrocious as her sense of spelling, she thought sometimes, and maybe the two things were connected, because knowing which way to turn was like when you were trying to spell 'failure' and you didn't know if it was 'faleyer' or 'fayelyor' or something quite else. You didn't know whether to go northeast or southwest at the choices of vowel. Her sense of direction was so horrible that she crashed her plane four times in I.T. They had stopped learning the home row of keys on the keyboard, and they were doing a Flight Imitator, or whatever it was called, and they were supposed to land a plane in the dark according to a map, and Nory simply could not read that map. Her plane shot up toward the stars, and the lights began going around, which meant she was in a death-spin, and she crashed. She crashed so many times that day she had a bad dream about it. So her sense of direction was not at all good. 'You're just a disaster, aren't you?' said the I.T.

teacher, but he said it in a very comforting way that made Nory feel better, in the same kind voice he used when he said, 'Good morning, ladies and jellyfish.' So anyway, Nory lost her sense of direction and got turned around and wasn't sure where she was headed, but Pamela, when Nory asked her for help that early time, wasn't in the least bit surprised that she didn't know the way back, and just treated it as a normal event and very nicely walked with her, having a nice indistinct conversation.

Another time Daniella Harding wanted to scratch 'D H' on the back of her watch, to stand for Daniella Harding—she was a pillish girl in some ways, no question about that, although not always—and she borrowed Nory's compass to use the point for scratching. Nory let her take it because it was flattering to be asked for something and to have it there in your pencil case, and of course, an hour later, the pencil in the compass was totally lost, gone, bye-bye. (Really the compass is called a 'set of compasses' and the things that stick out are called the 'arms of the compass.') And it was the only pencil Nory had just then, because somehow she'd lost the others, including even her mechanical pencil. That time, very nicely, Pamela let Nory borrow one of her pencils and helped her with some of her math. Nory was on the wrong track in her multiplication and was counting up all the numbers to the right of the decimal, including the numbers you add together to get the final number. Pamela showed her that it was much easier than that. You only had to count the number of numbers to the right of the decimal on the two numbers that you're multiplying in order to get the answer.

But even if Pamela had never once been nice to Nory, Nory probably would have said something, she thought, because Pamela had just as much a right as anyone else to

go off to school every day and not have her day be made
into a state of misery. Her parents were paying hundreds of
thousands of dollars to send her there, think about that.
Pamela said that she hadn't told her parents about any of it
because she hadn't found the time. Nory told her parents
about it and they said that it was brave of Nory to defend
Pamela. They thought Pamela ought to go right to the
teacher. But Pamela didn't want to.

And the thing that was so impossible to figure out, was:
Why was this happening? Pamela was never rude or
interrupting, she wasn't braggingly pleased with herself,
she was perfectly nice to everybody. Was it some chance
thing one day that made it happen that one kid decided to
pick on her and then everyone else did? Or was it that there
was something about the way she acted that made kids get
up on the wrong side of the bed with her? Her face was a
nice face—maybe a slight roundedness to it in the cheeks,
and her teeth were a little bit out of whack in maybe a
chipmunkish way. Or rather that was what two boys were
saying one time: that she had a rat-faced look, which is a
persistently rude and cruel thing to say, but those boys
were known for being rude and insulting guttersnakes
every chance they got. And her nose did have a pudginess
about it. But Daniella's nose had much more pudge to it
and nobody took the time to fuss her out. Actually Daniella
was one of the most popular kids!

Nory said to Pamela, 'Go to Mrs. Thirm, tell Mrs.
Thirm.' But Pamela said she'd gone to Mrs. Thirm last year
about something and Mrs. Thirm had said to her that she'd
done all kinds of things that she said she hadn't done, so
she couldn't go to Mrs. Thirm. Nory said, 'Well, then, go to
Mr. Pears.' Mr. Pears was the head of the Junior School
and an extremely nice man. He was the one who read them

about Hector. The problem with the story about Hector, however—or, not Hector, Achilles—the problem about Achilles, Nory felt, was that he was much more a likable heroine in the beginning, when he was a newborn infant. Later on, in the part about the battle, he takes a downturn and goes bad. The ending should have worked differently. He falls in love with somebody, and he kills hundreds of people, he drags a man around behind his wagon, and he sulks away the time in his tent and says he won't fight anymore. It's just not anywhere near as good. The better part is earlier when a person who was half deer and half human took care of him, and fed him with deerskin. No, the person couldn't have been half a deer, because he wouldn't be feeding him deerskin if he were a deer, that would be cannibalism. The person was half-oxen, half-human. This half-and-half creature fed him deerskin and cream. The deerskin was for good strength, and cream or sugar for good heart or health. Nory had not followed this part exactly, because she'd been inspired by it halfway through to have the idea of a detective story about a Batman ruler and a Barbie pencil. But Achilles was still good when he was having the cream and deerskin diet. He seemed like a much less good person when he got older.

Pamela said, 'Oh no, I can't go to Mr. Pears, because he'll go to Mrs. Thirm.' So she just didn't do anything. And it began to get gradually a little worse and a little worse, time by time. Kira kept saying to Nory, 'Whatever you do, do not speak to Pamela.' She said: 'Every time you speak to Pamela it will make you less popular.' She said, 'Just spend your time with me.' Nory liked Kira and was in the early part of a friendship when you are sort of under a person's spell a little, basically. So for two days she did stay away from Pamela more than she had—not completely, because she sat next to her for one lunch, but she spent most of the time with Kira. But it pulled at her, what she was doing, because she knew she was not helping Pamela and maybe hurting her feelings. Nory told this to her parents. They said that when a group of people decide to not speak to a person and pretend they don't exist it was called the Silent Treatment, and though it wasn't physically bullying in the meaning of punching someone or screaming at them it was a quiet mental torture and awful. They wanted to tell someone at the school about it, but Nory said that Pamela didn't want anyone to know about it. They said that the bad thing about bullying was that people who didn't ever imagine that they would be doing mean things to a person, people like Kira, ended up doing mean things, because it spreads. And the person who's being bullied gets kind of numb and bewildered and doesn't know how to take action.

So next break-time Nory sat on a wall side by side with Pamela. Kira was furious and stomped off. Nory found her later in the music room, with the headphones on, reading a book. Nory said, 'Kira! I've been looking everywhere for you! I've been in a state about it. I looked in the changing room, I looked in the classroom, I looked under the tree, I looked in the bathroom, I didn't even *go* to the bathroom because I was so busy looking for you. I even looked in the front field!'

Kira said, 'Oh, hm, yes.' She was not apologetic in any way and just sat there like a bump on a rug.

It hurt Nory's friendliness toward Kira that Kira had this character flaw of being very possessive and jealous and needing her all to herself. And the thing was, also, that Kira was generally in some ways a rough kind of punching friend—friendly punching. If Kira got mad at something, she would tighten up Nory's tie so afterward for a little while Nory's neck had a sweaty feeling from the itch of the collar. But when Nory went back to being friendly to Pamela, Kira began saying sharp sarcastic things, that were half-jokes, half not-jokes, like: 'Nory, do you like torturing people?' Nory was confused for a second because her parents had used that word and she thought Kira was talking about Pamela. She said, 'Um—do you?'

'No,' said Kira. 'But evidently you do, because that's what dentists do.'

'Kira!' said Nory, laughing, but not feeling particularly good. Her feelings were still hurt later when she thought about it. She could have said, still jokingly, but meaning what she was saying, 'How dare you insult the poor dentists, who are just trying to help. It's your fault. You got your own cavities. You should have brushed your teeth. Then the dentist would only have to put good old paste inside of your mouth, spread it around, and Mr. Thirsty would suck out all the saliva that gathered into a little puddle in your lower mouth.' Nory liked the feeling of Mr. Thirsty thirsting out the saliva, the hollow bubbling sound he made. Mr. Thirsty was just a name dentists gave to a certain little bended piece of suction tube, to make it seem friendlier to kids. And it worked. If you you kept it in too long, you might completely dry out your mouth, which would be an interesting experiment. Probably a dental researcher has tried it. Nory used to try to dry her tongue completely by sticking it out for a long time. If you lie there on your bed with your tongue out for long enough it will get so totally dry that it glues itself to your mouth when you pull it back in. But it's probably not good to do that too much. In one of her books about Egypt there was a horrible picture of a mummy curled up on its side with its tongue sticking out. They'd found the tongue in five pieces, dried up of course, and they'd carefully glued it back together. It was black and completely disgusting.

23. *Pot-stickers Are Not an Easy Thing to Make*

One boy, one of the three boys named Colin that Nory knew of—there was Colin Sharings, Colin Deat, and Colin Ryseman—started coming up to Nory after she was spending time with Pamela. He started saying, in a smeary little high voice, 'Oh, ho, Pamela's friend, oh? Pamela's *friend.*' Nory had saved up a little list of things that she could say back to this kind of person. Such as: 'Calling all police, calling all police, there's a grub in the classroom. Take it away, take it away.' There were lots of grubs in the yard of the Trumpet Hill house. They were white little wigglers, not very attractive, and if somebody stepped on them, they went all red.

If it was outside that Colin came up and said something unpleasant, then Nory could say that she had no idea that earthworms could talk.

Nory tried the earthworm one out on him one afternoon. 'My goodness, I simply had no idea earthworms could talk! Boy, did you prove me wrong.' Colin kicked some leaves and said, 'So you didn't know earthworms could talk, Pamela's *friend?* You don't know very much, do you, Pamela's friend?' Then he walked drearily away, chin on parade. It was sort of a tie. It's difficult because of the golden rule, you shouldn't ever say anything that's extremely rude, but you get angry, and you have to come up with comebacks that are not bad words, and not *too* insulting, not so insulting that it's really mean to bring them up. So for example you couldn't ever bring up Arthur's problem with the cavity in his bicuspid, because that's too true to make fun of. Colin Sharings had a pink mole on his ear, but you couldn't make fun of that, either. You had to come up with whatever you're going to say very quickly, too, because there you are, and there's the person who's said the rude thing to you, smirkingly looking pleased with himself, and the longer the rude thing is out on its own the more chance there is that people will laugh against you.

The first time Colin came up and mocked her for being Pamela's friend Nory wasn't prepared for it. She just said, 'Yes, I'm Pamela's friend. Is there a problem?' That worked quite well, except that Nory was standing with Kira when Colin said it, so Colin then said to Kira, because he was a fiend of badness, 'And you like Pamela, too-hoo,' using the grossest kind of mocking singing voice. Kira didn't say anything, so Nory said, 'No, as a matter of fact Kira doesn't like Pamela. So that shows how much you know about the whole kitten caboodle.'

But Pamela herself was nearby and probably heard Nory say that, and Nory worried afterward that that would hurt her feelings to have said that Kira didn't like her to Colin. Pamela didn't mention it next time they talked, though. After that crude awakening, Nory began saving up the comebacks so she wouldn't get tricked into saying something she wouldn't want to have said.

But the other problem, which was a bigger problem, was that some of why Nory wanted to be friendly with Pamela was because she thought Pamela truly deserved to have some friends who stuck with her, and she knew that if she was friendly with her it might be just that tiny straw that broke the camel's back of the habit that the kids had of ganging up on her. But Nory also had an idea that probably Pamela would never be a really close true friend, a dear friend, because they were quite different in certain ways. Other people were being bad to Pamela, and so Nory was feeling she ought to do her best to forfeit her obligation and be more of a friend than she would have been naturally, in real life, which made her feel a little artificial. When she walked back to the Junior School with Pamela they had all-right conversations but they weren't the kind of conversations about things that she would have had with Debbie, where they talked about how much fun it was to put Barbie shoes on 'My Little Pony' horses and dress up their manes with flower petals. Debbie loved those 'My Little Pony' horses, and you had to admit, seeing them all set up in a row, they looked pretty fancy in high-heeled shoes, with their puffy manes. And it wasn't the kind of wild-laughter conversations that Nory sometimes had with Kira or Janet or Tobi, at the Junior School, where somebody would keep trying to say something over and over and couldn't because it was so heroriously funny they couldn't finish the sentence. Pamela told Nory about everyone in her family. Very interesting: her uncles, her aunts, her cousins, her second cousins, what they did, what they looked like, what they watched on TV. Nory told Pamela about her family, but not in as much detail because it wasn't as impressive a family, since she only had four first cousins and a lot of her great-aunts and people like that had already died. They both agreed that chutney was fairly disgusting, but when Nory said that the thing she liked least in the world, par none, was fried chicken, Pamela said she liked fried chicken and that her Dad went out and bought fried chicken from Captain Chicken USA at least once a week. (Captain Chicken was a place that was trying to trick you into thinking it was Kentucky Fried Chicken, with the same red letters, and figuring that, 'Oh, you're English, you won't be able to draw a difference.') Nory hurried on to explain that probably she disliked fried chicken for a particular reason, which was that she'd had it so much at her old school, the International Chinese Montessori School, where it was piled up in large foil pans and got cold and was extremely dark-meatedly greasy. Nory had eaten too much Chinese fried chicken in her life for her to be able to stand another drumstick. The rest of the food had been pretty good, though, she said. No jacket potatoes, of course, because the Chinese are basically less interested in potatoes than America and England is. The jacket potato is a European dish. One time, Nory told Pamela, her whole class at the International Chinese Montessori School learned to make pot-stickers, which are difficult because sometimes you make the wrapping small and there's too much of the meat, or the filling, in the pot sticker, and sometimes you do too little filling. There are many problems and things that can go wrong. It's really difficult, and you have to seal it with egg.

Pamela asked what pot-stickers were, and Nory said they were a Chinese food filled with meat that can burn your mouth when you bite in on them. At her old school, they also learned to write in Chinese characters, Nory said.

Pamela laughed and said, 'In Chinese! You learned to write in Chinese?'

'Yes,' said Nory, feeling a little proud of being able to do that fairly unusual thing. 'We had to, because it was the International Chinese Montessori School. We spent half the day on Chinese, we did our multiplication tables in Chinese, lots of things. Would you like me to write something for you?'

Pamela said okay, so Nory got a piece of paper out of her backpack and sat down on the sidewalk and wrote her the character for 'hao.' Hao was made up of two parts. Half of it was part of the character for mother, and half of it was part of 'child,' because the Chinese think that mother plus child equals good. It's a good thing for a child to have a mother near her and a mother to have a child near her. So, sensibly, *hao* means good. In Chinese it looked like this:

好

Nory gave the paper to Pamela. Pamela looked at it and nodded. She said, 'How would you say six times seven in Chinese?' Nory said 'Liu cheng qi den yu si shi er. So six times seven is forty-two.'

'Oh,' said Pamela.

'If you know your numbers, it's really easy,' said Nory. 'Would you like me to show you how the Chinese character for two could have turned into our American-English number 2, and how the Chinese three could have become our 3?'

'Yes, but maybe another time,' said Pamela, 'because I think we have to go in.'

'Okay,' said Nory. 'Well, bye.'

'Bye,' said Pamela.

24. *What You Do and Don't Remember*

That afternoon Nory tried to reinstruct every tiny detail of the International Chinese School in her mind. Talking about it to Pamela showed her how much she was already forgetting. It was a lovely school, where the kids were nice, most of them. When she first started in Upper Elementary one of the kids, Carl, who should remain nameless, told her in detail how he was going to kill her by throwing her in a swimming pool filled with poisonous insects. Carl was a warped older boy who left after that year.

A number of kids ganged up on her in the very beginning of that year, which was just about the only time anything that an adult would call being bullied ever happened to her. It was distressing enough that she could connect it to what Pamela might be feeling. But then she tried to think, 'Honestly, was it a terrible thing that that boy, Carl, said all that mean stuff to me, and other kids mocked me?' In her memory it wasn't so unbearably bad because it was a very very long time ago. But that might be because it hadn't gone on and gone on. You remember things better that happen over and over again, like Stop, Drop, and Roll. Except when they happen so many times that you don't notice them whatsoever. Some parts of *Neverending Story*, the movie, she remembered very well, like the stone giant, and the flying dog that the boy meets. There's a girl in the movie who is a princess who is important in a way because she's going to die, but she's minor, actually: the heroine is the boy. Nory thought she must have seen *The Neverending Story* recently in an advertisement, maybe a preview before another movie that her mother rented for her, because parts of it she had in her mind very clearly and colorfully and parts of it were fogged in. At the beginning some bullies throw the boy into the garbage, and he comes back at the end and he throws them into the garbage, all three of them. And someone loses his horse, because it sinks into the swamp and dies. That could be in *Neverending Story II.* There was a story similar to that part in a booklet that Nory's father bought for her at the Cathedral shop. A man asks another man if he's seen a hat floating in a very muddy road. The other man says, 'Golly, no, I haven't, why?' And the first man says, 'Well, I suspect there may be a man sitting on a horse underneath the hat.'

At the time they were mean to her, Nory had told Ms. Fisker about the boys in her class. Ms. Fisker was the upper elementary teacher who taught in English, in the afternoon. (Bai Lao Shi taught in Chinese, in the morning.) But Ms. Fisker said Nory had to learn how to handle the older boys and work matters out for herself. 'Oh, Nory, I can see you're developing a long tail, I can see it growing'—that's what Ms. Fisker would say, because she was strongly not in favor of tattletales. The rule was: 'Don't be a tattletale for little things, do be a tattletale for big things.' Say if someone has broken someone's thumb in the door. Something major. But Nory's parents thought that Ms. Fisker probably should have ordered the older boys not to gang up on Nory. At some point the boys just stopped, though. And now it was just in her memory.

When Carl said that he would kill her by tossing her in the swimming pool with the insects she just disgustedly said, 'Carl, you're fat.'

Carl said, 'Well, not as fat as your butt.'

When Carl said that, Nory couldn't help giggling. Then he pointed at her and said, 'Haw, haw! You think it's funny! Haw, haw! I made you laugh!' So Carl won that battle face down, because it's really dumb-seeming to giggle at times. Carl just hated Nory, for some reason. And Nory hated Carl.

But a lot of what happened that year she couldn't remember nearly as well as that bit. 'That bit' is how they would say it in England, and if you asked your friend to come over, they would say that you asked her to 'come round.' These days Nory couldn't remember the order she had learned things at the ICMS or all the works she did—they called them 'works,' the little projects, like the number pyramid or a geography puzzle that they did. She couldn't even remember all the kids in the class. She remembered one very nice girl named Steffie who left later on, who had a birthday party at her swimming pool where Nory had floundered into the deep end and had gotten about a gallon and a half of water in her lung and thrown up a tiny bit on the grass. She gave Steffie a pair of tiny glass slippers, wrapped up in probably the best wrapping paper she had ever drawn, with a picture of a girl in a rowboat near a willow tree on it. She still thought about those glass slippers. They were paperweights that a glassblower made, but they worked as real doll shoes. She wished she had those glass slippers, they were amazingly wonderful. But Steffie's parents moved away to Lafayette and she started going to a different school. So that was the last birthday with Steffie.

It disturbed Nory very much to think that all she was going to know about what happened in her life was not very much at all. You only can really remember the things that happened when you were an older child and the things that happened to you now—that is, yesterday, or the day before yesterday, or late last week. You live your life always in the present. And even in the present, this day, dozens and hundreds of little tiny things happen, so many that by the end of the day you can't make a list of them. You lose track of them unless something reminds you. Say someone says, 'Remember when you dropped your ruler this morning?' And you do remember. But then that is lost in the tangle.

Now, some things you can just accept that you're not going to have the slightest chance of remembering. It would be nice, but you know that it would be basically impossible. For instance, being in your mother's womb, as it's called. Some people thought babies could remember that. Nory one morning asked Littleguy if he could remember being tucked away in Mommy's belly, long ago, and he said, 'Yes. It had all things there, in she's tummy. It had things that were called *steam trains*. It was filled with they. Filled with steam trains, City of Truro, Lord of the Isles, the Mallard. Pictures with steam trains, and toy ones, and jumping things, all. Filled, filled with they.' Well, of course there weren't toy trains in Nory's mother's womb, unless maybe he was remembering the small intestine chuffing around. Maybe he was remembering a freight train of food being digested going around and around him. But probably not.

Still, Nory thought it would be nice if you could think back at least to the age of three. It shouldn't be impossible. Three was older than Littleguy, and Littleguy could understand an amazing number of things. But Nory couldn't go back that far, really, except for a few scribs and scrabs. She remembered being eight, and back into being seven, and she went pretty much back to five, and then—it teetered a little bit. She only remembered her fourth birthday party, a Mermaid party, because she had watched the tape of it a number of times on TV.

One thing, though, she made a point of remembering and passing on to her older self. Every year that she got a year older she said to her parents, 'Remember when I was five, I said I was five going on six? Remember when I was six I said six going on seven? When I was seven I'd be going seven on eight? Then going eight on nine? Well, now I'm going nine on ten.' So each year the list of years got a little longer, but she remembered the earlier times that way, by saying the list over. Being thirteen would be very nice, because you're in your teens when you're thirteen, and you don't have to read a big sign that says, 'Children under the age of twelve cannot attend to this.' Another thing she made sure to bring along every year with her for a long time was the memory that there were many many little amounts of money that she hadn't paid back to her parents. Little collections of change she had found in the car and thought could be hers but maybe not, or times her parents had bought her a doll outfit or something when she told them she would reimburse them later when they got home from her own money, or gifts she bought other people with her own money, but borrowing it from her parents since she'd forgotten her purse. She would skip a week, not thinking of it, then still remember it and bring it into the next week, then skip a week, then bring it over. Finally she couldn't keep the amount in her head because it had been added onto and subtracted from so much, and it began to pull at her, and she thought, 'I know, I'll pay them a hundred dollars when I grow up, and that will surely make up for anything I borrowed along the way.' Then she didn't have to keep track of that.

25. The Last Straw

Ms. Fisker was a very good teacher with a humongously good memory. She could keep in the front-runners of her brain what each child knew and what they hadn't learned yet. And she could persistently keep the whole class quiet and doing their own work, privately. That's something you almost had to do as a teacher in a Montessori school because each kid is at a different level, learning some different scribbet of a thing, and there are lots of different ages of kids in a class. So for instance in Nory's class there were kids who were seven and kids who were eleven. Some were doing 'six plus five' kinds of things, some were doing 'numbers of seconds it takes a flicker of light to spark to the earth divided by the speed of light' kinds of things, and Ms. Fisker had to be totally on her toes about that. Some were learning how to break up words into syllables and some were learning that a noun was a large black triangle and a verb, which is an action, was a large red circle, and the reason why is because it's a red rolling ball, moving. And a proper noun was a long purple triangle, if Nory wasn't mistaken, and the the articles, like 'an,' 'a,' and 'the,' were either a short light blue or a short *dark* blue triangle. The adjectives were either short light blue or short dark blue, depending on what the articles were. The adverb is a smaller orange circle. Each of these things had to be learned, one by one, by coloring in the shapes over the sentences, and some kids were at the black-triangle stage and some were at the small-orange-circle stage. And there were keyholes and green half-moons, and on and on— Nory had never learned grammar out that far. Nobody at the Junior School knew about these grammar shapes because they were specially designed as part of the Montessori system, so all that time she had spent thinking about why a black triangle was like a noun, because it had a wide base and just sat there steadily being whatever noun it was, was just time that could have gone 'poof' away, as far as her teachers now were concerned. But she liked knowing that a red circle stood for a verb because it rolled. You could use it for other things you learned later, for instance you could say to yourself, 'Mass is a blue triangle, energy is a red circle.'

So each kid in Ms. Fisker's class had a different number of these shapes and math skills scrummaging around in their head, and Ms. Fisker had everything that they had in their heads in *her* head, at just the level that they had it, each of them, which was part of why she was such a good teacher. After Carl luckily left, Nory got used to the class and Ms. Fisker started to like her and told her things. The most amazing thing Ms. Fisker told her was that she was getting married and going to a different city. It was really amazing to think of Ms. Fisker, one of the proudest teachers, getting married, but she did. Of course, she had been married once before and had a son who was eighteen, but the class hadn't really taken that in. They didn't really know that very much. Ms. Fisker had a mischevious cat, and she would wake up, and the cat would prance around on her, and knock down her bottles. Her cat was a mischievous little thing. One time her son had had an operation on his knee and the cat jumped up on his leg and she said he almost went through the ceiling. If you were designing a teacher from scrap, you couldn't design a teacher better than Ms. Fisker. But Ms. Fisker's last day at the school was at the teacher-appreciation dinner at the end of the year. The main dish at the teacher-appreciation dinner was a huge fried pig. Its head was there on the big pan in the middle of the table. The head of a pig was not in Nory's opinion a good menu choice for a teacher-appreciation dinner since there were a lot of younger kids who might be very bothered by the sight of that head, not to mention older kids such as Nory herself who might be revolted as well. You could see its closed eyes. To be polite, she ate a taste of the pig, but only a taste. And that was the last she saw of Ms. Fisker for quite a while.

The teacher who came in place of Ms. Fisker was Ms. Beryl, who was good but totally different. She liked talking about herself a lot, whereas Ms. Fisker only told them a few careful things, such as about her cat in the morning. Ms. Beryl gave out extremely hard spelling lists with words like 'dicotyledon' and 'pinnate' and 'microeconomics' because she was probably more interested in the much older kids, the eleven-year-olds, and wanted them to be getting ready to go to college. It kind of slipped Ms. Beryl's mind that the younger kids were still trying to get it into their heads how to spell 'really' and 'tomorrow' and 'would' and 'unknown.' Nory had a custom of spelling 'tomorrow' as 'tomaro.' The math suddenly turned into a jostle of cube roots and algebra kinds of things, with x's and y's and breaking things down into their factories, when Nory was still trudging away with her times tables. As her friend Bernice said, 'When you wear a bra, you study algebra, not before.'

So Nory got exceedingly distracted, looking at the days of the week on the wall calendar and thinking 'SuMTWTHFRS, hmm, that could almost spell *smothers with furs*,' and from time to time she got into a state of click-laughing with Bernice, who was an easy person to get into a state of click-laughing. They positively could not stop, even though they were almost on the edge of crying, begging each other with their eyes not to start out on another huge laugh, and Ms. Beryl would get furious. Click-laughing is just when you laugh so heroriously that you only make little tiny sounds at the back of your throat. It set Ms. Beryl on fire, and one time, she wrote a note in Nory's booklet that said that Nory must make a more asserted effort on her concentration skills, because her constantly wanting to know what others were doing around her and her constantly being unable to resist distracting them from what they were working on by giggling was her FATAL FLAW. Ms. Beryl read her note to Nory's mother and underlined FATAL FLAW three times while she read. Nory was standing a short distance away, pretending to be thinking over other things or nothing, but she heard it near and clear. On the other hand, she wasn't exactly sure what a fatal flaw meant. But now that she had been going to Classics class at the Junior School and had learned about heroines like Achilles, she knew.

The fatal flaw was quite similar in what it means to the last straw, and the last straw was the straw that broke the camel's back. The last straw was NOT, REPEAT NOT the last straw in the machine at a restaurant that when it was taken meant the machine was empty and you would have to drink your milkshake sadly without a straw. Kids find out rather quickly that it is less fun to drink the normal way, with your mouth, because with a straw it's as if you have magical powers and are telling telling the drink, 'Kazam, kazaw, now climb the straw!'

Nory suspected that the straw that broke that camel's back was an unsensible idea anyway, because first of all, stop and think of that poor camel. How could it happen? Doesn't he have something to say about the situation? Also, camels' backs are pretty strong things. If you've ridden on them, you know that they can support at least two people, if not three. And if they are able to support two or three people, they should be able to support a lot, a lot, a lot of hay, because hay doesn't weigh very much at all, and some people weigh quite a bit. One single straw might weigh a thousandth of a gram, so two straws would weigh two thousandths of a gram, and three straws three thousandths of a gram, and so on, and so on. If they got enough straws together to weigh a very large amount of pounds, a massive knob of straw or a rectangle of straw like the ones that are out in the middle of the fields you see when you drive for what seems like hours and hours to Stately Homes, the huge shape would plop off before they got it all strapped on. Just stuffing the last straw under the strap of rope that was tying it all together, ever so gently, would make the huge heaviness start to tilt, and the straps under the camel's stomach would slip, which might give him an Indian burn, and the whole thing would thump to the side on the ground, unless they somehow had a machine that condensed every single bit of straw together into tiny blocks the size of sugar cubes that were so heavy you could barely lift them without a pulley and you put them all over the camel's back somehow. But that would be quite unusual.

And the other main point was, a camel is a mammal and a mammal is a sensible animal. He's not just going to freeze in place there. As soon as the load felt like it was getting uncontrollably heavy, he would fold his knees under him the way they do. He wouldn't stand there and have a major injury. When camels get cross they do something about it. They squirt large amounts of spit from their mouths, for one thing. That happened to Captain Haddock in Tintin one time. He was tickling the camel under the chin, and then suddenly, pshooo, his head is gone and a huge splash of camel saliva is in its place. So if you are the one in charge of putting the last straw on the camel's back, watch out for that risk. And also, if Nory was anywhere near by, watch out for Nory, too, because she had seen the camels at the zoo, which had hurt-looking gray places on their knees from having kneeled down on rough gravel all the time rather than soft sand, and she had cut her knee on a rock once while she was swimming, and then the cut had opened again and bled, leaving a bigger scar than she had expected, so she knew what it was like to have sore knees. She had enough empathy for camels that if she saw a camel in the desert that was being loaded up so much that its back might be broken she would walk out in front of the people who were doing it and she would just say, 'Stop, there is a fatal flaw in what you're doing. You're going to hurt the camel.'

Fatal flaw indeed! How dare Ms. Beryl say that? She was definitely a little chatty from time to time, but she had been chatty at every school she had ever been to, it was in her deepest nature to be chatty, and other kids were tons chattier, they actually shouted or threw things, and she was only eight at that time, eight going on nine. In Chinese class in the morning she did not have nearly so much of a problem with the 'fatal flaw,' but there too she sometimes did forget herself and talk a little to Bernice or Debbie. The Chinese teacher was much more strict, and a few times she got furious at Bernice and shouted in Chinese, because Bernice made fun of her sometimes by saying slangy things very softly in English that the teacher couldn't understand, but Bai Lao Shi was much calmer than Ms. Beryl. Every morning the kids stood on the field next to the school and did Chinese exercises, shouting out the numbers—yi, er, san—while Bai Lao Shi blew puffs on a silver whistle. Sometimes she held the whistle in her teeth. She had one silver tooth.

26. A Bad Dream That Joe, the Baby-sitter's Son, Once Had

Nory's parents were not completely happy about Ms. Beryl as a teacher, especially after she wrote them the note about the fatal flaw, and at the dinner table they had discussion after discussion after discussion about what they should do for the next year. The result of the discussions was they rented over their house, and presto, 'We don't mind if we do go to England!' The good thing about being in England was that there were lots of teachers at the Threll Junior School, and each one had things they did well and things they did less well. So you never got that feeling of too much Ms. Beryl. Each morning Nory's mother would take her and Littleguy to the school, Littleguy in his miniature uniform, which was very cute, and Nory in her jacket and tie and gray skirt and backpack, and each afternoon Nory's father or mother would pick her up and take her to tea at the tea place near the cathedral, where she had peppermint tea and a piece of chocolate cake with a little dopple of whipped cream next to it, while Littleguy slept in his stroller if they were lucky. Sometimes they read and sometimes they talked about the subject of the day, whatever it was.

Each person contributes something in this world. Some people make bricks, for example, and some make chocolate cakes. Some invent a new kind of powerful glue or maybe a marionette that works by magnets. Or they put the little ball bearings inside whistles that twirl around. Of course some people contribute more than others. Nory's contribution was going to be that she would be a dentist and help people with their teeth. Nory's mother's contribution was teaching Nory and Littleguy about everything, and how it's important to be honest and not hurt people's feelings. Nory's father's contribution was writing books that help people go to sleep. The books that Nory read to help her go to sleep were: Garfield comics, Tintin books, and sometimes a chapter book like *The Wreck of the Zanzibar*, although there was a description in that book of a cow lying on his back with his feet and arms extended in the air, cold and dead because it had been drowned in the water, that was not too pleasant. When she was just dozing off she liked something cheerful, with hand-lettered words, in capitals, nothing scary. Tintin was very popular in England, Garfield not quite as popular as in America. There was a Garfield cartoon in which Garfield has amnesia. He's talking about how he's upset that he's lost his memory, and how John is upset, and Garfield lies back on the table and turns his head back and puts his hand over like he's swimming backwards, just one hand, and he puts his finger up, and he takes a bit of the frosting of the cake off and says, 'Well, I remember being hungry.' Or no, maybe it was, 'Do I remember being hungry?'

You needed to give yourself the best chance of not having a bad dream by dozing off reading something cartoonish and happy, basically. But even then a bad dream can launch itself off in your head. It could just be something from a movie you saw. In Palo Alto, there was a girl in Girl Scouts whose mother was very big on letting kids see grownup scary movies. There was one movie about a mother who turns out to be evil, with yellow fangs and eyes with nothing but white. Nory had to be very careful not even to think about not thinking about that movie, because it could clamp onto her and she then would not be able to help thinking about it, and the only way to escape thinking about it would be to tempt herself by thinking up something even scarier, and the only way to escape from that was to think about sometime even scarier than that, until you were swamped with scariness and couldn't escape until morning.

Sometimes a movie isn't frightening at all, except for in one pacific spot, when you don't dream of expecting it, like that very good movie about a kid who's being flown over Canada in a plane, but the man who's flying him has a heart attack, so they crash, and the heroine has to survive by himself in the wild until he's rescued. All that is just fine. But nobody warned Nory that there was a scene in the movie in which the kid has to swim out to the plane, which is in the middle of the pond, to get something he needs, and dive under the water, and the dead man's horrible light purple staring face suddenly floats into the picture, with fear-music. Oh! It should say on the box, THIS MOVIE IS REALLY GOOD EXCEPT FOR ONE SCENE THAT WILL SCARE YOU OUT OF YOUR SHOES FOR THE REST OF YOUR LIFE NO MATTER HOW HARD YOU TRY TO KEEP FROM THINKING ABOUT IT. (ALSO ONE SCENE THAT IS DISGUSTING BECAUSE YOU SEE HIM EAT A GRUB.) The movie came back to her much less often nowadays, though. When you spend time in another country like England, there is so much new stuff coming pouring in that it even changes your nightmares. There was another movie about a boy who goes on a dogsled race. Everything's going along just fine, until for some reason the movie gets it into its head to have a corpse slide down on a dogsled at night. The corpse hits a bump and sits up, and there's his blank dead face, sheet-white, staring backwards at you.

Probably one thing that some kids do is that they watch the particular movie over and over until they go kind of numb and it doesn't scare them, because you're not supposed to be scared. Your brain toughens up, like the knees of the camels. But you have to stop at a point being tough, because there is definitely such a thing as being much too tough. There are other things you can do to help the situation, though. If you have a bad dream, and you wake up really frightened, and it's still dark, don't just lie there unhappy. You can finish the dream off in a good way. You tell yourself, 'This is my dream, it came from my own brain, I control it, and I have a chance now that I'm awake to make a few small, shall we say, adjustments to it.' Nory told this tip to Joe, who was Ruth the baby-sitter's son, when Joe told her a bad nightmare he'd had. Joe was Ethiopian, from the country of Africa, where he spoke a completely different African-American language, or rather African-African language, and he had learned to speak English quite well in only one short year in Palo Alto. His bad dream was that he and his dad were walking along, when a man jumped down from a tree and said 'Mfoya, mfoya!'—something like that—which means, 'Dead, dead!' The man pointed to some bones. Joe's dad thought the man was just Joe's friend, or just being kind of friendly. Then when his dad turned away the man bit Joe deep in the neck. Joe said 'Gah!' His dad turned around in surprise, and then he and the man fought, and his dad finally killed the guy by strangling him and hitting his head on a rock. But the guy's wife came out and she was very very angry. They were carnibels, or they seemed to be, anyway. The guy's wife ate Joe, finished him up, tooth and nail. So in the end Joe was only bones in the grass by the roadside.

Nory said to Joe, 'Okay, that's scary, I admit, but now you can finish it. Try this. Your dad sees your bones and thinks, "Gosh, I have to act fast, I have to get Joe to a hospital." He puts the bones in a bag and goes off. "Please could you help him get better?" your dad asks.'

Joe said: 'At the hospital they're going to say, "Sure, we'll do it, but you have to give us two thousand dollars." '

'Right,' said Nory, 'and your father just won the lottery, so he pulls out his wallet and he says, "This is your lucky day!" '

'And they put me in a machine that sticks all my parts back on me, arms, legs, a built-in heart, a built-in liver,' said Joe. 'And I wake up and I see my dad, and I say, "Dad? Dad? What happened?" '

27. Nory's Museum

That was back at the Palo Alto house, while Nory's parents were out for dinner and Ruth was there baby-sitting. Later on that night, Nory asked Joe if they had fake food in Africa, fake Japanese food, the beautiful kind that was in the window of Japanese restaurants, and he said they didn't. Japan wasn't important in Africa. Nory asked Joe if he liked fake Japanese food. He said he did. Nory told him her idea for a museum of fake food from all different lands. She would take very beautiful china plates, and place the food on them. It would be a small one-room museum, full of glass cupboards. She would go to all the Japanese restaurants, and call all the toy stores. There would be a children's area and a gift shop. And she would sell fake foods, for good prices, if she had duplicates, because thousands of toy stores would be sending her fake food at the same time. There would mostly be fruits and vegetables, and Japanese food, such as the one of seaweed shaped in a cornucopia, with rice tucked into it and crabmeat sprinkled over the rice. The children's area would have plastic plates, but beautifully painted also. 'Does that sound like a good idea for a museum?' Nory asked.

'Sure, yeah,' said Joe. He said a lady came into his school to do a nutrition demonstration, and she had tons of fake food. The chocolate chip cookie looked so real, Joe thought it was real at first. The meat was cool also, he said. It was red, but you could see light coming through it.

'Ah, the meat was translucent,' said Nory. 'Transparent is when you can see clearly through it, but translucent is when you can only see the glow of light but nothing in particular.' Joe nodded. It was amazing how much English he knew. You couldn't even tell he had ever not known English. Joe knew a huge amount more English than Nory knew Chinese, and she'd been studying it for four years. But they both had the same trouble with the multiplication table. Nory's parents gave their little red car to Ruth when they moved to England, and Ruth wrote a letter telling them that the car was running very well except for the fact that it needed a new engine.

28. Problems with Rabbits

So at night you could read Garfield or think about something happy-making, like a plan of having a fake-food museum, and arranging the fake loaves of bread on tiny plates, in order to try to be sure not to have a bad dream. But still they sometimes happened, and there was nothing you could do. Clang! Bad image. Fright. Run, wake up, lie in bed, panting. Nory's latest bad dream came after they went for a walk one day and saw hundreds of rabbits poking their heads out of holes. How could you get a bad dream out of something nice like that? And also, why would you want to? It had to do with the place that was just grass now, near the Cathedral, that said 'Monk's Burial Ground' on the map. So the monks were probably still under there even though their gravestones were totally and completely gone. In the dream she was a monk at first, who went out every day to feed the rabbits, wearing her hood. She fed them celery from a big white barrel. They were quite happy. But then a disease hit the rabbit families, a bilbonic plague with sores around their eyes. They started dying, even though Nory tried to care for them. She found the antidote, some yellow flowers in the forest, but then she died and was buried as a monk, in the monk's cemetery, under the grass. The rabbits got better and grew back after some time and they started digging tunnels. Nory was a rabbit in this part of the dream, nibbling her way through the ground. All of a sudden she came to a different kind of thing she nibbled through. What is this white crumbly stuff? Ugh! Bone is what it was. The earth trickled away and she was in a humongous underground tomb, where she saw that she'd just nibbled straight through the chest bones of a dead body that turned out to be the corpse of the monk. They had to cover over the corpse, because it was shrunken and awful to the eye. Plus it was starting to shiver or tremble. Then Nory was flying overhead in an airplane, but the airplane ran out of gas, and she couldn't find northeast. It went into a spiral, and she jumped out in a parachute and fell and was knocked out. The rabbits saw the parachute spread itself out on the ground and thought, 'Aha! Perfect material for covering the corpse of the dead monk!' So they took hold of the parachute in their teeth and started pulling it down, down, which of course dragged Nory down, too, into the hole, since all the parachute strings were still harnessed to her, and she woke up underground, with rabbits all bustled around her and with something lumpy and unnerving next to her hidden under her parachute. She pulled the parachute away and there was a dead shrively face whose eyes and mouth immediately opened, all together, and a tongue popped out that was totally black. That was where she woke up in real life.

Now that was not a particularly good spot to be in when you wake up from a dream and Nory was not in the least bit happy. She got up, tottled to the bathroom, which was also not a perfect experience because the lightbulb that was usually on over the mirror had burned out, so the only light was from the streetlight, and then she went into her mother and father's room and said: 'I had a frightening dream.' Her mother reached her hand out and squeezed her arm and hand and said in her murmury sleepy voice, 'I'm so sorry, my baby girl, try not to think about it, everything is all right, goodnight, my baby, love you.' She made kissing sounds with her lips.

'Goodnight, love you,' said Nory, and she stumbled back to her room, but she still had the fright living in her chest and when she saw the covers of her bed she thought, 'No, I definitely can't get back in there by myself,' and she turned around and went back to her parents' room and said: 'Can I sleep in your bed? I'm still scared.' But her parents almost never let her sleep in their bed, although they used to let Littleguy sleep in their bed until he was over two, which wasn't totally fair. Sometimes they let Nory come in in the morning and snuggle in, however. 'Tuck in, tuck in,' her mother would say then, lifting a corner of blanket, and that made her feel so happy.

Her father got up and said, 'I'll tuck you in.' He tucked her in her bed and stroked her head and said, 'Nothing is bad, everything's okay, pick something to think about with bright sunlight in it, Splash Mountain or having tea at the museum with the fan room or looking out from Oxburgh Hall over the fields. Or playing in the sprinkler with Debbie.'

'But I'm still quite scared,' Nory said. 'Can I read?'

'It's the middle of the night,' said her father. 'If you absolutely have to read to get your mind going in a different direction, go ahead and read. Goodnight, sweetie pie.'

'Goodnight,' said Nory. She clicked her light on and read a tiny amount of a book she was reading for the Readathon, which was a competition at the Junior School that gave money to leukemia depending on how many books you read. She was reading a book she liked about a hen who went on different vehicles, and with each vehicle she went on there was some disaster, and then the disaster was solved. For instance, the hen got stuck in a new road of tar and was almost rolled over by one of machines that press it flat. And whenever a person rescued her, the hen politely laid an egg for them, to say thank you. One time she laid an egg in someone's crash helmet. The book was called *The Hen Who Wouldn't Give Up*.

Nory was so frazzledly tired that she didn't want to read, even about this friendly hen, but she had to read, because she had to stay awake, since the thing was that if you wake up in the middle of an awful dream that is quite powerful and you go back to sleep too soon, the dream will heal over the cut you made in it and will finish itself. If you are very, very, very, very, very capable, and very determined, you'll be able to stay awake, just twelve, thirteen more minutes, and the bad dream will melt away, and you will have somewhat of a good dream instead, because the brain forgets and says, 'Hmm, that file is taking forever to finish, let's go on to the next file, ah, yes, fake food, very interesting, let's think about fake food.'

Nory struggled, but finally she couldn't read for one more second—couldn't read, and couldn't go to sleep. So what she decided to herself was: 'I won't read, and I won't go to sleep, I'll just think, because in reading you think and in dreaming you think, so that's exactly what I'll do—I'll think. And if the scary things come into my thoughts, fine, I'll change them.' What a bad dream does is turn something nice in your life, a simple plain event, like seeing some rabbits (including one dead one that was lying on the grass), or seeing a map of the Cathedral, into something dreadful. So all you have to do in going against the bad dream is turn it back into something nice again, since that's what it began from anyway. So she started up with her thinking, and of course, presto, the dead person from the dream came into her mind, but she said to herself, 'Stay calm, stay seated, let's figure this out.'

She went back into the dream a little bit and looked around. Ah, yes, she saw her mistake. It turned out that the dead monk was not really dead—it was just sleeping deeply, wearing a frightening mask. Really the monk was a girl, a princess of some kind, with skin as white as cream and lips as bright as boysenberries and long flowing golden hair, and she had only worn the frightening mask and the awful raggedy rotten clothes so that everyone would be scared away while she slept—everyone, that is, except for Nory who was brave enough to come and help her take off her mask. Nory turned the mask over and saw that it was molded plastic. The black tongue was made of paper mâché and had a little spring that made it pop out. The princess had waited there all those centuries until Nory came down, so that together they could help sick animals. 'I'm sorry for frightening you, my child,' the princess said. 'It was the only way.' Out of the rabbits' tunnel they climbed together, and over the next few months Nory learned many things about caring for animals from the princess. There was a dog with a broken leg, but they wrapped its leg in a special white cloth, and the next morning it was completely healed. There are three kinds of broken bones—simple, compound, and green stick. The princess knew all about them, because she was an expert in first aid. A green-stick fracture is when it bends like a flexible stick and makes a smuggled noise but doesn't break apart. A simple break is when it breaks in two, so that you can see two ends of bone if you look on an X-ray. A compound fracture is when some of the bone tears out of the skin. Compound is really bad, and grotesque to look at even for a doctor, probably. Jason from Nory's old school had gotten a simple fracture from jumping off one of the climbing structures. Flying squirrels jump from the climbing structures, but Raccoon is more careful.

Somewhere along the way of these ideas, luckily, Nory's thinking turned into good-dreaming.

29. Why Not Make a Quilt?

After that busy brainwash of a night you might think Nory would wake up terribly tired and alarmed, but no. Her eyes came easily open and she immediately wanted to work on a project in the Art Room—something like make a popup book of an airplane, which would have the little tables you could open and close, or make a teacup out of clay with the steam twirling up in spirals of rolled clay—since Littleguy squushed the last teacup she made—or tell a long story to her dolls while she changed their outfits, or draw a comic strip called 'The Two Bacteria' about the many adventures of two bacteria, French and Germ. She got the idea for the comic from a book about teeth which had a picture of some bacteria standing on a tooth. One of them says, 'Hey, hey, this looks like a perfect spot to dig for dentin.'

She lay under the covers moving her fingers and thinking about the things she could do that day, drawings, inventions, projects. She could make a booklet for Littleguy full of puzzles using things he liked, for instance a maze that would say: 'See if you can drive Solomon the Steam Shovel back through the mud to the construction site.' With her cousin Irene in Burlington, Vermont, she was working on a book of projects for kids. One of the projects Nory had already written down was: 'Make a Tree. Make a tree, every time you do something good hang a card on a branch saying what you did. It may make you happier.' Nory had never made a tree like that and hung cards on it, but it seemed like a good sort of a project. Another project was to make a ruler.

Make a Ruler:

What you will need:
cardboard
a Ruler
A pen & pencil
A Pair of scissors (For thin cardbord)
for thick cardboard: knife (ASK FOR HELP)
A clear space
A piece of paper & Tape
An Adult who is willing to help you out.

1. Take a thin or thick piece of cardboard and cut it
so it is about 4.7 in. Long and about 1.1 in. wide
2. Trace your cardboard
out on the pice of paper with a pencil & cut
along the side in in. and/or cm. and/or
m.m and Make a mark each time you
come to another one. and number it.
DON'T FORGET TO SAY IF IT'S
M.M OR I.N OR C.M.

Nory hadn't made a ruler herself, unless you count the one
she had drawn on the paper to illustrate how to make a
ruler in the project. Another project was a quilt: 'If you have
any rags, why not make a quilt? You could embroider it. It
would be very hard but worth a try.' Another project was:

WRITE A STORY!

Why NOT Write a story. It's very satisfying.

Here's some of mine: 'It was a cold icy freezie day in Autumn.
A poor girl dressed in rags shiverd, she was huddled bythe
side-walk.'

The project book was going at a slug's pace, though, because Irene was in Burlington, Vermont, and Nory hadn't sent off any of the pages she had made so far. Irene had a wonderful dog named Simone.

30. The Rest of the Story About the Icy, Freezie Day in Autumn

The story about the icy, freezie day in Autumn was quite different from Nory's other stories because she had written it down at Junior School, as an assignment for Mrs. Thirm, rather than just telling it aloud to one of her dolls. So unless she lost the notebook that it was in she couldn't possibly forget it. The story so far was:

Event One and Intorduction of Characters. It was a cold icy freezie day in Autumn. A poor girl dressed in rags shiverd, she was huddled by the side-walk. Long brown hair swept across her face, and tangeled though it was, if it had been brushed and combed it would be lovely hair. She could hear barking in the distance, she sighed, how nice it would be to have a dog to play with to always be at your side. 'Oh Well it probably already belongs to someone,' she thought. She blew the hair out of her face. The barking seemed to be geting closer by the minet. She lisened very cearfully and heard the raket came from a Sealyham she new alot about dogs they were her favorit thing in the world she used to get around at night by listening to the barking of the dogs now the barking was so close so could almost hear the padding of the dogs foot hit the ground. She turned in the direction she thought the barking was coming from there was a small black figure who seemed very pleased inded for making the loudest noise anyone could hear for miles, with no leash no person behind him only people trying to soo him away this what at the bottom of her heart she was wishing for. she couden't control her self she ran as fast as she could to him and throgh her self around his neack. and It was nice to feel his warm breath on her hands, and his soft fur on her face. The dog stoped barking, and looked at her out of his lovely black yees. He was a large dog for a Sealyham, he was also quite strong. She gathered her self and knelled by the dog. She smiled at him, What is your name? The dog looked content, then he barcked three times quickly, and it sounded like rour ran roph. Since he looked so content she figured he had sucsessfully told her his name was Ranrof. She sayed 'Ranrof is a lovely name.' She looked round her self and every one seemed to be staring so she and the dog slowly walked away. Mines Marielle she sayed how old are you she asked the dog, rine barked the dog. Which Marielle thout was nine, 'I'm nine too' she sayed. 'It's time we get somthing to eat' she sayed agin. They had come to a bush full of ripe berrys, they almost were more berrys than bush, and they had a lovely dinner of berrys.

Event two: the complecation. Marielle woke up from a long sleep to find that Ranrof was gone, she was upset 'Perhaps it was only a dream' she thought. how she longed for Ranrof, his beautiful black eyes, his soft fur and his warm breath 'I wish dreams came true' she sayed. 'It couldn't hurt calling for him' So she stood up and called ranrof again and again but nothing happened. So she sat down and looked for traces of him to, prove he wasn't a drea. there were footprints but it could have been something else. She fell back and was going to relas, When she notesed the ground was very soft in one part she sat up and saw that a trace of a what seemed dogs foot-print. but It seemed to be thear on purpose. Not just a dog was ramdomly walking and happened to step there, but really worked hard to make a deep foot-print. Mayby its a sort of signiture to say it was that dogs property but, maybe just maybe it was tring to take place of a card in which case there might be a present inside a sort of goodby persent. And she decided that it would be better to open it and have it not be hers, than it be hers and not open it because of corse if it wasen't herse she could cover it back up agin, and any way she wanted all the eviedence she could get to prove Ranrof wasn't a dream and if it was from any dog it might be as well from Ranrof.

Then she heard strage issing noises very cloes. She looked behind her and there were two large cats hissing and meowing at eachother they seemed to be arguing, hey hey she sayed dont argue but they kept on so she had to sit inbittween them so they couden't go on. Now now she sayed slowly for theas cats were sort of fritening becase they were so lage. The cats looked embarassed, and gave Marielle the look of 'what do you want.' So she ansered there look of 'what do you want,' with a look of 'you know perfectly well.' Then the cats seemed to be wispering at eachother. In fact they were wispering so quietly that she could almost hear her heart beeting, for it was beeting rather louwdly because of the size of these cats. Then a thout struck her mind, wouden't It be best to become friends with these cats maybe somehow they could tell her, somehow if they had seen Ranrof, and besides they were huge things. Itwas then that she deicided she should look at them becaus she hade been looking at the sky this whole time. They were onely showing off. They had their tails lifted high in the air (as they say) and where swaing while walking slowly cicleling her. They where going in oppisite directions so when they bumped noses, they would turn around at the same time and start off in the other direcion So they realy looked as if one was in the miore. She stood there for a few minutes just staring, and sometimes realy

did beleve that one was a riflection in a mior. Oh! because I
forgot to tell you they where totaly idenical and I bet they
could trick people as to wich one they were. After staring at
them for about 5 minets her eyes got tired and she glased
away for a minut, they sat down and curruld up as if that
was what they were wating for in wich case she wondered
what would happen if she had stared all night just then she
felt something lick her with their tounge.

Event Three. . . . . TO BE CONTINUED.

31. *Oatmeal*

Nory liked writing 'TO BE CONTINUED' at the end of
stories, and of course she could go right ahead and
continue them. But she had very old stories that she'd
written when she was seven and eight that had that in big
letters at the end, and when she came across them stuffed
in her desk in Palo Alto she thought, 'Wow, I haven't exactly
done what I said I would do, have I?' Basically, when she
wrote 'To Be Continued' at the end of a story it almost
always meant 'To Never Be Continued,' that is, 'To Be
Dropped Like a Hot Potato.' This made her a little sad
when she realized it. She had gotten the idea of 'To Be
Continued' from the movie *Back to the Future*, which ends
with those words in huge letters. *Back to the Future* was
another movie where the second movie, *Back to the Future
II*, was equally as good as *Back to the Future I*, like
Neverending Story and *Neverending Story II*.

So probably she wouldn't write any more of the story of
Ranrof, because by the time she got around to it she would
have become a little older and she would think some of it

was kiddish and she would be on to other unexceptional things. Also everyone had to read their stories aloud in class and when she she read hers some of the boys made low gurgles and snickers when she read the part about the girl throwing herself around the dog's neck. They thought it was girlish and sweetsy-cue, which didn't matter one bit because Nory liked the story. But it was true that after they gurgled she stopped working on it.

Her mother came in while Nory was still dozily under the covers thinking of what project she should do that morning and she said it was time for Nory to hop to. A few minutes after that her father came popping in and said, 'Let's go, kiddo, let's go, let's go.' So it was a school day, was it? Well well! How fair was that? Nory chatted to herself for not a very long time in the mirror, pretending to be surprised by her toothbrush flying in from the side, and trying out different surprised expressions. Then she tucked in all her dolls for the day, which took a good amount of time. She had only been able to take eleven dolls to England from America, not including Raccoon. By then her mother was calling out, 'Urgent call for Nory!' and her father was calling out, 'Extreme two-minute warning!' So she bustled on her school outfit and tied her tie and tucked the ends of it in her skirt, since they were always much too long to be becoming since basically the tie was too big for a child her age, and she went downstairs to have oatmeal.

The bowl was hot enough to burn your fingers from the microwave but the cold milk cooled its heels. Nory's father sometimes hummed to the sound of the microwave, because the microwave was extraordinarily loud, much louder than the one they had in America, which is named after Amerigo Raspucci, who made a map of America that was not terribly accurate because the technology that they had available in those times was not good, and the microwave sounded like the humming note of a bagpipe. He hummed a hymn that Nory liked from her school hymnbook, 'And did those feet, in ancient times.' Sometimes he hummed songs he made up, like 'Snort-victims on parade, exchanging glances.' But he had gotten into a very bad habit of also making a strange little humming sound when he put a spoonful of oatmeal in his mouth. He said the warmness of the oatmeal made him simply have to make that strange noise, but Nory's mother said she wasn't very fond of hearing that sort of moaning at the breakfast table before there was time for the coffee to work, and once Nory had to say to both of them, 'Fee, Fie, Fo, Fum, I smell the blood of an argument.' That was the way Nory got them to stop when they were going up the stages of having a fight, although it didn't work every single time. However, they didn't fight nearly as much as some of her friends' parents.

In America Nory ate cornflakes or frozen waffles with maple syrup. The cap of the syrup got congested with scrabs of dried syrup, which turned to pure sugar, so that you could barely get it on or off. But in England, no frozen waffles. In America Littleguy had Cheerios with bubanda, which was what he called banana. But here everyone ate oatmeal, everyone in her family, that is, and were quite content eating oatmeal in fact, and they quite happily sang hymns to the sound of the microwave while it cooked their breakfast. In the International Chinese Montessori School Nory wouldn't have dreamed of having a hymnbook. Yet here she had a prep book, a hymnbook, a reading logbook, and six or seven subject notebooks each of a different color. Her favorite was the 'English - Stories' notebook because it was a soft blue color, and she had sort of gotten used to the idea that she had made a mess-up and written 'Engish' first and had to quietly sneak in the 'l.' That was the notebook where she wrote down her stories for Mrs. Thirm, for instance the one about a girl who finds a dog.

Nory's family liked being in Threll because it made them do things not too differently but a little differently. Here Nory had tons more religion in her life than in America, since they never went to church in America except on Christmas and Easter, and maybe one or two other times when her grandmother visited, since she liked to go. But here the whole Threll School had a service at Cathedral once a week, on Monday usually. There was a great joke Nory knew about Friday. What is the fish's least favorite day? Fryday. That joke was probably invented in England, because England was a place that loved things swamped in hot grease. One day when they went out for breakfast and Nory's father ordered bacon and eggs and the bacon came out all clenched up in a little shape like a lettuce, and he said 'Jesus Christ, they deep-fat-fried it!' That was the day Nory had the idea of making a doll that would have an egg she would cook in a pan. It was not good to take the Lord's name in vain, or shoot the bird at anyone, for that manner, no matter what they do.

Every night they all said grace. They also said grace in America, but in America Nory always said the same thing, meal after meal, which was: 'Thank you, God, for this delicious dinner, bless the food on the table, Father, Son, Holy Ghost amen.' Nory's father didn't believe in God but he said that he liked the idea that other people did, and Nory's mother believed in the idea that God was the goodness in human beings but not that there necessarily was a certain particular god who knew everything everyone was thinking and worked us all like magnetic marionettes.

But Nory really believed in God as a thoughtful and extremely supreme person, and Littleguy believed that God was the driver of a steam train and the devil drove a diesel. And they all liked saying grace because it was just a calm and holy thing to do before you start munching away at your first bite, no matter what you thought about religion.

And here in England Nory was starting to say different graces, because she went to the Cathedral so much and had R.S., which is Religious Studies. 'Thank you God for this delicious dinner, and bless the Pope and the Bishop and all the people in the church, and Mr. Pears, and all the people who are sick in their minds or their bodies, and everything else, Father, Son, Holy Ghost amen.' Or, 'Thank you dear Lord for this delicious dinner, and thank everyone who was worked so hard in their lives and is still working hard now, and bless our lord and your son who we cruelly murdered amongst ourselves, and bless the Pope and the Dean and the Bishop and the Archbishop and all the chaplains, and everyone else in the church, please forgive these humble words of prayer, Father, Son, Holy Ghost, amen.' A different one every night, sometimes with little silent parts in the middle while Nory was thinking out what she wanted to say. And now Littleguy was coming in at the end saying, 'Now me: Holy Ghost, everyone in the church, amen!' When he said it he touched his chest in a dear way.

Then Nory's parents would nod and say 'Thank you, very nice,' and they would start eating. If before dinner they had been shouting at Nory to come right *now* to the table, the grace stopped any scolding of her by building a little wall between what had happened before dinner and what happened at dinner. No singing was allowed during the actual main part of the dinner but you could sing in between dinner and dessert, or if you had to demonstrate something you learned in drama class or something a kid did that you had to show by standing up, you could do that between dinner and dessert, as well. For instance, Roger Sharpless and Nory had had a pretend fight in which he had pretended to swop her in the face and she had ducked so that each time his fist would clong into the wall. That sort of event happened in Tintin a fair amount. Roger and she had Tintin in common, and they also both liked 99 Flake. 99 Flake is a candybar that you can't get all that easily in America. Actually 99 Flake is the name if you're talking about the ice cream made with the candy bar, and Flake is the name if you're just talking about the candybar.

32. Don't Forget Your Pencil Case

But back to the morning after the dream about the rabbits and the corpse. After breakfast there was a catastrophe of a broken mug that was holding apple juice, which was Littleguy's favorite drink. And Nory couldn't find the pledge sheet for Readathon, which she was supposed to have brought in ages ago. So they spent a lot of time dabbling up apple juice and looking in piles of paper for the Readathon sheet. Finally her mother found it tucked in the phone book. The apple juice had hurdled itself amazingly far away from the main place that the cup smacked into the floor. It was like a solar flare of apple juice. So they drove instead of walking, so as not to be late, since Nory's father had to go in to London anyway to look something up. Nory saw Pamela from the car hurrying up from the train station in her usual leaning-forward, staring-forward way. 'Pamela! Pamela!' Nory called out, but

Pamela didn't hear her, since they went past too fast for Nory to roll her window down, plus it was getting pretty cold these days for wide-open car windows.

Nory's father asked how things were going with Pamela.

'Mezzo-mezzo,' said Nory.

'Are people treating her a little better?'

'Not perfectly, no,' said Nory.

'Shouldn't we talk to Mr. Pears about it?'

'I think Pamela really doesn't want that,' said Nory. 'Please not yet.'

'Okay,' said Nory's father. 'I'm very sorry you had that awful night last night.'

'Oh, thanks,' said Nory. 'I was just agitated. Bye Littleguy! Bye! Love you!'

'Bye Nory! Kisses and hugs! Now off to *my* school,' said Littleguy.

Nory was a tiny bit late when she got there, and the office, where you go to be ticked off when you're late, had nobody in it, and Nory had a total brainwash and couldn't find the list for her house, Lord Lamper. There were five houses in Junior School, Bledingsteale, Beaston, Morris-Sirrer, Lord Hivle, and Lord Lamper. The sheet for the Lord Lamper kids had slid under Morris-Sirrer, and Nory, spinning around trying to find it, went out of the office, back in, out, in, thinking, I'm going to be horribly late, until finally she saw Betty in the hall, who was always nice to her. Betty said, 'The list is in the office.' Which was not all that helpful, but what can you do? Then a woman who sometimes helped Nory with spelling sorted her out, as they say, and she went to the classroom, but on her way she saw Mrs. Thirm talking to Shelly Quettner. Mrs. Thirm gave her the nicest, nicest smile. Why in the world did

Pamela not like Mrs. Thirm? Mrs. Thirm was a really nice housemistress. Shelly, who was not always the greatest of kids, called out, 'Tutoring is in Mrs. Hant's classroom today, I'll show you where it is.' Nory couldn't resist that offer, even though, yes by all means she knew that there was maths tutoring and yes also knew where Mrs. Hant's class was, because it's always pleasanter to arrive at a slightly out of the ordinary classroom with someone you know, even with Shelly, who was the girl out of all the girls at that school probably who did the worst thing that anyone had done to Nory so far, which was when she told the class, 'Nory fancies Jacob Lewes.'

But that didn't turn out to be so much of a bad thing anyway. A few weeks after Shelly had said that she had said 'Nory bad-worded Belge Coleman.' Using the most horrible bad word there is. Nory said, 'I did not!' She did not say, 'At least, I don't think I did.' For a tiny second she thought about saying, 'Well, maybe I did, but I don't think I did,' because you forget so many tons of things in your life and you don't want to tell a lie about a thing you mistakenly forgot, but then she thought, 'No, in this case, I know for sure,' and she just said, 'I did not!' Only a few girls heard it, none of the boys, and basically nobody believed Shelly anyway, in this case, because think about it: Shelly was obviously the one who fancied Belge Coleman in real life and nobody else would stand a chance of fancying him because he was one of the two kids in the class who were kind of thought of by the whole class as pests. Belge Coleman that same day had plucked away Nory's snack, which was a wonderful Flake, and said, 'Oh, thank you,' in a Vampire accent and squeezed it and squeezed it. Nory struggled it from his hand, and it fell on the ground. It was broken in half. The good thing was that Nory gave the other half to Kira, because it was broken in half so conveniently. But still, it wasn't so nice of Belge Coleman and nobody if they knew could understand why Shelly would ever like someone as idiotic a nitwit as him, but she did, and Nory knew it because Shelly even told her straightaway, 'Some days I go mad over boys.' And she told her, 'I really fancy Belge Coleman and I just go mad about him some days.' Shelly was saying that Nory had horrible-bad-worded Belge Coleman because she was bothered that he was paying attention to Nory by stealing away the snack from her and using typical Vampire behavior. She was jealous, basically. The thing about Shelly was that she was from New Zealand and it could be that nine-year-olds were more teenagery in New Zealand. You could know very easily that Shelly was a jealous kind of person because her sidekick, Tessy Harding, one time told Nory a story about how she was showing off and Shelly climbed a tree and started throwing chairs at her! Nory was shocked that anyone would bully someone by throwing chairs at her, since that could really injure you if the chair fell on you a certain way, or even kill you, if, say, one of the legs of the chair hit you in the soft spot on the side of your head next to your eye, which was like an Achilles heel of your head. Later she found out that it was just cherries, that Shelly had thrown, not chairs. But still.

So Shelly wasn't a complete and utter delight as a person, but never mind, Nory was happy to go with her to maths tutoring. Shelly said, 'Wait, I just have to go get something.' Nory said quickly, not to interrupt her with Mrs. Thirm, 'Okay, I'll meet you right here.' Shelly came back and they started going to the class and suddenly Shelly said, 'Your pencil case! You need your pencil case!'

Nory froze and said, 'Oh, gosh, my pencil case! You mean, we need *our* pencil case.' Because Shelly seemed to be totally empty, nothing on her. But no, Shelly said that hers was already in the class. So Nory said 'Wait for me here, all right?' And Shelly said okay. Then Nory rushed to the other classroom to get her pencil case but when she was leaving Mrs. Copleston said, 'Nory, where are you going? You're supposed to be in here.'

Nory said, 'Oh, right, okay,' and sat down.

Then Mrs. Copleston looked at her book and said, 'I'm sorry, you're right, go to Mrs. Hant's class, my mistake.'

So Nory went partway to Mrs. Hant's class. Then she remembered she was supposed to be meeting Shelly. So she went where Shelly had been. But Shelly was gone by this time. So she went to Mrs. Hant's class. Mrs. Hant hadn't gotten there yet and Shelly wasn't there. 'Is this Mrs. Hant's tutoring class?' Nory asked.

'Yes, you're not supposed to be in here,' said one of the kids.

'Yes, I believe I am,' said Nory. Then she looked around and realized that true, she had her pencil case but in her brainwash she'd forgotten her notebook, so she popped up and said, 'Oh no, I forgot something!'

'You're an Americayan,' people started saying in an exaggerated accent.

Nory said, 'Yes, and I'm glad of it, but first, excuse me, I have to get something,' and she shot out the door. In the hall Mrs. Thirm said, 'Are you getting things sorted out?' Nory said she was just going back for her notebook.

'And then you'll be going to Mrs. Copleston's class?' said Mrs. Thirm.

Nory said, 'Ah, no, I think I'm supposed to be in Mrs. Hant's class.'

'Oh yes, yes, you're right,' said Mrs. Thirm, waving. 'And I believe I'm your last port of call today.'

When Nory got back to Mrs. Hant's class, Mrs. Hant was there. 'She's not supposed to be here,' said one of the kids.

'Are you sure you're supposed to be in here?' said Mrs. Hant.

'I'm not completely positive, but I think so,' said Nory.

But then Mrs. Hant said, 'Ah, yes, I see, you'll be spending the class with me, yes.' So finally Nory was in the right class with the pencil case and the notebook. And then Shelly came storming in and sat down. So everything was settled, and they did maths for ages and ages of time. And then it was over and they went to English class.

English class was devoted to Readathon because the school wanted the kids to read as many books as possible for Leukemia, and that night was the end of the time period for the Readathon. Kira was in Nory's English class and she was a passionate reader. Every spare second, Kira was there nonstop, reading, reading, whistling through book after book. Her father had pledged twenty pounds per book, she said, and she wasn't like Shelly Quettner or Bernice from last year where when they tell you something you never know what's true and what isn't. Shelly Quettner brought in a book about simultaneous human combustion that had a picture of a bloody piece of leg where a man had blown up for no reason, and she expected everyone to believe that it had happened, and everybody did, for a while, until they began thinking about how simple it would be to fake it. But when Kira said something had happened, it had happened. Nothing bothered her while she read, she just read like a hot butterknife, totally emerged in the page, because she wanted to have read more books for

Readathon than anyone else in fifth year, and she had a good chance of doing it, too. She never talked about what she read, she just read. Nory couldn't read that fast and when she read one book like *The Wreck of the Zanzibar* in a day she had a staring wobbling sensation as if she'd been playing too long with the screensavers on the computer.

The English class read their Readathon books pretty well for a while, although there had to be *some* chatting. Absolutely no chatting was a little bit hard to ask. Then the teacher went out of the room, and the chatting turned to a muttering and a chittering and a smattering and a fluttering in every direction, because when the teacher goes out, let the rumpus begin. The two main chitter-chatterers for most of the time were Paul and Ovaltine, who was called that because his first name was Oliver, and he liked Ovaltine—or maybe he was just a good sport and said he liked Ovaltine, since basically everyone liked Ovaltine and you wouldn't normally make a big thing out of liking it and, for instance, stand up on a chair and say, 'Hi, everybody, I like Ovaltine!'—and his last name was Dean, and his face was oval, and maybe another reason that Nory couldn't remember, but that covered most of it. Paul and Ovaltine were friends but they couldn't stop talking and arguing, on and on and on and on. As soon as the teacher was gone they started fighting, and they actually drew on each other's cheeks.

Then the teacher came back in and everybody dove headfirst back to the Readathon. And then the bell rang and it was time for the next lesson, which was Classics. But unfortunately Classics was totally devoted to Readathon, too, so no chance for Nory to ask her questions about Achilles.

33. Unexplained Mysteries

Her questions were: The only place that Achilles wasn't immortal was in the back of his ankle, in what's known as his heel, because his mother did less than a perfect and less than a gentle job of dipping him. So, Nory felt, the only place he absolutely has to wear armour was around his ankles. He could fight in whatever strange underwear they had back in ancient times except for two huge gold and silver dust-ruffles around his ankles. Nory knew a little about ancient underwear because of the movie, *Ji Gong,* about the crazy monk. In it a rich, rich, rich man got naked in clothes that he would have worn very long ago. If you were rich in China your underclothes would be little shorts and a huge apron over your chest that tied in the back.

It would not matter how many times Achilles was stabbed in the neck or the heart—those parts were totally immortal. He would never have to fight back with Hector, he could just stand there with his hands at his sides and let Hector stab and jab the day away. But then you would miss the good part later, when they fight so fast and were so good at swordfighting that the crashing together of the swords made sparks, and the light of the sparks could be seen for miles in the night sky. But probably that wasn't true. It was probably two stumbling men, swamped with blood, shouting bad words at each other and fighting in the mud until one slumped down. Nory hated when people said that oh yes, so-and-so 'bit the dust,' because what it meant was that the person lost his balance and fell at a point of being so faintingly weak and near dying that he couldn't even put his hands out to stop himself when he fell, and so his teeth hit and dug a little way into the mud or dust or dirt, which was sad and a little disgusting to think about. But say a young child had been crouching in a doorway watching, a frightened young thing. She would have seen the fight, and then seen everyone else stab each other and die off, and when she was older her child would ask her, 'Mommy, tell a story of a bad thing that happened to you as a child,' just the way Nory herself always used to ask her mother and father that same question, so many times. 'Tell me a bad thing that happened to you as a child.' Nory asked it, year after year, and her mother and father told their stories of getting stitches in their thumb or getting hit by a car while running after a paper airplane or being kicked under the sinks in the school bathroom or mocked for long hair or falling one floor down and getting a concussion and then having to stay awake all night hearing *Winnie the Pooh* so they wouldn't doze into a coma (this last bad thing happened to Nory's mother when she was four), until her parents ran dry of bad things and had to start all over again with one of the early ones.

The girl who saw Hector get stabbed to death would say to her young child that she saw Hector and Achilles fight and Hector die, and the child would say, 'What did they look like fighting?' The mother wouldn't want to say what it really looked like when a sword puncture-wounded deep into someone's body, since it was a plain basic gruesome thing like the sight of the butterfly's little head when she made the mistake with the lid, and she would think around for something else, and would have an instinct to say ah, that she saw the swords sparkling each time they smashed together, something nice like that, because maybe there was a poem already in Latin or some African-American language that people spoke in those days, or ancient Chinese, about swords sparkling. When you're asked to say how you saw something you almost have to give up the idea of doing it exactly, since whatever bad thing happened had a happy ending because here you are, an everlasting grownup, happily holding a child.

'But all right,' Nory thought, 'let's say that the story is obviously made up in certain aspects, the way that legends so very often are.' Myths were totally made up from scrap, according to Mr. Pears, but legends were a combination of made up and true-to-life. Even still, just to have it be a working legend, you need to know the kind of way that Achilles was immortal, and the story doesn't provide you with that. Say Hector tried to stab him in the chest. There were three possibilities of what could happen. The sword could just not be able to go into Achilles at all, even an eighty-sixth of an inch, because his skin would be incredibly durable and unable to be cut in a good, sensible immortal way. Or the sword could go in just as deep as it would be in a normal human and hurt him very badly, so badly that he would have to be in the hospital, since you can be severely badly injured and be under intensive care in the hospital and still not die. Or the sword would swish completely through the chest as if it was the chest of a realistic ghost and Achilles would only feel a little sense of tickling inside, like when you swallow a very cold, pure, sour glass of cran-blackberry juice and feel it pouring down your ribcage in a waterfall.

But that's not really even the difficult part of the question. Achilles is definitely killed by a poison arrow. Mr.

Pears stressed that they had to remember that it was a *poison* arrow. The arrow goes into the mortal part of him, his heel, making a nasty puncture wound. But if the poison killed only his heel, he would survive just fine, since you can survive losing your whole foot or even your whole leg. If your head dies, you die. If your heart dies, you die. If your liver dies, even, you die. But if your ankle dies? It would hurt, no question about that, it would not be a comfortable or cozy experience at all, at all, because you would probably have to have your foot chopped off above the ankle so there wouldn't be any gangrene. Gangrene was a situation that Nory knew about from Debbie, who said mountain climbers usually got it. Debbie made up a pretty funny joke about it. When you had gangrene, the doctors all crowded around your foot, if it was your foot that had it, and shook their heads and said, 'It's green, gang,' and then, *chop*, off goes the foot, in the trash, two points. Debbie had a tape of an expedition to climb a very difficult-to-climb mountain, Mount Everlast. One guy fell and his foot broke so that it bent back against his leg in not a natural way, and it got badly infested, because the bone was projecting out, and they ran out of antibiotics, so they had to put plastic tubes all through the injury at his ankle, so water was pouring through his ankle every second. But he was all right once he got back to civilization.

So Achilles would not be able to kill as many people after they had to cut off his foot, since he would have to fight hopping to and fro, or rolling around in a wheelchair, or a wheelchariot, going 'Charge! Rip, slash, stab, rip,' at people and then frantically pushing the wheels. But he wouldn't die. He would not die and be buried underground because the immortality wouldn't let him. So you have to assume that it's the poison spreading that does it. But this can't be exactly correct because remember, if you're Achilles, every cell in the rest of your body is immortal. Totally immortal. If you looked through an electronic microscope on the highest power, each molecule of the poison would be there with a little sword of stabbing chemicals pointing harshly at each cell, and each cell would be fighting harshly back, and you could see the sparks for millimeters around, but each cell would win each fight. The cells wouldn't die. And then you have to think of this as well: in real life, your cells do die, and you get a whole new crop of cells every year, or every five years. The old cells get dissolved and get sent down by your blood to your bladder, and your bladder takes it from there. If you were Achilles, no cell would die, so you would get bigger, and bigger, and bigger, since your bones would be adding cells on, and no cells would be leaving, and your muscles, same thing, and your skin, same thing, every part of you would be growing in size and expanding like the expanding universe so after a little while you would be this absolutely huge monstrous thing just because you were immortal.

34. Things to Rem

So those were the basic questions that Nory wanted to ask Mr. Pears but couldn't, and instead of asking them, she finished her book about the hen who wouldn't give up. She wrote down on her Readathon sheet that she'd finished the book, and she saw her plain old ruler in her pencil case, which was made of plain clear and red plastic, and she listed through all the fancy rulers she had back in Palo

Alto. She had a whole collection—two Lisa Frank rulers, a Pompeii ruler, a Little Mermaid ruler, a ruler that had liquid in it that fishes slowly swam through, and the Hello Kitty rulers from the Sanrio store in Japan Center, and on and on, maybe twenty feet worth of rulers, and all of that was *plus* a whole separate collection of erasers. Maybe this wasn't quite as good as having a collection of fake food but it was something that Nory thought she should really be more pleased about. She kept her erasers in a blue ice-cube tray, not in the freezer of course, but it was a way of keeping them neatly in place, one eraser per ice place.

One time she was trying to earn some money to buy Underwater Barbie. Underwater Barbie, as many may know, kicked her legs in the bathtub. It was pretty good when she got it although the problem with it was that its motor made a massive amount of noise, so you couldn't tell a story about something that happened to Underwater Barbie while you had her kicking gently along under the water, which was what ahead of time Nory expected she would be doing. But she was really desperate for Underwater Barbie, and she had almost enough, and to earn the last bit of money she did a lot of different things. One of them was to set up a poster-making store with different styles of lettering for sale and different kinds of pictures to go along with them, but the customers, who were of course Nory's mother and father, mainly, chose what they wanted it to be a poster of. Nory's father asked for a poster of five important sayings or mottoes, which could be sayings or mottoes that other people had said or sayings that Nory herself said. So Nory wrote a poster titled 'Things to Rem.' She ran out of space for the rest of *Remember* so she made a thought-cloud and had the *Rem* remembering the *ember* part as if it was a contented memory. She only charged for ten headline letters because of that mess-up—three cents for each letter. The sayings were:

A Home Made Gift is Worth More than a Pot of Gold

Things May Not Be How You Rember Them

Things That You Take for Granted others May Treasure

Some Thing That you Think is Good
Another pearson Will think is bad

She only did four sayings, not five, because she was almost out of room and couldn't think of any more, but Nory's father liked the poster and wanted to pay extra for the border design but Nory said that was included free, and the total was 84 cents for the sayings at 2 cents per word and 30 cents for the headline, which came to $1.14. The saying Nory liked best was 'Things That You Take for Granted others May Treasure' because that might be true of something like her eraser collection or her ruler collection, especially her ruler collection, which even she took for granted up to now and didn't even bother to think of as a collection except that now at the Junior School she only had this one plain red ruler that said, 'Helix.' Rulers were useful for drawing the cubicles of a cartoon properly.

Nory drew a face on her fingernail and then smeared it away, trying to figure out how you would draw a cartoon picture of a girl thinking about clouds. You'd have to draw the thought-cloud with the usual three puffs leading promptly down from it to the girl's head, and then in the cloud you'd draw a cloud, and you'd have to shade the background of the thought-cloud with a different color, maybe, to draw the clear distinction between it and the real cloud that the girl was thinking about—but anything's possible with a pencil and paper, just about. Nory had in general two favorite types of clouds. One was the low flat steamy gray ones that you can walk right up to, and the other kind was the fat puffy ones that seem to have no end.

35. Break

Then the bell rang and Classics was over and Nory went to her break. She had been spending a lot of breaks with Kira, so to balance things out this break she spent with Pamela, who gave her some prawn chips which have a very dry feeling on your tongue, as if they're pulling out all the water from the tastebobs completely, but being infinitely delicious at the same time. They didn't have that awful glittery added-salt taste. Kira stopped by where they were sitting, under a conker tree, and said to Nory, 'Come on, let's go.'

'Take a seat and join us, Kira,' said Nory. 'We're having our break here.'

Kira said, 'I'll be back in a bit.' That was what she said when she wanted to go away but didn't want to say so. She didn't want kids to see her near Pamela. Pamela was quiet. Pamela didn't like Kira, because Kira didn't like Pamela, and Kira didn't like Pamela because nobody else liked Pamela.

Colin Sharings came up and said to Pamela, 'Have you ever gone bungee jumping?'

'No,' Pamela said.

'Good,' said Colin, 'because you'd probably break the cord and make a mess on the rocks.'

'That is an idiotic, nitwitted, dumb, and very stupid thing to say,' said Nory.

'Are you *friends* with Pamela?' Colin asked, pretending to be amazed.

'Yes, I am,' said Nory. 'And you are quite attractive. For a dead monkfish.'

'Oh, thank you, little American girl,' said Colin, who had a curly little mouth. 'Little Americayan. Take care that your *friend* Pamela doesn't get on any boats. They'll sink to the bottom as soon as she goes aboard. And as you may know, we dead monkfishes are quite hungry.' Having finished up with his insults for the day, he walked off with his nose aimed high.

'Colin Sharings is just awful,' said Nory.

'With a knob of butter and some parsley on his head,' said Pamela, 'he would look quite fishy.' She held out the bag of prawn chips for Nory to have another.

'These are infinitely delicious prawn chips,' said Nory. 'Where do you get them?'

'My mum gets them from Tesco,' said Pamela.

'We go to Tesco, too,' said Nory.

'It's quite a popular place to shop,' said Pamela. 'I think we probably should go in now.'

36. A Bird Problem

After break it was on to the next event, because each school day was packed with tons and tons and tons of events—good events, bad events, mezzo-mezzo events, confusing events, alarming events. The next event was I.T., where the class was trying to land their airplanes on an island. Nory mostly taxied around the airport, which was quite enjoyable. Finally she got her plane to take off down the runway, but then she started having some trouble. She pressed on one of the arrow keys, and if you held on to it for too long (which she was desperately doing to steer her plane back in a straighter direction) the plane went into an acute turn, which is the opposite of an obtuse turn, and would not ever turn back, it would just crash. So she crashed, as usual, but this time she not only crashed her own plane, she somehow curled persistently all the way around and crashed the plane that was following along behind her. Mr. Stone, the teacher, shook his head and said: 'Millions of pounds of expensive technology, sinking to the bottom of the ocean.'

Mr. Stone was a very nice teacher and probably the only teacher Nory had who hadn't yet said shutup to the class. All the teachers said shutup, even Mr. Blithrenner, the history teacher, who was a delight and knew every strange fact you could imagine. No grownup would have said shutup at the International Chinese Montessori School, but here, boy oh boy, the word was all over the place. Mr. Blithrenner was explaining, half jokingly, that there simply had to be bloodshed in the Aztec religion each and every day because the sunsets and sunrises were much redder and darker in America, and the Aztec religion was a religion of the sun. So blood had to be shed every day or the sun would become angry and simply refuse to rise, which would be a disaster. That explained the confusion. But two of the boys were being very disruptive and chitter-chatting about human sacrifices, and finally Mr. Blithrenner reached his limit and said, 'Colin, Jacob! Just—shut—*up!*' And they did.

Mrs. Thirm said shutup, too. The first time she did she put her hand up to her mouth, and the class was in shock, thinking, 'Wait just a tiny minute, teachers don't say that.' But now they'd gotten used to hearing it: 'Shut *up!* Shut *up!*' Not that often, though. At least the teachers didn't say, 'Shut your trap,' which was something Nory sometimes said to other kids, even though she knew she shouldn't. Sometimes she was noisy and interrupting in class, too, and then she felt guilty and when one of her parents picked her up at the end of the day she said, 'I can't have tea because I was not particularly good today. I talked a lot and laughed a lot and drew madly on my fingernail.'

But Mr. Stone, the I.T. teacher, never said shutup. Nory one time called the little rectangle that was in the middle of the screen the Bermuda Rectangle, because inside it were five little green blobs that were islands and on one of the five islands was the little landing strip—and Mr. Stone liked that name for it and started calling it that, too, which made Nory feel proud. If you can imagine trying to land a huge airplane on a popsicle stick, that's what it felt like to approach the Bermuda Rectangle. There was a ninety-percent guarantee that they would crash. Nory liked the old unit of I.T. better, when they were doing touch-typing, where if you make a mistake and typed a j for a k it just made a fly-buzzing sound and said 'Try again.' The next unit would be good, though: they were going to put on black hats with visors that plugged in and do Virgil Reality using the four new computers that were set up especially for multi-mediorite.

Then all the fifth-year kids went to lunch. No jacket potato for Nory this time, sadly enough, because Nory's mother was quite firm about how Nory had to have something meaty from time to time. Fortunately they didn't have the ham on display as a possibility. 'Oh, the ham,' Nory thought, 'the salty ham of last week.' She wanted to make an 'ulll' sound in her throat when that ham sprang to mind. It was a flat round thing with a narrow border of fat almost all the way around it, a capital G shape of fat, and it was dead cold and pale red. Actually it started out hot but got cold later. Nory was going to put it away and not eat it after one tiny bite. One of the people serving the food had said, 'Ham?' and given Nory such a nice tender smile that Nory said, 'Yes, please.' She should definitely have said, 'No, thank you.' But she felt that the person serving the ham might have her feelings hurt, so she said, 'Yes, please.' Also there didn't seem much like anything else she would like that day, so she got the flap of ham. But one taste and she was salted off her rocker. The music teacher came by and said, 'You should eat more of that delicious *ham*, what a waste.' Nory ate it and ate it. The teacher came by again and said, 'You should eat a little more.' So Nory ate a lot more, chewing endlessly, about two thousand and one chews of ham. Kira was whispering advice the whole time. 'Hide some of it, Nory, hide it in here,' she said, pointing to Nory's pencil case. Nory said no way could she hide the ham in her pencil case, not after all she'd been through with that pencil case. Finally she finished most of it. Maybe it was Danish ham. Mr. Blithrenner told his class one day that he didn't buy Danish ham these days because Danish people keep the young hams locked up in tiny lockers when they're alive and don't let them get any light or fresh air. Or rather, the young pigs. That was when he was talking about salting meats. The important thing people should know about the tip of finding the right direction to sail to shore by throwing the pig overboard is that you had to pull the pig back onto the ship very fast, because pigs have sharp what's-known-as trotters and could injure their face by desperately swimming. Pigs can smell mushrooms underground very well, amazingly well, in fact, so maybe even way out on the ocean they are smelling the underground mushrooms and that's why sailors can use them as compasses. Trotters are the things they trot on, sort of like hooves.

Fingernails are our hooves. Littleguy had a problem with his fingernails when he was a tiny newborn child—he would wave his arms around so clutchingly that he would scratch his face with his fingernails. Nory's mother and father had to be careful to cut his nails all the time so there wouldn't be too much scratching, but, poor little man, he sometimes scratched himself anyway. Nory's fingernails got to be a problem for her at the International Chinese Montessori school, an opposite sort of problem, because Bernice had a total habit of biting her nails until they were bare round nubs, and then nibbling off the skin of her tips of her fingers, too. Since Nory was best-friends with Bernice at that time, Nory began biting her nails as well, out of friendship, because when you're friends you start doing many of the same things. Now that she wasn't best-friends with Bernice anymore, presto, her nails were just their usual length, if not longer. Same thing with Kira. Kira had the habit of always jumping the last three steps of any stairs she went down, for instance the stairs in the dining hall, and now that Nory was becoming better and better friends with Kira, Nory had gotten in the habit of jumping down the last three steps, too, and she was starting to find she couldn't stop jumping, just like with biting her nails: she got near the bottom of the stairs, and before she had time to think about it, she was in the air and landing. Nory's mother had told her strongly to stop, because her landing made a huge thud of a noise at home, but usually she would forge ahead without thinking, and then have to call out, 'Sorry, I forgot myself!'

Debbie she hadn't been best-friends with for long enough for that to happen, or maybe Debbie just didn't have any weird habits like that. Another habit Nory's brain got into was writing a letter 'e' after words that of course had no 'e'—like 'had' or 'sad.' Before she would be able to remember to tell herself 'Stop, all systems stop, don't curl the little curl,' she would curl the curl. This was very maddening because she'd have to use the ink eradicator. 'Said,' however, was not spelled 'sayed' as she had been under the impression it was, until Mrs. Thirm wrote it on the markerboard, but with an 'i.'

One time just before she went to sleep, there was a bad thing that wouldn't stop thinking itself. She started in a perfectly ordinary way going out in a rocket into the universe, and landed at the edge, on some grass, and kept on walking. She walked over the field with cows and squishy places, and came to the Great Wall that was at the far edge of the universe, and naturally she climbed that wall, and at the top, she saw another field with more cows, lighter brown this time, and grass that was a little different, too. She crossed that field, and came to a moat, and another Great Wall, climbed that wall, saw another field with more cows, black and white spotted cows this time, and she kept walking and climbing, climbing and walking, getting more and more bothered by the infinity of it. She looked behind her and there was a crowd of angry cows. They knew a way through the walls. Some of them had a look as if they were about to pull back their lips and show their teeth. Finally she went downstairs and found her mother and father talking in the kitchen in the quiet casual way that grownups talk after kids are in bed, and she said 'A bad thing is in my head and I just can't get it to stop. It's like a bad screensaver.' Nory's mother took her back upstairs and put Cooch close to her cheek and told her not to worry, when you're sleepy your brain sometimes repeats things for no reason. She said when she had trouble like that she sometimes thought about how she would furnish a dollhouse, going from room to room, because your brain needs a simple problem to give it something to work with. That helped enormously. She thought about the fake food in the cabinets of the dollhouse, the tiny boxes of oatmeal, with tiny packets inside, the tiny roast hams.

But fortunately, no ham whatsoever today for lunch! Instead there was a wonderful piece of some kind of brown meat, totally soft, so that you could use it as a piece of bread and just wobble it all around. Nory said, 'Jennifer, it's really good, taste it,' and when Jennifer bit into it she said, 'Mmmmm, that is delicious.' Jennifer was just a girl who was amazingly gifted at drawing horses. So it was a good lunch, and after that came after-lunch break, which Nory spent with Kira because she'd spent the whole first break and some of lunch with Pamela and she thought it was hurting Kira, although, honestly, it wasn't fair that Kira wouldn't be with Nory when Nory was with Pamela. That break was when the bad thing happened. It was almost the worst thing that happened that whole day, except for a worse thing that happened later on. They were making a conker-pile, and Kira started saying—again—that whenever Nory was with Pamela it made her unpopular, which Nory was sick as a dog of hearing. Suddenly Nory wanted passionately to climb a tree, so she went over to the one that she'd been looking at that looked like the perfect tree-climbing tree, and started to try to climb it, even though a skirt and tie wasn't the ideal outfit for doing that. She looked up, happily, and suddenly there was a discreet thud on her face. She thought, 'Boy, quite a pinecone, oh dear.' It felt hard, because things that are really light can feel really hard when they fall from a distance. 'Oh, my, what a pinecone,' Nory thought, 'and what a lot of sap, too.' And then she wiped with her finger and took a look at it. 'This is *not* good looking sap,' she thought. 'This is not the kind of sap I'm used to. This is brown sap with a berry-skin in it.' Then she realized what it was and said, 'Kira! A disgusting bird took its leisure on me!'

Kira came running over and looked at her. 'Oh, Nory,' she said. 'Oh, dear. Oh, yuck. Come on inside.' Nory held her face out so that the rest of the bird leisure wouldn't drip on her jacket and Kira led her to the bathroom. They spent quite a good amount of time cleaning up.

'Smell my hand, does it smell okay?' said Nory.

Kira smelled it. 'It just smells like soap.' Then she thought for a moment. 'Wait, let me sniff it again.' She sniffed it again. 'You're fine, just soap.'

They were a tiny bit late for French class, but when they explained to the teacher what had happened, she said, 'Fine, fine.' The French teacher was a young, short-haired, dark-haired, short-bodied, stylish-dressed person. She had a wonderful way of saying 'superb' and she said it a lot, probably too much for some people's taste.

37. Pig Bladders

Then there was drama class, where they were doing
sword fighting. Sword fighting is useful to know because
you never know when you might be in a play in which there
was sword fighting. Although that was as if a student said,
'I.T. is useful because you never know when you might
need to spend the morning taxiing all over the airport in an
airplane.' The drama teacher warned them again that you
have to be very very careful with sword fighting, because
even though the swords aren't sharp, they're heavy. And
they were heavy, they weighed about five hundred grams,
Nory thought. The teacher told a story about going to see a
play by Shakespeare where a man had a rib broken by a
wooden sword because he was supposed to take three steps
one way and he forgot and took three steps in the opposite
way by mistake and wound up in exactly the wrong place. A
wooden sword plunged through a curtain, for some reason
in the play, and slammed right into his ribcage and he had
to go out on a stretcher, not as an actor but sincerely as an
injured person. Shakespeare was famous for writing plays.
Boy were they ever plays, and boy were they ever long.
Nory's aunt and uncle took her to a Shakespeare play
outside in a park one time, *Romeo and Juliet*. It might have
been very interesting for a twelve-year-old, but for an eight-
year-old, which was how old she had been when she went,
it was impossible to understand, too long, and extremely
boring. Thank goodness for the Inman Toffees that Nory's
aunt brought along—Nory ate quite a number of them and
thought about what it was like to chew them. Sometimes

you think when the candy sticks to your teeth that maybe your teeth will be plucked right out, but they're stuck into the gums pretty strongly.

Shakespeare's name was probably William R. Blistersnoo but he thought he needed a preferable name in order to be famous, and since there was tons of stabbing and spearing of people with swords in his plays he thought, 'Let's see, William Swordjab, no. William Fight? No. William Killeveryone? No. William Stabmyself? No. Aha! William Shakespeare! Yes, that will be just the thing.' In Shakespeare's plays what they would do, according to the drama teacher at the Junior School, is they would have an outfit on and they would sew a pig's bladder in a little tiny place under the outfit that would have a little mark on it so that the person knew right where to stab. The guy would go *king!*—stabbing lightly right at that particular spot, and blood would instantly coosh out from the pig's bladder.

'But wouldn't they run out of pigs quite quickly?' Nory thought to herself. 'And therefore run out of pig's bladders, and therefore could not do another play?' Shakespeare would have to go on stage before the play and say, 'As you may know, we cannot do any of the blood we were going to do tonight, because we have run out of our lovely pig's bladders. We checked in the cupboard this morning, but due to good business, and a number of highly gruesome plays, we have run out. Please enjoy the show. You can have your ticket refunded if you would rather not see the show without blood, since early next week we will have more fresh pig's bladders shipped to us. We are also going to be getting some big, fat, juicy cow bladders in stock that we will be using for some extremely disgusting effects in a play I will be finishing soon. So please, dear friends, sit back, and enjoy the show.' And say if somebody was in too much of a rush and forgot to empty out the urine and pour in the blood? In the big swordfight Shakespeare would stab the guy. 'Die like a filthy scoundrel, you midget!' And then, *pssshooo*, oh dear, that blood's a bit on the yellow side, hm. 'Oh, yellow blood, is it?' Shakespeare would say. 'You monstrous, yellow-blooded confendio master! Hah-hah! Return to your imperial distinctive land!' Hack, chop. And a little later he would take a smug giggle and walk off the screen.

After drama there was Sciences. They looked through microscopes at different kinds of line—pencil line, crayon line, colored pencil line, medium-nib fountain pen line, and one other line. Biro line, they call it. A Biro is just a normal kind of everyday pen that you would use next to the phone to write out a phone message. In class they used an eraser on the lines to see what happens when you erase. The amazing thing was that the pencil left big gaps of white paper in its line, sort of the way an eraser will jump in a rubbery way in little tiny bounces if you pull it lightly over the paper, and the eraser left twisted shapes like something an insect would leave behind. One kid, Peter Wilton, was still in a state from drama class and was fidgeting all over the place. He was obviously in a Shakespeare mood of wanting to chop something up, and so he looked down at his desk and thought, 'Here's something.' He had a whole nice beautiful green pen in front of him. He sawed a quarter of it off, using his ruler, and then another quarter, and then a whole half of it. Nory shouldn't have smiled but it was quite cute, this tiny shrub of a pen, just enough for the cartridge to fit in, which he tried to write with. Then he got carried away and took the cartridge and sawed that in half. Now that was not a brilliant idea. As you can imagine, the cartridge went *plume*, everywhere. He said, 'Mrs.

Hoadley, my pen leaked.' But Jessica—who was sitting right next to him and rather exasperated by this point since it's very hard to look in a microscope even when things are calm and peaceful because your head moves and you push the thing the wrong direction and lose what you're looking at, or the light gets boffled up—so Jessica had lost her patience and she said to the teacher, 'Yes, it leaked because, ahem, he was sawing it into a-tiny a-little a-pieces.' The science teacher got steamingly angry when she got the picture and breathed through her nose in a furious way after everything she said. She said, 'Peter, that is unacceptable behavior, bup bup bup bup bup bup bup bup bup.'

'May I go wash my hands?' he asked.

'No, you may never wash your hands,' said the teacher. 'Your hands will stay blotched for the rest of your life.'

Which was a little joke by Mrs. Hoadley, although in fact she didn't let him wash his hands. But it was really nice to see the pencil lines and to think how many adventures happen to a pencil line while you're just writing a simple word.

38. More Things That Happened to Pamela

The next thing in the order of the day was that they were supposed to go to music class, and that's what Nory was in the process of doing, but she went by a place near the auditorium where there were some wooden boxes, because she took the wrong turn in the hall, and she found some boys crowding around saying 'Feeding time, Pamela.' Pamela was shoved back behind one of the boxes and she was hiding there. It was just after the sixth year kids' drama class. Nory couldn't understand exactly what was happening except that Pamela couldn't come out and wouldn't come out, and the boys were saying stuff about 'Eat,' and saying 'Are you hungry, Pamela?' One of them said: 'Feed the monster.'

Nory said, 'Let Pamela out! Stop it, let her out!' But they wouldn't. Then the French teacher walked by and the boys went into a quick flutter. They said, 'Sssh, don't let her see.'

'Pamela, please come on out,' said Nory, while the teacher could hear, so she would notice the situation. The boys were all pretending to be doing something else. The teacher said, 'Pamela? Are you there? Come out.' So Pamela did. Nory said, 'Hi, Pamela, come on, let's get our stuff.' Nory got her hurried away and waved to the French teacher who waved back. The French teacher probably didn't know much of what was going on, but that was good because Pamela did not want any teachers to know, because then they would have a word with Mrs. Thirm, and then she would have to have a word with Mrs. Thirm, and she thought Mrs. Thirm thought she'd done all those bad things last year.

Nory said, 'Pamela, you've got to go to Mr. Pears, because Mr. Pears is very nice. You've got to complaint to him. If you don't complaint to him nothing will get better. It'll just keep getting worse.' But Pamela said she couldn't find the time to complaint to him. The problem was that if you get bullied for a certain amount of time, you start thinking that it's average to be bullied and you end up stopping being able to fight back for yourself. It's like having a cold for so long that you start thinking its normal to have a stuffed-up nose. Nory didn't want to say that to Pamela because it wasn't the perfect thing to say. Pamela had the sound of almost-but-not-quite-crying in her voice when she said, 'I have to get my stuff,' and she went off.

The next thing that happened, not counting music, which was fairly anonymous, was that everyone was outside, waiting to be picked up. Nory was out with a bunch of other kids, including Kira. Pamela came out and sat down nearby with a big sigh and slumped her backpack down, and everyone froze and went dead quiet. Pamela concentrated on doing a strange thing, which was: taking off her shoe and sock and checking on an orange Band Aid that was on her toe. That was such an unexpected thing for Pamela to do that all the girls started to laugh at her, and then Nory couldn't help it and she laughed, too, although she felt it was mean. Jessica said to Nory, 'Can you please get her to go away?'

'Why should I?' said Nory. 'She's happy there. No, I can't get her to go away.'

Kira grabbed her arm and pulled her over and said, 'Nory! The more on her side you are the less popular you'll be.'

'Kira, is that all you can think about in this school?' said Nory. 'If you're my friend and Pamela's my friend I'm just fine in the area of being popular.'

'You're not thinking!' said Kira, in a whisper-shout, which is when you shout, but you do it in a whispering voice rather than a shouting voice.

'Oh, puff,' said Nory. She went to sit down next to Pamela and said, 'Hi, Pamela.' Pamela said 'Hello,' and kept checking away at her bandage, which had that old bandage look to it. Then she put her sock and shoe back on. Kira was waving to Nory very urgently, over and over, saying, 'Nory! Come *over* here!' with her mouth. Nory shook her head in refusal as if to mean 'Pardon me, but

I'm *sitting with Pamela*.' To Pamela, she said, 'You should tell the teacher about those girls.'

Pamela said, 'Girls? The girls are the least of my problems, it's the boys who are giving me a headache.' She pointed over at some of the boys who were in a little group on the steps pointing at her and pretending to throw up at the sight of her. But you could tell that it hurt Pamela that the girls had laughed at her when she looked at her Band Aid, including Nory, because you could hear the same crying in her voice, unless that was just the way she talked when she was angry, with a little sort of trembling. She'd wanted to be near the girls but she knew they wouldn't want her to be there, so she'd made up this idea of checking her Band Aid, maybe, which turned out to be so unexpected of a thing to do at that second that it worked out even less well than if she'd just walked over and said hello to everyone and nobody had answered. Pamela didn't understand that the girls were just as bad as the boys, not in shoving her into the boxes, but in just going along with this whole Porkinson Banger of an idea that Pamela was for no convinceable reason a kid who should be put into a state of misery every born day she went to school. Or probably Pamela did understand it, but didn't want to admit it, because obviously you don't want to think that everyone dislikes you. Nory told herself, 'Forget it, just forget it, don't talk to her about the other kids, just talk to her about something totally separate from the meanness that's going on, and show the other kids that Pamela is a kid like any other kid at the Junior School who can have a friend who will sit down next to her and talk to her normally.' So Nory told her a joke she remembered from Garfield. Garfield was her favorite comic strip, because it was really hilarious and really well drawn. Garfield went up in a tree to catch a bird in a nest. He had it clutched in his hand and was just about to eat it, when a mother bird the size of an eagle came in the back yard and glared at him with a vicious glare. Garfield looked up, still squeezing the bird in his hand, and said, 'Um—chirp? Chirp?' The eagle pecked at him wildly and Garfield got down from the tree and was all touseled and ruffled and bruised from the eagle. He said, 'Well, it was worth a try.'

Pamela nodded a little and managed a sad little grin of a smile. Then Nory asked her what books she was reading for Readathon. Pamela took a big breath and said, 'Well, I'm reading *The Call of the Wild*.' She started telling Nory the plot of the story, which was about a magnificent dog who gets stolen away, and then she hopped up and said, 'I've got to go, I'll miss my train.' Then she said, 'Thanks, Nory, bye,' and nodded at Nory a little, which made Nory happier and made her stop feeling the guiltiness she had been feeling about being magnetized into laughing at her when Pamela had first taken off her sock. Pamela seemed definitely more cheered up by the time she dashed off. Then Nory sat back down on the wall and waited to be picked up by her mother or her father. Kira didn't come over to sit next to her, but that wasn't too surprising, only a little saddening.

There was a humongous sign in one of the halls that said 'Bullies Are Banned' in balloon writing. Balloon writing was a very, very thick kind of puffy writing.

39. Reading Tintin to Her Babies

That night, after Nory's mother read to her and her father brought her up a glass of water, Nory bundled

Cooch and Samantha together in bed with her, with a plan of reading some *Tintin in Tibet* to them, because they were just about ready for that level of book now, as long as you explained some of the words. The difficult thing about reading to any of her dolls, as you may imagine, was that it was hard to keep both children sitting up so that they could see the book. They tended to slide down or over, and then Nory would have to tilt the book so that if Samantha was staring off toward a corner of the ceiling she could still have the chance to see the pictures, as long as Nory held the book right down over her head, and the same thing with Coochie. In the case of Tintin books you really had to be able to see the pictures—in fact if you were the one reading you had to point to each person's head in each square as you read what they said so that the person you were reading to would know who was talking. The pictures were very important to the story, because Hergé was such a good drawer, especially of mountains and people climbing mountains wearing backpacks. His dreams were very realistic. Captain Haddock dozes off while he's walking along and dreams a number of strange things that change from one picture to the next as he's walking. Nory had only sleptwalked a few times. One time she sleptwalked into the closet in Littleguy's room when she was eight and was under the general impression that it was the bathroom and so she peed carefully there, pulled up her pajama-bottoms, and went straight back to her bed.

The hard thing about holding the book so that Cooch and Samantha could see was that then it was not all that easy for Nory to see, and her arms and shoulders got so tired that they started to have a case of the sparklies, and couldn't hold the book up for one more second. Luckily

Cooch and Samantha both corked off in a very short time and she could relax the book and scoot down in her bed. Nory felt sleepy, too, but not quite enough to go to sleep herself. She didn't feel that there was any major bad dream getting itself ready to bother her—probably the last bad dream had been bad enough that she might not have any more for a month or two. So she wasn't bothered about that. But she wasn't completely sleepy, and she didn't want to start another Jill Murphy book about the Worst Witch, even though it was Readathon, because her brain was stuffed to the gizzard with reading for Readathon, and yes, by all means, leukemia was a horrible disease to strike a small innocent child but she would read more Jill Murphy books at another time, since they were very, very good books. Sometimes the problem with telling someone about a book was that the description you could make of it could just as easily be a description of a boring book. There's no proof that you can give the person that it's a really good book, unless they read it. But how are you going to convince them that they should read it unless they have a glint of what's so great about it by reading a little of it?

It was a challenge, but worth it because it was much better when somebody else has read a book you've read and you can talk about it, unless they try and be cool by saying something like, 'Oh sure, I read that ages ago, that was really easy and kind of stupid.' Kira had read all four of the Worst Witch books and about a hundred books besides that and she said she liked them but she didn't seem to want to talk about them too much, as usual. She sort of read a book, *bzzzzzzz*, as if she was sawing through it, and then on to the next. Nory felt a little jealous of how fast she could read. It was nice to talk to Roger Sharpless about

Tintin books because he had read them a lot and had them filed away in his brain, and you could play a game of describing a scene with five or six clues—say, falling out a trapdoor of an airplane into a wagon full of hay—and he would say, *King Ottakar's Scepter!* because he was so fast at identifying which book had which scene. You could say just three words, 'Acting the goat!' and he knew that you were talking about *Destination Moon.*

When Nory closed her eyes she saw the little red and yellow and orange dots that spread out on the computer screen to show that you've crashed the plane in I.T. If you forgot that they were the sign of a massive crash, the dots were as pretty as a screensaver. She lay there for a while, thinking about little snibbets of the day, I.T., playing with the conkers with Kira, then Kira helping her clean off the bird leisure, which had been very nice of her, and her smelling her hand, also very nice. But she didn't want to think about the day very much because in some ways it was such a dirty-clothes-heap of a day, all twisted around and garbled and wrinkled. She wanted to close her eyes peacefully and be told an unexpected story, but since she'd already been read to that wasn't much of a possibility, so she picked up the small Chinese doll on her bedside and looked at its eyes. They were painted with different colors than they used to paint Barbie's eyes, which are blue and purple. Then she imagined that maybe she could tell herself a story—maybe a short emotional story of the kind that Mariana, the girl who had been in the burning rain, would tell herself. So she did.

40. Amnezia and the Dragon

In ancient days, even before there were hot and cold faucets that can offer something of a problem in England because the hot comes storming out of one faucet and the cold comes freezing out of the other one that is about a foot and a half away from the hot, and they don't mix, and the hot is screamingly hot, hot enough to boil tea, so that if you want to wash your hands you have to move back and forth very fast, hot-cold-hot-cold-hot-cold-hot-cold, to imitate the sensation that it's warm water, which is by the way how the art of claymation works—you move one tiny pinch of clay and then walk over to the camera and take a picture and move another tiny movement, move-click-move-click-move-click—but long before there was any of that kind of advanced modern technology, there was a girl. Her name was Amnezia. Amnezia's mother told her when she was only very little that the Dragon of the Fourth Continent would come. There were seven huge pieces of land in those days, and are now, distributed around the world, and the Fourth Continent was good old Asia. The Seventh Continent is Antarctica, which is a landmass with a huge thing floating underneath it called Magnetic South which is made up of magnets and tons and tons of anonymous rock.

So the Dragon of the Fourth Continent would come, Amnezia's mother told her. 'Only to very special people like yourself,' whispered her mother, who was herself from the Western region of China a thousand miles from the Great Wall. This was when the child was two, one night, and she asked to be told a story. The story turned out to be true and about her own life in the future. 'We'll have to defeat the dragon,' her mother said. 'The dragon will try and come to get you. He will try and eat you. But you are strong, dear child, he cannot win.'

Then the mother whispered, even more quietly, 'I have experienced it, just like your grandmother, and her mother and her grandmother, and back and back.'

But there was one thing that the mother did not know: that her daughter would have to meet the dragon *two times*.

Many years later, when the child was about eight, it happened. Now she was a very pretty child. Her black hair was shinier than ever, and very, very long. It could almost touch her ankles. The experience happened at nighttime. She was doing her studying, she was learning what is now known as botany. It was very late at night and there were no sounds at all except the rustle of the dried plants she was looking at through what is now known as a microscope, but then was known as a Chenker-Pah and made of jade and mother-of-pearl. (A grain of sand is an orphan-of-pearl, because think about it: a pearl is made from a grain of sand held in the loving home of an oyster, and if it never gets a loving home, it will never get the mucousy stuff to harden around it and will never become a pearl.) Amnezia was sitting on her bed, writing on the little table on which she kept her face towel and the equipment she used for her late night studying. She stopped to dip her pen in the ink, for this was long before the days of cartridges, but just as she was about to take it out of the ink, everything changed.

Her bedside table disappeared, her room vanished. Her house, everything. She was on a black ground with millions of people, including her own parents and her. A huge dragon was coming. She touched her shoulder and fell back on her bed. Then in a split second she realized it was coming. All these grownups had come to watch her defeat the dragon. They were all holding candles, beautiful caramel-colored candles. She looked at her mother with pure fear, but her mother smiled at her, as if to say, 'Everything's all right.' It was then that she remembered the time when her mother said, 'It will happen, the dragon will come, but you will defeat him.'

She clutched her shoulder even harder. She thought to herself hard, 'Amnezia, gain up all your courage, just like your mother told you!' Now she could feel dust and hot air brushing against her face from the steps of the monster, it blew in every direction, but all the adults didn't seem to care one whiff. Now his hand was almost grabbing her. He grabbed tightly now, without her even being able to do as much as take a breath.

She was very smart. She decided she would scoot out from his hand. But it was not as easy as she thought it was. He clutched hard, and what would have been his thumb if he was a human had a very sharp nail. It was an inch away from her arm. She knew it would scrape her if she slithered down. But then she thought, 'No, it's better to be alive than not to have a long scrape across you.'

So she began to squirm. She bit the monster, she kicked and punched. But he did not move, he was looking around curiously at everyone else. And foolishly enough he was very preoccupied. She squirmed and squirmed. She managed to slither out. But now she started to turn this way and that. His thumb scraped her all the way down her chest to her hip. Finally only her head was caught in his hands. She pushed off his hands as hard as she could, and fell. It seemed like only five minutes that she fell, and then everything blacked out.

The next day, she woke up. Her mother came in. She spoke softly, just in the same voice she did when Amnezia was only two. 'You did it, you did it, Amnezia,' said her mother. She seemed very pleased. Amnezia was glad. She had been scared of that moment for ages.

Then she went off to a boarding school. She went there for five years. She came back when she was thirteen, a very learned girl now. She was ready to become what she had dreamed of for months, years, and what seemed like a decade to her. She was ready to be a professor. The day she came back, it happened again. She was thirteen now, and still just as pretty as she was when she was eight.

She stood taller than ever, her mother's eyes shined when she came back. She had never seen her mother look so happy in all her life. That night, she was washing, helping her mother wash, when it happened again. The basket in her hand did not disappear this time. She found herself in the black place she had been in before, kneeling down on the same flat blue pillow, holding a basket of clothes. There was her bed, behind her. She sat back on it, scared. But not as scared as the first time. Now many people were there. Thousands of them, not all adults, but also children. There was a woman holding a baby. Holding her tight. Amnezia had a shock. 'The baby is the only one here who is also supposed to defeat the dragon,' she thought to herself. 'The mother is scared. How could a baby do it?'

The mother set the baby down beside her and smiled at Amnezia. Then Amnezia thought, 'I am only brought here to protect the baby. I was chosen to protect her.' She looked around her. Now all the candles everybody was holding were not caramel-colored but a baby blue. 'It is a ceremony for an infant,' she thought. So they used blue.

Then she felt the dust from the monster's foot again. She put the baby behind her and lay with her body protecting her. She used all her chest-power to scream at the monster, 'Don't try and eat her, try and eat me. I am so much bigger than she is.' The monster got a strange look on his face, as if he understood. He picked up Amnezia and took her away.

And no one ever saw her again, because now she is in heaven.

That was what Mariana told to herself, as she sat on the big cozy bed. She sang softly, 'She'll be coming round the mountain when she comes.' She got up, picked up her two dolls Heleza and Releza, yawned and decided to read herself a book, the end.

41. In Real Life

'It was only pretend,' Nory said to reassure Samantha and Racooch when she was finished whispering herself the story—in case one of them had been only dozing lightly and caught some of it, or was only pretending to sleep, as Nory sometimes did herself, so she could hear a glimpse of things she wouldn't normally hear. 'In real life there are no dragons with long fingernails,' she said to her dear babies. 'There are, it is true, many terrible things in real life, but you two are young and you don't need to know about all of them yet. There will be plenty of time for that. You just need to try to do your best to be as good as I know you can. I will cradle you away from anything that might harm you, because I love you very much, as you know.' She kissed them in their sleep, and then it was unavoidably time for her to conk.

42. *The Lady Chapel*

Littleguy called the morning the good-morning time, because that was what Nory had called the morning when she was Littleguy's age, and Nory's parents still did. Nory didn't have the slightest memory of ever calling it that, though, because of how much you undoubtedly forget, she just knew about it from her grandmother telling it. One time their plane was cancelled and Nory and Nory's mother and her grandmother were all in a hotel room near the airport. They got in bed very late and turned out the light. The two grownups had just finally closed their eyes and dozed away when Nory stood up in her crib and said brightly, 'Dood morning!' Little children say 'dood' instead of 'good' and 'breaksiss' instead of 'breakfast' because some sounds are not all that easy for them to make and sometimes they give up trying to teach their tongue to make, for instance, a 'g' sound and think to themselves, that's dood enough for now. But later on they hear it so many times as 'g' they can't help it and they finally say 'good morning.'

A little kid calls it the good-morning time because you don't have the slightest idea of what time of day it is then, but you *do* know that at a certain particular time of day people always say 'Good morning' to you, so sensibly it's not just plain morning time, but good-morning time.

So in the next good-morning time Littleguy woke up very, very early, before Nory's mother and father were up, and Nory and he closed the door to their mother and father's bedroom and snuck into the Art Room together and closed that door. The Art Room was a true multi-purpose room. It was actually a tiny extra kitchen in the upstairs of the house where there were markers, and a stapler, and Scotch tape and scissors and all kinds of supplies like that, including a sink where you could do water projects. You could play egg-beater games in there or make things with clay or just be by yourself and do anything. 'Littleguy, what do you want to make?' Nory whispered, because again today the idea of doing some kind of project was burning a hole in her pocket, and since Littleguy was there and wanted to be involved, well, she would make a project with Littleguy.

'I want to make a auger driller,' said Littleguy.

So they made one, together, extremely early in the morning, out of an empty cracker box and a small empty Legos box and some paper rolled into a tube. They decorated it with drawings of all four of them, and put it in a shopping bag and when Nory's parents got up they said, 'Here's something for you.' When you give your parents a present and they are very appreciating of what you've done and say that it's the most beautiful thing they've ever seen, it can give you a undescribable feeling in your chest, a certain kind of opening feeling, as if your heart's a clock in a furniture museum with little doors that open up and a clockwork princess twirls out for a short time. While Nory and Littleguy had been working on the auger driller Littleguy stopped once and said, 'I'm sho happy!' So she did get to do a project and it turned out well.

But that day was a Saturday, which meant—because this was something that was very different between England and America, at least at this school—it meant, school in the morning. So, put on shirt and skirt and tie, tuck tie in skirt, brush hair and teeth, oatmeal, rush to school. While they were walking there, the swans came up hunching their shoulders in a threatening way, and Nory's mother asked, 'How's Pamela doing?'

'Not exactly perfect,' Nory said, and told some of the details. Her mother said Nory should tell the teacher that these bad things were going on, but just not use Pamela's name since Pamela didn't want to be mentioned. She could just say, 'I have a friend who keeps getting treated badly by other kids, and she doesn't want me to bring her up to you, but I really think someone has to know about it at the school because it's bad, and what should I do?'

Nory said okay, maybe that was a solution. They got there almost on time, and first there was R.S., then history class. In R.S. they were given the assignment of designing a piece of stained glass for the Lady Chapel, in a drawing. Nory drew the Virgin Mary in a blue dress with puffy sleeves and the golden thing over her head, holding up two fingers, but the fingers were quite stubby because Nory did the drawing in a cartoony style, since when she did her very precise style she often made mistakes from trying to do it too perfectly, like the painters you see in the Fitzwilliam. When she used her realistic style a lot of times she got into trouble with the eyes, making one of them too bulging, or the nose too nostrilly. A cartoon style was a set style she knew how to do, and when she used it she was pretty sure that the face would turn out all right and have a loving look which you need for the Virgin Mary and not have one side that looked like an off-kilter monster face or hands that looked like chicken claws or something like that.

There was a whole separate part of the Cathedral called the Lady Chapel that was dedicated to the Virgin Mary, but it had only a tiny bit of stained glass in it. That's why they talked about it in R.S.—what kinds of decoration would you want in a Lady Chapel? You could have the seasons of the year or other important nuns and lady saints, or do scenes from Mary's life. Long ago it had been painted rich colors, but right now the Lady Chapel definitely had problems, in Nory's opinion. It smelled very coldly of stone. Probably that was because the stone powder was always falling, since there were so many places that the stone was broken open, and over the years it kept falling from them, like pollen. It was a sad bare place, the exact opposite of what you would want in a church devoted to the Virgin Mary, since it was a place to honor the memory of the mother of the Lord Jesus Christ, Mary, and her job had been to shelter the baby Lord Jesus in her cradling arms. As we know, the stone had been broken up very tiresomely by the people in Threll who got out their hammers and started breaking things in the churches because they had a sudden powerful brainwash and came to the decision that they were totally against the monks.

Nowadays if you walked up to any statue in the whole Mary Chapel you saw that there were very few heads on them, so it was almost impossible to enjoy looking at them, since they were just pathetic little carved stone dolls about the size of Samantha dolls except not quite as plump, that stopped at the shoulders with no expressions whatever. The most important part of a doll, or a sculpture, or a drawing is, by all means, the face, because all your senses come from your face, except for your sense of touch, and even that is included on your face, if you think about it, since your skin can feel, and even your teeth can feel although it's not exactly touch when your teeth are very sensitive to the pain of having a huge ball of ice-cream in your mouth, but it's not taste either and it's not touch, it's another sense that only your teeth have, maybe, that dentists study. Sometimes you can have the feeling that your face is the only part of your body. Some people think there's another sense in your chest, though, in the oystery place around your heart, and maybe it would be possible for you to think with your heart.

Littleguy was a good example of how important faces were in art, Nory thought, since he was just starting to make his first really good drawings of people. Before he had drawn two big circles and connected them with a line he called the driving bar to make the two wheels of a steam engine and he would very happily say, 'That's a steam engine!' But now he was drawing the same two circles and the same line, but now they were the two eyes and the mouth and he would say, 'That's Juliana!' Juliana was a girl who he was best-friends with in Palo Alto that he missed very much, even though he was going to school here in Threll, too. He was even drawing the legs now, the way little kids do, with the feet poking off in one direction and capturing the movement and not the other aspects that you learn later, like the knees.

A sad thing to think about was all the little heads from all the little statues lying on the floor of the Mary Chapel at the end of the day, after the nitwitted men had finished slamming around with their hammers and gone away. Maybe then an old nun would have come in by a side door with a broom made of straw bundled up. Shaking her head sadly, she would have swept up all the little bumbling stone angel-heads very carefully into a cold little pile, like a pile of brussels sprouts, and maybe she would have scooped them into a velvet bag and taken them out into the Bishop's garden and planted them. Each little head would grow into a rare tulip or a lily or a conker tree in the spring, probably a lily since the lily was Mary's special plant, especially devoted to her. The passion-flower is a vine that was Jesus Christ's plant because you can see a cross inside it if you look at it close up. Someday Nory thought in a hundred years someone would go around the Bishop's garden with one of those wands with the little halos at the bottom that they use to find things underground—a sculpture-detector—and discover the heads and dig them up. They would wash them off very gently with certain chemicals they use to do that kind of work, and glue them back in place one by one, so carefully you couldn't even be able to tell where they had been broken off, and the whole place wouldn't seem so destroyed. UHU was the name of the glue people used most often in England, but they pronounced it as 'You-hoo,' not 'Uh-huh.'

If Nory grew up to be a stained-glass maker and not a dentist or a popup-book maker she would design each window in the Mary Chapel to tell the story not just of Mary's life but of the digging of the stone for the Mary Chapel and the whole construction of it and the story of the people who came around one Thursday afternoon for no reason smashing the stained glass and the statues, and she would illustrate her own story of the woman who saved the heads and the flowering of the heads and the gluing back on of the heads with UHU. Then the place would be filled with the colors of the stained glass again and not seem cold at all. The idea of the heads growing up out of the ground wasn't her own idea. It came from something they talked about in Classics class, the planting of an army out of teeth by Jason.

Now it was almost all clear glass in the Lady Chapel, in little square pieces going all the way up each window, and near the bottom of each window it said a name, like 'Lord Chinparm' or 'Lloyd's Bank' or 'Tesco.' Tesco was the name of one of the food stores in England. There was Tesco and Waitrose and Asda and Safeway. Safeway was exactly the same name as in America. It was a good name for a supermarket because it gave you the idea of very calm smooth aisles of food that were so wide that you would never have an accident with another shopping cart and would always be able to buy your groceries quickly and safely. Each window of the Mary Chapel had a name on it because that was who originally gave money to put up that piece of transparent stained glass, or rather unstained glass. So now it just said TESCO, plain and simple, with no picture of Mary, not of Adam and Eve, not of Solomon or the ark or Jonah or Jesus Christ going down into H-E-double-hockey-stick.

So this is what happened to a visitor now. You went in and looked around, and thought, 'Hmmm.' You might not want to look at the headless sculptures, because you didn't want to think about people doing that with hammers each by each, so you looked up at the glass, and then you saw LLOYDS BANK and you thought, 'Oh, right, that reminds me, I need to get some money at the cash machine,' and you turned around and walked out. Or you saw TESCO and you thought, 'Oh, right, I need to get some brussels sprouts and some dwarf cauliflower for dinner,' and you turned around and walked out. You didn't necessarily think of how the Virgin Mary protected her son because she loved him. She would have died for him, as any mother would. That's why she was so important! She would have died for her son just because she loved him so infinitely much, even if he hadn't been Jesus Christ but just simply her own child—but the way the Catholic religion had adjusted the story a little was that it had her son dying up on the cross out of love for the world, to save it, as if it was his dear child. His own personal dying was a symbol for the kind of love that Lady Mary had for him. Long ago it would have been a much, much more Mary-Mother-of-Goddish sort of building when the stained glass was there, because the colors would be red and blue and you might feel you were in a humongous stone kangaroo pouch. There is such a thing as warm colors and cold colors, so that even if a place is cold in a temperature sort of sense it can be quite heartwarming. Though your heart is always fairly warm anyway because think how much exercise it's getting.

Once at Christmastime when she was seven, Nory made a nativity scene using the miniature baby from Babysitter Barbie as the Baby Jesus and dressing one of her Barbies in a blue dress with a crown as the Virgin Mary and then arranging the Three Wise Barbies, one blond, one dark-haired, and one African-American, in front with pipe cleaners decorating their heads and show that they'd come from foreign lands. The Three Wise Barbies couldn't kneel, so they had to kind of lie there near the gifts they brought, which were in little Polly Pocket suitcases. But that was sensible because in Roman days people very often ate dinner lying on the couch.

43. A Talk with Mrs. Thirm

So that was what Nory did in Religious Studies, drew the Virgin Mary. This made a little bit of a strange comparison with History, where they were still busy discussing the Aztecs and investigating the way the Aztecs sacrificed their people in order to feed the blood-red sunsets. There was a picture of them sacrificing in the textbook. First of all—and Nory thought that it was good of them to do this, at least—they made the person who was going to be sacrificed very drunk, so drunk he almost fell asleep waiting in line to be killed. Then they held both his legs—two people holding his legs and one person holding his arms. In other words, one person holding one leg, the other person holding the other leg. There was one person in the middle, on one side, who had a spear and a skull on his outfit. His hand was all red from killing people and he held a sword that was all red, and his sleeves were soaked with blood to the elbows. There was a wooden block that they had the person lie on. Blood was dripping down the stairs they had to walk up, slobbed all over the place, because what they did in order to sacrifice them was to cut their heart out while it was still beating.

Nory thought that it was really nothing to be proud of, this type of behavior, nothing that should allow the Aztecs to have elaborate costumes and solid, proud faces. Of course it was a picture that was painted many years after the sacrifices happened, but still—they weren't smiling, so they didn't look totally wicked, neither did they look very very upset. And what they were doing was unspeakable. It was not just unspeakable. It was unsingable, it was unchattable, it was unsignlanguageable. It was way, way past the limit. However, maybe it was good to learn about at school because kids love gory things, especially boys and certain girls, like Bernice, and it wasn't something especially made up to scare your living dits off, like *Tales of the Crypt* or *Goosebumps*, it was something that was a part of real-life history, which was why it was being taught in Mr. Blithrenner's class. And, really, being sacrificed on a wooden block was not the worst way to die, if you had to die in some fancy way other than old age. There were three worst ways to die in this world. One was to be on one of those posts with a fire under you that trickles up your legs. The second was to be smuggled by surprise with a hand over your mouth. And the third was to drown.

At break Nory discussed this with Kira, who pretty much agreed, except that she said that the absolute worst-of-all-worsts way was: being buried alive. Pamela came over and said there were some fresh conkers under the tree, and this time, quite amazingly, when Nory said, 'Come on!' to Kira, Kira came along. She didn't play with Pamela, exactly, but Pamela and Kira both played with Nory, in a sort of separate way. Pamela said that she thought the worst way to die was probably to fall off a cliff onto needle-sharp rocks, and both Kira and Nory had to admit that, yes indeed, that was a pretty unattractive way to die, as well. So there was a tiny spark of Kira and Pamela maybe starting to get along. But meanwhile a few other kids came over for the conkers and Kira went over to them. So obviously she was still embarrassed to be with Pamela. And then, on the way to lunch, Kira asked Nory out of the clear blue sky if maybe Nory could come over to her house the next day and play, and Nory said she would check with her parents, because it couldn't hurt to ask.

Just before Nory left she had a horribly nervous moment of talking to Mrs. Thirm. She told her that there was a girl, a friend, who was having one bad experience after another with bullying. Not physically bullying so much as mental bullying. She told her about the time with the jacket and the time that day with the boys, and the girls not talking to Pamela and laughing at her, and a few other times, like the time one of the boys kept throwing Pamela's duffel coat

down and hanging his duffel coat on her peg. 'This friend
doesn't want me to say her name,' said Nory, 'but she is
quite, quite bothered that this is going on day and day
out, and I was just wondering if you might have a
recommendation on what to do about it.'

'I suppose you mean Pamela,' said Mrs. Thirm.

'Well, I can't exactly—I mean—she's a friend,' said Nory.

'Thank you for mentioning it, Nory,' said Mrs. Thirm.
'We'll keep an eye on it.'

'Thank you, because it does really bother her,' said Nory.
She breathed the hugest blast of a sigh of relief because
she had been worried all day about saying something to
Mrs. Thirm about Pamela, and lo and behold it turned out
that the teachers already knew about the situation. And
fortunately Nory hadn't had to give out Pamela's name,
although it was a close call.

44. Six Extra Brains

Her mother picked her up from school at twelve-thirty,
and Nory asked right on the spot if she could go over to
Kira's house the next day. Nory's mother and father
discussed it. The difficulty was that they were going to
drive to Wimpole, which was a Stately Home, the next day.
'Couldn't Kira come with us?' Nory asked. Nory's mother
and father looked at each other and made their 'I don't see
why not' expressions. So Nory scrummaged around in her
backpack and found Kira's phone number on a little folded
piece of paper in her pencil case. She called the number:
'Hello, this is Eleanor, could I please speak to Kira?' Then
Kira came to the phone and Nory invited her to come

with them to Wimpole. Nory heard Kira shout, 'Can I go to Wimpole tomorrow afternoon?' Then she heard, 'Wimpole!' Then, 'WIMPOLE!' Then, 'With Nory.' Then she heard, 'A girl from school. Yes.' Then after a second Kira came back on and said, 'Yes, I can go, but my mother would like to talk to your mother to sort out the logistics.' So it was all settled that Kira was coming over an hour before they left so they could play a little, as well. And Wimpole was a good place to go because Nory's mother said it had a farm with a number of endangered species of cows and pigs and goats, which made it good for kids of all age groups. Nory was so happy to hear the good news that she cleaned up her room for Kira from the northeast corner to the southeast corner, like a hot butterknife. And what usually happened happened again as usual, which was that as she cleaned she began rearranging her dolls, and thinking of little events that could happen in their adventurous everlasting lives. So while Littleguy took a nap in a little clump on the couch she came down with two dolls and sat next to him and started to tell herself a story of Mariana. But she kept getting distracted by the idea that Kira was coming over, so she put it on the back of the stove.

Kira's mother dropped Kira off and Nory felt the surprise of 'Wow, this is very strange to have Kira in my house,' because of course she was used to seeing her at school. They were a tad-bit shy with each other for a few minutes, but then everything turned pleasantly chatty as can be, except for one very big hitch. Kira was being brought up, through her whole childhood, without any TV allowed in her house, so of course as soon as she came over to Nory's house she was desperately craving a long juicy watch of TV. She knew precisely what was on, and she knew what she wanted to see. It was an American cartoon called *Space KeBob* 7.

Space KeBob 7 was about a fifteen-year-old named Space KeBob with a huge skull that was built up using bone grafts. Six extra brains were stored inside his skull, which had little partitions in it sort of like the chambered nautilus, and he was able to connect up to each of the brains by unplugging a wire and connecting to the next brain, so that if he wanted to think like, for example, a wise old Native American man, he plugged into that plug and connected up to that brain, and if he wanted to think like a falcon, he connected up to a tiny little falcon brain. The six extra brains plus the boy's personal brain he was born with equals seven, which was why 'Space KeBob 7' was the most logical name for the show. Nory wasn't wild on seeing it, because she had seen plenty of the episodes and they usually had some sort of enormous space-dragon with a gargling voice. Also it didn't make sense because if you were the bad guy it would be quite easy to take a little dab of modeling clay and press it into a couple of the boy's brain plugs and Space KeBob 7 would immediately be Space KeBob 5, and a little more clay stuffed in a few more sockets, he'd be Space KeBob 3, then Space KeBob 2, and then he would be right back down to his own brain, with nothing else to rely on, and it wouldn't be a popular show anymore and would just be a shy little slip of a cartoon about an average kid in space.

But Kira was passionately interested in seeing it, since she almost never had an opportunity to, so they watched it from start to finish. Nory got very sleepy. She had woken up early that morning, and again gone right to the Art Room with Littleguy. Littleguy had seen some styrophone packing chips in a box and said, 'They look like tato chips.'

So Nory stapled together a bag of pretend potato chips out of them that said:

EVER LASTING
CRISPS

** Now Even Freasher **

Nory wasn't allowed to eat the kind of Prawn chips that Pamela usually brought in for break except on special occasions because they had an artificial fragrance of sugar in them and Nory's parents didn't want her to possibly get brain damage from a chemical molecule that dressed up in a sweet disguise as if it was sugar when really there was nothing sugary about it, so that your brain didn't know how to clean itself out after the feeling of sweetness was gone from your mind. Kira didn't care for Prawn chips—but they really were wonderful because they dissolved on your tongue almost as if they were that kind of super-sour candy that foams up on your tongue.

Finally *Space KeBob* 7 was over and Nory and Kira went up to Nory's room and Nory showed Kira her dolls. Kira was polite about them, but not as interested as she might have been. She did like the little metal cars on the edge of the bathtub that changed color depending on whether they were dipped in cold water or hot water. So they played with the color-changing cars for a while. Kira didn't seem to want to try to get a story going about them, though, the way Debbie probably would have.

45. Nogl Erylalg

Wimpole House was a long quease of a drive away. The farm was good. Some of the rare cows had huge heads and quite bulging eyes that looked as if they might plop out onto the hay. That might explain why they weren't as successful as the kinds of cows farmers used now. One black cow nipped Littleguy's finger when he was feeding it some green pellets and the finger turned red. Littleguy cried but then he bravely went on to feed the goats, which turned their heads to fit their horns under the bars of their cage—their lips were soft and speedy over your hand, taking the crumbles of food, and they stretched their necks out so far sometimes that they cut off their breathing a little against the bars and you heard them making choking noises, like a dog when he pulls at his collar. But because there were bars you didn't feel nervous the way you could feel with the beady-eyed swans by the river.

The house had a crunchy stone path going up to it. Crunchy paths were very important to this kind of fancy palace-house because then when you walked into the house the feeling of walking on a real floor or a real rug would feel unusually wealthy and very hush-hush. Also the gravel helped to clean off any dung or mud or other nonsense from your shoes, although there was much less anonymous dung nowadays than in the days of the wives of Henry the Eighth, for example.

While they were walking up, a little girl bumped her head on a place under the stairs up to the house and cried without any exaggeration, for it had been quite a sharp bump. Nory's father bought two children's guidebooks, so Nory and Kira could both have one. The Wimpole children's guidebook wasn't quite up to the snuff of the Ickworth children's guidebook, but what could you do? The main thing about the afternoon basically was that it was a totally different experience going around a Stately Home with Kira because Kira was infinitely competitive, so that if the guidebook said, 'Can you find such and such a teeny little bell-pull they used to attract the servants?' then Kira was off in a frantic dash and scrabble to find it before Nory did.

Tables and paintings and chairs and hidden doors went flittering by from room to room that Nory couldn't look at because she was trying to keep up with Kira. She didn't want to race, but then again she also didn't want to lose if Kira *did* want to race, and Kira definitely wanted to race. Not that they were running, either, just going as fast as they could while pretending to be very calm and smooth and angel-may-care. They came to a picture of a girl walking her dog. 'Oh, what a lovely painting,' said Kira, but Nory looked at her out of the corner of her eye because she wasn't so completely sure Kira actually liked the painting all that much. Kira was just pleased to have gotten there first, possibly, since it was mentioned in the children's guidebook and Kira was so competitive. Nory had wanted to arrive at the painting at least at the same time as Kira, so that she could admire it without a feeling of having lost a race, because she was a fan-and-a-half of dogs in things like paintings and statues, mainly because she so very much wanted a dog of her own, craved for one, and couldn't have one, and Kira did have one, a golden retriever, which was just exactly the kind of big, hairy, smelly dog that Nory desperately wanted and couldn't have because, for one thing, the English government locks up every single dog that comes into England for six months to make sure it doesn't have a plague.

So, because Nory felt a trifle cross, she said, when they were both in front of the painting of the girl walking her dog: 'Hmm. Her shoes aren't perfect, and the dress could go higher up.' Then she said, 'Let alone the strange pink sleeve floating out behind her. Also, her hat could be improved. It looks like it's about to jump the gun. The dog looks a bit vicious, too. He could be improved.'

'Well!' said Kira, with some chin in the air and some humphing in the voice. 'I guess you don't like that painting very much at all, do you?'

'I like the ground quite a bit,' said Nory, 'and the light catching on the rocks. The bush is good, and the houses, there's plenty I like, but it's true—the whole middle part of the picture, including the girl and her hat, is not exactly my taste.'

Kira went back to her guidebook. She was much, much better at the word-puzzles in the back than Nory was, because Kira was a wiz of a speller, and Nory was a speller from Mars, if not from the Big Dipper. Kira knew right on the spot that NGOL ERYLALG was a scramble of LONG GALLERY.

46. Some Chandeliers

On the stairs they passed by a painting of dead birds, which was called a still life because the birds are not moving or flying, but are just there, still as glass, which makes them easier to paint. 'Still deads' would be a more realistic name for them than 'still lifes.'

'Ulg, I think I just lost my appetite,' said Kira.

'Wouldn't they go a little rotten while they were being painted?' asked Nory. She was remembering something Mr. Blithrenner told them in History about the Aztecs, which was that once the priests were done with a sacrifice, they let the person's brains rot in his chopped-off head. That was somewhat like what they did to Oliver Cromwell for chopping off the king's head. They dug him up a few years after he was dead, then cut his head off of his by now totally disgusting body, and put it on a spike on a building so that any child passing by would point at it and say, 'Mom, what is that strange black lump with teeth?' Once again, nothing to be proud of.

The people who figured out Ickworth House had a better idea of what you would want to pass by on the stairway every day and instead of a big painting of dead birds they put up a woman holding a fan. The real-life fan that was painted in the picture was attached to the wall above the fireplace in one of the rooms upstairs, so you could compare the painted fan and the real fan and see how good a job the painter had done. He had done a fine job. Some fans used to be made from chicken skin, though, so they would qualify as being still lifes, too.

The Yellow Drawing Room of Wimpole House was quite reasonable, and it had a dome that was shaped like the Jasperium of the Cathedral, but with a chandelier hanging down from it that was slightly on the scrawny side. Ickworth had a humongous chandelier over the dining room table. A man there had explained that it used to be at a different house but it had suddenly plundered from the ceiling one day for some reason and they'd had to prune it down, like a huge bush that was run into by a tractor. They carefully saved all the good pieces, and threaded it with new string, and now you couldn't possibly tell that it wasn't the way it was meant to be when you looked at it, since it was an extravaganza of sparkles as it was. Kira found out from the children's guidebook that it wasn't actually a chandelier but a 'gasolier,' running on gas power.

'Is it a diesel?' Littleguy asked.

Nory suddenly remembered the bathrooms at the restaurant of the Ritz-Carlton hotel in San Francisco where she had gone to lunch one day with her parents. Each stall of the bathroom had a chandelier above it. She told Kira about it.

'Wow, your own personal chandelier,' said Kira. 'That's pretty incredible.'

Nory was quite content to have impressed her with a known fact about America.

45. *The Bad Sister and the Good Sister*

In the car home from Wimpole House, Kira licked Nory on her face, pretending to be one of the rare kinds of cow. Nory happened to be squeamish about being licked on the face and said, 'Kira, stop.'

'Let's not have any saliva games in the car, please,' called Nory's father from the front seat.

That made Kira stop, and instead she and Nory played a game in which you pass a little orange ball back and forth, and whoever has the ball has to tell the next part of the story. Kira started it off.

'Once,' she said, 'there was a good girl and a bad girl. They were identical sisters. One day the bad girl decided to play a trick on the good girl. This trick was . . .' And Kira passed the orange ball to Nory.

'Oh dear, I've come unbuckled,' said Nory, fixing her seatbelt. 'Okay, the trick was for the bad girl to put her foot down on the girl's dress in a very fancy party that she was going to suggest to her mom that they have. She was spoiled and knew as a matter of course that her mom would agree. If she stepped on her good sister's dress, her good sister would be embarrassed in front of everyone and be very upset. And so . . .' Nory passed the ball to Kira.

'So the mother let them do it,' said Kira, and gave the ball back to Nory.

'Let them have a big garden party,' said Nory, and passed the ball back to Kira.

'Have a huge garden party,' said Kira. 'But there was one desperate problem, and that problem was . . .'

'That it was raining on the day they were going to have the garden party,' said Nory.

'So they decided to have the party inside,' said Kira. 'But there was another problem as well. The bad little girl, whose name was . . .'

'Kuselda,' said Nory.

'Kuselda,' said Kira, 'was feeling rather sick. And the party went like this.'

'The first part was successful,' said Nory. 'The good little girl was fussed over, everyone was nice to her, she was superb. Everything went well, until the bad girl decided that she would stagger out and she would still carry out with her plan. She suggested a dance, saying, "Of course I have to be with my beloved sister." And the sister said . . .'

'The sister said, "All right," ' said Kira. 'And they had the dance. But when Krusella was just about to do it, something else happened.'

'What happened was,' said Nory, 'the bad girl felt horribly sick. She felt so sick and faint she was almost too weak to press down hard enough with her foot on the dress. And yet she still decided she would try. But the mother, thinking it wasn't intentional, called out, "Careful Kruselda, don't step on your sister's dress, you're about to." '

'So Kruselda had to not carry out her plan that night,' said Kira. 'But will she carry it out later? Find the answer.'

'She decided firmly she would,' said Nory. 'She had made a plan and she was going to carry it out. She was so angry that she didn't get to do it all that night she couldn't sleep, and she was so tired that . . .'

'She couldn't get up for a week,' said Kira. 'Her plan almost slipped out of her mind, but at the end of the week, constantly thinking about how she could get revenge, she decided to . . .'

'Not only step on her good sister's dress,' said Nory, 'but somehow make her good sister's hair come out of place and fluff up, in such a way that the good sister wouldn't know it happened, just before she went out, so she would look just dreadful, and it would be just as well as she stepped on her dress.'

Kira whispered to Nory, 'You still have to say *when* she would do this and *how* she would do this. Would she have another party, or what?'

'But she didn't know how to do carry out her plan,' said Nory. 'Then she finally thought of it. She'd have to . . .'

'Have another party,' said Kira. 'But this time everyone was supposed to come all dressed up so you couldn't guess who they were. If you guessed who a person was, the person had to . . .'

'Duck for apples!' said Nory. 'And that would be pretty embarrassing at such a fancy wonderful party . . .'

'Because you had to stick your head in the water,' said Kira.

'And because,' said Nory, 'the water would have food coloring in it, that made your face turn a awful color of pale green for a day, which would be extremely embarrassing, for this was a very rich and dignified family. So the bad girl asked her mom, who said sternly . . .'

' "Yes," ' said Kira.

'The bad girl sang a carol at the first part,' said Nory, 'just to make herself more popular. A goose could have sang it better than she did. She sang it like a wild chicken.'

'Then the dance was to begin,' said Kira. 'The two sisters, not knowing each other of course, because they had chosen different outfits deliberately and not telling each other what they were being and what they would look like, chose themselves. They danced with each other.' And then Kira whispered her advice to Nory: 'The bad girl has to fall.'

'First their steps went quickly,' said Nory, nodding. 'The good girl, Emmerine, had swift lovely steps. But the bad girl, Kruselda's steps were big and bulgy, slow and ugly steps. They danced on together for a long time, until Kruselda finally remembered what she was to do. She was just about to do it, but there was a corner of the rug that was flipped back. She tripped on the rug, fell on her chin, and made her nose be an awful shape, which looked so awful and swollen that no one wanted to look at her for the rest of the day, so she decided to sing . . .'

'But then decided no, she would not sing,' said Kira, quite strongly. 'Instead her mask and fake hair came off, and everyone knew who she was and she had to . . .'

'Duck for apples!' said Nory. 'She ducked and ducked and ducked, but her face was so dirty and ugly from the beginning that it turned an awful red, and . . .'

'No one would look at her and she was in disgrace,' said Kira. 'And she learned to be nicer. The . . .'

'The Dog was important to the story, too,' said Nory, because she didn't want to say, 'end,' which Kira of course wanted her to say.

'No, the end,' said Kira.

'The end!' sang Nory. 'The end—the end, the end, the end, oh way-ay-end! And then—and then—and then and then and then and then and THEN!'

'Then that was the end,' said Kira.

Nory's parents called out 'Nice story' from the front.

'I have a story to tell!' said Littleguy, waving his hands in his car seat. 'It's about two girls and it's the story you telled. There are two good girls. One's bad and one's good. They cide to to something. The end.'

'I like it, good,' said Nory.

'But it's not the end,' said Littleguy. 'There's something they had to make up, their momma said they can make marshmellons, they cide to make something, and it's something they made. They made two engines, the Flying Scotsman and the Mallard. Steam engines! And there was something in the party. It was a double-decker jelly cake, a double-decker bus, to eat. Like a double-decker bus. When it went in the sun, it rolled out, it drived, when it was on the grass it drove!'

'A double-decker jelly cake,' said Nory, 'Good story, Littleguy.'

'Not quite yet,' said Littleguy. 'It's a big digger, the scooper, scooper, it goes, kksssh, scooper, scooper, digger. And then there was a big thing there, a dumptruck, auger driller, a front loader.'

'Yay, good story,' said Nory.

'Not quite yet,' said Littleguy. 'And there was something in the story, once upon a time, I have another story, I have another story too! Another story!'

'Okay, just one more story,' called Nory's mother.

'Once upon a time were two flat holes, and there was a big digger truck came over and ran over they, and got dirty dirt on they. They washed their feeties and eyes and toesies and they were all clean, the end.'

They dropped Kira off at her house and the outing was over.

46. Marks

About a week later the Threll School stopped for a vacation. Nory and Pamela shook hands, as if to say, 'We made it.' Kira went with her family to a place nearby London, so they didn't see each other. Guy Fawkes Day happened during the break. There was a huge enormous bondfire and life-size models of Guy Fawkes were thrown into the bondfire. Nory was expecting the models to be little voodoo dolls of Guy Fawkes, not huge floppy heavy dolls the size of people, but life-size was how they did it. Guy Fawkes was a strongly Catholic man who had snuck barrel after barrel of gunpowder down into the basement, and he was just about to blow up the king when he was caught. So they burnt Guy Fawkes in a bondfire and now they have fireworks to celebrate that. Guy Fawkes Day is much more important a holiday in England than Halloween. Possibly they first chopped off Guy Fawkes's head then burned him in the bondfire, Nory wasn't clear on that, but that would certainly have been Nory's preference, because she was not attracted to the idea of being burned. In any case, he was severely punished, in a way the Aztecs would understand quite well. Nory burned her finger on a sparkler in the backyard after the fireworks were over, because the metal got remarkably hot. The skin turned white where it was singed but it felt better when she put an ice cube on it.

No letter from Debbie came in the mail during break, but something else did: Nory's marks. At International Chinese Montessori School they didn't have marks at all, just a special conference with Nory sitting there with her parents. The teachers always said this and that: 'Eleanor, oh, yes: bright, nice girl, talks too much, though, and she has to work harder on her spelling.' The principal, Xiao Zhang, translated for the Chinese teacher, since Nory's parents didn't understand Chinese. There was never a piece of paper with marks on it that said good or bad, the way there turned out to be at Threll school. Threll sent out a sheet of paper with a list of Nory's different classes and a set of boxes for either Excellent, or Good, or Satisfactory, or Weak, or Poor. Nory got all checkmarks for Satisfactory, except for one Good, in History. No Excellents whatever. She was a little disappointed not to get a Good in Classics because she had liked that class more than all the others and listened like a demon when Mr. Pears read to them. But she was relieved because she had been very worried that she was going to get a Weak in French because the French was completely refusing to stick in her head. Her goal for the year, she decided, was never ever to get a Weak or a Poor. But still, she was a tiny bit sad about English, because she thought her story about the girl and the dog wasn't just a drab old Satisfactory. It wasn't just the minimum you had to do, it was actually somewhat above the bare necessities and was possibly in the Good category.

But probably the objection for Mrs. Thirm was that Nory was supposed to write a shorter story that she would finish, and instead she'd written a longer one that ended with TO BE CONTINUED, and also of course her spelling was a disgrace-and-a-half, although Nory's father said Nory spelled better than anyone did a thousand or two thousand years ago, because back then they had about eight different ways to spell every English word, and people just chose whichever way they felt like. They would say, 'Today I think I'll spell *chair* as *chayer* and tomorrow *chayrre* and the day after that, hmm, *chaier* might be nice, and the day after that I think it will be *chere*.' Now it had to be *chair* every time, no matter what mood you were in.

47. Three Forbidden Words

One other reason Nory might have only gotten a Satisfactory and not a Good in English was that it turned out that Mrs. Thirm was not terribly fond of 'nice' and 'then' and 'said.' When they went back to school after break Mrs.

Thirm told them that from then on they had to try whenever they could not to use 'nice' or 'then' or 'said' in their assignments, because they were extremely overused and she was tired of seeing them in their books. Nory felt a little discombobbledied at hearing that, because she used 'nice' and 'then' and 'said' quite often. There were only so many different ways you could say, 'he laughed,' 'she giggled,' 'he answered,' 'they whispered,' and so forth and so on, before you suddenly felt, 'Okay, ladies and jellyfish, it's time to go back to good old *she said*.' And without 'then' Nory had to use 'the following day' or 'the next thing that happened was' or 'later that week' or 'Three days passed,' which were fine, but so was 'then.'

Also Mrs. Thirm turned out to not like rhymes in poems, and the poems Nory had written for her had a fair amount of rhymes. One of her poems was:

I Went to a Poor Man's House

I went to a poor man's House yes,
The First thing I did was to Look at the poor man's Dress
    yes,
The second thing I did was to look at the Horrible big mess
    yes,
The Third thing I Did was to stand up and confess yes
'What a Horrible Big Mess' yes.
The Poor man looked down at the Horrible big mess yes
And spoke up But did not confess but merely said 'yes'!

Another one was:

Please Don't Frighten Little Birdies Away

Proud people walk through
The little Birdies' Feast.

And make them fly away.
And make it so they
Can not come back to where
They could have played
All day So please don't
Frighten the little birdies
Away.

The poem she wrote most recently for Mrs. Thirm was:

I am trapped in a waterfall
And can hear the singing fishermen's call,
But through the waves and
In a dark and gloomy cave,
I am enjoying what the world gave.

Basically all of Nory's poems had rhymes in them somehow or other. And then Mrs. Thirm suddenly said: 'I particularly don't like poems that rhyme, but it's just a matter of opinion.' She told everyone, 'It's so difficult, there's really no point.' Nory raised her hand to suggest that one thing you could do would be to make a list of all the words that are rhyming words, which would make finding the rhymes a lot easier.

'Yes, yes,' said Mrs. Thirm, 'but it's such a waste of time to make the list, and then you're right back where you started, aren't you?' So Nory's poems were not exactly the poems Mrs. Thirm would have naturally preferred. She was still perfectly nice about them, though. She didn't gnaw her teeth and say 'Not more disgusting rhymes!' Teachers in England weren't like teachers in America writing 'Great Job!' and 'This is a gem of a story, Eleanor!' and whatnot, and stamping cat-chasing-a-ball-of-yarn stamps around on the page—they just made a quiet checkmark to prove that they'd seen what you did and sometimes corrected the spelling in the margin. Once in a great while they wrote 'Good' or 'Excellent prep.' They weren't as emotional.

The complete and total ban on 'said' and 'then' and 'nice' was hard for Nory, though, and it got harder. Poetry they didn't do that much of in class, but they did unquestionably do a fair amount of story-writing, and Nory would sit writing her story and come to a place where she needed to say, 'he said' and she would spend five minutes trying to figure out a way not to say it, and by then the thing she had in mind to write next had disappeared in a chuff of steam, as Littleguy would say. Sometimes she would even write the 's' of 'said' and then think, 'Oh, I'm too tired, I just can't possibly go through the effort of pulling the top off the ink eradicator at this moment,' and so she would try to imagine a word that began with 's' but wasn't 'said,' like 'he smiled' or 'he smirked' or 'he shouted.' But then whatever it was that 'he' did changed his personality totally and he became this very unaturally smiley or smirky and shouting person that didn't fit in with the story. Another thing you could do was change the comma to a period and change the 'h' into a capital 'h' and then go on with a new sentence about what he was doing. Say as an example you by mistake wrote:

'Mmm, this coliflower looks delishous,' he s

You're all the way to the 's' of 'said' and suddenly you remember, 'Oh no, I've done it again, Mrs. Thirm said no *he said*!' Well, then just go around and around the comma with the point of your pen, turning it into a big and very circular and very confident period, and then just change the lower-case 'h' to a capital 'H,' which is easy to do since you just have to straighten out the rounded part of the 'h' and make the short part long—and then have him doing something casually beginning with 's.' So it would become:

'Mmm, this coliflower looks delishous.' He spooned out a large amount for him self and breathed-in the steem.

That was just an example. But that way of solving it also could cause confusion in the story because often it worked out that when you read it out loud to people you couldn't tell who was talking and it sounded jerky. That was why it drove Nory totally bonkers to have the ban on 'said.'

As for 'nice,' well, yes, Nory did use 'nice' a lot, quite frankly. But 'nice' was a very, very important word for kids in fifth year, which is fourth grade in America, and it was important to the younger kids of Littleguy's age as well, and kids in general, because if you think about a kid's language, it can mean about eighty million different things. You can say a person is nice or a school is nice or a way of spending an afternoon is nice. It's not as definite as 'fun'—say a few things went wrong in your afternoon, so it wasn't completely and frolickingly 'fun' but it was still a very 'nice' afternoon. Or say Littleguy made a drawing of the Lord of the Isles, a distinguished steam engine, and gave it to Nory as a present. So basically two little circles and a big circle and some driving bars. If you said, 'Oh, Littleguy, that's very *kind* of you,' it could almost sound a little sarcastic, or too fancy, but if you said 'Oh, Littleguy, that's so nice of you,' you were saying what you intended to say. If you said a person at school was very kind, you could just mean that they were very kind to you, and yet maybe you wouldn't say they were very nice because for some reason you didn't want to be with them because they had a different set of interests or maybe they were not very kind to some other person, like Pamela. And furthermost, it was the exact word that kids used, and Nory was writing conversation that kids had, so she would come to a point in the sentence where obviously the word that the child would tend to use was 'nice' and she would suddenly remember, 'Alert, alert, no "nice" allowed' and she would be ready to tear her hair out by the roots.

Actually Nory wouldn't be ready to tear her hair out by the roots because it was almost impossible to tear out your hair, from Nory's point of view, either by the roots or by the bare tips, because you would pull on one big grab of hair, but only some of that would come out, since you never have quite as much of a grip on the whole thing. And besides you can't have the willpower to pull hard enough to make it all come ripping out like a plot of grass. You could of course cut your hair so that it looks like it's been teared out if you want to be included in a chapter in one of those books that include all the amazing, but luckily untrue, things in the world. That would be 'tearing your hair' to some extent. But the only time Nory ever pulled even one hair out was not when she was going crazy over something like having to not use 'nice' in her prep, but when she was thinking very very carefully about something, and as she was thinking she would anonymously take a tiny piece of hair in her fingers and pull at it ever so very slightly, testing how much pulling it could take. Sometimes possibly one hair would finally go *poink* and come out but that was it, nothing drastic.

48. Another Bad Thing That Happened to Pamela

Thomas Mottle's hair was cut straight as a pin in back, so that when he walked it moved with a bobbing motion. He was a chorister, like Roger Sharpless, and he looked like such a pearl of a boy, but really inside he was the kiss of the devil, basically. And one day, which wasn't the finest of days anyway, Thomas Mottle did something to Pamela that made Nory want to tear out some of *his* hair, it made her so steamingly angry. It began as a good day because Nory and Kira got into a state of herorious giggling by pretending to worship Nory's almighty ink eradicator, after Nory got it to balance upright on the table. Actually Nory laughed before Kira noticed, but quite quickly they were laughing the exact same amount, and the funny thing was that Kira hadn't seen Nory do the thing that was actually funny, she only heard Mrs. Thirm say 'Nory, what may I ask are you doing?' Nory had been bowing her head in worship before the ink eradicator and then she and Kira starting saying, 'No, no, no, no, you can only worship one god,' so they pretended to attack it and punch it without their hands touching it, because they didn't want to knock it over.

That was extremely fun, as you can imagine, but then the bad part of the day was that Mrs. Thirm gave them a Mental Maths test in which Nory got one answer right out of fifteen. Mrs. Thirm was saying the multiplication problems aloud very fast in a way Nory didn't understand, since English people say double-naught or triple-three sometimes when they mean 'zero zero' or 'oh oh' or 'three

three three'—let alone when they say 'M-I-double-S-I-
double-P-I' for the spelling of Mississippi, which always
tempted Nory to want to write a letter d for 'double' or a
number two, depending on whether it was numbers or
letters, that is. Mrs. Thirm was doing something similar,
but not exactly that, and Nory couldn't conceivably figure
out what in the Blue Blazers Mrs. Thirm was asking the
class to do—so bingo, one right answer out of fifteen in
Mental Maths, which is not a very good record. So that
made it not the finest of days. And then after lunch along
came Thomas Mottle.

The bothering of Pamela was continuing steadily
anyway, and getting worse. It had progressed to the stage of
barking Pamela's shins. But the kids who did it were clever
kickers and never did anything when a teacher would catch
sight. 'Barking your shin' is what it was called because it's
as if the bark came off. In other words, the skin was
scraped. Pamela told Nory about it but she only saw it with
her own eyes a few times, because they didn't do it when
Nory was there.

Then that afternoon Nory watched Thomas Mottle
sneak up behind Pamela and kick her very viciously in the
back of the leg and then try to dash off. He was probably
thinking he would disappear as quick as lightning, which is
what the boys would normally do. Naturally Pamela fell
down and her books splattered out on the path. She turned
bright red this time, and she cried a little, too. Nory was a
ways away with some other kids so she only saw it off from
a distance, and she was on her way over to help Pamela,
when one eighth of a second after Thomas kicked, Mrs.
Hoadley, the science teacher, appeared from out of
somewhere, and stepped up to the plate. Thomas Mottle
saw her and completely changed. He was a different child.

Very purely and simply he helped Pamela up and picked up her books, one by one. By the time Nory got there she heard Mrs. Hoadley saying, 'Thank you *very* much, Thomas.' That was they way they acted, these blasted bullies—not just kicking someone in the shins, but then as soon as the teacher was on the spot, pretending to be sweet as pie, nicely helping the person.

'You should have told Mrs. Hoadley that Thomas was the very one who made you trip!' said Nory to Pamela. 'Now she probably thinks you tripped on your own two feet! You have to tell them!' But Pamela was still thoroughly mum's-the-word. That's why she was having the absolute worst year of her life, while Nory was having the absolute best year of her life, just about. A few people teased Nory about her accent or said she was ugly, but nobody would ever possibly dare to sneak up on her and kick her, because if someone kicked her, oh boy, she would be off like a rocket and chase them down and kick right back just as hard, and if they hid her jacket she would wring whoever's neck who hid it, and if somebody tried to capture her duffel-coat peg with their duffel-coat she would scrummage fiercely for it and get her duffel-coat peg back, no questions asked. But Pamela never fought. It was not her personality to fight, or if it was, they'd changed her personality bit by bit since the beginning of the year by being constantly awful to her. When Nory said to two of the kids, 'You better stop being mean to Pamela or she's going to tell Mr. Pears,' they just laughed, they didn't bother to stop, because they knew that Pamela wasn't going to Mr. Pears. She never had and never would. Again and again Nory said, 'Pamela, it would really be much better if you told somebody,' but she didn't want to at all. So no matter how much Nory wanted to take one of them by the scroll of the neck to Mr. Pears, she couldn't, since Mr. Pears would have a word with Mrs. Thirm, and so on and so on. So the bullying went its merry way.

Nory planned out things she could say to the people who were doing it, but words didn't really help because the boys kicked and then disappeared, and whatever insulting thing you wanted to say couldn't be said in time for the person you wanted to insult to be insulted. Nory did try to fight back at Thomas Mottle by calling him Cinderella's stepsister a few times, since one time in drama class Thomas had played the part of one of Cinderella's stepsisters, wearing a big blond wig. 'Just the sort of thing Cinderella's ugly stepsister would do,' Nory said to him.

'Hardly!' he said. And that was that.

49. Word-Fighting

Even Julia Sollen was a little shocked and a little bit nice to Pamela after she saw her being kicked by the revolting Thomas. If you hear that somebody took a kick at somebody, you just think, 'Oh, I see, that's bad.' But if you see it eye to eye, the sneakiness of it, the pure meanness of it, it is something quite else besides. Nory was furious to think that a kid could have a basic urge to kick in his impudent mind and then get away with doing it, just because he knew from his observations that Pamela wouldn't be the type of person to kick him back, so he was safe from punishment. Maybe there was so much constant kicking of shins in England because all the boys wanted to be footballers when they grew up. That was what they said that they wanted to be in class, anyway, except for a few kids like Roger Sharpless, who said that he wanted to go to

Durham and learn to make barometers. In football, which is actually soccer, you use your feet more than your hands, so you have all this practiced ability with your feet that you could easily use for barking up the wrong shin.

So a few of the kids were beginning to go over to Nory's side and be a little nicer to Pamela. And Roger Sharpless always had been nice to Pamela. However, Kira was still trying her hardest to get Nory to stop being Pamela's friend. She'd say things like, 'Nory, you do know, don't you, that you're the only person in the whole school who likes her.'

'I don't know if that's quite true,' said Nory.

'Yes, it is true,' said Kira. 'Nobody else is her friend, nobody.'

But Pamela did definitely have other friends from time to time. One time she waited a very long time to meet one of her friends who was in sixth year. Nory waited with her—Pamela said it was just a quarter of an hour they waited but Nory thought it was more like fifteen minutes. And even if Nory was the only one in the whole Junior School who was steadily Pamela's friend, that wasn't necessarily a *bad* thing, she thought. What in the world was so bad about being Pamela's one and only real friend?

Also, Nory liked being Pamela's friend, because she liked planning out with Pamela what kind of vicious attacks she could use to fight back for Pamela, and she admired that Pamela was good at maths, since if you were good at maths it allowed you to go on and do so many different things in science or dentistry, and she liked that Pamela had unusual aspects about herself, such as being double-jointed. Pamela couldn't use certain kinds of pens, she told Nory, because she was extremely double-jointed. Her thumb was a whole level further of being exposable than most normal people. She had to use a special other kind of pen. It looked like a simple everyday kind of medium-nib fountain pen to Nory, but she didn't say so. So there were surprising things like that about Pamela that Nory liked, and she also just liked Pamela's very hush-hush way of talking to you— Pamela always spoke very softly and had quite a lot to say but you had to listen very carefully because she only spoke to one person at a time and she was very particular about who she told things to, which in this old day and age is probably a good thing.

Nory's parents got extremely upset when they heard the news from Nory that Pamela was having an even worse time of it now than ever. They said that things had gotten utterly untolerable and something just had to be done. The mistreatment of Pamela was something that they personally had to go to Mr. Pears about, they said, or straight to Pamela's parents, because it simply couldn't be allowed to go on. Nory cried at the dinner table and said that it was Pamela's choice and nobody else's, and Pamela absolutely, definitely did *not* want the teachers or her parents to know, and she had made Nory promise, so please, please, please not yet. But Nory did promise to go to the teacher again herself, at least, and announce that physical shin-kicking was now going on. And her parents promised Nory, not exactly as a trade (since they wanted her to get one, too), but sort of as a trade, that she could have a gum-guarder. A gum-guarder was a thing you use to keep your teeth from getting knocked out. If a hockey stick whams into your mouth and you have a gum-guarder on you would get a fat lip, but no particular tooth would fall out. Nory wanted the gum-guarder because other kids had them and she thought it would make her feel stronger and more able to stop the bigger kids from being bad to Pamela, even when she wasn't wearing it. She could think, 'Aha, I have a powerful gum-guarder, nobody can bother me now!' Also she wanted to be sure that none of her teeth tumbled out onto the Astroturf. If you want to be a dentist your own teeth are kind of an advertisement of your work, and it's important that there is nothing strange about them, or people will say, 'Oh no, I won't go to that dentist to have my teeth fixed, because take a gander at hers.'

Nory went ahead and told Mrs. Thirm that she had a friend—a friend who was quite possibly the same friend as she had talked to her about before, who was now being— no question about it—bullied. Nory had promised her friend not to say what the exact bullying was, but 'Let's put it this way,' she said. 'It involves a boy's foot, and a shoe, and a shin, pure and simple.' Mrs. Thirm said, 'Thank you, Nory, it's good of you to let us know.'

Sometimes it was quite efficient to tell two boys, say, who were being bad to Pamela that they were 'imbecile-idiot-numbskull-nitwits,' saying the words super-fast, or tell them, 'Gee, I hope you don't sleep on your side at night, because your pea-brain might tumble out your ear.' But some of the older kids had a style of word-fighting that Nory couldn't do anything against, because it was just too confident. Pamela asked Nory one time to help fight back against an older girl named Janet who was constantly saying mean things about Pamela's cheeks. Nory said to the girl, 'Excuse me, would you please do me a favor and stop being mean to Pamela or take a long deep dip in a dump?'

The girl looked at Nory for about a minute and a half and said, 'Turn around, I don't like looking at your face.'

'Well,' said Nory, 'I don't like looking at your face!'

'If you don't like it, don't look at it,' said the girl.

'Well, if you don't like looking at my face *don't look at my face either!*' said Nory. The girl laughed and flossed off to the library because she fancied one of the librarians, a boy in seventh year, and the next time Pamela asked Nory to fight back with words against that girl Nory said, Gee, she could try, but she just didn't think she could do all that much against her, because the girl was so sure of herself and so able to think quickly in those kinds of tense moments.

50. The Core of the Friendship

In Geography they began doing the countries of Europe—in other words, Sweden, Denmark, Norway, Holland, Finland, Greenland, Iceland, Ireland, Scotland, Lapland, the UK or United Kingdom, and of course, not to be forgotten, England itself. Land after land. There were an amazing number of big and little lands all fitting nicely tucked together, and when you concentrated in on one, you tended to forget about the others, although there was just as much going on in them, too, every day of the week. And when you concentrated on all of them, the low countries and the high countries and the medium or 'mixed-traffic' countries, as Littleguy would call them (if he knew clearly what a country was), since he called a plain donut with chocolate frosting on top a 'mixed-traffic donut' on the idea that an engine like James the Red Engine that can pull either passenger cars or freight cars is a 'mixed-traffic engine'—when you concentrated on Belgium and Barcelona and whatnot (those are just examples), you forgot about America, something that you would think would not be all that easy to forget. One day Nory almost lost her geography book and had to take out everything from her backpack, looking for it. She found it, finally, but she also found, way down at the bottom, some Flake 99 wrappers and six old conkers. They were turning rotten. They were black in some places and white in other places and they were wet soggy things that when you touched them you wished you hadn't. They smelled extremely good, though, because they were becoming peat.

Nory missed playing with Kira under the conker tree, all those weeks ago—or not that many weeks, actually—and she had a feeling that she and Kira were not such good friends now as they had been then. Kira had something of an idea of being friends, true, but not the whole idea. A friendship was like the core of something, not a conker but something really basic like an apple, and there were all these things around it—the peel and the leaves and the wax they put on the peel to make it shiny, and whatnot. The shiny peel is a fun part, but the friendship has to go down and down into the very core, and Kira didn't seem to understand what that core should be. Or maybe she just had a different opinion of what it should be than Nory did. Nory believed that the core was not just to stick together and be friendly from time to time, as the case may be, and *definitely* not always to be in a competition every second, and not to just be tomboyishly friendly, but also to be able to empty your heart out to the person. Say, for instance, you had the horribly embarrassing secret that you were keeping inside that you really loved playing with Barbies, and you were afraid to tell anyone because boys, especially, not to mention some girls, are vicious about instantly making fun of anybody who likes Barbies and they laugh at you for liking them. To a real friend you could casually empty your heart out by saying, 'You know what? *I really like Barbies.*' And there would be no problem. They would be able to be trusted not only not to tell anybody but not to laugh at you, either. And a real friend, if you had another friend that people were being awful to, wouldn't say 'Stop being friends with that person, nobody else is friends with her, stay away from her.'

Mostly it was connected with Pamela. Kira was never directly mean to Pamela the way the other kids were. Then again, she was never directly nice to her either. But Pamela still didn't know how strict Kira was about things like not eating at the same table with her. It was probably a good thing she didn't know. When Pamela steered toward a table where Kira was sitting, Nory would say, 'Oh, er, Pamela, that table looks a little full, um, why don't we go to that other table over there?' And of course Kira when that happened would be furious that Nory would prefer to eat with Pamela at a separate table and not with her. But really it was Kira's choice, not Nory's, since Nory would have been happy as a horse to eat with them both if they got along together. One time Kira and Nory were walking to lunch together and Pamela came up to walk with them, and Kira said, 'Oh, Pamela, your backpack! You forgot to put away your backpack, better hurry back! Nory, we'll go on ahead! Hurry and put away your backpack, Pamela!'

'I don't absolutely *have* to put it away,' said Pamela.

'But you really ought to,' said Kira. 'It's so clumsy, really you shouldn't take it along. Go on and put it away, Pamela! Go on!'

'She doesn't have to if she doesn't want to, Kira,' said Nory, because she could see that Pamela's feelings were a ways down the path toward getting hurt.

Kira then grabbed Nory's arm and said, 'Come on, let's go.' But Pamela grabbed Nory's other arm and said, 'Stay, Nory, stay.' Both pulled, Pamela on one arm and Kira on the other arm, and they started circling around. It was almost fun. Then Kira gave up and asked Nory if she could borrow two p. Nory gave her the two p and Kira went off to be with Shelly and Daniella, and Nory went to lunch with Pamela.

'Does Kira secretly hate me as much as the others do?' asked Pamela.

Nory decided it wouldn't be such a smart idea to admit straight out that Kira didn't like Pamela, since she'd already made that mistake once before, and after all there was still plenty of ways Pamela could be hurt, even now. Even if Pamela basically knew something was true she didn't have to have it rubbed in her nose. So Nory said, 'You know, I don't understand Kira one bit. Sometimes she's as nice as a friend can be, and then sometimes she's so competitive about who is friends with who and who walks with who and who sits with who and bup bup bup bup bup bup bup bup bup. From how she reacts to me being friends with you I would say that she likes her friends to be only her friends and nobody else's, like she's got the copyright on that particular friend. She is so marvelously in awe of how other kids act that she can't think privately what would be the obviously right thing and draw her own conclusions.'

'I'll be very glad when we reach the end of term,' said Pamela.

Nory was suddenly reminded of something she had thought of in the mirror brushing her teeth. 'You know what we should do?' she said. 'Okay, you don't want to tell the teachers or your parents. But we could still write a book about your whole experience, every good or bad thing that somebody did, Thomas kicking you in the shin, hogging your duffel peg, every single thing. We could make a timeline, first this happened, then that happened.'

Pamela shook her head fiercely. 'It isn't something that I want to think about any more than I have to.'

'Oh, but think about it: you would be thinking about it not in the unhappy way of having it just anonymously happen to you, but in the way of telling it,' Nory said. 'And then other kids could read it and know what happened, the story of one girl, or two friends. We could do it together.'

'I can't imagine that it would interest people, and I wouldn't dream of doing it,' said Pamela. 'I like to write about nice things.'

'Okay,' said Nory, 'how about—not a book about the present, but a book about the future. Say when we're both eighteen and we go off to college and have adventures.'

Pamela gave it a second of thought and nodded. 'Okay,' she said, 'but I can only come up with the adventures because I'm double-jointed and don't particularly like writing as it hurts my thumb. But I'll give you hints for some of the adventures. For instance, we could visit a live volcano together and have an adventure. I once visited a live volcano.'

'That's perfect!' said Nory. 'What name do you want for yourself?'

'Claudia,' said Pamela.

Before bed Nory wrote the first page of the book, which was called 'The Adventures of Sally and Claudia.'

The Adventures of Sally and Claudia

'Mom I'll need my file as well,' Claudia screamed up the stairs. In her freshly washed uniform, she looked as if she was going to a disco rather than Oxford University. She was 18 very smart, and especially keen on maths and the study of vulcanos. She had only just left Threll Senior School and missed it alot and so she might as she had started there when she was in year six and never missed a year. One of the reasons she missed it so much was because of her best friend Sally who had been her friend from her first day at Threll School to her last.

Sally was a very tall girl who was extreamely interested in dentestry and was American. She was know going to Stanford University while her brother borded at Threll School and was a prephect. He was taking a class in model bildiung, where he was bilding a large balsa wood model of the Mallard, which as many are aware is a preticular kind of high speed steam traine. For this whol life he had been interested in everything about traines and it looked as if that woud continue into his double-digets.

If Claudia only knew that Sally was sitting at a table even now and thinking about her, while she did her studying! Claudia was still thinking about Sally as she set off for school on the wet path with her hair sopping wet because of the rain.

As she reached school she could almost see Sally as she had been in Year Six in her school, she felt she could give anything to see Sally agin. So did Sally, who was now hard at work writing a letter to Claudia It went like this:

Dear Claudia,
    I miss you so much and think about you every day. I had a maths exam today and I did all right but I could have done better if I hade seen you befor. How are things in England?

                                        Love,
                                        Sally, your friend

TO BE CONTINUED. . . .

Nory showed the page to Pamela the next day, and Pamela read it over twice carefully. 'One very important thing you should know is that here we don't say *Mom*, we say *Mum*, and we spell it with a *u*,' Pamela said. 'And I think you shouldn't describe Claudia by her interests, but by how she looks. You probably should rewrite the beginning including a bit more about her appearance.' That was Pamela's complete reaction. She didn't say 'Good,' or 'Nice try,' or 'Well done,' or anything like that. (If you fell or dropped something, sometimes the boys would call out, 'Well done!')

Nory thought to herself, 'If you don't want to write it, Pamela, fine, but don't refuse to help write it and then tell *me* to rewrite it. I did the best I could.' But maybe Pamela was a little embarrassed by the mention of the two of them being best friends, since they'd never actually talked about being best friends.

They chatted about the book quite a number of times after that, but the first page was the one and only page that got written down. Oh well.

51. The Wind

Mostly Nory and Pamela spent more and more time together at school as friends. Actually at times there were four friends total, since Pamela had an I.F. named Leyla (I.F. stands for Imaginary Friend), and Nory thought it would be a friendly gesture to have an I.F. herself, too. She thought for a long time and came up with Penny Beckinsworth as her new I.F. She liked the name Penny, and Beckinsworth sort of sounded like a person you would think was worth beckoning for. She made up a song that she sang to the rhythm of 'She'll be coming round the mountain': *Penny Beckinsworth I reckon is a friend. Penny Beckinsworth I reckon is a friend. Penny Beckinsworth I reckon. Penny Beckinsworth I reckon. Penny Beckinsworth I reckon is a friend.* But Nory had never been too good at keeping up with imaginary friends. For example, if you write an I.F. a letter, you never get one back, unless you write it, too, which takes some of the fun out of it. On weekends in particular, Nory sometimes missed having someone real over to play with. Just simply to play with, period, end of discussion. It hadn't happened very much this year, strangely enough. Her parents were happy to watch her perform a play in which she dressed up Littleguy as a dog or a swan or an airplane engineer, and they were happy to listen to a story she had made up or play Battleship with her, and Battleship was quite fun, even when you were hit, because you could think up a new way to say you were hit, such as 'Ouch, I seem to have developed a yawning hole in my forecastle,' or 'Yikes, hoist out the rubber dinkies, she's a-going down!' But it wasn't the same as having your very own friend over to play. Littleguy also missed his best friend from school in Palo Alto. His new friend Jack spit onto the steam engines and that was not good to do, he said. But he had a different friend, Oliver, who he said was 'a very nice shy boy.' Littleguy had gotten into the usual habit of walking up to a stranger in the toystore and saying, 'Hello, I'm shy.'

Nory played some with her dolls but she was desperate just to have another nice girl her age in her room. Pamela refused to give Nory her phone number because she said she wasn't supposed to give out vital information such as her phone number unless her parents said it was okay, and she kept forgetting to ask them if it was okay. Her number was ex-directional, which means that you can't get it by calling 192. 192 sounds like it would be the same as 911 in America but actually it's the same as 411. Nory had Kira's number but she and Nory were not getting along all too well. They had just enough of a shred of friendship left to want the other person to act the way they wanted them to, rather than just not caring.

On Sunday afternoon Nory's mother took Nory and Littleguy to a playground near the Cathedral. There was a nice little child who was Littleguy's age for him to play with, but as usual, no child Nory's age. Nory's mother went over to supervise Littleguy on the slide, and Nory swang on the swings, which always made her feel lonely feelings unless there were tons of other people swinging on them, and then she sat anonymously on the bench. She started flipping through a catalog that her mother had brought along. There was a wind that day, and Nory liked the wind. Whenever she had a chance in a drawing or a painting, she included a tree with long flexible branches being blown by the wind, because it was one of her favorite things to paint or draw in all art. She noticed the pages of the catalog rustling and thought, 'I know, I can try being friends with the wind!'

She held the catalog open on her lap. She asked the wind, 'So what do you think, do you think I'd look good in this dress?' And the wind would either turn the page or not turn the page, or rattle the page a little without completely turning it. If the wind didn't turn the page, it meant yes, it liked the dress. If the wind only rattled the page, it meant that it still hadn't reached a decision. And if it did turn the page, Nory would look at the new page and say, 'Oh, so you think I'd look good in that dress? How interesting. I'm not so sure, but maybe.' The wind was not all that chatty, but it seemed nice and it had definite ideas about the fashions Nory should wear. That was kind of fun, although it had something of a lonely feeling to it, too.

That night Nory had a bad dream, not horrible, but not exactly enjoyable. It came to her probably because the light in her bathroom had burnt out again and it was windy, which meant that squeakings kept coming from outside. She dreamed her winding way through old dark and deserted buildings and found a room where there was a giant ring of black metal, with black metal hooks all the way around it. She knew they were the hooks you use in a slaughterhouse, where you would hang up the meat. The ring was turning, slowly, but it looked as if nobody was in the building except Nory. That was the frightening thing.

She got up and paddled into her parents' bedroom and asked them if it was morning, or if it wasn't morning could she possibly read because she'd had a scary dream. They lifted their heads and croaked out that they were sorry she'd had a scary dream but everything was all right and yes, she could read. She went back into her room and turned on the light to read some of *Puppies in the Pantry*. Then she stopped reading and remembered a really good speech at Cathedral service. Mary, Jesus's mother, had been frightened and someone told her, Do not be frightened, the Lord is using you as his servant, and we all must do as Mary did and strive to serve the Lord and be helpful to him. 'I will strive to serve the Lord, I will strive to serve the Lord,' Nory said to herself, and when she had said it she felt infinitely happier and smiled her way deep down into the pillow and closed her eyes. Before she went back to sleep, she had a strong wish to tell a quick story to herself about a girl who met a princess. Nobody had anything else for her to do, since it was plum in the middle of the night, so that's what she did.

52. *A Story About a Girl Who Meets a Princess*

It was a bright, sunny day in May. A girl, by the side of a large creek, sang. She was happy and playing. She was totally content. She was an orphan; she lived on the street, or places like that. She ate wheat straight from the kernel, and whatever she could find in her wanderings. Except meat, which she did not care for.

She was not very big for her age. She was what's known as a small, young girl, to most people. To herself, she was not young at all. She was very smart and had lived awhile. She had no recollection of what had happened in her younger days, but when she was ten years old, she got her dog, a big golden retriever. He was the person she looked after, and he looked after her. He was the person she knew best in the world. She loved him. He came along wherever she went. They were content.

Now she was in her thirteenth year, with jet black hair that hung in huge sausage curls down her back, which were tied up at night with long grass peels, and were wetted by pure lake water. Her hair was as gleamy and fresh-looking as ever. And when she tied it up with grass, she was careful to put basil in it, that would take the odors from the wet lake away from it, and make it smell so good you would want to just take one of the locks and eat it—maybe. She had never thought of doing that, but other people must have.

And now, she was playing. Playing, singing, and finding conkers, throwing them across the country to her beloved dog, Flame. He would jump and collect them, and run back with them. It was wonderful. He would be very careful not to miss the conker, for if he did, it could fall into the lake, and then he would not be able to have a conker, or a horse chestnut. We'll call them conkers. Real chestnuts were harder to get, for though the horse chestnuts came in spikey shells, they were not so spikey that you couldn't get them out. The chestnut shell was so spikey that you had to stamp on it. And when you tried to get the chestnut out after the shell was cracked open, it still could prick your finger. So the dog was being very careful not to lose them in the lake. And indeed he was good at jumping and catching them. He caught them almost every time.

Suddenly something awful happened. She threw the conker and it hit a tree, which rumbled and shook. Tons of conkers fell on the poor dog. She'd hit the largest conker in the largest conker tree, so that it had made the branch shake and all the fresh conkers in it fall all over poor Flame. Oh, how it bruised him, for they were huge ripe conkers. The girl picked up every single one. 'Oh, I'm so sorry,' she said. 'I'm so sorry.' Then Flame rolled over and they laughed together. That would be a good dinner for them, all those conkers. They were not very tasty on their own, but she found that if she let them sit in the sun all day, then put some parsley in, which grew very near by, mixed it with corn, and then added a bit of pepper in, it made a good dinner for them. Pepper was hard to buy, but she could get a job, whenever she wanted, and work, and buy some. As soon as she had enough to get the pepper she would say, 'Thank you very much,' keep on working for a while, and then go off.

As she picked the conkers up under the tree, she noticed something. There in the grass was a large purse of blue silk, with ruffles on it. Inside it were a number of precious things like a silver brush, and a tiny sewing kit, with scissors in the shape of a bird, and spools of gold and silver thread, and thimbles and needles so bright you could see them a mile away. She wanted to confiscate that purse, but she knew she could not. Just then, a ringing bell charmed in her ear. She looked up. What she saw was nothing but a lovely princess about her age.

The princess had neatly, neatly brushed hair. Her hair was in thick curls, and it was yellow. Shiny yellow hair. The girl loved the sight of that hair. The princess's shoes were fancy and her dress, oh her dress, it was the most beautiful lavishing color of blue—turquoise blue. It was a lovely blue. Puffy sleeves, so gorgeous, and it reached down at her ankles. And little roses at the end. It was puffy beyond belief!

'Hello,' the princess said quietly. 'What's your name?'

'Oh, ah, um, uh—' The girl was speechless. She was dressed thoroughly in rags and did not think it was a good idea to talk to this distinctive person. But then she thought she must answer. She didn't have a name, though, she'd never had one. What *was* her name? she wondered. 'Ah, mm, I don't have one,' she said finally, stuttering. 'Um, your majesty,' she said. For the princess was obviously of royal vintage.

'Hah, don't bother about it,' the princess laughed. 'Don't bother. I'm not very much a relative of the Queen, you see. My dad's brother was related to the Queen so I trace back from the Queen, yes, it's true, but not really closely . . .' she said.

'Oh wow,' said the girl. 'But, please—your name?'

'Oh, um, just call me, um, just call me—' The princess seemed to be thinking, too. 'Just call me, well, most people call me Mademoiselle Saram Shi-Kah, but just call me Shee, for Shee-Kah.'

'All right, Shee,' the girl said. 'Shee, how is it spelled?'

'Oh, Shee,' she said, 'well, it's spelled as She is normally spelled.'

'And, and how is that?' The girl looked a little scared.

'Well, to be quite honest,' the Princess said, 'it could be spelled "she" but that's probably not how it's spelled. To be quite honest, I've never thought of it. I think I'd like it if you'd spell it, S-h-e-e. Notice the doubled e.'

'Oh, right,' the girl said, 'Of course. And—what does an "e" look like?'

The Princess took the ruffled purse that the girl handed her and opened it up. In it she found the most beautiful notepad, with lovely marbled silk outside, and if you lifted the silk off there was beautiful Chinese paper, embroidered. 'Do you like it?'

'Oh yes,' the girl said.

The princess wrote down a lovely 'e'—the kind of 'e' that only princesses would learn how to write. It was a gorgeous letter. 'That's how I write it. But you know some people write it this way.' She gripped her pen; it was a lovely quill pen, too—a blue one to match her outfit—and wrote a smaller 'e,' not as fancy.

It seemed ordinary to the girl. 'Yes, yes, that's the one I'd be able to write,' she said.

'Right,' the princess nodded. 'That's the one that most people write. But impress people with this one,' she said, pointing to the one that she'd drawn first. 'It's really fun. It makes you seem so royal,' she said. 'What would you like me to call you?'

'Well, um, well, I think my last name is . . .'

'Oh, come on, don't tease me,' the princess said laughing, with a whiff of her hand. 'You have to have a name.'

'Well, I, er, don't,' she said. 'You see, I'm, um, er, call me, um, Sorsumpon . . .' She tried to make up a name. 'That's what you should call me.'

'Where does that name come from?' the princess asked.

'Um—my brain,' the girl said nodding. 'I don't have a name. I'm a servant, I'm a peasant girl, an orphan,' she said. 'And, well, I don't have a name at all. I wish I did, though. If you'd like, I'll tell you what I'd like to be— actually, I think what I'd like is, call me Sally. It's a nice name, I like it. It's the only one I know,' she confessed.

Then she talked the grownup way, the way she loved to talk, the way that she didn't talk when she was scared. The more mature way, not the scared, childish way, but the grownup way—she spoke: 'Now would you care to have some fresh conkers cooked in the heat of the sun?' she asked.

'Oh,' said the princess nodding. 'I, I'd love to. But I must return to the castle. Please come with me. Oh, but wait, I can't go in the dining room with my hair like this.' She touched one of her beautiful curls. 'I just can't, I can't go in with my hair curled. Oh, why can't mine be straight like yours?'

'I was just thinking why can't mine be curly like yours?' the girl said.

'Oh, you wouldn't want curly hair,' the princess said. 'You'd be too embarrassed to go into a dining room with it.'

'I'll switch hairstyles with you,' said the girl. 'I'll tell you how I keep it down—because I used to have somewhat frilly hair—and you tell me how you keep it up.'

'All right,' said the princes. 'I just tie it up every day with silk bows. Oh, but you wouldn't have any, would you?' And she handed the girl five silk bows, one blue, one red, and one TO BE CONTINUED.

53. *Good Result*

The very next day two unusually wonderful things happened. First, Nory was the lucky getter of a letter. The mail in Threll was delivered by men on bicycles with big red packs strapped to their handlebars, and it came early in the morning, before breakfast-time. Littleguy brought the envelopes into the kitchen, saying 'Mail livery! Mail livery!' Nory's father stopped singing to the microwave and said, 'Something for you, Nory.' She read it:

Dear Eleanor,
    How are you? Ive been making lots of strange things with FIMO latley, including tarts pies and cakes. I miss you too. I wish I could pay a visit but that's not even a possibility. So when are you coming back? Ms. Beryl is moving away so Ms. Fisker is coming back, maybe!!! I won second place in the soccer turnemint. Love from your friend, Deborah.

'Aw, that's so nice,' Nory said, folding the letter to herself. It made her suddenly strongly love Debbie and miss her, and made her think, 'How could I be letting such a good friend trickle away from my thinking just because there's so much going on here in England?' She hummed Ji Gong, the song about the crazy monk, on the way to school, looking down at her feet and remembering every detail about Debbie and her panda collection, and she thought about going back to school at the International Chinese Montessori School, and of how fun it was to know Chinese and to be able to point out to her parents some Chinese characters on the sidewalk in Chinatown that said something like 'Warning, telephone here' in orange paint.

Then, Wonderful Event Number Two, at school: towards the end of the day, Mrs. Thirm came up to Nory outside and said, 'I'd like to give you this.' It was a small piece of paper with a seal on it and a signature.

'Thank you,' said Nory, not by any means grasping what it was all about.

'It's a Good Result for being kind to Pamela,' Mrs. Thirm said.

Nory's face got a totally flabbledigastered look of complete amazement on it. She said, 'Wow, you're kidding, thank you, thank you!'

Nory only knew a little bit about Good Results. A Good Result was one of the best possible things you could ever get at the Junior School, higher than getting an Excellent, and if you got five of them in a row, you got a gift certificate to buy a special book of your choice. Good Results weren't too unusual, though, since quite a few of the girls had gotten them for different things, like for music or science projects or maths or handwriting. But still, Nory had never even come close to getting one, and she never knew that it was possible to get one for something like being nice to Pamela. She was standing in some mud in a dazzle-and-a-half of pure delight, when Mr. Pears came up to her and pointed to the piece of paper and sort of gave her a wink and said, 'That's my favorite kind of Good Result, for kindness.'

'Thank you,' Nory said. She was in a state of triumph, pleased out of her gourd, and she hopped up and down and told everyone who was nearby her, 'I got my first Good Result, I got my first Good Result!'

'Really?' said Shelly Quettner. 'What for?'

'For being kind to Pamela,' Nory said. But then she thought, 'Oops,' because it didn't feel quite right to tell. On the other hand, she wanted to tell everyone, because it proved without a doubt that if you went against the bad things that kids were doing a good thing could un-expectedly happen to you when you least expect it. She ran over to Kira.

'Kira, I got a Good Result for being nice to Pamela!' she said.

'You didn't,' said Kira.

'Yes, I did,' said Nory. 'If you don't believe me, look at this.'

Kira looked at the paper and got angry and said, 'It's not as good a Good Result as if you'd got one for a particular subject. Many people get those.'

'No,' said Nory. 'Mr. Pears said that this was his favorite kind of Good Result. He seemed to think it was somewhat unusual. You're jealous.'

'I am not!' said Kira.

'You most certainly are!' said Nory.

'I most certainly am not!' said Kira.

'Okay, I'll take your word for it, Kira,' said Nory. 'You're not jealous.'

Later Roger Sharpless came over. Usually what he did was to pretend to kick Nory in the shins, so that Nory could get back at him by pretending to kick him: onk, *conk*, onk, *conk.* Or they would do a strange kind of punching in which they would punch at each other's fists and then say, 'Ow!' and walk around making a huge production of their injured hand, flapping it around, even though it wasn't injured the least bit. But this time Roger just said: 'I think you ought to know that Pamela is unhappy because Shelly Quettner told her that the reason you've been being nice to her is that you've been trying to get a Good Result, and according to Shelly you've finally got what you wanted.'

Nory turned as red as a piece of origami paper. 'That's not true!' she said. 'Yes, I did get a Good Result, but I didn't plan on it, I didn't even know you could get a Good Result for something like that!'

'I told Shelly she was a nitwit,' said Roger. 'But you should have a word with Pamela.'

Nory tried to find Pamela but she couldn't find her anywhere. The next day she sat with her at lunch but Pamela was quiet. 'What Shelly said is totally, totally not true,' said Nory.

'You have been very nice to me,' said Pamela.

'But do you believe me?' Nory asked.

'Believe you about what?'

'That it's totally untrue?'

'I believe you,' said Pamela, 'but I'd prefer to talk about something else.'

'What do you want to talk about?' Nory asked.

'I have no idea,' said Pamela.

'Well, what's your favorite color?' Nory asked.

'Turquoise,' said Pamela.

'Ah yes, turquoise, good.' Nory pretended to note it down in an imaginary notebook. 'And what's your favorite vegetable?'

'Spinach.'

'Spinach, ah yes, very interesting.' Then there was a long silence. Finally Nory said, 'Okay, what's your favorite piece of potato chip on this plate?'

'That bit,' said Pamela, and ate it.

'That was chip number 1306B, yes, yes. I have that noted down. Now, what's your favorite water molecule?'

'What do you mean what's my favorite water molecule?' said Pamela. 'What's your favorite water molecule?'

Nory put her eye close to Pamela's glass of water and peered in. She said, 'It's a difficult case, but I believe my very favorite is that particular one there, sort of near the top. See it? A little to the side of the tiny air bubble. That one. What's yours?'

Pamela poked her finger straight into Nory's glass of water. 'That one,' she said.

Nory laughed. 'Which one?' said Nory.

Pamela pulled her finger out of the water and flicked it so that a drop or two splashed on Nory's face. 'That one,' she said.

'Ah yes, that one,' said Nory.

54. End of Term

The day before the last full day before the End of Term, everybody in the school was told to pack up everything in their backpacks and kits and take it all home. Every book, every notebook, every pen, every pencil case, every netball outfit and pair of shoes—home. The next day, the science teacher passed out strange dull little pencils, since of course their pens were no longer available, and told them to spend the class finding as many words as they could in *scientific* and *cathedral*. This was the kind of thing that Nory was never good at, and in 'scientific' she only found words like 'in' and 'it' and 'sit.' For 'cathedral' Roger Sharpless gave her the very useful hint of starting at the end and going backwards, and she luckily found 'lard' right off the bat, which was a more important word in England than in America, and 'death.' Roger said afterward that you could easily have gotten 'teach' from the word, too, but her brain unfortunately didn't work that way. During break Nory and Roger were pretending to chop off each other's heads with their bare hands when a boy came up and blurted out, 'You like Pamela, don't you?'

'My, you are slow,' said Nory. 'I've already answered that question about four separate times.'

'Of course Nory likes Pamela,' said Roger to the boy. 'Pamela is a hundred times nicer than you are. You are a sorry bowl of soup.'

The boy made a delighted expression and skipped off. Soon after that, when Nory was walking to I.T., a few people came up and smirked wildly at Nory. They said, 'You fancy Roger Sharpless! You fancy Roger Sharpless!'

Nory thought of saying 'I certainly do not!' But she didn't want to lie. So she said, 'Well, I do like him, yes.'

When they were gone Nory was quite relieved to remember to herself, 'I've got this secret that's burning a hole in my pocket and I need to talk about it with someone, and I can't talk about it with Shelly or even Kira, but I can with Pamela, because she's a friend and she can be trusted with the situation.' So later she went ahead and told Pamela, 'You know what? I used to fancy Jacob Lewes, because I'm attracted to boys who are my height or taller than me and highly intelligent and a tiny bit mean and kind of ugly in a particular way. But now, guess what? I fancy Roger Sharpless.'

'Oh, yes, Roger Sharpless is beautiful,' said Pamela. 'I fancy him too.'

'No way!' said Nory. 'I'm quite shocked!'

'Just kidding,' said Pamela. 'I think.'

On the very last day of term, all they had was house meetings and then Cathedral. Then each kid was supposed to meet their parents. Nory gave cards to Mr. Blithrenner and Mr. Stone and Mrs. Hoadley and Mrs. Hant and all her teachers, and to Mrs. Thirm she gave chocolates that she and Littleguy had made the night before. They made the chocolates by melting down a big chocolate bar and pouring it into little plastic molds. One of the molds had turned out to be of an owl. 'But not a scary owl,' Littleguy said, when he saw what it was. 'A chocolate owl. A chocolate owl is not a scary owl.'

In return Mrs. Thirm gave all the kids in class chocolates each, or caramel candies each, from a box, whichever they wanted. Someone said, 'Let's say thanks to Mrs. Thirm!' Everyone shouted, 'Hip hip hooray! Hip hip hooray! Hip hip hooray! Hip hip hooray!' Then everyone put their chairs up on the tables for the last, last, last time that term, and while Nory was lining up the little metal sliders on the legs of her chair on the tabletop so that it was perfectly straight, since that was how it would sit, in just that precise position, until she came back after Christmas, she had a strange feeling of never wanting that term of school to be over but wanting it to go on and on to an endless limit. She slipped Pamela a little present of a pop-up card, home-made, which had a cutout of herself and Pamela in their school clothes standing on top of a little volcano, and she made it so the volcano leaned forward a slight extent when the card opened, which you can do fairly easily by cutting two little slices in the folded-over edge so that the place where you cut can be folded outward the opposite way as a little ledge for something to be attached to. The Pamela pop-up and the Nory pop-up each had one flexible arm that waved back and forth when you pulled the two louvers at the bottom that ran all the way up the back of the card as two strips of paper and sometimes got completely out of whack. They both were saying, 'We made it!' and a bird was tucked conveniently halfway in a pocket of paper that was shaped as a cloud.

A little while later Nory remembered something Mr. Pears quite sternly said about not enough people saying thank you personally to the parents who organized the party before the fireworks on Guy Fawkes Day, so she personally said, 'Thank you for the chocolate,' to Mrs. Thirm. But she said it quietly, while Mrs. Thirm's back was turned, because sometimes it makes you shy to say thank you in person before anyone else has cleared the path by saying thank you. Shelly Quettner heard her say it and spun around and said much more loudly, *'Thank you for the chocolate, Mrs. Thirm!'* Mrs. Thirm turned and smiled at Shelly and said, 'You're welcome.' But that was quite all right because it isn't the giving, it's the thought that counts. 'On the other hand, if the other person doesn't know that you've thought the thought, how *can* it count?' Nory wondered.

Everyone streamed up the path toward the Cathedral and Nory looked at them walking. Each kid had their own particular personality, good or bad or mezzo mezzo, and each personality, no matter what it was, was interesting in some way. Sometimes a kid lost their personality for Nory when all they seemed to want to do was to be cruel to Pamela—then they just became a dull, boring idiot, shuffling through the day—but just lately some kids were getting more preoccupied in other things and losing interest in being cruel to Pamela, to a certain extent, though not totally. Maybe a little bit of the reason was because they saw that Nory was persistently going to be Pamela's friend, and so they began to notice that it wasn't necessarily the absolute end of the world to be Pamela's friend as well or at least not be her vicious enemy.

Inside, since it was a very bright cold day, the green light blasted in through the Jasperium and onto quite a few kids, including Nory. She didn't exactly think God's thoughts, but she thought: 'Frankly, I love school.' 'Love' was one of the most important of all the words that seemed to be spelled wrong on purpose, just to confuse you. It should be spelled 'lov' because the rule is that an *e* makes things long, and there is no long *l* or long *o* or long *v*. For example, it's not 'I loave school,' it's 'I lov school.' But however it was spelled, it was true. The best thing about school was that there were so many teachers teaching different things, so that you learned about how to get stabbed in drama, or about the Aztecs, or the Virgin Mary, or how to type or how to not cry when your plane crashes six times in a row, or about Achilles being dipped into the water, or the friction in a brick, or any amount of things, and there were so many hundreds of kids, and each kid was given quite a bit of responsibility. They were treated as if they were hundreds and hundreds of adults pouring in to work at a factory, wearing a jacket and tie, with that level of independence. You walked to and from Cathedral and to and from lunch, and during break you could choose to go to the art room or the library or back to your classroom or stay outside, whatever you wanted, and you would run into all of the people you knew, and each time you saw someone you had a particular thought, like 'Ah yes, Colin, who is always asking to borrow my eraser,' or 'Ah, Kira, how are you? Haven't seen you in a while!'

A sad thing was that Kira and Nory had stopped being very, very good friends because of Pamela. But it wasn't really Kira's fault or Pamela's fault. It was the fault of all the people who had decided not to like Pamela. If they hadn't been at the Junior School, then there would have been no problem. Of course you could say that there wouldn't have been much of a Junior School, either, since almost everyone was part of the meanness from time to time. But now that some of the kids had decided that they liked Pamela better, or weren't going to bother to hate her, presto, Kira was liking Nory better again.

While Nory was by the South Door of the Cathedral waiting for her parents to pick her up, Pamela came by to give her a note. She didn't want to leave but she had to because her parents said they had to go or they would miss their train. The note said, 'Dear Nory, Thanks for being my best friend, Love Pamela.' And it had her phone number on it, for once. So things were working out rather well. Not to mention that for the first time in a very long time Nory had a wonderful loose tooth. If she bent it past a certain position, she could feel the sharp edge of it that was usually hidden under the gums, and there was a distinct salty taste of blood in her mouth.

The End.